The Formation of a Modern Rabbi

Program in Judaic Studies
Brown University
Box 1826
Providence, RI 02912

BROWN JUDAIC STUDIES

Edited by

David C. Jacobson
Saul M. Olyan
Rachel Rojanski
Michael L. Satlow
Adam Teller

Number 371
THE FORMATION OF A MODERN RABBI
by
Samuel Joseph Kessler

THE FORMATION OF A MODERN RABBI

THE LIFE AND TIMES OF THE VIENNESE SCHOLAR AND PREACHER ADOLF JELLINEK

by
Samuel Joseph Kessler

Brown Judaic Studies
Providence, Rhode Island

© 2022 Brown University. All rights reserved.

No part of this work may be reproduced or transmitted in any form or by any means, electronic or mechanical, including photocopying and recording, or by means of any information storage or retrieval system, except as may be expressly permitted by the 1976 Copyright Act or in writing from the publisher. Requests for permission should be addressed in writing to the Rights and Permissions Office, Program in Judaic Studies, Brown University, Box 1826, Providence, RI 02912, USA.

Library of Congress Control Number: 2022948936

For M.L.

Song of Songs 8:5

One hundred tongues speak one language: namely, the Science of Judaism is bound up with faith. Wherefore the latter lives actively in the hearts of the Jews, literature finds support and encouragement, and thus we can infer the warmth of faith among the Jews based on the favorable or unfavorable conditions [they] afford to science.

—Adolf Jellinek,
"Eine Wanderung durch jüdische Bibliotheken" (1853)

Contents

Acknowledgments xi

Note on Place-Names and Translations xiii

Introduction 1
   A New Shoot from the House of David:
      Adolf Jellinek at the Fulcrum of Jewish Modernity 1
   Adolf Jellinek and Jewish Modernity 3
   Modernity in Jewish History 8
   Central Europe in Jewish History 12
   Urbanization and the Rabbinic Sermon 15
   The Historiography of a Transformed Rabbinate 16

Chapter
1 **On the Threshold of Modernity: Jellinek's Early Years** 21
   A Tale of Three Brothers 21
   Jewish Society and Emancipation in
      Turn-of-the-Century Moravia 25
   Ungarisch-Brod: Religious Life in Rural Moravia 27
   Proßnitz: Moderate Religious Reform after the Haskalah 30
   Prague: An Early Urban Model 33

2 **Town and Gown: Jewish Leipzig and the**
   Wissenschaft des Judentums 37
   The Jewish Community of Leipzig 37
   Creating *Wissenschaft des Judentums* 43
   Jellinek's Scholarly Interests 50

3 **Breakthroughs in Scholarship: Jellinek's Studies**
   on Kabbalah 55
   Jellinek's Earliest Scholarship 55
   The *Zohar*: Authorship and Lineage 60

viii   Contents

4   Attraction to Rabbinic Innovation:
     Jellinek and Midrash 69
     Bet ha-Midrasch: *Context and Conception* 69
     Scholarly Friendships and Theoretical Precursors 70
     Key Themes in *Bet ha-Midrasch* 80
     The Values of Medieval Exegesis 85

5   Divided Loyalties: Jellinek between
     Scholarship and Communal Leadership 89
     Early Thoughts on the Future of European Judaism 90
     Divided Loyalties 95
     Taking Up Communal Leadership 98

6   A New Synagogue for a New Suburb: Jellinek in
     Vienna's Leopoldstadt 103
     The City of Vienna and Its Jewish Migrants 104
     The Idea and Aesthetics of the Monumental Synagogue 111
     Jellinek's Dedication of the Leopoldstadt Temple 117
     The Vienna Rite 120

7   Tradition and Change in the Rabbinic Persona:
     Jellinek's Context and Innovations in Vienna 125
     A New Rabbinic Persona 125
     The Development and Transformation of
       the Rabbinic Sermon 129
     The Nineteenth-Century Sermon 134
     Jellinek the Preacher 137

8   Major Themes in Jellinek's Sermons 141
     Judaism Plus Liberalism in a Viennese Setting 143
     The Possibilities of Midrash 148
     The Hebrew Language 150
     Between Orthodoxy and Reform 154
     Jellinek's Rhetorical Method 155

9   Jellinek's Sermons: Justice, Care of the Stranger,
     and Ethical Universalism............................. 159
     Truth, Freedom, and Justice 161
     Loving the Stranger 164
     Jews and Christians 168
     Judaism in Modern Times 177

Conclusion.. 187
    Making Twentieth-Century Connections:
        From Central Europe to Anglo-America 187
    Genealogical Connection: Jellinek, Hertz, Sacks 190

Selected Bibliography of the Works of Adolf Jellinek............. 197

Bibliography 201

Index... 225

Acknowledgments

As Rabbi Elazar said that Rabbi Hanina said: Whoever reports a saying in the name of he who said it brings redemption to the world. As it is stated: 'And Esther reported to the king in the name of Mordecai.'

(b. Megillah 15b)

One acquires many debts in the writing of a book: to friends, mentors, institutions, funders, and a myriad of seen and unseen librarians and archival staff.

To begin, this book would not exist at all if it weren't for a research fellowship from the Simon Dubnow Institute in Leipzig in summer 2013, for which I was encouraged to apply by the ever gracious and knowledgeable Yaakov Ariel. It was in Leipzig that I discovered the world of Adolf Jellinek and began to get a sense that bringing together the rise of *Wissenschaft des Judentums*, the changing rabbinate, and Jewish urbanization might make for an interesting project. A subsequent meeting with the eminent Rabbi Dr. Ismar Schorsch pointed me firmly in Jellinek's direction. And as the project continued to take shape, I was encouraged by both Randall Styers, whose profusion of recommendations landed me the various grants I required, and Malachi Hacohen, who firmly believed that a book on Jellinek had something new to offer historical scholarship. Above all, however, I am indebted to my teacher, Jonathan Hess, z"l, whose graciousness, generosity, kindness, and intelligence embodied the noblest ideals of the professoriate. He is greatly missed.

I owe much thanks to the staff of the various centers and libraries with whom I worked personally: Mandy Fitzpatrick, Carina Röll, Grit N. Scheffer, and Marion Hammer of the Simon Dubnow Institute, Leipzig; Klaus Fitschen and Stefen Hoffmann of the University of Leipzig; Peter Honigmann and Eva Blatter at the Zentralarchiv zur Erforschung der Geschichte der Juden in Deutschland, Heidelberg; and Emily Buss, Christian F. Ostermann, and Zdenek David of the Woodrow Wilson International Center for Scholars, Washington, DC. And I owe thanks to the staff and archivists at whose institutions I have researched and written: the National Library of Israel, Jerusalem; the Universitätsarchiv, Leipzig; the Stadtarchiv, Leipzig; the Albertina Bibliothek, Leipzig; the Bundesarchiv,

Koblenz; the Davis Library, University of North Carolina at Chapel Hill, Chapel Hill, NC; Duke University libraries, Durham, NC; the Library of Congress, Washington, DC; the Center for Jewish History, New York City; and the New York Public Library, Dorot Jewish Division, New York City (and especially my friend, now retired librarian Eleanor Yadin).

Many colleagues and friends supported this work, as conversation partners, helpful translators, and readers: Brian Britt, Marcia Bunge, John Cha, Thia Cooper, Blake Couey, Alexander Dickow, Casey Elledge, Matthew Gabriele, Mary Gaebler, Abigail Gillman, Talia Graff, Jerry Heverly, Cornelius Ludwig, Fuad Naeem, Annegret Oehme, Timothy Parrish, Robert Porwoll, Bharat Ranganathan, Sarah Ruble, Peter and Sarah Saulson, Maren Scheurer, Leif Tornquist, and Lucy Lopata-Varkas. To my teacher, colleague, and dear friend, George Y. Kohler, I owe uncountable thanks. Beside him I seek to uphold the dictum of Rav Nachman bar Yitzchak, who said, "Just as a small piece of wood can ignite a large one, so too, minor Torah scholars can sharpen greater ones" (b. Ta'anit 7a).

Finally, in the decade I spent working on this project, my family has changed and grown. My parents read every page of the earliest drafts of this book. Their love of Judaism and of the life of the mind set me down the scholarly path. For that, and to them, I will be forever grateful. As Rabbi Nachman of Bratslav writes, "This and this correspond—a majestic countenance and becoming an elder, that is, because an elder is one who has acquired wisdom" (*Likutei Moharan* 27:6). When my wife and I traveled in the Caribbean for her MA research a decade ago, it was just before I discovered my fascination with Jellinek. Little did we know then that he would be with us all these years later. And in the last two years, as I have finished work on this manuscript and the world has been convulsed by pandemic, we have been blessed with two beautiful children, Nathaniel Oz and Paloma Hodaya. Beyond all else, I pray that they follow in the steps of Rabbi Abraham Joshua Heschel of Apt, who strove to embody the principle of *ohev yisroel*, one who loves all Israel.

But to my wife, for her patience and endurance, and for the purity and depth of her love, I dedicate this book.

Versions of portions of this work previously appeared as "Translating Judaism for Modernity: Adolf Jellinek in Leopoldstadt, 1857–1865," *Simon Dubnow Institute Yearbook* 14 (2015): 393–419; and "Rediscovering the Study of Spanish Kabbalism in *Wissenschaft des Judentums*: Adolf Jellinek in Leipzig, 1842–1856," *PaRDeS: Zeitschrift der Vereinigung für Jüdische Studien* 24 (2018): 125-44.

Note on Place-Names and Translations

I refer to historical locations using their German name (e.g., Pressburg instead of Bratislava), although upon first use I include any alternate or contemporary terms as well (e.g., Breslau [Polish: Wrocław]). If Anglophone readers are most familiar with a particular name (e.g., Vienna instead of Wien) I use what is familiar. For other places, I use a period- or linguistically appropriate name and spelling (e.g., Leopoldstadt instead of Leopold City).

In the nineteenth century, Christian and family names often contained slight differences depending on location, language, and typography. For Jellinek, a vast majority of modern scholarship spells his first name "Adolf." He himself, however, was not consistent. In Leipzig, his printed and manuscript works often spell his given name "Adolph." Jellinek's Hebrew name was Aaron, which he inherited from his maternal grandfather. (In German, Aaron is rendered "Aron.") In the body of the text I use the modern spelling, Adolf, while in quotations and bibliographical citations I retain whichever form appears in the original.

Unless otherwise noted, German, French, and Hebrew translations are my own.

Introduction

A New Shoot from the House of David: Adolf Jellinek at the Fulcrum of Jewish Modernity

> The chief advantage derived from a study of Jellinek's life and work is a better understanding, a clearer grasp, of the noblest ideal of a modern rabbi.
> —H. G. Enelow, *The Jew and the World* (1921)

A vast transformation has occurred in Jewish communal existence over the course of the last two hundred years, one that separates the Jews of the contemporary moment from their coreligionists of preceding millennia. A Jew who traveled between Pumbedita and Marseille in the tenth century, or from Strasbourg to Alexandria in the fifteenth, would certainly have encountered Jewish communities materially and linguistically distinct. What that sailor or merchant or rabbi would not have found, however, were the demographic, theological, and political divisions that began to fragment European Judaism in the latter decades of the eighteenth century and resulted in fundamental changes to the nature of Jewish religious practice and self-understanding by the turn of the twentieth. European modernity has altered almost everything about Jewish religious and communal existence: its governance and organization, the location and aesthetics of the synagogue, its vernacular languages, the role of women, the centrality of Torah, Talmud, prayer, and religious law, its rural–urban demographics, and the role of the rabbi. For an observer from a more distant past, much about Jewish practice and thought in the twenty-first century would seem to have undergone a fundamental change.

Nineteenth-century Central European society encapsulated the multitude of dynamics that European Jews encountered in the era of high modernity. In those mid-century years, communal and religious leaders recognized that unalterable transformations had already overtaken Jewish social and cultural life, ones that would permanently end age-old assumptions and usher in an era of remarkable possibility and challenge. In a broad sense, this book, *The Formation of a Modern Rabbi*, driven by the life and works of Adolf Jellinek (1821–1893), is a social history of changes in Jewish religious expression in German-speaking Central Europe from about 1830 to 1870. At a more detailed level, it is a narrative centered particularly on the transformation of Jewish ritual experience, and especially of the role of the rabbi as the shaper of modern Jewish religious self-expression through the advent of academic historical scholarship and the weekly Sabbath sermon. The changes chronicled in *The Formation of a Modern Rabbi* were permanent and fundamental; they established forms of communal organization and theological assumptions that organize the religious lives of the vast majority of Jews in Europe and America to this day.

The Formation of a Modern Rabbi begins in the opening decades of the nineteenth century with the new developments in politics, philosophy, and economics that have come to define our idea of modernity. In nascent form in the seventeenth and eighteenth centuries, ideas such as liberalism, ethical universalism, and philosophical rationalism found real and widespread influence only in the wake of the Napoleonic Wars, when they were taken up not just by intellectuals but by young politicians and the social elite. Further, starting in the 1840s, radical technological and economic developments (railroads, factories, stock markets) led to widescale urbanization with the migration into cities of hundreds of thousands of Europeans in just a few decades. The social and cultural dynamics of the continent being as they were, Central European Jews were among the largest blocks of modern urban pioneers. Indeed, in the 1850s and 1860s, the Jews of Germany and the Habsburg lands moved in such large numbers that within mere decades, the formerly rural and parochial character of Central European Jewry was entirely displaced and the modern stereotype was born: that of the Jews as a distinctly urban and cosmopolitan people.

As a result of this demographic shift in the Jewish population of Central Europe, that region became the first on the continent to construct monumental communal synagogues. It was in these buildings, erected in large and small cities alike, where the modern rabbi as rhetorician came of age. These Jews called their rabbis "preachers," adopting a Christian term as both indicative of and a gesture toward a reimagination of the rabbinic role in modern times. Jewish communities in urban spaces expected their rabbis to speak in grand gestures on behalf of Jewish tradition, to be involved in the political and social needs of the community, and to oversee ritual life inside the synagogues. In the medieval and early modern periods, the synagogue was almost exclusively a place for men's prayer, with ritual life overseen by lay leadership and rabbis (especially in Ashkenaz) expected to speak only on religiously significant occasions (e.g., Shabbat HaGadol and Shabbat Shuvah); in the middle of the nineteenth century, communal leaders (often following or in tandem with their Christian counterparts) reimagined the weekly Sabbath service as a pedagogical as well as religious experience, calling on the rabbi to shape the feelings and ideas of the congregation. Before modernity, women practiced Jewish ritual life at home and were the primary conveyers of Judaism's everyday traditions to the children; in the newly constructed synagogues, women's attendance was expected in a sizable, visual way, and the home lost much of its particularistic religious character. In nearly all aspects, Central European Jewish communities were the first in urban modernity to experiment with both a new role for the synagogue and a new idea of the rabbi.

In focusing specifically on Adolf Jellinek, chief rabbi of Vienna and the most famous preacher in Central Europe in the second half of the nineteenth century, *The Formation of a Modern Rabbi* offers a unique window into the earliest, formative years of the new communal synagogue as urban religious space and demonstrates how the Sabbath sermon came first to suggest, later to compel, and finally to embody the transformative dynamics of Jewish religious modernity. Urban migration brought these communities into existence. The sermon made the rabbinic role one of rhetorical traditionalism: the rabbi was now the chief vocalizer of Jewish history and morality, responsible for articulating a Jewish vision of modern life. In a world that was rapidly losing the felt and remembered past of premodern Jewish society, the rabbi (with Jellinek as prime exemplar) took hold of the sermon as an instrument to define and mold Judaism and Jewish values for a new world.

Adolf Jellinek and Jewish Modernity

Adolf Jellinek was born and raised in small-town traditional Jewish society in the Habsburg province of Moravia. His intellectual and geographic peregrinations—yeshiva in Prague, university in Leipzig, rabbinate in Vienna—offer a powerful map through which to trace Judaism's religious adaptations and experimentations in European modernity. Jellinek was both a creator and an observer of these changes within the Jewish community of German-speaking Central Europe. He was the recipient of a world that (relatively suddenly) lacked many of the legal and cultural discriminations that had prohibited his parents and grandparents from a more robust participation in European cultural and civic life. Likewise, his biography overlapped with a momentous transformation in European economics and technology, one that witnessed the rapid growth of industrialized cities and the subsequent urbanization of culturally diverse rural populations, a demographic shift seen most dramatically among Jews but witnessed in Catholic and Protestant communities as well. Jellinek's obvious intellectual virtuosity, coupled with a dedication to community organization, Jewish social cohesion, and theological continuity, made him one of the most well-known and widely respected religious leaders of nineteenth-century German Jewry.

This book constitutes the first major intellectual biography of Jellinek in almost a century[1] and the only work that critically engages with both Jellinek's scholarship and communal activities in the context of the origins and nature of Jewish religious modernity. During his lifetime, Jellinek was broadly recognized for his intellectual contributions to the study of Jewish history, including his myriad philological and biographical articles in scholarly journals, his editing and publishing of midrashic manuscripts (resulting in, among other books, the six-volume *Bet ha-Midrasch*, still in use today), and his groundbreaking work in the critical analysis of medieval Jewish mysticism.[2] However, a number of factors have led to his general disappearance from historiographical accounts of the development of Jewish scholarship, chief among them his subject (mysticism) and the dominant role played by Gershom Scholem in crafting a narrative of "this derelict area."[3] Scholem, as is well known, overtly downplayed the many contributions of nineteenth-century scholars to the study of Jewish mysticism, including, and perhaps most egregiously, that of Jellinek, who did more than any other to pave the way for Scholem's own groundbreaking work. Instead, in his narrative of the study of mysticism up to his own era, Scholem chose to highlight those historians whose ideas he sought most to overturn.[4] This obfuscation on the part of Scholem has been compounded by a remarkable lack of Hebrew-language scholarly interest in Jellinek.[5] In the end, outside the present author's own publications, only in 2019 did Jellinek's many contributions to the study of Jewish mysticism first receive serious analysis and contextualization.[6]

---

1. Moses Rosenmann, *Dr. Adolf Jellinek: Sein Leben und Schaffen* (Vienna: Schlesinger, 1931).

2. See, e.g., Isaak Markus Jost, *Adolph Jellinek und die Kabbala ein Literatur-Bericht* (Leipzig: Colditz, 1852), which appeared even in the midst of Jellinek's most important work on the *Zohar* and its context.

3. Gershom Scholem, *Major Trends in Jewish Mysticism* (New York: Schocken, 1995), 3.

4. See Scholem, *Major Trends in Jewish Mysticism*, 1–2; and Scholem, *Ursprung und Anfänge der Kabbala*, Studia Judaica 3 (Berlin: de Gruyter, 1962), 1–9.

5. The two exceptions are Moshe Idel, "Al Aharon Jellinek ve haKabbalah," *Pe'amim* 100 (2004): 16–21; Boaz Huss, *Ke-Zohar ha-raḳi'a: peraḳim be-hitḳablut ha-Zohar uve-havnayat 'erko ha-simli* (Jerusalem: Ben-Zvi Institute, Bialik Institute, 2008) (Engl.: *The Zohar: Reception and Impact*, trans. Yudith Nave [Portland, OR: Littman Library of Jewish Civilization, 2016]).

6. George Y. Kohler, *Kabbalah Research in the Wissenschaft des Judentums, 1820–1880: The Foundations of an Academic Discipline*, Europäisch-jüdische Studien: Beiträge 47 (Berlin: de Gruyter, 2019).

As a rabbi and a preacher, rather than as a scholar, however, Jellinek is somewhat better remembered. Jellinek's death prompted fond obituaries in the leading Jewish publications of the Euro-American world, and into the twentieth century his name continued to be mentioned among the leading rabbinic figures of the prior generation. In 1921, for his continued fame as a rhetorician of Jewish modernity, he merited a chapter in the American scholar Hyman G. Enelow's popular work *The Jew and the World* (where he was held up alongside no lesser figures than Moses, Jesus, and Napoleon).[7] And in 1931, Moses Rosenmann's biography appeared to acclaim in Jellinek's home city of Vienna. But broader interest soon waned, and Jellinek's rabbinical career became the purview of niche scholarship on the German Jewish experience. In 1990, Robert Wistrich's magnum opus on the Jews of Vienna included dozens of references to Jellinek and some pages on his public career as a preacher.[8] A Jellinek family biography appeared eight years later, in which Adolf is an important but not major figure, though the work helped ground his life within the broader themes of Jewish Central European modernity.[9] The past three decades have seen modest but continuous scholarship on Habsburg and Viennese Jewry, with important but not frequent mention of Jellinek.[10]

This book returns the focus squarely onto Jellinek, who lived and worked through the peak period of change for Central European Jewry. Throughout his life he paused to reflect on the historical role of the rabbi, and he recognized early that the entire structure of religious Judaism was being radically altered both intellectually and materially, by liberalism, on the one hand, and urbanization and industrialization, on the other. True, Jewish reformers as early as the 1810s and 1820s had already embarked on ritual modifications and set up some communal structures to adapt Jewish religious practice. The Hamburg Reform Temple, the Neuer Israelitischer Tempelverein, was established in 1817 and adopted a siddur that modified liturgical language related to the restoration of the Jerusalem Temple. But even with the religious developments enacted among the Reform, Jellinek

---

7. Hymen G. Enelow, *The Jew and the World* (New York: Bloch, 1921), 97–106.

8. Robert S. Wistrich, *The Jews of Vienna in the Age of Franz Joseph* (Oxford: Littman Library of Jewish Civilization, 1990), esp. 98–130.

9. Klaus Kempter, *Die Jellineks 1820–1955: Eine familienbiographische Studie zum deutsch-jüdischen Bildungsbürgertum*, Schriften des Bundesarchivs 52 (Düsseldorf: Droste, 1998).

10. See esp. Marsha L. Rozenblit, *The Jews of Vienna, 1867–1914: Assimilation and Identity*, SUNY Series in Modern Jewish Literature and Culture (Albany: State University of New York Press, 1983); Rozenblit, "Jewish Identity and the Modern Rabbi: The Cases of Isak Noa Mannheimer, Adolf Jellinek, and Moritz Güdemann in Nineteenth-Century Vienna," *Leo Baeck Institute Year Book* 35 (1990): 103–31; Björn Siegel, "Facing Tradition: Adolf Jellinek and the Emergence of Modern Habsburg Jewry," *Simon Dubnow Institute Yearbook* 8 (2009): 319–44; Siegel, "The Temple in Leopoldstadt and Its Function in Habsburg Vienna: The Role of History in Fashioning Jewish Modernity," *Austrian Studies* 24 (2016): 109–23.

realized that the broader, continent-wide transformations were far more wide-reaching and fundamental, altering the Jewish national self-narrative itself, along with such long-held traditional assumptions as those concerning the responsibility of Jews to non-Jews, the relations between synagogue and home, yeshiva and university, city and countryside, halakha and parliament, and Talmud and literature.

As *The Formation of a Modern Rabbi* will argue, Jellinek was one of just a handful of figures in the middle decades of the nineteenth century whose actions and writings actively created the underlying framework, assumptions, and scope of the rabbi and synagogue in modern urban Jewry as we understand them today.[11] As Jellinek wrote in 1866, "But this new, great, and glorious time—of which our ancestors in their seclusion had little idea—sets on us new obligations and presents for us new challenges on whose fulfillment we are want to use our ability."[12] Jellinek sought to chart a path of religious synthesis, integration, and nondestructive transformation, a path that would embrace the newly liberalizing culture of the densely urban industrial city without demeaning or forgetting the small traditional towns and lives that these Jewish migrants (and that he himself, in fact) had only recently left behind. And to a great degree, he succeeded. His ideas and innovations concerning the roles and responsibilities of the rabbi in urban Jewish modernity have become, almost completely, the model for non-Haredi rabbis and their communities in Europe and America today.[13]

It remains important to note that Jellinek was as much responding to the larger dynamics of his era as he was a leader and molder of them. At every juncture Jellinek found the world opening a multitude of new possibilities and presenting a fresh array of challenges. The story told in

---

11. Jellinek's peers as early pioneers of the modern rabbinate included Michael Sachs in Berlin, Solomon Tiktin and Abraham Geiger in Breslau, Isaac Bernays and Gotthold Salomon in Hamburg, Samuel Hirsch in Philadelphia, David Einhorn in Baltimore and New York, Isaac Mayer Wise in Cincinnati, and Isaac Noah Mannheimer (Jellinek's predecessor) in Vienna.

12. Adolf Jellinek, *Predigten*, vol. 3 (Vienna: Herzfeld & Bauer, 1866), 4.

13. Jellinek's importance as a rabbinical pioneer was already recognized a century ago: "Jellinek felt that Judaism contained truths of everlasting value, that its institutions and the life of its adherents were meant to be beautiful, that its teachings were designed to produce the noblest ethical and spiritual results. But he knew, also, that in order that this end might be wont, Judaism in the new age required an expression appropriate to the times and different from that of the ages which had preceded and during which conditions of Jewish life were entirely different. To this theme Jellinek returns repeatedly. And he returns to it because it is vital. The people of his age had emerged from the ghetto. They loved beauty. They sought culture. They needed ethical and spiritual sustenance. Could they find these things in the old religion, which many of them associated, though wrongly, with ugliness, narrowness, and rigid legalism? Jellinek considered it as his first duty to demonstrate that Judaism did contain these things, and that to find them it was necessary only to go down to the heart of Judaism, where its treasures were hidden" (Enelow, *Jew and the World*, 99–100).

The Formation of a Modern Rabbi is certainly not the only one that has been or should be written about Jewish modernity. There was no predestination in the narrative of Jellinek's life when he set out from Moravia to attend school in Prague and then Leipzig, no logical end point of a great trans-historical struggle when he took over the rabbinate in Vienna and sought to keep a fractious and diverse community from splintering into denominations and sects. Instead, we will encounter Jellinek and his peers partly as individual actors, confronted by rapidly changing political, social, intellectual, and economic worlds. Yet their individuality stopped at the shore of Jewish historical memory and continuity. Jellinek and his fellow religious leaders loved Judaism. They valued its rituals, believed in its teachings, and cherished its texts. Though they lived in a world of almost unimaginable cultural flux, they clung to the idea that, even in all this, Judaism, too, could flourish. Though they often approached the goal from different angles, nearly everyone described in these pages was dedicated to the religious idea that Judaism was an inheritance from their ancestors, who were (perhaps divinely) accountable for handing it on to their children. Their choices—and their quarrels—must be understood within that framework.

As Jellinek experienced it, out of what must have felt like a ceaseless cascade of historic events and challenges ("in the midst of the pounding waves of the present" was how he described it in 1849[14]) a particular set of new communal and religious structures began to emerge in the period of high modernity, ones built atop premodern Jewish models but adapted and transfigured (sometimes through the co-opting of non-Jewish norms and assumptions, sometimes through internal innovation) to fit dramatically altered circumstances. At the dedication of the new synagogue in Leopoldstadt, for example, Jellinek compared its erection with nothing less than the rebuilding of the Second Temple under King Herod, pointing to the ways past, present, and future all found favor in that moment:

> As at the time when the Herodian Temple was built, according to an ancient account, rain poured down on the seed fields at night, and warm sunshine in the morning made Jerusalem's places dry, that neither the fertility of the land nor the sacred building should be disturbed; so the ground of our congregation did not lie fallow outside of this house: old institutes were preserved undiminished; new ones came into being during construction."[15]

The Formation of a Modern Rabbi is about exactly this: how Jellinek, in the company of friends, allies, and opponents, engaged in the practice

---

14. Jellinek, "Drei Gräber" (Leipzig: Fritsche, 1849), 15.
15. Jellinek, "Zwei Reden zur Schlußsteinlegung und zur Einweihung des neuen israelitischen Tempels in der Leopoldstadt" (Vienna: Knöpflmacher, 1858), 7.

of modifying and rebuilding Jewish religious life for urban modernity—what they experienced in their youths and adulthoods, what they learned at university, what they saw in their communities, and what resources in the Jewish and non-Jewish pasts they drew upon to imagine and invigorate a European future for religious Judaism.

In seeking to tell this story, I examine key aspects of ritual Jewish religious culture as it formed in urban centers and university towns in the decades from approximately 1830 to 1870. By focusing on Jellinek, I attempt to explain the processes through which the foundational intellectual and social components of today's religious Judaism came to be constructed. The persona of the rabbi, the intellectual culture of the *Wissenschaft des Judentums*, the urbanization of Jewish communities, the centralization of the synagogue as the primary location of Jewish worship and theological experience in new urban neighborhoods, and the weekly sermon—these are the key sites in this book's narrative about the formation of modern Jewish religious practice. By the book's end, we will have seen how a number of Jellinek's specific insights—that midrash was the best narrative genre suited to melding historic Judaism with the ideals of modern science and *bildung*; that political liberalism was the key to the future of European Jewry; that the development of a vernacular vocabulary of Jewish nationhood meant Jews could seek to retain their separate practices while being accepted among the diversity of Western peoples—have become essential, even foundational assumptions for nearly all modern Jewish communal and rabbinic leadership in the Anglo-American world, Reform, Conservative, and Modern Orthodox alike. As Jellinek wrote in 1861, "The Torah stands as the greatest world book, whose spirit must be understood by the people if they do not want to be condemned in the name of religion to a monotonous standstill. This should be the task of today."[16] One would be hard-pressed to find a graduating rabbi at any of the major Anglo-American rabbinical schools today who disagrees with that sentiment. Taken together, the practical religious changes Jellinek devised or promoted in the 1850s and 1860s were essential to the dramatic evolution in the role and idea of the rabbi and synagogue (and therefore the entire urban Jewish religious experience) in the modern era.

Modernity in Jewish History

The adjective *modern* and its noun *modernity* have and continue to have a multiplicity of definitions. In one common academic form they refer to the long nineteenth century (1789–1914). In another, they mean the years

---

16. Adolf Jellinek, *Predigten*, vol. 3 (Vienna: Herzfeld & Bauer, 1866), 312.

from the Franco-Prussian war to the end of Weimar (1871–1933). When the Museum of Modern Art in New York adopted the word *modern*, it canonized a specific period in the progress of Euro-American artistic expression beginning with the 1880s and extending to the present. When used to describe warfare, architecture, or film, the term can span from the Renaissance (the early development of guns and the European rediscovery of dome construction) to the present. Modernism, a particular mode of expression that characterizes forms of fine art, literature, and music, is again a separate noun entirely.

Each of these usages is valuable in its own way, and all should be understood as having an influence on the meaning of the term in this book. Still, instead of offering another definition, *modernity* in these pages is meant to act as a signifier of the pace and character of nineteenth-century change. Separating or identifying historical moments, actions, or ideas as modern or premodern is not the goal. Instead, *modern* is used to suggest a particular type of movement and action. It is a rhetorical indicator, pointing out that a new form of thought or social existence is taking shape at a particular moment or place in nineteenth-century Europe.

Modernity in these pages is therefore an activity and not a state of being. *The Formation of a Modern Rabbi* follows those who theorize the modern as an act of becoming, as about the dynamic transformation of landscapes, rituals, and ideologies by individual persons, their inhabited communities, and the built environment.[17] In one instance, modernity is about the imaging of entirely new forms of unity. As Barbara Hahn writes, for example, in 1834 there appeared in print the possibility, quite entirely without precedent, of suggesting "what appear to be entirely contrary meanings can suddenly be thought together ... [Jewish] and German ... not in opposition; [instead,] the one appears to strengthen the other.... If a Jewish woman can be the German Pallas Athena, contraries have been united."[18] Hahn's point is that modernity represents an unmooring and reclassifying of categories, a chance of unmaking and making again, a shakeup of the jar of reifications such that what falls out are categories that, though previously as unmixable as oil and water, are newly homogenized, such that what could not before be seen is now not only visible but

---

17. See Jürgen Osterhammel, *The Transformation of the World: A Global History of the Nineteenth Century*, trans. Patrick Camiller, America in the World (Princeton, NJ: Princeton University Press, 2014), esp. 59–67; Christopher Bayly, *The Birth of the Modern World, 1780–1914: Global Connections and Comparisons* (Malden, MA: Blackwell, 2004); Charles Taylor, *A Secular Age* (Cambridge: Belknap Press of Harvard University Press, 2007); Eric Hobsbawm, *The Age of Revolution. 1789–1848* (1962; repr., New York: Vintage, 1996); Hobsbawm, *The Age of Capital, 1848–1875* (1962; repr., New York: Vintage, 1996); and Hobsbawm, *The Age of Empire, 1875–1914* (New York: Pantheon, 1987).

18. Barbara Hahn, *The Jewess Pallas Athena: This Too a Theory of Modernity*, trans. James McFarland (Princeton, NJ: Princeton University Press, 2005), 5, 8–9.

in some ways (perhaps most ways) erases and makes strange the gaze of the past it has displaced.

Hahn's is one aspect of modernity. Another, as Jonathan Hess has observed, is that

> "Modernity" ... is not simply a period or a process. It is not merely something [that people] were subjected to nor can it be grasped as a process of social, economic or political transformation whose conformity to an abstract standard might be quantified. It is, rather, a *discourse*, a mode of envisioning a new and secular world that claimed its legitimacy not with reference to the various traditions and legacies of the past it sought to overcome but solely in relation to itself, to the break it performed with tradition to insist on its right to institute and follow its own norms.[19]

As we will see throughout *The Formation of a Modern Rabbi*, modernity was much more a method to be used than it was an ideology to be encountered. It is certainly true that, by the second half of the nineteenth century, much that was invented or reinvented as modern was too overwhelming to ignore (such as the bureaucratic state, railroads, capitalism, and liberal political norms), and that modernity did eventually become a force that acted on people even against their wills. In this sense, Louis Dupré was correct to note that "cultural changes, such as the one that gave birth to the modern age, have a definitive and irreversible impact that transforms the very essence of reality. Not merely our thinking about the real changes: reality itself changes as we think about it differently. History carries an ontic significance that excludes any reversal of the present."[20] Yet in the decades covered by this book, modernity had not yet acquired its full ontological powers. Modernity was still something one got caught up in and, by dint of acting, further helped to create. As Hahn poetically writes, "a productivity outside all genealogies. A productivity that manifests structures—but how?"[21] The fundamentally transfigurative effects of modernity were not monolithic entities that Jews encountered and to which they adjusted. Instead, modernity was the act of engaging with transformation itself, the construction and imagining of a new set of values, signs, regimes of meaning and appreciation, and built environments that altered the Jewish relationship with its past and (attempted, at least) to outline the contours of its future.

In the specific case of the Jews, modernity, as scholars are still seeking to uncover and decode, took on many faces. As we will see, for Jellinek

---

19. Jonathan Hess, *Germans, Jews and the Claims of Modernity* (New Haven: Yale University Press, 2002), 20–21 (emphasis original).

20. Louis Dupré, *Passage to Modernity: An Essay in the Hermeneutics of Nature and Culture* (New Haven: Yale University Press, 1993), 6.

21. Hahn, *Jewess Pallas Athena*, 11.

it meant uniting the histories and purposes of two civilizations, European and Jewish. Modernity became, then, for Jellinek, the realization of a shared liberal, universalist, ethical heritage, followed by their slow interweaving (through the warp of scholarly history and the weft of cultural intermingling—modernity as the creation of a new mantle for all of Europe to wear, a new civilizational fabric). In this regard, we can read Jellinek as an exemplary figure along one branch of Jewish modernization, branches sometimes aware of and responsive to others, but often as not simply moving in parallel with similar Jewish modernities happening elsewhere on the continent or in other parts of the Jewish people.[22] Ultimately, the aspect of Jellinek's modernity that will be discussed extensively in this book (and which has been less discussed in recent scholarly literature) is that of urban modernity, and specifically the ways in which the synagogue and the rabbi were shaped by these forces in European life and culture.

The question remains, however, how to justify calling the nineteenth century "the modern era." In the usage of this book, the nineteenth century is called "modern" because of the potent combination of three interrelated factors: its specific time line (roughly 1800–1900); the breadth and magnitude of change within that time line (no part of European society remained untouched over the course of the century); and the stark difference in individual human lives at the time line's beginning and end (daily life was virtually unrecognizable from the first year to the last). Observing European society circa 1800 one can immediately identify many of the threads that allowed for modernity. But each of those threads arose at a different historical moment and had yet to come together to constitute widespread change at the most individual level. In 1800 it was still possible (and still normative) to assume a daily existence very nearly identical with that of one's parents, grandparents, and great-grandparents. By 1900, such seamless historical consistency was almost impossible anywhere in Central or Western Europe. In not a single village, town, or city from the borders of the Russian Empire to the shores of the Atlantic Ocean could an individual live a social, intellectual, or economic life unaffected by the developments of the previous century.

And what, exactly, were those developments? To name a few: government-mandated general primary and secondary education (and eventu-

---

22. On modernization of traditional Jewish life, see, e.g., Eliyahu Stern, *The Genius: Elijah of Vilna and the Making of Modern Judaism* (New Haven: Yale University Press, 2013); on sexuality and cultures of the body, see Benjamin Maria Baader, Sharon Gillerman, and Paul Lerner, eds., *Jewish Masculinities: German Jews, Gender, and History* (Bloomington: Indiana University Press, 2012); and on citizenship and nationality, see Malachi Hacohen, *Jacob & Esau: Jewish European History between Nation and Empire* (New York: Cambridge University Press, 2019).

ally, mandated university-granted doctoral degrees for rabbinic leaders); Jewish access to the civil judiciary; the mechanization of essential industries like sewing, farming, and transportation; political and theological assumptions influenced by Enlightenment liberalism; revolutions in the biological and geological sciences; reforms in university curricula and the promotion of the concept of rationalism and objectivity; and massive urban migration. It can be argued that no previous century witnessed this number of fundamental daily-life changes affecting so many people in such a brief time frame. It was in the nineteenth century that many earlier developments and ideas found their fullest flower and fruition, altering not only the physical environment (jobs, homes, villages) of the daily European experience but instantiating and codifying an entire regime of social and intellectual ideologies that together forced a reconsideration of much that Europeans had traditionally assumed to be timeless truths. By the end of the century, modernity was the communal creed that fostered these changes and gave them the simulacrum of new truth. (As has been convincingly argued, even what we think of as "orthodox" denominations—across the religions—are recent interpretations, composed of parts only possible within the world created by modernity.[23]) It was the shared dogma that gave to Europeans the immense energy that made possible the physical, emotional, and spiritual transformation of their world.

Central Europe in Jewish History

Why Central Europe? For any number of reasons this region and era hold little space in the imagination of the contemporary Anglophone world. Not until one begins a conversation about the 1880s and 1890s do Viennese music and science begin to compete with Parisian art and literature in well-known histories of prewar Europe. Such is also the case for Jewish history in this region, where early nineteenth-century Central Europe is but a few bars in the much longer symphony of *La Belle Époque*, Weimar, and the Shoah. Without Moses Mendelssohn and the Haskalah (Jewish Enlightenment) in the mid- to late eighteenth century, Central Europe would be a niche topic in the history of Judaism, the domain of but few scholars of the *Wissenschaft des Judentums*, emancipation, and the Reform

---

23. See, e.g., Adam S. Ferziger, *Exclusion and Hierarchy: Orthodoxy, Nonobservance, and the Emergence of Modern Jewish Identity*, Jewish Culture and Contexts (Philadelphia: University of Pennsylvania Press, 2005); Mordechai Breuer, *Modernity within Tradition: The Social History of Orthodox Jewry in Imperial Germany*, trans. Elizabeth Petuchowski (New York: Columbia University Press, 1992).

movement. In other words, in the popular Anglophone imagination, Central Europe before Sigmund Freud and Gustav Mahler barely registers at all. (And even Freud barely appears in popular discourse anymore. Mahler, mercifully, remains a symphonic staple.)

Yet, throughout the middle decades of the nineteenth century, Central Europe was at the forefront of the sort of modernity defined above, engaging with and being shaped by every one of the larger economic, social, intellectual, and theological forces that affected the entire European world by the turn of the twentieth century.[24] This is as much the case in the spheres of industrialization as in philosophy, in imperialism as in nationalism, in liberalism as in anti-Semitism, in immigration as in urbanization. Politically and militarily weaker than their neighbors to the east and west, neither the German states (before the empire) nor the Habsburg monarchy maintained serious colonial possessions beyond the borders of geographic Europe.[25] For residents of both the German and Habsburg lands, imperialism was a homegrown commodity, as was its result: large urban centers filled with people who spoke and acted differently one from another. In 1860, London and Paris were almost entirely populated by native British and French, respectively.[26] Vienna had Austrians and Budapest had Hungarians, certainly, but both cities also had large communities of Czechs, Slovaks, Romanians, Serbs, Italians, Poles, Ruthenians (Ukrainians), and Jews. The same can be said for all the cities of the Habsburg Empire's borderlands in East Europe. Every kind of people over whom Vienna and (eventually) Berlin ruled came to live in their respective metropolises. What we now think of as the constituents of the European fin de siècle — mass urban migration, ethnic cosmopolitanism, the give and take of liberalism and conservatism, political anti-Semitism, religious adaptation and innovation — were all first seen in the capitals and provincial cities of

---

24. The most important new book to argue for the centrality of the Habsburg Empire in the making of modernity is Peter Judson, *The Habsburg Empire: A New History* (Cambridge: Belknap Press of Harvard University Press, 2016).

25. Beginning in the seventeenth century, Prussia and the Habsburgs maintained small colonial possessions overseas, including Ghana, Mauritania, Benin, and various islands in the East Indies. Following the establishment of the German Empire in 1871, however, Berlin ruled territories in the Pacific as well as in sub-Saharan and East Africa.

26. For an overview of urban migration in Britain and France in the second half of the nineteenth century, see Friedrich Lenger, *European Cities in the Modern Era, 1850–1914*, trans. Joel Golb, Studies in Central European Histories 57 (Leiden: Brill, 2012), 67–94. What Lenger shows is that most urban migrants in the nineteenth century came from the same province as their destination city. For example, London and Paris drew peasants from the vast rural regions surrounding them. Even Berlin drew from the predominantly German regions of Brandenburg and greater Prussia (the Mark) to its east. The ethnic crowding of the Habsburg Danube Valley necessarily made for greater immigrant diversity.

Central Europe decades before they were encountered in France, England, and America.

Jews were in some ways the drivers, but in most ways the beneficiaries, of modernity's early arrival in Central Europe. And modernity affected the Jews differently than it did their gentile neighbors. Any list of changes to Jewish life in the middle decades of the nineteenth century will certainly remain incomplete, but Michael Meyer provides a starting point. For Meyer, Jewish modernity is defined by the amalgamation of an idea of "religious autonomy of the individual"; the need for "freedom from religious control"; the pursuit of economic and professional advancement; the expansion of educational opportunities; the institutionalization of communal governance; and the rationalization and moralization of theology.[27] With this list, we see already the emphasis on the individual over the collective—the civil and cultural acceptance of Jews (as people) by non-Jewish Europeans without an analogous social sanction of Judaism (as a religion). Even the institutionalization of communal governance and the expansion of education were, counterintuitively, innovations that promoted the individual over the collective. In rural Central Europe, interlocking networks of families had long formed the core of Jewish self-governance and communal continuity, with the responsibility for the education of children and the upholding of traditional norms and values incumbent upon families working together within a shared localized framework. With the creation of overarching communal polities in cities, the family unit was no longer the responsible party for the continuation of Jewish tradition and practice. Jewish children, as individuals, became the focus of organized education, with parents ceding oversight to elected or appointed institutional boards. Overall, families became members of communities that existed without their direct contribution and prayed at synagogues that were maintained regardless of their personal, financial, or temporal investment.

---

27. Michael A. Meyer, "Reflections on Jewish Modernization," in *Jewish History and Jewish Memory: Essays in Honor of Yosef Hayim Yerushalmi*, ed. Elisheva Carlebach, John M. Efron, and David N. Myers (Hanover, NH: University Press of New England, 1998), 372–75. See also Jonathan Sheehan, *The Enlightenment Bible: Translation, Scholarship, Culture* (Princeton, NJ: Princeton University Press, 2005), esp. xi–xii. See also Peter Hanns Reill, *The German Enlightenment and the Rise of Historicism* (Berkeley: University of California Press, 1975). Reill distinguishes between the German Enlightenment and its Western cousins, the French and British Enlightenments, noting the uniquely *"bürgerlich"* mentality of the German Enlightenment: "Piety, respect for education, moderation in speech and dress, disdain for the extravagances of the feudal code of honor, and, sometimes, frugality were the hallmarks of the *bürgerlich* mentality" (5). Alongside their non-Jewish peers, we can observe a cultivation of this set of characteristics reflected in writings of early German Jewish maskilim (Jewish members of the Enlightenment).

Urbanization and the Rabbinic Sermon

A major instigator of this shift in religious practice and the rabbinic role was the migration of Central European Jewish communities to cities.[28] With this movement, the loss of village-based religious societies forced a radical restructuring of normative religious practices and assumptions. As Jews began dressing and acting more like their gentile neighbors, synagogues evolved from being places primarily designated for men's prayer to locations where Judaism could be most forcefully and openly expressed. Because urban Jewish neighborhoods were not like their rural counterparts, the synagogue began to represent one of the last places where Judaism could always be found. City streets did not have the same sort of Jewish character as those in towns. The shops did not all close on the Sabbath. Families did not have generations-long histories with their neighbors.[29] To many liberal-leaning governments, urban Jews were not a semi-autonomous community, viewed as a group, but were instead semi-citizens, viewed as individuals.[30] The synagogue became a marker of continued Jewishness and Jewish presence, a place to go to experience Jewish continuity.[31]

---

28. On a theoretical level, what we see happening during this Jewish demographic shift was what some scholars have called the "transnational migration of identity." As Peggy Levitt writes, "In [modernity], religion's fundamental universality and globalism often take precedence over its national forms. Religion, like capitalism or politics, is no longer firmly rooted in a particular country or legal system.... God needs no passport because faith traditions give their followers symbols, rituals, and stories they use to create alternative sacred landscapes, marked by holy sites, shrines, and places of worships" (*God Needs No Passport: Immigrants and the Changing American Religious Landscape* [New York: New Press, 2007], 12–13). See also Levitt, "'You Know, Abraham Was Really the First Immigrant': Religion and Transnational Migration," *International Migration Review* 37, no. 3 (2003): 847–73.

29. Still, it is important to remember that the memory and relationship with historic towns and villages retained a strong influence in a family's new settings. "[S]ometimes migration is as much about the people who stay behind as it is about people who move.... The immigrant experience is not a linear, irreversible journey from one membership to another. Rather, migrants pivot back and forth between sending, receiving, and other orientations at different stages of their lives" (Levitt, *God Needs No Passport*, 23–24).

30. For a comprehensive discussion of the Jewish transition from communal autonomy to national citizenship, see David Sorkin, *Jewish Emancipation: A History across Five Centuries* (Princeton, NJ: Princeton University Press, 2019).

31. Carsten Wilke's work focuses on the dramatic change in the Central European rabbinate, though mainly from the perspective of rabbinical education and yeshiva culture. Little attention is paid to the broader economic movements that uprooted Jewish communities across the continent. See Wilke, "Modern Rabbinical Training: Intercultural Invention and Political Reconfiguration," in *Rabbi – Pastor – Priest: Their Roles and Profiles through the Ages*, ed. Walter Homolka and Heinz-Günther Schöttler, Studia Judaica 64 (Berlin: de Gruyter, 2013), 83–110; and Wilke, *"Den Talmud und den Kant": Rabbinerausbildung an der Schwelle zur Moderne* (Hildesheim: Olms, 2003).

As part of this urban shift, one of the key innovations was the development of the rabbinic sermon. For most of medieval and early modern history, the vast majority of community rabbis were concerned with the inner workings of Jewish law and belief, and synagogues were places predominantly for men's prayer and study. With the advent of the new style sermon, for the first time in Jewish history the local rabbi gained a mass public forum. The idea of the preacher is itself a Christian concept, tied to a theological notion (most dominant in strands of Lutheranism) that words far more than deeds are the way humanity corresponds with divinity. The sermon gained traction within Protestant communities through the Reformation and the Enlightenment because it suggested that ideas were the most powerful actors in human culture. Jewish preachers read Protestant ones (and to an unknowable extent, presumably vice versa). Yet when the content of those Jewish sermons became about the history of the People of Israel, about Jewish ritual and practice, and about the stories of the rabbis, we begin to observe a historical transformation. The sermon became a way of using a new public medium to promote the particularities of Jewish morality and philosophy. It evolved into the main organ through which communal rabbis argued for a deep connection between Jewish beliefs and non-Jewish cultures, histories, and practices. Importantly, these sermons were directed at everyone: men and women, adults and children, religiously learned and secularly educated. The sermon was not the single cause of the new communal values, but it is one of the most obvious and useful markers for tracking the evolution of Jewish thought and practice at the height of modernity.

The Historiography of a Transformed Rabbinate

This books traces in detail the life of just one man, whose education and interests, life span and place of birth, opened the way for him to be a leading player in the formative years of the creation of the modern rabbinate. But Jellinek's story, as we will continue to see in the forthcoming pages, is part of a much broader one that scholars have been trying to understand for the better part of the last century. Histories of Jewish modernization often note the significant differences between the role of the rabbi and the synagogue in, for example, 1750 and 1850, or 1600 and 1900.[32] As all these accounts make clear, there is significant divergence in practice and philosophy between the rabbinate and synagogues of the premodern and

---

32. See Simon Schwarzfuchs, *A Concise History of the Rabbinate*, Jewish Society and Culture (Oxford: Blackwell, 1993); Jacob Neusner, ed., *The Rabbinate in America: Reshaping an Ancient Calling* (New York: Garland, 1993); and Jack Wertheimer, ed., *The American Synagogue: A Sanctuary Transformed* (New York: Cambridge University Press, 1987).

modern periods. All the modern biographies of key rabbinic figures of this era note the broader contextual transformations, though none attempts an authoritative description or analysis of the distinctions that arose, what they entailed, or why their implications were so profound.[33]

As this book demonstrates in fuller detail, it was only beginning with the decades of mass urban migration from about 1850 onward that large numbers of culturally distinct Jews encountered one another in a single religious setting.[34] The image of a rabbi standing at a lectern before a multitude of people whose extended families he (and often today, she) does not know, and who are themselves each descended from a different, more localized tradition with its own liturgy, music, languages, clothing, and food, has little historical precedent before the middle of the nineteenth century.[35] In 1957, Max Gruenewald published a description of the rabbi that succinctly captures the nature of the modern position.

> Already towards the end of the [nineteenth] century rabbis and large communities encountered excessive demands on their time....[Abraham

---

33. There are some very good biographies of nineteenth-century rabbis, all of which comment on the evolving role of rabbis and religious institutions as it contextualizes their subject. But none of these works attempts to make a larger claim about the transformation of the rabbinate during this period. See Michał Galas, *Rabbi Marcus Jastrow and His Vision for the Reform of Judaism: A Study in the History of Judaism in the Nineteenth Century*, trans. Anna Tilles, Jews of Poland (Boston: Academic Studies Press, 2013); Roland Tasch, *Samson Raphael Hirsch: Jüdische Erfahrungswelten Im Historischen Kontext*, Studia Judaica 59 (Berlin: de Gruyter, 2011); Susannah Heschel, *Abraham Geiger and the Jewish Jesus*, Chicago Studies in the History of Judaism (Chicago: University of Chicago Press, 1998); Sefton D. Temkin, *Creating American Reform Judaism: The Life and Times of Isaac Mayer Wise* (Portland, OR: Littman Library of Jewish Civilization, 1998); and Noah H. Rosenbloom, *Tradition in an Age of Reform: The Religious Philosophy of Samson Raphael Hirsch* (Philadelphia: Jewish Publication Society of America, 1976).

34. During the premodern period, especially in trading centers, it was not uncommon for small numbers of culturally distinct Jews to live in the same neighborhood. In the centuries after the establishment of the Venice Ghetto (1516), the Jewish community in that city had at least half a dozen synagogues maintained by culturally distinct Jewish communities: the Scuola Italiana for the Venetian locals; the Scuola Grande Tedesca for the Ashkenazim, or German Jewish merchants who had made their home in the republican city-state; the Scuola Canton for Jews from Southern France; and the Scuola Levantina and the Scuola Spagnola for Sephardic Jews from other parts of the Mediterranean. What we do not see until the middle of the nineteenth century are the large numbers of culturally distinct Jews coming together to practice in the same synagogues and listen to the same rabbis.

35. Indeed, the nineteenth century might be equated with one other moment in early modern Jewish history, when so many families moved from one place to another: the expulsions from Iberia at the end of the fifteenth century. No migration on that scale had taken place since the second century. However, if we combine the economic migrations of the nineteenth century with the war-related dislocations of the twentieth, nearly every Jewish family in the world is now living in a different place from where its ancestors were born a mere two hundred years ago. That is a historically unprecedented level of Jewish communal movement.

Geiger noted that] in a small *kehillah* [community] the rabbi is not only a teacher but also peacemaker in family quarrels, initiator and founder of charitable associations, in short, here he is in the true sense a *seelsorger* [pastor].³⁶ During the second decade of our [twentieth] century, the rabbi who was a student above all, became a faint memory. Henceforth, he had to fight for leisure in order to continue with his studies or to fill the gaps in his background. In addition to his representative duties, to speechmaking and a heavy teaching and lecturing schedule a large part of his time was spent in helping needy people and coming to the aid of an ever increasing number of distressed families that had met with the business failure and face ruin.... For the orthodox rabbi there has to be added supervision of *Shechitah* [kosher butchering] and *Kashruth* [all food preparatory laws], the stream of ritual questions some of which came before his Beth Din [rabbinic court]. Considering the tasks to be shouldered, the heavy programme and short holidays of the rabbi, it is the more remarkable that so many of the rabbis continued to study and to publish.³⁷

But how did we get here? Put simply, before this book there has been no analysis of the creation of the modern rabbinate that contextualizes it within the economic, intellectual, and demographic transformation (often newly possible because of liberal political reforms) taking place in post-Napoleonic Central Europe. Nor has there been a study that describes such a direct line between the practices of contemporary Euro-American Jewry and the innovations and contingencies created by mid-nineteenth-century Central European rabbis.³⁸

The Formation of a Modern Rabbi partially fills this gap. It focuses on changes in ritual practice and theological assumptions, as well as the built environment of the new urban centers. Through Jellinek's particular story, this book traces how, as the nineteenth century progressed, the rabbi increasingly took on the role of being a public preacher and translator of contemporary ideas into a Jewish idiom, someone who conveyed a theological and moral message that might very well have differed with the personally held beliefs of particular congregants. Being a rabbi became about the public performance of Jewish practice and dogma.³⁹ The urban

---

36. A literal translation of the German gives a more textured feel for the word: "one who listens to the soul."

37. See Max Gruenewald, "The Modern Rabbi," *Leo Baeck Institute Year Book* 2 (1957): 85–97, here 90–91.

38. A number of earlier works have examined various aspects of this phenomenon. See Margit Schad, *Rabbiner Michael Sachs: Judentum als höhere Lebensanschauung*, Netiva 7 (Hildesheim: Olms, 2007); Wilke, *"Den Talmud und den Kant"*; Andreas Brämer, *Rabbiner Zacharias Frankel: Wissenschaft des Judentums und Konservative Reform im 19. Jahrhundert*, Netiva 3 (Hildesheim: Olms, 2000); and David Ellenson, *Rabbi Esriel Hildesheimer and the Creation of a Modern Jewish Orthodoxy* (Tuscaloosa: University of Alabama Press, 1990).

39. See Naomi W. Cohen, *What the Rabbis Said: The Public Discourse of Nineteenth-Century*

communal synagogue with which the rabbi became intimately associated was a place for the display of religion, in a context in which the outward demonstration of piety or commanded practice was rapidly lessening.[40] For Jews in Central Europe, from the start of the nineteenth century to its end, the public practice of sacredness—of declaring the presence of God in one's midst—became ever more confined to communal synagogues. On the one hand, because the rabbi was a weekly preacher, a wider segment of the community heard his message; on the other, he became mainly associated with the synagogue and its bureaucracy, and his intimate presence in the lives of families diminished. In this new urban setting, the rabbi took on the role of performing traditional belief and action rather than arbitrating within a community governed thoroughly by Jewish law.

The contemporary scholarly historiography of European Jewry has led us to a place where we can begin to write a more unified history of nineteenth-century Jewish social and religious transformation, one that weaves together the diverse strands of urban migration, social integration, communal synagogue formation, the adoption of the language of liberalism, and the reimagination of the role of the rabbi. By concentrating on the life, works, and ideas of Adolf Jellinek, *The Formation of a Modern Rabbi* offers a focused and detailed narrative framework for understanding the crucial junctures that fundamentally transformed Jewish religious life in the past two centuries. It explores how modern Jewish practice came about—what led up to it, when the choices were made, and for what reasons.

American Rabbis (New York: New York University Press, 2008). Cohen does not stress the novelty of the rabbinic sermon and its place in the fundamental restructuring of communal Judaism. Similarly, Gruenewald's study of the modern rabbi focused narrowly on theological and teaching seminaries and did not address any of the broader demographic or cultural issues central to this work; see Gruenewald, "Modern Rabbi."

40. This was true in Central Europe by the 1870s, and eventually across the continent and the whole Anglo-American world in the twentieth century. Jews in any number of national settings could find a religious space in the synagogues of foreign towns and cities. "In today's postmodern era, religious communities have become vigorous creators of an emergent transnational civil society" (Susanne Hoeber Rudolph, "Introduction: Religion, States, and Transnational Civil Society," in *Transnational Religion and Fading States*, ed. Susanne Hoeber Rudolph and James Piscatori [Boulder, CO: Westview Press, 1997], 1–24, here 1).

1

On the Threshold of Modernity: Jellinek's Early Years

A Tale of Three Brothers

Adolf (Aron) Jellinek was born June 26, 1821, in Drslawitz (Czech: Drslavice), a small town northwest of Ungarisch-Brod (Czech: Uherský Brod) in what was the Ungarisch Hradisch (Czech: Uherské Hradiště) region of the Habsburg Crown Land of Moravia.[1] He was the oldest of three brothers in a family we might now consider of lower-middle-class means. The boys were raised in a characteristically traditional Jewish home: the family celebrated the Sabbath and festivals, and the children attended the local *cheder*, or Jewish boys school, in Ungarisch-Brod, where they learned to read and write in Hebrew and memorized passages from Torah and Mishnah.[2] As late as the 1820s, the life of a Jewish family in

---

1. For overviews of Jellinek's life, see Kempter, *Die Jellineks 1820–1955*; and Rosenmann, *Dr. Adolf Jellinek*. See also Josef Bartoš, *Uherský Brod: Minulost i současnost slováckého města* (Brno: Blok, 1971). For an overview of Czech history, see Jaroslav Pánek and Oldřich Tůma, *A History of the Czech Lands* (Prague: Charles University Karolinum Press, 2009). For accounts of Czech Jewry, see Martin Joachim Wein, *History of the Jews in the Bohemian Lands*, Studies in Central European Histories 61 (Leiden: Brill, 2015); Hillel J. Kieval, *The Making of Czech Jewry: National Conflict and Jewish Society in Bohemia, 1870–1918*, Studies in Jewish History (New York: Oxford University Press, 1988); Kieval, "Texts and Contest: Myths of Origin and Myths of Belonging in Nineteenth-Century Bohemia," in Carlebach, Efron, and Myers, *Jewish History and Jewish Memory*, 348–68; Kieval, *Languages of Community: The Jewish Experience in the Czech Lands* (Berkeley: University of California Press, 2000); Kieval, "Choosing to Bridge: Revisiting the Phenomenon of Cultural Mediation," *Bohemia: A Journal of History and Civilization in Central Europe* 46 (2005): 15–27; Kieval, "Imperial Embraces and Ethnic Challenges: The Politics of Jewish Identity in the Bohemian Lands," *Shofar: An Interdisciplinary Journal of Jewish Studies* 30, no. 4 (2013): 1–17; and Michael L. Miller, *Rabbis and Revolution: The Jews of Moravia in the Age of Emancipation*, Stanford Studies in Jewish History and Culture (Stanford, CA: Stanford University Press, 2011). For a collection of primary sources translated into English about Judaism in Bohemia and Moravia from the eighteenth century to the twentieth, see Wilma Abeles Iggers, ed., *The Jews of Bohemia and Moravia: A Historical Reader* (Detroit: Wayne State University Press, 1992).

2. For an account of traditional *cheder* education, see Ephraim Kanarfogel, *The Intellec-*

Moravia more or less resembled that of one from any of the preceding four or five centuries, and Adolf's parents, Isak Löw and Sarah Back, were typical members of this rather unpretentious Jewish community spread across the southern Czech lands. Isak and Sarah, therefore, had little reason to suspect that theirs would be the last generation where historic norms prevailed: by their boys' teenage years, the social climate of Moravian Jewry had changed so drastically that it was not unusual for the brightest sons of rural Jews to go to school in Prague or Berlin, or for young men born to peddlers and cloth-makers to run businesses in Budapest. The generational transformation that occurred during this period was dramatic simply on this individual scale. If, as Adolf would quite quickly come to believe, rabbinic Judaism itself were to survive in modernity, it would need to change as well.

Sarah never lived to see the world her sons would come to have a significant hand in building. She died in 1826, leaving Isak, a brewery attendant, to care for their three children. Sarah was the granddaughter and daughter of two Moravian rabbis, Tzvi Hirsch Broda and Aron Back, respectively, and her marriage exemplified the mostly classless society that existed among Moravia's Jewish families at the turn of the nineteenth century.[3] Denied many of the rights that would have allowed industrious individuals to accumulate wealth, and without the major cities that often create economic divisions between urban and rural communities, the Jews of Moravia lived more or less on equal measure with one another.[4] While religiously observant, Isak had likely not received an extensive Jewish education himself, though he clearly knew its value: he sent all three boys to grade school and university, encouraging their interests and intellectual causes both at home and through extensive correspondence.

As in many families that found themselves caught up in broader cultural upheavals, sibling rivalries and petty antagonisms played out against the backdrop of international politics and shifting social opportunities. Adolf and his younger brothers Hermann (1822–1848) and Moritz (1823–

---

tual History and Rabbinic Culture of Medieval Ashkenaz (Detroit: Wayne State University Press, 2013).

3. Zvi Hirsch Broda, who was born in Ungarisch-Brod, died in 1820, unmet by his grandsons. He was the son of David Broda, rabbi in Szenitz (Slovak: Seneca), Slovakia, and in Burgenland, Austria, in the closing decades of the eighteenth century.

4. Adolf Frankl-Grün, *Geschichte der Juden in Ungarisch-Brod: Nebst Biographien von R. Moses Perls, P. Singer, Ad. Jellinek, P.F. Frankl &c. Nach Archivalien Dargestellt* (Vienna: Waizner, 1905), 49–51. As Grün explains the family tree: "Rabbi Pessach Singer had two sons-in-law: Simon Hamburger, the father of the family Hamburger-Singer in Proßnitz; and Aron, son of his sister, the wife of Rabbi Hirsch Broda in Kittsee. After the death of his first wife, Rebekka, R. Aron married the daughter of his brother-in-law, Isak Löw [no relation to Adolf's father.] He was head of the Jewish schools in Brod, later rabbi in Kojetein, and the grandfather of Dr. [Adolf] Jellinek, who bore his name.... [Adolf's] mother, Sarah, was the granddaughter of Rabbi Hirsch Broda in Kittsee and the daughter of Rabbi Aron Back."

1883) were, each in his own way, emblematic of the diverging paths that European modernity was creating for its Jewish minority. All three boys received their educations in Ungarisch-Brod, Proßnitz (Czech: Prostějov), Prague, and Leipzig. Adolf stayed on in Leipzig, earning his doctorate in Near Eastern languages and becoming a leading scholar of the early *Wissenschaft des Judentums* (see chapters 2 and 3). The youngest of the three, Moritz, studied economics in Leipzig and Vienna before settling permanently in Budapest. Moritz quickly rose to prominence in the Hungarian capital, helping found the city's first streetcar system and running it as its president, as well as organizing a Budapest stock exchange. For his successes, he was named a member of the Hungarian Academy of Sciences.[5]

After his initial schooling, Hermann, the middle brother, traveled across Central Europe in a peripatetic life of writing and campaigning for the cause of political liberalism.[6] In Prague, he studied philosophy and theology; in Leipzig, economics, politics, and (outside the university) socialism.[7] After receiving his doctorate, Hermann left Saxony for Vienna in 1847. Arriving in a city on the brink of turmoil, his polemical style and sharp mind were highly regarded by the capital's liberal intelligentsia.[8] Participating in the March 1848 revolution, Hermann authored, in the following months, a long treatise, *A Critical History of the Vienna Revolution from the 13th of March to Its Constituent Parliament*,[9] linking the Enlightenment ideals of the French Revolution of 1789 to those promoted by his compatriots in Vienna in 1848.[10] A harsh critic of Austrian politics and culture ("Austria has produced no philosophers, no politicians, no economists who have any creativity. Its poetry cannot be attacked since its only object of pleasure is the factual, and it exercises no influence on the masses of

---

5. Michael L. Miller, "Going Native: Moritz Jellinek and the Modernization of the Hungarian Economy," in *The Economy in Jewish History: New Perspectives on the Interrelationship between Ethnicity and Economic Life*, ed. Gideon Reuveni and Sarah Wobick-Segev (New York: Berghahn Books, 2011), 157–72.

6. Hermann's story is told in detail in Kempter, *Die Jellineks 1820–1955*.

7. In this era, the connection between socialism and Judaism (and therefore with anti-Semitism) had not yet been made. See Robert S. Wistrich, "Socialism and Judeophobia: Antisemitism in Europe before 1914," *Leo Baeck Institute Year Book* 37 (1992): 111–45.

8. On 1848 and its impact in Vienna, Germany, and across Europe, see Hans-Joachim Hahn, *The 1848 Revolutions in German-Speaking Europe*, Themes in Modern German History (Harlow, UK: Longman, 2001); R. J. W. Evans and Hartmut Pogge von Strandmann, eds., *The Revolutions in Europe, 1848–1849: From Reform to Reaction* (Oxford: Oxford University Press, 2000); Mike Rapport, *1848: Year of Revolution* (London: Little, Brown, 2008); and Jonathan Sperber, ed., *European Revolutions, 1848–1851*, 2nd ed. (New York: Cambridge University Press, 2005).

9. Hermann Jellinek, *Kritische Geschichte der Wiener Revolution vom 13. März bis zum constituirenden Reichstag* (Vienna: Sommer, 1848).

10. See Salo W. Baron, "The Impact of the Revolution of 1848 on Jewish Emancipation," *Jewish Social Studies* 11, no. 3 (1949): 195–248.

the nation"[11]), Hermann's ringing credo was "We have translated the feelings of the Revolution into thoughts,"[12] by which he meant that, despite setbacks in achieving changes to policy or governance through action, the ideology of liberalism as an idea was sure to persist. Tragically (and no doubt needlessly), in November 1848 Hermann, along with a handful of his compatriots, was executed in a Viennese prison for actions committed against the Habsburg crown. They were some of the very few agitators to lose their lives in what was (by comparison with the response of other municipalities in Europe) a fairly bloodless political uprising.

The relationship between Adolf and Hermann had become increasingly strained throughout the 1830s and 1840s. Hermann felt that Adolf was insufficiently devoted to the liberal cause, and of the personal notes he wrote his family before his execution, Adolf appears to have received nothing. Still, Adolf's love for Hermann overrode their mutual grievances; he named the youngest of his three sons after his departed middle brother, and penned an emotional essay on the occasion of the tenth anniversary of Hermann's execution.[13]

Adolf spent his school years in Ungarisch-Brod and the nearby city of Proßnitz, whose Jewish communities still mostly functioned like the traditional rural societies that had come before them. Yet change, both philosophical and political, was rapidly approaching. Moving to Prague in 1838, Jellinek joined one of Central Europe's most dynamic and innovative Jewish communities, led by rabbis who encouraged their students to study at the city's Charles University and read maskilic (Jewish Enlightenment) tracts. In Prague, Jellinek learned with rabbis who sought to actively and peacefully integrate the newest philosophical developments emanating from universities in Berlin, Jena, Weimar, and Paris, with traditional Jewish texts and philosophical systems. Still, while its leaders were innovative and experimental, the social and political dynamics of the Prague community were very much those of a more traditional Judaism, and the rabbis at the city's main yeshiva were not the communal educators and activists that would, within a few decades, define modern urban Judaism.[14]

---

11. H. Jellinek, *Kritische Geschichte*, iv–v.

12. H. Jellinek, *Kritische Geschichte*, v.

13. Max Hermann Jellinek (1868–1938) followed in his father's scholarly footsteps, pursing a doctorate in philology at the University of Vienna. In 1900 he was appointed assistant professor, and from then until his death received numerous honors and awards. In 1968, the street "Max-Jellinek-Gasse" was named in his honor in the Floridsdorf neighborhood of Vienna. (Alongside letters to their father, Isak Löw, Adolf Jellinek retained in his collection letters from his brother Hermann's youth. See NLI ARC 4* 1588 [folder 58]).

14. While in Prague, Jellinek almost certainly encountered Rabbi Michael Sachs, whose residence in the Bohemian capital (1836–1844) made him one of the most famous preachers among German Jews, and a leading advocate of a form of traditional Judaism. See Schad, *Rabbiner Michael Sachs*.

Therefore, when Jellinek left Prague for Leipzig in 1841, he had yet to see a model of the rabbi as we might recognize it today—in fact, neither had Jellinek seen an exemplar of the man he would become nor had he yet realized the role he himself would play in the creation of modern Jewish rabbinic leadership. Instead, in Leipzig, Jellinek sought to become a scholar, and his early years there were devoted almost entirely to the causes of *Wissenschaft des Judentums*, at whose methods and practices he greatly excelled. Not until he was asked to take up leadership responsibilities for the growing Leipzig Jewish community in the late 1840s did his focus begin to shift away from scholarship and toward the future of the rabbinate (see chapter 5). By the time he moved to Vienna in 1857, Jellinek was consumed with the need to find a Jewish voice within European modernity, one that felt in congruity with Jewish tradition but was also honest about the importance and monumentality of the changes brought by advances in fields such as the natural sciences and liberal political philosophy.

It is clear that, each in his own way, the Jellinek brothers spent their lives engaged with the questions raised by political activism and intellectual liberalism. Yet what is as astounding as the arc of each of their careers is the fact that such options were open to them at all. That three young Jewish boys, born in the early 1820s in rural Moravia, could grow up to attend university, publish books in German, become political activists, city planners, stockbrokers, and scholars was nearly inconceivable a mere two decades before their birth. Such a social revolution had profound effects on the religious and cultural life of the Jewish communities of Central Europe.[15]

Jewish Society and Emancipation in Turn-of-the-Century Moravia

To an outside observer, Moravian Jewish life in the early decades of the nineteenth century would have appeared remarkably similar to that of a century or more previous. Yet some parts of modernity—in the guise of philosophy, the whisperings of emancipatory ideas, and technological innovations—were, even in the rural villages, already a part of the conversation. As early as the 1790s, Habsburg political reforms dictated that modern subjects be taught in Jewish primary schools in Bohemia.[16] Though Moravia differed from Bohemia in its lack of central Jewish authority and its

---

15. See Ruth Kestenberg-Gladstein, *Neuere Geschichte der Juden in den böhmischen Ländern*, Erster Teil: Das Zeitalter der Aufklärung, 1780–1830, Schriftenreihe wissenschaftlicher Abhandllungen des Leo Baeck Instituts 18 (Tübingen: Mohr Siebeck, 1969).

16. As Hillel Kieval describes it, despite "deep-seated suspicions on the part of Prague's rabbinical leadership of both the motives and effects of [modernization], figures such as Ezekiel Landau (1713–1793) and Elazar Fleckeles (1754–1826) ultimately gave their approval to

exceedingly rural character, the effects of these educational reforms nevertheless made their way to the small towns of the southern half of the Czech lands. By Jellinek's birth, the rabbis at the Proßnitz yeshiva had already been writing about enlightenment for the better part of three decades.[17]

Emancipation, we might say, began for Moravia's Jews on two different dates, separated by a quarter of a century: January 2, 1782, and December 2, 1805. On the first date, Holy Roman Emperor Joseph II (1741–1790) issued an "Edict of Toleration for the Jews of Lower Austria," which granted to them a list of civil rights nominally equivalent to those enjoyed by their Christian coinhabitants.[18] Extended to the Jews of Bohemia, Moravia, Silesia, and Hungary during the following months, Joseph's initial edict signaled to Habsburg Jewry that their sovereign was willing to act on his promise of eliminating inequalities in the empire's legal code.[19]

Though it would take until the reforms following the 1848 revolution to witness wholesale change in the Jews' civil status, and all the way until 1867 for full equality under law in the Habsburg Empire, Joseph's edict suggested that the philosophical liberalism—at least where it concerned educational and employment opportunities—being advocated in the salons of Berlin and Paris was making an impact on the governance of the lands of Central Europe as well.[20] Ideals of republican liberalism, in combination with the various other elements of modernity, created the framework upon which fundamental change could be imagined and then instituted.[21] According to data collected by Stefi Jersch-Wenzel, by 1848 these reforms would have affected a Habsburg Jewish population of about 108,000 (out of 34 million total crown subjects), mostly concentrated in Jellinek's home provinces of Bohemia and Moravia.[22]

---

the educational reforms. Between 1790 and 1831 ... some 17,800 children received a Western-style education at the Prague [Jewish] school" (*Making of Czech Jewry*, 6).

17. See Ruth Kestenberg-Gladstein, "A Voice from the Prague Enlightenment," *Leo Baeck Institute Year Book* 9 (1964): 295–304.

18. See Jacob Katz, *Out of the Ghetto: The Social Background of Jewish Emancipation, 1770–1870* (Cambridge: Harvard University Press, 1973), 161–66.

19. See Rachel Manekin, "Praying at Home in Lemberg: The *Minyan* Laws of the Habsburg Empire 1776–1848," in *Jews and Their Neighbors in Eastern Europe since 1750*, ed. Israel Bartal, Antony Polonsky, and Scott Ury, Polin: Studies in Polish Jewry 24 (Oxford: Littman Library of Jewish Civilization, 2012), 49–69. For a lengthy discussion of the reforms of Joseph II, see Judson, *Habsburg Empire*.

20. See Arno Herzig, "The Process of Emancipation: From the Congress of Vienna to the Revolution of 1848/1849," *Leo Baeck Institute Year Book* 37 (1992): 61–69 and Sorkin, *Jewish Emancipation*, ch. 12.

21. The lands of the Russian Empire, including those of the Polish-Lithuanian Commonwealth, lie outside this study. Their history, while in some ways reflecting that of Central Europe, is ultimately quite distinct. Generalizations made here should not be assumed to apply to lands east of the Habsburg frontier.

22. Stefi Jersch-Wenzel, "Population Shifts and Occupational Structures," in *German-Jewish History in Modern Times*, vol. 2: *Emancipation and Acculturation, 1780–1871*, ed.

The second date that modernity came to Central European Jewry was in December 1805, and this time is was through the barrel of a gun. On the second day of that month, outside the rural village of Austerlitz (Czech: Slavkov u Brna), Napoleon Bonaparte's Grand Army defeated the combined forces of the Russian and Holy Roman Empires. The House of Habsburg, accepting defeat, signed the Treaty of Pressburg, granting Napoleon rule over its vast territories in the heart of Europe. In turn, as part of his consolidation of power, Napoleon imposed new laws on the conquered regions, including one of equal citizenship for the Jews.

Most European Jews around the turn of the nineteenth century were born into a world of small, rural townships where Jewish families were deeply reliant on one another to provide the religious and social backbone of communal life. Yet the French left behind cultures changed by occupation, and by the 1820s, what for the Jews had been centuries of relative social segregation was rapidly dissolving. Though short lived, Napoleon's rule over Central Europe gave rise to a series of liberalizing reforms whose effects quickly came to transform the historical expectations of Jews and open possibilities for widespread educational and social advancement unprecedented in the history of Christendom. Certainly, many cities and principalities sought to turn back the Jewish emancipatory laws they felt had been illegally forced upon them during the occupation.[23] But with the brief implementation of Napoleonic law, as well as the unforeseen consequences of Europe's technological revolutions (only moderately felt and certainly little understood at the time of the Napoleonic Wars), the forms of Jewish traditionalism highly dependent on semi-isolated rural life were in the process of vanishing forever.

Ungarisch-Brod: Religious Life in Rural Moravia

The village of Drslawitz, where the three Jellinek brothers were born, was too small to host a synagogue of its own. The more formal community existed in Ungarisch-Brod, the larger town three miles to the southeast.[24]

Michael Brenner, Stefi Jersch-Wenzel, and Michael A. Meyer (New York: Columbia University Press, 1996), 50–89, here 51 and 54.

23. See Stefi Jersch-Wenzel, "Legal Status and Emancipation," in Brenner, Jersch-Wenzel, and Meyer, *German-Jewish History in Modern Times*, 2:7–49; and Reinhard Rürup, "German Liberalism and the Emancipation of the Jews," *Leo Baeck Institute Year Book* 20 (1975): 59–68. For a specific example, see Dagmar Herzog, "Anti-Judaism in Intra-Christian Conflict: Catholics and Liberals in Baden in the 1840s," *Central European History* 27, no. 3 (1994): 267–81.

24. An image of a later synagogue (constructed in 1875 in neo-Romanesque style) from

It was in Ungarisch-Brod that the three Jellinek brothers attended a formal Jewish school, which was likely run not by a rabbi but by a learned lay member of the town's community. Still, as the boys grew older and as Adolf showed promise and interest in rabbinic learning, Ungarisch-Brod's rabbi would have become an increasingly central presence in the young man's life. Nevertheless, it is important not to impose the contemporary vision of "communal rabbi" onto these figures. They were neither community leaders nor activists, and certainly did not play a central role in creating the cultural "Jewishness" that made these Moravian Jews distinct from their gentile German and Czech neighbors.

We can get an interesting picture of rural Jewish life in the pre-emancipation period by tracing the places of employment of the rabbis of Ungarisch-Brod. In his pamphlet on the history of the Jews of Ungarisch-Brod, Adolf Frankl-Grün describes the Moravian rabbinate as being something of a world unto itself.[25] Often spending their entire lives in this one province, these men married daughters of other rabbis or local respected families and traveled often among the villages and towns of the countryside. The three rabbis who held court in Ungarisch-Brod while the Jellinek's were children provide a simple example of this much wider phenomenon. Moses Jehuda Rosenfeld (1755–1828) was rabbi in Ungarisch-Brod from 1806 to 1828. Born in Piesling (Czech: Písečné), he was probably raised in Jamnitz (Czech: Jemnice), after which he lived in Proßnitz (where he was a private tutor alongside Moses Sofer [1762–1839]) before moving to Ungarisch-Brod—all Moravian towns).[26] In 1829, Israel Wolf (d. 1830), originally from the little village of Koritschan (Czech: Koryčany) in Moravia, succeeded Rosenfeld.[27] David Buchheim (d. 1841), rabbi from 1830 to 1841, replaced Wolf after the latter's untimely death. Buchheim was born in Proßnitz and studied at the yeshiva there. He married a woman from the Moravian town of Kremsier (Czech: Kroměříž) and was rabbi in the nearby villages of Kojetein (Czech: Kojetín) and Hranice before mov-

---

the region of Ungarisch Hradisch (Czech: Uherské Hradiště) can be found in Arno Pařík et al., eds., *Symbols of Emancipation: Nineteenth-Century Synagogues in the Czech Lands* (Prague: Jewish Museum in Prague, 2013), 60. For a history of the town, see Frankl-Grün, *Geschichte der Juden in Ungarisch-Brod*.

25. Frankl-Grün, *Geschichte der Juden in Ungarisch-Brod*, 46–75. The capital of Moravia, Brünn (Czech: Brno), hosted one of the more sizable Jewish communities in the territory.

26. See Michael Brocke, Julius Carlebach, and Carsten Wilke, eds., *Biographisches Handbuch der Rabbiner*, Teil 1: *Die Rabbiner der Emanzipationszeit in den deutschen, böhmischen und großpolnischen Ländern, 1781–1871* (Munich: Saur, 2004), 751. Rosenfeld had close ties to the Back family. He is likely the rabbi who married Isak and Sara, presided over the births of Adolf, Hermann, and Moritz, and paid a call at Sara's untimely funeral. Moses Sofer (born Moses Schreiber), also called the Chatam Sofer, was one of the most influential rabbis in Central Europe. He was a sharp critic of modernity, and his writings and responsa continue to influence Orthodox Judaism today.

27. Brocke, Carlebach, and Wilke, *Biographisches Handbuch*, 1:911.

ing to Ungarisch-Brod. (One of Buchheim's few known publications is a response, published in German, to the writings of Moses Sofer, the onetime colleague of Rosenfeld.)[28]

These three brief summaries exemplify how truly small the world of Moravian Jewry was in the centuries before modernity. The near distances of these locations and the relative infrequency of long-distance travel not only reveal the difficulty of movement in that era but also emphasize the vastly different expectation of what a Jewish life was or should be—all of which should underline the enormous social disruption that accompanied the first generation of Jewish sons who engaged the new possibilities of travel in modernity. Starting in the 1820s, the brightest (or wealthiest) children of Moravian Jewry were leaving for universities and professional careers elsewhere in Central and Western Europe, often to different kingdoms or empires. Instead of using their talents to help their neighbors or devoting their attentions to the advancement of their own home communities, they were far away, thinking about lofty ideals or building new machines.

For its size, Ungarisch-Brod was unusually fertile ground for Jewish life in the decades before Jellinek's birth. In hagiographical terms, Frankl-Grün wrote, "The rabbis [of Ungarisch-Brod] first discovered the abilities of gifted children of the community to the study of the law.... Their contributions are why it has long been recorded that Ungarisch-Brod was 'a city full of sages and scribes.'"[29] The senior rabbi of Ungarisch-Brod at the time of Jellinek's birth, Moses Rosenfeld, undoubtedly fostered this intellectual vibrancy.[30] Rosenfeld maintained the town's tradition of cultural exchange with Proßnitz, the larger city fifty miles to the northwest, which housed a well-respected yeshiva long dedicated to a form of traditional rabbinic education that engaged in the debate and study of non-Jewish philosophy and writing.[31] (All three Jellinek children, because they showed intellectual promise, were sent to study at the yeshiva in Proßnitz. As Adolf remembered much later, however, he was the only one of the brothers who demonstrated a deep interest in Torah study.[32]) Rosenfeld's intellectually vibrant court certainly provided the young Adolf with a chance to see and hear much about the changes coming to European Jewry.

---

28. Brocke, Carlebach, and Wilke, *Biographisches Handbuch der Rabbiner*, 1:215.
29. Frankl-Grün, *Geschichte der Juden in Ungarisch-Brod*, 47.
30. See Brocke, Carlebach, and Wilke, *Biographisches Handbuch der Rabbiner*, 1:751.
31. See the discussion of the rabbis of Jellinek's youth in Frankl-Grün, *Geschichte der Juden in Ungarisch-Brod*, 69–71.
32. Moritz Eisler, "Feuilleton: R. Moses Katz Wanefried: Eine Reminiscenz aus dem Leben des Herrn Dr. Adolf Jellinek von einem Jugendgenossen," *Die Neuzeit* 21, Friday, May 22, 1891, 205–7, here 207.

Proßnitz: Moderate Religious Reform after the Haskalah

Until age thirteen Jellinek continued both his Jewish and German educations in Ungarisch-Brod, after which he left to live and study at the Proßnitz yeshiva, under the tutelage of Rabbi Moses Katz Wanefried (d. 1850), a disciple of Moses Sofer.[33] When Jellinek left Ungarisch-Brod in 1833, Buchheim had been the town's rabbi for three years, most significantly during Adolf's bar mitzvah, the celebration of his attainment of Jewish adulthood. That Jellinek would come of age under a series of rabbis with close ties to both the (comparatively) progressive yeshiva in Proßnitz and the antimodernist thought of Moses Sofer offers a compelling metaphor for the promises and hazards of modernity.[34] In Proßnitz, and later in Prague, Jellinek had his first chance to see how the newest generation of religious leaders had responded to the call of religious reforms, the opportunities afforded by modernity, and the new demands of "enlightened" states. Though many of the factors that would lead to the immense changes of the mid-nineteenth century and that would make his decades as a rabbi so significant (economic reforms, large-scale urban migration, the emergence of a German-speaking Jewish bourgeois class) were still some decades off, nevertheless, a new *shulchan aruch*, a new set table of Jewish intellectual modernity, was most certainly being laid out.

During Jellinek's residency there, Proßnitz was a thriving commercial town with a (relatively) large Jewish population whose leaders were central figures in a moderate form of the Haskalah—what Michael L. Miller has called the "rabbinic Haskalah."[35] What they were moderating was an ideology begun in the later decades of a the eighteenth century by a group of avant-garde Jews committed to philosophical progress and a mutual

---

33. See Bohuslav Eliáš, "Zur Geschichte der Israelitengemeinde von Prostějov (Proßnitz)," *Husserl Studies* 10 (1994): 237–48.

34. In this respect, Hillel J. Kieval writes, "[The Czech] lands provide a kind of historical laboratory in which to observe both the power and the limits of traditional Jewish authority and of conservative responses to transformative change. [A yeshiva like Proßnitz's offered] not the reactionary conservatism of [Moses] Sofer's Hungary; its resistance operated, rather, as a succession of brakes on the pace and extent of change … an effort to maintain a strict separation between educational streams without standing in the way of state-mandated progress, a valiant endeavor to marry Jewish Enlightenment to halakhic observance and respect for rabbinic authority" ("The Unforeseen Consequences of Cultural Resistance: Haskalah and State-Mandated Reform in the Bohemian Lands," *Jewish Culture and History* 13, no. 2 [2012]: 1–16, here 12).

35. According to Michael L. Miller, "Proßnitz was not only a center of traditional Jewish learning but also a center of the conservative 'rabbinic Haskalah' and of moderate religious and educational reforms" (*Rabbis and Revolution*, 9).

attraction to the new ideas of the European Enlightenment.[36] The movement, called the Haskalah, and its adherents, called maskilim, came from across the ideological spectrum of Judaism, and for most of the eighteenth century remained a small but vibrant group of like-minded scholars, writers, doctors, and teachers—a Jewish Republic of Letters. Born predominantly in villages along the German and Polish borderlands, these men and women sought to establish a place for Jews and Jewish ideas in the traditionally hostile or forbidden intellectual circles of cities like Berlin, Frankfurt, and Vienna. By publishing articles, starting journals, and engaging in public debates, these early maskilim inserted themselves into the cultural world of late eighteenth-century imperial Prussia and Austria.

Maskilim were not, however, Jews interested simply in joining non-Jewish intellectual circles. They also hoped their ideas would reform Judaism in ways practical and theological.[37] Contesting the preeminence of the rabbis in matters of Jewish education, many of the leading teachers in the growing cities of Central Europe were in some way associated with the maskilim. The Enlightenment had a profound effect on traditional Jewish philosophical and theological assumptions. By the decades of the late eighteenth century, biblical and rabbinic texts were increasingly being subject to critical readings based on rationalist explanations. Thus, the Haskalah played a key role in undermining the traditional rabbinic narrative of Judaism at the beginning of modernity.

Observing the ways that yeshivot like the one in Proßnitz responded to the Enlightenment is one of the key factors in differentiating the histories of Central and Eastern European Jewry in the early decades of modernity. Miller notes that "the students who flocked to Wanefried's yeshiva found an environment that was particularly open to secular studies."[38] In 1891, six decades after his years in Proßnitz, an interview with Moritz Eisler allowed Jellinek—by then an old man—the chance to recall his student days learning under Wanefried. According to Eisler, "the yeshiva of Rabbi Moses Wanefried differed from other yeshivot: besides its excellent performances

---

36. See Simon Grote, "Review-Essay: Religion and Enlightenment," *Journal of the History of Ideas* 75, no. 1 (2014): 137–60, here 142–44.

37. See Shmuel Feiner and Natalie Naimark-Goldberg, *Cultural Revolution in Berlin: Jews in the Age of Enlightenment*, Journal of Jewish Studies: Supplement Series 1 (Oxford: Bodleian Library, 2011), 1–2: "As a new intellectual élite, the maskilim set themselves up as educators, providing alternative ideological leadership in competition with the rabbinic, scholarly élite that thus far had held a complete monopoly over knowledge, books, values, education, supervision over norms and behaviors, and guidance of the public."

38. Miller, *Rabbis and Revolution*, 91. It was also from Proßnitz that Moritz Steinschneider (1816–1907) emerged, who would sojourn briefly in Leipzig before Jellinek's arrival there, and whose work in Oriental studies and Jewish history greatly influenced Jellinek throughout his life. On moving to Proßnitz, Jellinek had begun studying secular subjects—French, Italian, the sciences—with the doctor and private tutor Gideon Brecher.

in the Talmud, its advantage was that it allowed the students to deal with disciplines other than the Talmud.... Here young people came together to study Jewish literature as well as the ancient and modern languages."[39] In the interview, Jellinek reminisced that Wanefried "was a tall figure, with large eyes that exuded of spirit. He lectured before about forty young people, and the students looked at their teacher as a higher being. [On Jellinek's first day at the yeshiva, Wanefried] threw a question to the students, only one of whom had the courage to dare shyly to try an answer."[40] That student was, of course, Jellinek, and over the next three years the two grew close, with Wanefried calling Jellinek "my Ahronle" (a diminutive, friendly nickname). Jellinek also credited Wanefried with fostering his interest in the history of Jewish mysticism (see chapters 3 and 4), even when many of the leading Jewish intellects of the age were opposed to its academic study.

Wanefried's stewardship of the Proßnitz yeshiva, especially his embrace of modern languages and literature, was not, however, the only route taken by Jewish leaders in Europe at the dawn of modernity. In an example of an almost entirely opposite approach, Shaul Stampfer describes the reorganization of the Lithuanian yeshivas in the early nineteenth century. As modern ideas and values began to enter Eastern Europe, those rabbis sought

> their complete organizational and sometimes even physical isolation from the local Jewish community. In the past, yeshivas had been communal institutions, but the new type of Lithuanian yeshiva was independent of the community.... [While] all the great yeshivas of the past had been located in large cities, some of the most important of the Lithuanian yeshivas were to be found in small towns.[41]

While rabbinic thought and practice were fairly uniform from the Seine to the Vistula until the latter half of the eighteenth century, by the middle of the nineteenth century these communities were creating very different religious responses to the European Enlightenment.[42]

Such a contrast between the rabbis of Central and Eastern Europe is striking. Previously allowed to live only in small towns or provincial vil-

---

39. Eisler, "Feuilleton: R. Moses Katz Wanefried," 206.
40. Eisler, "Feuilleton: R. Moses Katz Wanefried," 206.
41. Shaul Stampfer, *Lithuanian Yeshivas of the Nineteenth Century: Creating a Tradition of Learning* (Oxford: Littman Library of Jewish Civilization, 2012), 3.
42. For recent studies of Lithuanian rabbinic modernity, see Gil S. Perl, *The Pillar of Volozhin: Rabbi Naftali viz Yehuda Berlin and the World of Nineteenth-Century Lithuanian Torah Scholarship* (Boston: Academic Studies Press, 2012); and Stampfer, *Lithuanian Yeshivas of the Nineteenth Century*.

lages, once granted access to larger urban centers the Jews of Germany and the Habsburg lands never returned to their rural heritage. The few yeshivot that already existed in cities (e.g., Prague) grew in size and number of students, and the seminaries founded in Central Europe in the nineteenth century were all built in major urban centers (e.g., Berlin, Breslau, Frankfurt, Budapest). These new schools professed to speak to and for the larger Jewish community—ironically, they did this at the very moment when the Jewish culture they existed in was fracturing in historically unprecedented ways. The rhetoric emanating from these new, often progressive, liberal (or simply moderate) yeshivot was one of universal inclusion, and often advocated for students to take dual degrees, one at the local university and the other at the local rabbinical seminary.[43]

This fact—that many, if not yet a majority, of young Jewish men were pursuing more advanced secular educations—had a profound effect on the composition of the rabbinic elite in Central Europe by the middle of the nineteenth century.[44] Many in the new generation felt tied to the social communities that existed around universities and in urban spaces, where salon and café culture dominated, rather than to their rural hometowns. Even in a small city like Proßnitz the impulse of the rabbis was to engage with modernity rather than retreat into the countryside. This decision would prove fateful for Jellinek's life: Jewish learning, he came to believe, followed the Jewish people. And when a majority of Israel was moving to the city, so too should their religious leaders and institutions.[45]

Prague: An Early Urban Model

After five years in Proßnitz, Jellinek traveled north to Prague, a city that, even more than Proßnitz, was an innovative center of the rabbinic Haskalah.[46] Attempting to bring together traditional and modern texts, the rabbis in Prague encouraged their students to attend both their own lectures and

---

43. See Hillel J. Kieval, "The Social Vision of Bohemian Jews: Intellectuals and Community in the 1840s," in *Assimilation and Community: The Jews in Nineteenth-Century Europe*, ed. Jonathan Frankel and Steven J. Zipperstein (Cambridge: Cambridge University Press, 1992), 246–83. See Carsten L. Wilke, "Modern Rabbinical Training: Intercultural Invention and Political Reconfiguration," in *Rabbi – Pastor – Priest: Their Roles and Profiles through the Ages*, ed. Walter Homolka and Heinz-Günther Schöttler (Berlin: de Gruyter, 2013), 83–110.

44. Hassidism did not gain many adherents in Bohemia or Moravia. Rabbi Samuel Shmelke Hurwitz (1726–1778), chief rabbi of Moravia, appears to have been one of the few rabbinic leaders in the region to fully devote himself to the movement.

45. See Marsha L. Rozenblit, "Creating Jewish Space: German-Jewish Schools in Moravia," *Austrian History Yearbook* 44 (2013): 108–47.

46. See Hillel J. Kieval, "Jewish Prague, Christian Prague, and the Castle in the City's Golden Age," *Jewish Studies Quarterly* 18 (2011): 202–15.

those at Charles University, the city's famed institution of higher learning. Jellinek embraced this dual mandate, and its legacy remained with him throughout his career.

In 1800, Prague was home to the largest urban Jewish community anywhere in the German lands, numbering 8,500 souls.[47] A third brief interruption (the first and second were in 1551 and 1557 under Ferdinand I) in Prague's Jewish occupation had occurred from 1744 to 1748, when Maria Theresa (1717–1780), then ruling sovereign of Bohemia and Moravia (nominally at the pleasure of her husband, Francis I [1708–1765], Holy Roman Emperor), promulgated an edict of expulsion for the Jews in the regions along the borders with Prussia, purportedly for their collaboration with the empire's northern enemy, Frederick the Great (1712–1786), during the Second Silesian War. The edict was rescinded after four years, and only the Jews of Prague seem to have been displaced; those who lived on manorial estates or in villages remained materially unaffected. (On the return of the Jews to Prague in 1748, however, Jews in the whole territory were forced to pay a Toleration Tax for the right to continue living in the two provinces.)[48]

A number of scholars have noted the peculiar social position of the Jews of Prague.[49] As a population neither Czech nor German, the Jews occupied a liminal space in the city's ethnic and linguistic hierarchy, a social stratigraphy that was fast changing over the course of the nineteenth century. Prague's status as a German-speaking city, in a Czech-speaking countryside, in an empire in which German culture was predominant, make it a unique geographical space with which to study the effects of modernity on Central European Jewry. Thomas Simons Jr. noted that, because of its large size, Prague's "unusual metropolitan character gave it an uncommon sensitivity to new developments elsewhere."[50] He argued that such urbanity among the city's Jewish elite led to a number of high-profile conversions to Catholicism, and his work sought to uncover the Prague-specific milieu that made such social transitions possible (and desirable). Still, while individual cases of conversion are interesting, their statistical importance remains limited. What these incidents do reflect, however, is

---

47. Jersch-Wenzel, "Population Shifts," 55.

48. For an account of the activity of Jews in an attempt to halt the expulsion order, see Barouh Mevorah, "Jewish Diplomatic Activities to Prevent Expulsion of the Jews from Bohemia and Moravia in 1744–45," in *Binah: Studies in Jewish History* 1, ed. Joseph Dan (New York: Praeger, 1989), 143–58.

49. See Eduard Goldstücker, "Jews between Czechs and Germans around 1848," *Leo Baeck Institute Year Book* 17 (1972): 61–71; Michael Anthony Riff, "Assimilation and Conversion in Bohemia: Secession from the Jewish Community in Prague, 1868–1917," *Leo Baeck Institute Year Book* 26 (1981): 73–88; and Hans Tramer, "Prague—City of Three Peoples," *Leo Baeck Institute Year Book* 9 (1964): 305–39.

50. Thomas W. Simons, Jr., "The Prague Origins of the Güntherian Converts (1800–1850)," *Leo Baeck Institute Year Book* 22 (1977): 245–56, here 247.

that, by the turn of the nineteenth century, the Prague Jews were already mixing with non-Jewish society. By the 1840s, a sizable Jewish bourgeois class had developed, and it, too, learned to be similarly comfortable in gentile-dominated environments.

When Jellinek arrived in Prague in 1838, Solomon Judah Rappaport (1790–1867) had just recently been appointed head of the city's Landau yeshiva. The new rabbi expressed a deep interest in ensuring that his curriculum included both the newest developments of *Wissenschaft* alongside traditional Talmudic study.[51] Yet Rappaport was not the first chief rabbi of Prague to inculcate a liberal view toward secular learning. The city had a series of rabbis whose views on gentile knowledge (especially concerning the natural sciences) diverged from mainstream rabbinic dogma. These included Judah Loew ben Bezalel (1520–1609), called the Maharal;[52] David Ben Abraham Oppenheim (d. 1736);[53] Ezekiel ben Yehuda Landau (1713–1793), called the Noda bi'Yehuda;[54] and Rappaport. Each of these rabbis left his unique imprint on the community.[55] Beginning with the Maharal, Prague's legacy was as an epicenter of traditional but broadly inquisitive Jewish learning, a convention that continued well into the nineteenth century.[56]

The Prague of Jellinek's student days was certainly confronted with its own seeming crossroad in Jewish history. The opportunities witnessed under and afforded by the Napoleonic invasions, not only as they played out in Republican France but as they were implemented, to varying degrees of immediate success, across occupied Europe, gave Jews a sense

---

51. We know that Rappaport's intellectual model remained foremost in Jellinek's mind for many years to come, for on November 15, 1867, the Viennese Jewish newspaper *Die Neuzeit* featured a multipage obituary for Rappaport, with the lead essay penned by Jellinek. See Adolf Jellinek, "Erinnerungen an den verewigten Oberrabb. S. J. Rappaport," *Die Neuzeit*, November 15, 1867, 531–33. See also Adolf Kurländer, *Biografi S. L. Rapoport's* (Pest: [Self-published], 1869).

52. Born in Posen (Polish: Poznań), Poland, the Maharal was *Landesrabbiner* in Nikolsburg from 1553 to 1573 before spending the rest of his life in Prague. By the nineteenth century, his legendary creation of the Golem—a clay figure meant to protect the community from attacks during the reign of Rudolf II (1552–1612; son of Maximilian II), Holy Roman Emperor—had become a staple of Jewish mythology, and it remains so to the present day.

53. Oppenheim began as Landesrabbiner of Moravia in Nikolsburg. The emperor named him chief rabbi of Prague in 1702.

54. Landau was appointed chief rabbi in 1754. See Sharon Flatto, *The Kabbalistic Culture of Eighteenth-Century Prague: Ezekiel Landau (the "Noda Biyehudah") and His Contemporaries* (Oxford: Littman Library of Jewish Civilization, 2010).

55. See Kestenberg-Gladstein, "Voice from the Prague Enlightenment," 135.

56. See Pavel Sládek, "Judah Löw ben Betsalel—the Maharal of Prague: A Theologian with Humanist Bias," in *Jewish Studies in the 21st Century: Prague – Europe – World*, ed. Marcela Zoufalá, Jüdische Kultur 29 (Wiesbaden: Harrassowitz, 2014), 59–83, here 82. See also Byron L. Sherwin, *Mystical Theology and Social Dissent: The Life and Works of Judah Loew of Prague* (Oxford: Littman Library of Jewish Civilization, 2006).

of what it might be like to participate (almost as equals) in the broad civic life of their communities. But at what cost would that participation come? A cautious embrace of modernity seemed like a sensible approach for many of Rappaport's generation. But as it turned out, Jellinek discovered, modernity was not something that often arrived in moderation.

2

Town and Gown: Jewish Leipzig and the *Wissenschaft des Judentums*

The Jewish Community of Leipzig

Unlike Bohemia, long part of the Habsburg domains, Saxony remained a quasi-independent territory (called an Electorate before 1806) into the nineteenth century, with the princes in Dresden managing a difficult set of alliances in the shifting social and military landscape of Central Europe.[1] Saxony's wealth came primarily from trade and farming, but in the sixteenth and seventeenth centuries the ruling house invested heavily in the arts and humanities, and Dresden gained great fame and honor for the splendor of its Baroque artistry. Considered one of the most beautiful cities in the world, at the turn of the nineteenth century the Saxonian capital boasted pleasure gardens along the river Elbe, an imperial museum displaying curiosities of natural history, and a fine arts gallery open to an inquisitive public.

Leipzig, seventy miles to the northwest, was the overshadowed sibling. As a center for trade and crafts from the Middle Ages, at the end of the eighteenth century Leipzig was best known for its fairground, which attracted merchants from across Central Europe.[2] Yet the mercan-

---

1. For histories of the territory, see James N. Retallack, ed., *Saxony in German History: Culture, Society, and Politics, 1830–1933*, Social History, Popular Culture, and Politics in Germany (Ann Arbor: University of Michigan Press, 2000). For a mid-nineteenth-century account of Saxony, see Henry Mayhew, *German Life and Manners as Seen in Saxony at the Present Day with an Account of Village Life, Town Life, Fashionable Life, Domestic Life, Married Life, School and University Life, &c., of Germany at the Present Time* (London: Allen, 1864). Following the defeat of Napoleon at Waterloo in 1814, the princes of Saxony sent representatives to the Congress of Vienna, which allotted them—until Saxony's absorption into the Prussian Empire in 1871—status as a fully autonomous kingdom.

2. For a discussion of the Leipzig fairs, and the Jewish part in them, see Wilhelm Harmelin, "Jews in the Leipzig Fur Industry," *Leo Baeck Institute Year Book* 9 (1964): 239–66; and Robert Beachy, "Reforming Interregional Commerce: The Leipzig Trade Fairs and Saxony's

tile character of Leipzig changed dramatically in the opening decades of the nineteenth century. Leipzig was occupied by Napoleon, and this brief foreign rule was enough to introduce the city's inhabitants to the more urbane pleasures of cosmopolitan life. In these mid-century decades, Leipzig expanded greatly, partly because the city government early on recognized the economic importance and political power of the railroad.[3] In 1833, Friedrich List (1789–1846), a German-American industrialist and economic philosopher, proposed a pan-German railway system.[4] While residing in Leipzig as the American consul, List became instrumental in establishing the Leipzig–Dresden rail line, which officially opened in 1839.[5] In 1842 the city inaugurated the Bayerischer Bahnhof, the first of many grand terminals that would solidify the town's importance as a center for industry, commerce, and travel conducted by rail.[6] Located outside the old city walls, the new Bahnhof anchored a set of neighborhoods stretching south and east of the town center, accessible by streetcars and wide promenades. By 1851, the rail lines outside of Dresden had been completed, connecting passengers and goods in Leipzig with such major Central European cities as Prague, Budapest, and Vienna.[7]

Trains aided the rise of a local bourgeoisie, whose adoption of salon and café culture, with its voracious appetite for literary periodicals, stimulated the rapid expansion of the city's schools and intellectual institutions. By the 1830s, Leipzig University (along with the university in its neighboring city, Halle/Saale) had become a leader in key areas of modern

---

Recovery from the Thirty Years' War," *Central European History* 32, no. 4 (1999): 431–52. See also Exhibition Committee of the Textile Industry, *The Textile Industry of Saxony and Its Importance, Appendix: List of Exhibitors Interested in the Textile Industry of Saxony* (Leipzig: Leipziger Monatschrift für Textil-Industrie, 1893).

3. Rainer Fremdling et al., eds. *Statistik der Eisenbahnen in Deutschland, 1835–1989*, Quellen und Forschungen zur historischen Statistik von Deutschland 17 (St. Katherinen: Scripta Mercaturae, 1995), 26, 33; and Albert Wiedemann, *Die sächsischen Eisenbahnen in historisch-statistischer Darstellung* (Leipzig: Thomas, 1902).

4. Fremdling et al., eds., *Statistik der Eisenbahnen in Deutschland*, 33; Friedrich List, *Ueber ein sächsisches Eisenbahn-System als Grundlage eines allgemeinen deutschen Eisenbahn-Systems und insbesondere über die Anlegung einer Eisenbahn von Leipzig nach Dresden* (Leipzig: Liebeskind, 1833).

5. Roy E. H. Mellor, *German Railways: A Study in the Historical Geography of Transport* (Aberdeen: Dept. of Geography, University of Aberdeen, 1979), 10. The German Democratic Republic (East Germany) issued a 150-year commemorative stamp of List and the Leipzig–Dresden line in 1989.

6. See Rolf Bayer, *Die bayerische Bahnhof in Leipzig: Entstehung, Entwicklung und Zukunft des ältesten Kopfbahnhofs der Welt* (Berlin: Transpress, 1895). Building terminals, where tracks end, instead of stations, where trains pass through, meant that Leipzig became a shipment and transit hub as well as a market center.

7. For statistics on the Leipzig–Dresden line between 1837 and 1875, see Fremdling et al., eds., *Statistik der Eisenbahnen in Deutschland*, 101, 167, 233, 324, 448.

scholarship, including Orientalism and higher biblical criticism.[8] It had also liberalized its admittance requirements, allowing Jews to study and earn degrees. Further, by the middle of the century, the city had become a center of the German book trade. All these changes taken together were enough to attract the young Jellinek away from Prague to the still modest but rapidly modernizing Leipzig.

The Jewish community of Leipzig was small and new when Jellinek arrived in the city in 1842.[9] Unlike what we saw in Moravia in the previous chapter, for many centuries there were no Jews in Saxony at all. The Jews who populated Leipzig after Napoleon's departure arrived from farther afield, primarily but not exclusively the German principalities directly abutting Saxony to the north and west. Jews had, however, been allowed to commute to the major Saxon cities during seasonal fairs, and by the 1820s the few urban Jewish communities that continued year-round were located in or around Dessau and Dresden, in the latter city of which the chief rabbis resided.[10] The first Jewish cemetery inside the Leipzig municipality was established in 1811, and the Jewish population in the city continued to be semi-permanent into the 1820s, following the annual cycle of city fairs.[11] The first permanent synagogue structure in Leipzig, the Bet-Jacob Betschule, was completed in 1820 and catered to these transient Jewish traders: it was opened during the fairs but closed otherwise. Interestingly, from the beginning, the Bet-Jacob Betschule conducted services in the so-called "Berlin-Hamburg style," which meant that it followed a semi-reformed liturgy and allowed the playing of an organ on the Sabbath.[12]

---

8. Halle (Saale) is now home to the library of the Deutsche Morgenländische Gesellschaft (German Orientalist Society), founded in Leipzig in 1845.

9. For an overview of the history of the Leipzig Jewish community, see Ephraim Carlebach Stiftung, *Judaica Lipsiensia: Zur Geschichte der Juden in Leipzig* (Leipzig: Edition Leipzig, 1994); Kerstin Plowinski, *Die jüdische Bevölkerung Leipzigs 1853, 1925, 1933: Sozialgeschichtliche Fallstudien zur Mitgliedschaft einer Grossgemeinde* (Diss., Leipzig, 1991); and Stephan Wendehorst, ed., *Bausteine einer jüdischen Geschichte der Universität Leipzig* (Leipzig: Leipziger Universitätsverlag, 2006).

10. Neighboring regions, such as Brandenburg-Prussia, had many more Jewish families. The Jews of the western regions of Saxony, called Saxony-Meiningen, did not fair nearly as well. As late as 1811 they faced expulsion, a recurring phenomenon for that community from the Middle Ages. See Franz Levi, "The Jews of Sachsen-Meiningen and the Edict of 1811," *Leo Baeck Institute Year Book* 38 (1993): 15–32.

11. Harmelin, "Jews in the Leipzig Fur Industry," 242. Harmelin records a long history of strenuous opposition on the part of gentile fair-goers and Leipzig residents to the Jewish presence, however minimal and transient, in the city. But city officials appear to have enjoyed the high taxes and rents paid by Jewish merchants, and so were more tolerant of the Jewish presence. Dessau's most famous Jewish son is Moses Mendelssohn, born there in 1729.

12. Leopold Zunz (1794–1886), the seminal figure in the origins of *Wissenschaft des Judentums*, gave the synagogue's inaugural sermon.

The relative paucity of permanent urban Jewish life in Leipzig in the first decades of the nineteenth century was characteristic of the great majority of the smaller, early industrializing cities across Central Europe.[13] But the rapid and widespread Jewish urbanization of the 1830s and 1840s created a growing Jewish presence in these historically non-Jewish spaces. While much is made of Moses Mendelssohn's participation in the Berlin Wednesday Club in the 1780s, Mendelssohn's conspicuousness as a public figure underscores the absence of Jewish social life across the German-speaking lands more generally.[14] An increase in Jewish social inclusion in the nineteenth century was made possible partly by gains in legal civil rights in the first decades of the new century.[15] Often, these changes allowed Jews greater freedom of movement into and out of urban spaces, as well as prompted (or enforced) educational reforms, with the result being that Jewish students spoke Yiddish to their parents and German to their peers. Further, Jewish access to the public sphere was made possible by the widespread disruption in urban social spaces more generally. This was caused principally by economic developments across the continent, including the growing industrialization of manufacturing, and, eventu-

---

13. In many places across the German lands of Central Europe, the gains toward emancipation (and therefore free movement) made by Jews under Napoleonic occupation were halted or reversed in the decades between the Congress of Vienna and 1848. Yet, as Arno Herzig writes, "It is not immediately apparent why, in their development towards becoming modern economic states, most German states chose to place restrictions on their economically active Jewish minorities and thereby, as in Prussia, incurred significant administrative expense. The reason for this lay partly, perhaps, in the role which the Jews played as an anti-symbol for broad sectors of the population during this turbulent period of economic and social upheaval. For most social groups, the Jewish minority was perceived as symbolically embodying the dark side of the new system and its insuperable difficulties" ("Process of Emancipation," 64–65). This can certainly be said for the treatment and view of the Jews of the Leipzig fairs. Governments found the Jewish traders productive and taxable, but the Christian merchants and their customers generally disliked the Jewish presence.

14. For a discussion of Mendelssohn and the Wednesday Club, see Deborah Sadie Hertz, *Jewish High Society in Old Regime Berlin* (Syracuse, NY: Syracuse University Press, 2005), esp. 75–118. Saying that there was minimal Jewish presence in broader German society is, of course, different from saying that "Jews" or "Jewishness" as topics of intellectual life were likewise absent, since quite the opposite was the case. As Ronald Schechter notes about eighteenth-century France, "[After counting the texts,] the sheer number suggests that historians have vastly underestimated the importance of the Jews to non-Jewish writers, their readers, as well as to political actors and their audiences in eighteenth-century and early nineteenth-century France. They suggest that Jews mattered or, more precisely, that images and perceptions of Jews mattered" (*Obstinate Hebrews: Representations of Jews in France, 1715–1815*, Studies on the History of Society and Culture 49 [Berkeley: University of California Press, 2003], 6–7. Similar numbers can be found for Germany. The "Jewish Question" was addressed by all the major figures of the German Enlightenment, even when few of them spent any time with actual Jews, or showed particular interest in other aspects of Jewish life or thought.

15. See Sorkin, *Jewish Emancipation*, 148–61.

ally, the advent of the train, which employed central depots for the assemblage and distribution of goods.

In the first half of the nineteenth century, Jews were not the only Europeans reacting to modern educational reforms and economic changes, and certainly not the only populations migrating toward cities. But the noticeable cultural differences of Jews from rural Christian migrants, as well as the historic exclusion of Jews from daily urban life, made their growing numbers an obvious marker of profound social and demographic transformation.[16] Such a transformation—from relative Jewish absence in the public sphere to an overt Jewish presence in it—had many effects, not least of which was on the opportunities afforded to Jewish youths. By the 1830s, young Jews were participating in many of the same public activities as their gentile peers. Focusing specifically on Dresden, Christopher Friedrichs describes the life of a young Jewish man, Louis Lesser, which contained few distinctly "Jewish" elements.[17] Lesser, Friedrichs tells us, worked at a bank and spent his free hours in public parks and gardens, at home with friends, or in the various museums and galleries of the capital. While he did not work on the Sabbath or during festivals, Lesser appears to have spent little time thinking about religion and, except for the inherited fact of his Jewishness, lived a life not dissimilar to that of many other twenty-something gentile inhabitants of Dresden. (Nevertheless, Lesser's family was entirely Jewish, that is, not inter-married; he himself married a Jewish woman; and he lived in a neighborhood specifically designated for Jews.)

By the end of the 1840s, the experience of Jewish youths in Leipzig came ever more to resemble that of Louis Lesser. "At the time," noted the *Illustrirte Zeitung* with its usual enthusiasm, "Leipzig was the refuge of all free spirits who could not live in Austria under the pressure of the Metternich-atmosphere."[18] Jewish students attended the university by the score. Jewish publishing houses were established, inaugurating what

---

16. Perforce, as Uri R. Kaufmann writes, by 1815, "a Christian-Jewish public sphere came into being [... where] Jewish lay leaders saw themselves as part of the larger German society, believing that the time had now arrived when 'Israel should not dwell alone.'... Such social interactions between Jews and Christians did not exist before 1800" ("The Jewish Fight for Emancipation in France and Germany," in *Jewish Emancipation Reconsidered: The French and German Models*, ed. Michael Brenner, Vicki Caron, and Uri R. Kaufmann, Schriftenreihe wissenschaftlicher Abhandlungen des Leo Baeck Instituts 66 [Tübingen: Mohr Siebeck, 2003], 79–92, here 81).

17. Christopher R. Friedrichs, "Leisure and Acculturation in the Jewish Community of Dresden, 1833–1837," *Leo Baeck Institute Year Book* 56 (2011): 137–62.

18. *Illustrirte Zeitung*, no. 2637, January 13, 1894, 45–46, here 45. By the 1840s, there was, no doubt, pressure on Jellinek to take the Leipzig community farther to the left. The Hamburg Reform community was already well established, as were others in Berlin and Frankfurt. In Leipzig itself, the preacher at the messe-synagogue in the 1820s had been Leopold Zunz, whose personal preferences leaned to the religious left. See Alexander Altmann,

became one of the most important centers for the Jewish book trade in Europe until the mid-twentieth century. Jewish merchants and their families also settled permanently in the city, allowing the opening of perhaps half a dozen small synagogues catering to distinct provincial traditions. These new Jewish migrants lived primarily in the neighborhoods being constructed west of the historic center, and it was there, in 1855, on Gottschedstraße, that the community consecrated its first central synagogue, called the Neue Israelitische Tempel (later the Große Gemeindesynagoge).[19] Yet, until Jellinek was hired in the mid-1840s, Leipzig had no permanent resident rabbi of its own. Historically, the rabbi in Dessau would follow Jewish merchants each season to the fairs and preside over their religious activities. And in the 1830s and 1840s, Zacharias Frankel (1801–1875), then chief rabbi in Dresden (1836–1854), would make trips to Leipzig to attend to the community's needs.[20] But by the late 1840s, the community had become settled and wealthy enough to build a grand central synagogue and hire its own chief rabbi—the young Adolf Jellinek. During his sixteen-year residence in Leipzig, therefore, Jellinek witnessed not a Jewish demographic transformation but a demographic creation. Where formerly there had been no permanent community, no synagogue building, and no Jewish presence in public life except as merchants during fairs, by Jellinek's departure for Vienna in January 1857, Jews in Leipzig had attained sizable representation among the students at the university, in the city's mercantile classes, and in the regional publishing industry.[21]

Importantly, however, as Steven M. Lowenstein has argued, the urbanization of European Jewry was not necessarily coterminous with its religious liberalization.[22] As Lowenstein writes, "Jewish life in urban communities was at least as heterogeneous as life in the villages."[23] This observation points in two directions. First, traditional rural Judaism did

---

"Zur Frühgeschichte der jüdischen Predigt in Deutschland: Leopold Zunz als Prediger," *Leo Baeck Institute Year Book* 6 (1961): 3–59.

19. For a description of the synagogue, as well as architectural images and drawings, see Otto Simonson, *Der Neue Tempel in Leipzig: Entworfen und Ausgeführt* (Berlin: Riegel, 1858). This synagogue was destroyed on November 9–10, 1938. A memorial now occupies part of the square where the building once stood.

20. A copy of the Leipzig Jewish community's logbook is kept at the city's *Stadtarchiv*. It records the various births, celebrations, and decisions of the community. When in town, Frankel would write notes in the book as well.

21. The Leipzig Jewish community was almost entirely destroyed in the Second World War. A Leipzig Jewish diaspora exists, mainly resident in Israel and the United States. The current community numbers in the hundreds, composed primarily of immigrants from the former Soviet Union. Its current rabbi, Zsolt Balla, a native of Budapest, was educated at the Lauder Yeshiva in Berlin.

22. See Steven M. Lowenstein, "Was Urbanization Harmful to Jewish Tradition and Identity in Germany?," *Studies in Contemporary Jewry* 15 (1999): 80–110, esp. 82–83.

23. See Lowenstein, "Was Urbanization Harmful,?" 82.

not exemplify a unified religious orthodoxy. Prior to modernity (and certainly to conventional accounts of "shtetl" life[24]), a high level of diversity in religious practice existed within local Jewish communities. Second, Jewish urbanization was not concurrent with Jewish secularization. Jews migrated to cities for many reasons, some of them ideological, but many others social or economic. The diversity of Jewish religiosity encountered in a place like Leipzig in the 1840s would therefore have been comparable to that found among the towns of Moravia. What differed, of course, was everything else. The lifestyle and the legal system that sustained a coherent Jewish identity in rural Central Europe were entirely absent in industrializing Leipzig. As we will see over the course of this book, the task of creating a new form of Jewish religious life that reflected urban modernity was something that took time, creativity, and an immense amount of faith in the inherent, enduring power of Jewish texts, stories, and rituals.

Creating *Wissenschaft des Judentums*

In the first decades of the nineteenth century, as the politics and economics of the continent were changing, a new movement was being developed, following on some of the innovations of the Haskalah but employing a decidedly different ideology and set of scholarly practices. Called *Wissenschaft des Judentums*, or the Science of Judaism, the movement was an outgrowth of the same intellectual impetus that created the academic disciplines of Orientalism, biblical criticism, archaeology, and philology, and its pioneers were trained at universities in the newest forms of scientific, historical, and linguistic scholarship.[25] The creation and shape of the other new, modern disciplines were fundamental in

---

24. For a reevaluation of premodern rural Jewish life, see Yohanan Petrovsky-Shtern, *The Golden Age Shtetl: A New History of Jewish Life in East Europe* (Princeton, NJ: Princeton University Press, 2014).

25. The importance of philology to the development of *Wissenschaft des Judentums* remains to be more thoroughly investigated. See Kerstin von der Krone and Mirjam Thulin, "*Wissenschaft* in Context: A Research Essay on the *Wissenschaft des Judentums*," *Leo Baeck Institute Year Book* 58 (2013): 249–80, esp. 261–62. For some preliminary research, see Anthony Grafton, "Juden und Griechen bei Friedrich August Wolf," in *Friedrich August Wolf: Studien, Dokumente, Bibliographie*, ed. Reinhard Markner and Giuseppe Veltri, Palingenesia 67 (Stuttgart: Steiner, 1999), 9–31; Grafton, *Defenders of the Text: The Traditions of Scholarship in an Age of Science, 1450–1800* (Cambridge: Harvard University Press, 1991); Dirk Hartwig, "Die 'Wissenschaft des Judentums' und die Anfänge der kritischen Koranforschung: Perspektiven einer modernen Koranhermeneutik," *Zeitschrift für Religions- und Geistesgeschichte* 61, no. 3 (2009): 234–56; and Gregor Pelger, *Wissenschaft des Judentums und englische Bibliotheken: Zur Geschichte historischer Philologie im 19. Jahrhundert*, Minima Judaica (Berlin: Metropol, 2010). As German interest in Arabic and Farsi grew, so too did the study of Sanskrit and the Indian subcontinent. See Pascale Rabault-Feuerhahn, *Archives of Origins: Sanskrit, Philology, Anthro-*

determining the scope and character of *Wissenschaft*. Around the turn of the nineteenth century German universities began to systematically overhaul their research methodologies, philosophical ideologies, and bureaucracies based on the Enlightenment's premise that rational investigation, definition, categorization, and philological precision could reveal deep, inerrant truths about the world.[26] Pioneered in Germany by the University of Berlin under the leadership of Wilhelm von Humboldt, these educational reforms emphasized the concepts of empirical study in scientific scholarship, moving beyond strictly philosophical speculation.[27] They likewise reorganized the hierarchy of disciplines, accentuating philosophy (what we now call Humanities) and the practical disciplines (law and medicine) over theology—the traditional focus of medieval and early modern university curricula.[28]

The nearly complete disinterest of even the most Judeophilic Christian scholars in the study of Judaism after the death of Jesus meant that rabbinic history was entirely open to young Jewish *Wissenschaft* scholars.[29] They were eager to fill the niche, not least because it provided a way of reinserting rabbinic Judaism into the European story—a central project of *Wissenschaft*. Salomon Munk used Maimonides to demonstrate the Jewish presence in the reception history of Aristotelian thought in Europe.[30] Abra-

---

pology in 19th Century Germany, trans. Dominique Bach and Richard Willet, Kultur- und sozialwissenschaftliche Studien 9 (Wiesbaden: Harrassowitz, 2013).

26. "For the first time it is not history that must prove its utility to Judaism, but Judaism that must prove its utility to history, by revealing and justifying itself historically. [With the term *Wissenschaft*, one] has in mind specifically the new critical historical spirit and historical methodology that were sweeping Germany and that would soon become one of the hallmarks of nineteenth-century European ... thought." See Yosef Hayim Yerushalmi, *Zakhor: Jewish History and Jewish Memory*, Samuel and Althea Stroum Lectures in Jewish Studies [Seattle: University of Washington Press, 1982], 84.)

27. According to von der Krone and Thulin, "... science, or rather the German appreciation [of] *Wissenschaft*, intended a historical, application-oriented understanding of knowledge based upon measurable, verifiable and objective standards and judgments" ("*Wissenschaft* in Context," 249).

28. See Immanuel Kant, *Der streit der Facultäten: In drey Abschnitten* (Königsberg: Nicolovius, 1798).

29. For an early argument for Jewish scholarlship on Judaism to oppose Christian (mis-)reading of Jewish history, see Salomon Formstecher, *Die Religion des Geistes: Eine wissenschaftliche Darstellung des Judenthums nach seinem Charakter, Entwicklungsgange, und Berufe in der Menschheit* (Frankfurt am Main: Hermann, 1841), esp. 1–16. A notable exception to the Christian scholarly dismissal of rabbinics was Johann Andreas Eisenmenger (1654–1704), a German student of Hebrew. Eisenmenger is best known for his book *Entdecktes Judenthum* (Judaism Unmasked, 1700), which, alongside a great deal of learning, described and interpreted in lurid detail a great many unpleasant things said by the rabbis of the Talmud. *Judaism Unmasked* remains a source for anti-Talmud and anti-Jewish polemicists to this day.

30. See Salomon Munk, *La philosophie chez les juifs* (Paris: Bureau des Archives Israelites, 1848); and Munk, *Mélanges de philosophie juive et arabe* (Paris: Franck, 1857).

ham Geiger wrote avidly (if somewhat polemically) of the Jewishness of Jesus. Jellinek promoted the idea that some of the central tenets of liberalism were part of Europe's biblical inheritance, as opposed to the Greek and Roman love of art, sport, and war. In these early and middle decades of the nineteenth century, non-Jewish Europeans were actively creating (they saw themselves to be "discovering" or "revealing") the idea of a trans-European history, a story of a continent that overrode the specific developments of its constituent, often geographically diffuse empires, and that all but erased such traditional actors as the Byzantines or Umayyads and promoted previously inconspicuous peoples like the Saxons and Magyars. So, alongside them, Jewish scholars of the *Wissenschaft* adopted their new geographic boundaries and historiographical languages, writing about "Europe" and its Jews as if they were transhistorically recognizable entities. In this way, the specific notion that the Jewish people and its ideas had long been part of the "European story" was a radical innovation of the *Wissenschaft*. Further, as the findings of *Wissenschaft* came to be ever more deeply assimilated into the discourse of Europe's urbanizing and acculturating Jewish communities, such political-scholarly discussions took on new valences and had far-reaching implications. With the development of *Wissenschaft*, Judaism and Jewish society in Central Europe gained a new class of learned and honored person: the university-trained intellectual. By the 1840s, no longer were the only leading figures of Jewish thought rabbis or heads of yeshivot. Historians, philologists, and editors, all in some way associated with the new field of *Wissenschaft des Judentums*, were creating another sort of Jewish *gaon* (genius), one with cosmopolitan, scholarly credentials and a dedication to participating in the wider conversation of modern European culture.

Wissenschaft was at once both a cultural and an ideological creation. In the context of cultural phenomena, Jews in the early nineteenth century were participating in the modernization and cosmopolitanization of society in much the same ways as were other educated members of European society. Often looking to distance themselves from what they perceived to be the insularity of rabbinic (and specifically yeshiva-centered) culture, these young Jewish men sought another way of interacting with Judaism, one that would be more in line with, and better able to contribute to, the many philosophical and methodological developments being discussed in the scholarly circles of Europe.

As an ideology, *Wissenschaft* was about integrating Judaism into the larger narrative of European history—a history, we have noted, that was itself just then being constructed by thinkers in Western and Central Europe. *Wissenschaft* was not about dismantling Judaism, or about proving it false. Rather, it was about subjecting Judaism to the same intellectual rigors as Christian scholars were doing to the classical world. It was also about demonstrating the innumerable links between Christianity (and

Islam) and Judaism, going back to the time of Jesus and the Gospels and Muhammad and the Arabian conquests of the Near East.[31] *Wissenschaft*, many of its early adherents believed, could prove to be the intellectual knot that tied Judaism together with Christianity, and therefore justified the Jews' presence in Europe and their moral and intellectual equality in a gentile-dominated society.

The early figures of *Wissenschaft*—Leopold Zunz (1794–1886), Immanuel Wolf (also known as Immanuel Wohlwill, 1799–1847), and Julius Fürst—began publishing in the 1820s and 1830s.[32] Zunz conducted pioneering work on Jewish liturgy and edited the *Zeitschrift für die Wissenschaft des Judentums*, the discipline's inaugural journal.[33] Wolf was a preacher and philosopher. Fürst wrote a series of important dictionaries on ancient Near Eastern languages and a history of the Jews and the Greeks; in addition, he edited the journal *Der Orient*. Perhaps more than any other publications from that period, *Zeitschrift* and *Der Orient* created the matrix out of which an independent discipline of Jewish studies could be formed.[34] The men who published in these journals, or whose books were reviewed in them, were almost all university-trained Jews, with aca-

---

31. See S. Heschel, *Abraham Geiger and the Jewish Jesus*, esp 50–105.

32. See Nils H. Roemer, *Jewish Scholarship and Culture in Nineteenth-Century Germany: Between History and Faith*, Studies in German Jewish Cultural History and Literature (Madison: University of Wisconsin Press, 2005); Henri Soussan, *The Science of Judaism: From Leopold Zunz to Leopold Lucas* (Brighton, UK: University of Sussex, 1999); Ismar Schorsch, "From Wolfenbüttel to Wissenschaft: The Divergent Paths of Isaak Markus Jost and Leopold Zunz," *Leo Baeck Institute Year Book* 22 (1977): 109–28; Michael A. Meyer, "Jewish Religious Reform and Wissenschaft des Judentums: The Positions of Zunz, Geiger and Frankel," *Leo Baeck Institute Year Book* 16 (1971): 19–41; Nahum N. Glatzer, *Leopold and Adelheid Zunz: An Account in Letters, 1815–1885* (London: East and West Library, 1958); Nahum N. Glatzer, *Leopold Zunz: Jude, Deutscher, Europäer: ein jüdisches Gelehrtenschicksal des 19. Jahrhunderts in Briefen an Freunde*, Schriftenreihe wissenschaftlicher Abhandlungen des Leo Baeck Instituts 11 (Tübingen: Mohr Siebeck, 1964); Samuel Solomon Cohon, "Zunz and Reform Judaism," *Hebrew Union College Annual* 31 (1960): 251–76; Luitpold Wallach, *Liberty and Letters: The Thoughts of Leopold Zunz* (London: East and West Library, 1959); E. D. Goldschmidt, "Studies on Jewish Liturgy by German-Jewish Scholars," *Leo Baeck Institute Year Book* 2 (1957): 119–35; Fritz Bamberger, "Zunz's Conception of History: A Study of the Philosophic Elements in Early Science of Judaism," *Proceedings of the American Academy for Jewish Research* 11 (1941): 1–25. Zunz's most important scholarly works are *Die gottesdienstilichen Vorträge der Juden, historische entwickelt* (Berlin: Asher, 1832); *Zur Geschichte und Literatur* (Berlin: Veit, 1845); and *Die synagogale Poesie des Mittelalters*, 2 vols. (Berlin: Springer, 1855–1859). Zunz also translated the Hebrew Bible into German. The *Zeitschrift für die Wissenschaft des Judentums* only published three volumes (1822/23), but it nevertheless had a decisive impact on the future course of Jewish studies.

33. See Ismar Schorsch, *Leopold Zunz: Creativity in Adversity*, Jewish Culture and Contexts (Philadelphia: University of Pennsylvania Press, 2016).

34. Eduard Gans (1797–1839) was also a founding member of the Verein für Kultur und Wissenschaft der Juden, and a friend and colleague of Jost and Zunz.

demic credentials that, if allowed, would have granted them professorships across Germany. (Zunz, Wolf, and Fürst themselves received some of the first degrees granted to Jews following the initial period of emancipation: from Halle, Kiel, and Halle, respectively.) Their efforts created a thriving, and at times biting, community of Jewish intellectuals, whose (mostly) shared ideology fostered a continuous stream of students and contributors well into the twentieth century.[35]

As something of an opening coda for the discipline, in 1822 Wolf penned the opening essay for Zunz's *Zeitschrift*. Published in Berlin for the Verein für Kultur und Wissenschaft der Juden (Club for the Culture and Study of Jews, whose opening in 1819 is often identified as the founding moment in Jewish Studies), the *Zeitschrift* (which published only one volume, in three installments between 1822 and 1823) included articles on (among other things) Jewish legislation in the Roman Empire (Edward Gans), the Jewish idea of the messiah (Lazarus Bendavid), Rashi (Zunz), and the psychology of the Jews in the Talmudic era (L. Bernhardt). Wolf's essay, entitled "Ueber den Begriff einer Wissenschaft des Judentums" (On the Concept of a Science of Judaism), gave form and substance to the varied content of the journal, as well as offering an overarching ideology for what had until then remained a relatively informal gathering of like-minded scholars. The article, began with a definition:

> If we are to talk of a science of Judaism, then it is self-evident that the word "Judaism" is here being taken in its comprehensive sense—as the essence of all the circumstances, characteristics, and achievements of the Jews in relation to religion, philosophy, history, law, literature in general, civil life and all the affairs of man—and not in that more limited sense in which it only means the religion of the Jews.[36]

With these words, Wolf turned away from the philosophical and cultural formulations favored by the Haskalah, whose members had sought to bring together Judaism and modern thought, especially with the aestheticism of the late eighteenth century. Contemporary European philosophy was never really the primary focus of *Wissenschaft*. Instead, in the view of the *Zeitschrift*, Judaism was a historical culture, and the Jews were

---

35. Important among these early *Wissenschaft* scholars was Solomon Rapoport (1786–1867), Galician-born Czech rabbi. Though writing in Hebrew (and not German), Rapoport's scholarship on medieval Jewish philosophy and piyyutim was broadly recognized as a significant contribution to the new critical historical style.

36. Immanuel Wolf, "On the Concept of a Science of Judaism (1822)," *Leo Baeck Institute Year Book* 2 (1957): 194–204, here 194. Originally published as Immanuel Wolf, "Ueber den Begriff einer Wissenschaft des Judentums," *Zeitschrift für die Wissenschaft des Judentums* 1, no. 1 (1822): 1–24.

a unique nation; neither was just a set of intellectual conjectures. *Wissenschaft*, therefore, was not a competing theological claim but a scientific method aimed at uncovering the past.

Zacharias Frankel (1801–1875), born and raised in Prague, was another central early figure in the conceptualization of *Wissenschaft* and one of the most outspoken voices of religious moderation in the discipline.[37] In 1851, while living in Dresden, he became the founding editor of the journal *Monatsschrift für Geschichte und Wissenschaft des Judentums* (Monthly Journal for the History and Science of Judaism). Aimed at both educated lay readers and scholars, *Monatsschrift* proved to be the most enduring publication to arise during the early period of the movement. (It was continuously published in Germany until 1939.) Being a rabbi and scholar in Dresden (and later Breslau), Frankel had no interest in seeing *Wissenschaft* become a conflicting ideology with religious Judaism.[38] He sought instead to defend Judaism, not only against Christians who denigrated the Jews as backward and legalistic, but against radical Jewish reformers who saw in *Wissenschaft*'s historicization of Judaism the potential to dismantle rabbinic (both legal and intellectual) power.[39] Regardless of their personal identification with the religious lifestyle of traditional Judaism, the founders of *Wissenschaft* were dedicated to the creation of a body of texts that truthfully reflected the multifaceted complexity and ancient chronology of the Jewish people. *Wissenschaft* was not an attack on revealed religion per se. But it likewise did not seek to draw any boundaries beyond which its investigations could not tread, least of all into the development of Jewish beliefs or practices. In this way, *Wissenschaft* differed fundamentally from some of the core philosophy of the Haskalah, and especially with Moses Mendelssohn. *Wissenschaft* was meant to be, no more and no less, an objective investigation (according to the best methods of its time and place) of the past and present world of the Jews.[40]

---

37. See also Esther Seidel, *Zacharias Frankel und das Jüdisch-Theologische Seminar / Zacharias Frankel and the Jewish Theological Seminary*, Jüdische Miniaturen 144 (Berlin: Hentrich & Hentrich, 2013); and David Rudavsky, "The Historical School of Zacharia Frankel," *Jewish Journal of Sociology* 5, no. 2 (1963): 224–44.

38. For a firsthand account of the Breslau Seminary, see Caesar Seligmann, "Breslau Seminary 1881," *Leo Baeck Institute Year Book* 5 (1960): 346–50. See also Gruenewald, "Modern Rabbi," 85–97; and Moshe Carmilly-Weinberger, "The Similarities and Relationship between the *Jüdisch-Theologisches Seminar* (Breslau) and the Rabbinical Seminary (Budapest)," *Leo Baeck Institute Year Book* 44 (1999): 3–22.

39. See Ismar Schorsch, "Zacharias Frankel and the European Origins of Conservative Judaism," *Judaism* 30, no. 3 (1981): 344–54.

40. See Michael A. Meyer, *The Origins of the Modern Jew: Jewish Identity and European Culture in Germany, 1749–1824* (Detroit: Wayne State University Press, 1967); Shmuel Feiner, *Haskalah and History: The Emergence of a Modern Jewish Historical Consciousness*, trans. Chaya Naor and Sondra Silverston (Oxford: Littman Library of Jewish Civilization, 2002); Amos Funkenstein, *Perceptions of Jewish History* (Berkeley: University of California Press, 1993),

With their early journals, Zunz, Fürst, and their fellow contributors sketched the foundations of a new academic discipline.[41] But that was to be only the beginning. In the 1840s and 1850s, dozens of young Jews, among them Heinrich Graetz (1817–1891), Ludwig Philippson (1811–1889), Abraham Geiger (1810–1874), Moritz Steinschneider (1816–1907)[42], and Jellinek, would take up the mantle of *Wissenschaft*, forming a second generation of scholars. In 1855, Jellinek himself defined the still-nascent field as "the scientific treatment of vast, comprehensive, and manifold subjects, written down in various languages and hidden in remote libraries of Jewish literature."[43] But the discipline was, he went on, "still very young, and the resources for its pursuance still very few."[44] Often trained in Central European yeshivot before entering the university, these men were eager to participate in the wider discussion of the German university, and especially its innovative scientific methodologies. Their university years, spent in places like Halle, Berlin, Jena, and Leipzig, also provided them with some of their first consistent encounters with Christians, Christianity, and a host of newly developing urban social institutions, such as the coffee house and literary salon.[45] Still mostly excluded from the more rarefied gatherings and private events of German intellectual life, Jewish university students banded together, founding magazines, journals, and reading groups, and formed lasting friendships with one another and with the handful of professors who expressed an interest in their education.

220–56; Michael Brenner, *Propheten des Vergangenen: Jüdische Geschichtsschreibung im 19. und 20. Jahrhundert* (Munich: Beck, 2006); and Roemer, *Jewish Scholarship and Culture in Nineteenth-Century Germany*. See also Georg G. Iggers, "Historicism: the History and Meaning of the Term," *Journal of the History of Ideas* 56, no. 1 (1995): 129—52.

41. Isaak Markus Jost (1793–1860) warrants mention here in the founding generation of *Wissenschaft*. He is perhaps best remembered for writing the first comprehensive history of postbiblical Judaism: *Geschichte der Israeliten seit der Zeit der Maccabäer bis auf unsre Tage*, 10 vols. (Berlin: Schlesinger, 1821–1847); and *Geschichte des Judenthums und seiner Secten*, 3 vols. (Leipzig: Dörffling & Franke, 1857–1859).

42. See Reimund Leicht and Gad Freudenthal, eds., *Studies on Steinschneider: Moritz Steinschneider and the Emergence of the Science of Judaism in Nineteenth-Century Germany*, Studies in Jewish History and Culture 33 (Leiden: Brill, 2012); Petra Figeac, *Moritz Steinschneider, 1816–1907: Begründer der wissenschaftlichen hebräischen Bibliographie*, Jüdische Miniaturen (Berlin: Hentrich & Hentrich, 2007). For Steinschneider's most lasting bibliographical work, see his *Catalogus librorum hebraeorum in Bibliotheca Bodleiana* [*Bibliotheca Hebraica Bodleiana*] (Berlin: Friedländer, 1852–1860).

43. Adolph Jellinek, *Bet ha-Midrasch. Sammlung kleiner Midraschim und vermischter Abhandlungen aus der ältern jüdischen Literatur*, vol. 3 (Leipzig: Vollrath, 1855), viii.

44. Jellinek, *Bet ha-Midrasch*, 3:viii.

45. See Robert Liberles, *Jews Welcome Coffee: Tradition and Innovation in Early Modern Germany*, Tauber Institute for the Study of European Jewry (Waltham, MA: Brandeis University Press, 2012).

Jellinek's Scholarly Interests

In 1842, at the age of twenty-one, Adolf Jellinek arrived in Leipzig from Prague. Attracted to the city primarily for its well-regarded Faculty of Oriental Languages, and especially the ability to study with the Arabist Heinrich Leberecht Fleischer (1801–1888)[46] and with Julius Fürst, Jellinek resided in the Saxon city until the end of 1856, when he was recruited by the Viennese Jewish community to become its rabbi in Leopoldstadt.

In a remarkable demonstration of Leipzig's transformation from regional market town to modern city, nearly every *Wissenschaft* scholar of the middle decades of the nineteenth century (with the exception of Abraham Geiger, who passed through only for brief visits) either learned at or spent significant time in Leipzig. This is not a surprise. As described in the opening pages of this chapter, in the first half of the nineteenth century Leipzig was among the earliest German municipalities to begin a process of modernization that was uniquely suited to the formation of Jewish intellectual and cultural life in an urban setting. Its university accepted Jewish students through the doctoral level. A number of its professors were interested in the Jewish contribution to modern scholarship—especially the advanced linguistic training in Hebrew and Aramaic those students possessed.[47] Leipzig's history as a trading center provided the ready-made infrastructure for its rapidly multiplying publishing houses, as well as guaranteed that the university and city libraries would contain the newest writings from across the continent. In addition, the absence of an established Jewish community meant that arriving students encountered no entrenched politics or ideologies. They were free to form Jewish associations on their own terms.

Still, Leipzig's university and those like it across the continent remained as much an intellectual impediment as a resource for young Jewish scholars. German universities were confessional institutions, meaning that one needed to profess the same faith as the theological orientation of the school to be hired as a professor.[48] In the middle of the nineteenth century, there was simply no way for Jews to receive professorial appointments anywhere in the German lands. Aside from its obvious social implications,

---

46. See Ismar Schorch, "Beyond the Classroom: The Enduring Relationship between Heinrich L. Fleischer and Ignaz Goldziher," in *Modern Jewish Scholarship in Hungary: The 'Science of Judaism' between East and West*, ed. Tamás Turán and Carsten Wilke, Europäisch-Jüdische Studien: Beiträge 14 (Berlin: de Gruyter, 2016), 119–56.

47. It was in Leipzig, in the newly founded department of Oriental Languages and Literature, that many of *Wissenschaft*'s second generation encountered the famed orientalist Heinrich Leberecht Fleischer (1801–1888).

48. Following the First World War, the German parliament passed laws that superseded this requirement. But as late as the twentieth century, to be considered for an academic appointment Jews were made to convert to Christianity.

this fact also had profound scholarly reverberations. In German universities, the work being done on "Jewish" topics (e.g., Hebrew Bible, Second Temple literature, the Apocrypha) overwhelmingly originated from Christians. Moreover, Christian academics focused almost exclusively on ancient Israel and its related literature. Christian scholarly interests in and knowledge of post–Second Temple Judaism, including rabbinic theologies and languages, were almost entirely absent. *Wissenschaft* scholarship, therefore, existed on the periphery of the German university, with access to its resources but without institutional support. *Wissenschaft* scholars were sometimes tutors at the university or of university students, but they never held professorships or chairs, and their journals were independently published. In Jellinek's case, as in them all, the lack of advancement within the university after the end of one's student years was clearly determinative for the course of one's scholarly life. Many *Wissenschaft* scholars were community rabbis.[49] Others pieced together careers as teachers, tutors, or librarians,[50] and a few became part of the Jewish Theological Seminary in Breslau (founded by Frankel in 1854).[51] In many ways, the modern German university was essential for the formation and growth of *Wissenschaft*, but even into the early twentieth century it was never a scholarly home for the movement—and certainly not as it was for other modern scholarly endeavors in the humanities and human and natural sciences. Importantly and interestingly, during its first few generations, the innovative heart of *Wissenschaft* lay almost entirely in the pages of its journals and the monographs published by those journals' contributors.

Jellinek was an immensely prolific scholar during his residence in Leipzig, contributing dozens of short- and medium-length articles and book reviews to *Der Orient* in the 1840s; publishing eight booklet- and book-length works on the history and philology of Kabbalah in the first half of the 1850s; and beginning a project that would, in total, take him over two decades to complete, the six-volume *Bet ha-Midrasch*, a collection of previously unpublished rabbinic texts ranging in subject from biblical exegesis to mysticism to historical narrative told in metaphor. In Saxony, Jellinek became one of the leading voices in *Wissenschaft* and, specifically, in the history of Jewish mysticism, the origins of the *Zohar* and related literature, and medieval midrash. (As has become the focus of recent scholarship, Jellinek's scholarly accomplishments in Leipzig exemplify a widespread academic interest in Jewish mysticism.[52])

---

49. E.g., Solomon Formstecher (1808–1889); David Einhorn (1809–1879); Moritz Güdemann (1835–1918).
50. E.g., Jost; Joseph Dernburg (1811–1895); Philippson; Steinschneider.
51. E.g., Graetz; Manuel Joël (1826–1890).
52. See Kohler, *Kabbalah Research in the Wissenschaft des Judentums*, 63–64: "During the almost fifteen years of his stay in Leipzig, [Jellinek] became the leading and most industrious

One overriding question arises from even this brief recounting of Jellinek's publications. Why was he so deeply interested in the history of mysticism, and of medieval Jewry writ large? We cannot, of course, comprehensively answer any question that contains more than a hint of personal idiosyncrasy. But two modes of inquiry go some lengths toward an explanation. First, the history of Kabbalah revealed certain historical phenomena in which Jellinek was particularly interested: those concerning Jewish philosophy and its non-Jewish influences; Jewish theology and its development and transformation across the ages; and Jewish accounts of value, meaning, and ethics outside of biblical exegesis and halakhic codes. All of Jellinek's publications in Leipzig point toward his deep fascination with the interplay of Jewish and non-Jewish intellectual and linguistic motifs. For Jellinek, medieval mysticism (especially in its Spanish kabbalistic variety) was an unexamined entrée into the vast cultural diversity of historic Judaism, one that was often obscured by more Bible- and Talmud-centered narratives.[53]

The other answer as to why Jellinek was interested in the history of mysticism focuses less on the specifics of the numinous tradition itself. Instead, it understands Jellinek's fascination as related to his observations concerning contemporary developments in German Judaism. In other words, during his years in Leipzig (and then even more so during his first decade in Vienna), Jellinek was seeking new modes of language and rhetoric for connecting contemporary German Jews to the narratives and moral principles embodied (he believed) in the Jewish tradition. Jellinek interpreted the mystical tradition as part of the more general project of theological expression known as midrash. It was in midrash, Jellinek hoped, that one might find an authentic and uniquely Jewish rhetorical posture, one that could appeal to urban, acculturating (liberal) Jews. For Jellinek, mysticism was a deep and complex form of midrash, just one

---

German-Jewish scholar of kabbalistic thought of his time, probably even of the entire nineteenth century." For an introduction to and overview of *Wissenschaft* engagement with the history of Jewish mysticism, see David Myers, "Philosophy and Kabbalah in Wissenschaft des Judentums: Rethinking the Narrative of Neglect," *Studia Judaica* 16 (2008): 56–71.

53. As early as 1852, Isaak Markus Jost had written about Jellinek's interests in these unusual facets of Jewish history: "One might also judge about the value of the Kabbalah itself—we ourselves regard it as one of the many aberrations of the human mind, that pleases in the unusual, especially when one can train it by extraordinary thinking and seclusion. One cannot deny that it is a great phenomenon on which knowledgeable and profound thinkers gave their lives, and that it presents a very noteworthy direction of human activity, which, by the way, exercised an unmistakable influence on the edifices and customs of the people, and in part makes even the moral side of whole masses comprehensible.... It is very meritorious, therefore, [for Jellinek to] give information on the nature and content of such a profound mental activity, especially since its products are accessible to so few researchers, and so much misunderstood in previous attempts" (*Adolph Jellinek und die Kabbala*, 14–15).

of a myriad of its strands, each of which illuminated a particular Jewish apperception of the world and represented a distinctive Jewish adaptation or appropriation of non-Jewish ideas and insights. Indeed, as the years progressed and Jellinek participated less in scholarship and more in communal leadership, it was to this enormous body of midrashic texts that he returned time and again for rhetorical inspiration and moral guidance. During his career as a preacher and community rabbi, he came to hold that midrash was the key that could rejuvenate Jewish belief and practice in a world of urban modernity.

In Leipzig, Jellinek wrote about two separate but related topics, first, the genealogy of Spanish Kabbalah and, second, the various traditions of midrashic development from antiquity to the Middle Ages. To fully understand why Jellinek was interested in the Kabbalah and midrash we must take a closer look not only at these writings but at his intellectual context—at the modes of historical critique employed by *Wissenschaft* scholars themselves; at what Jellinek was reading and to whom he was speaking during his years in Leipzig; and how *Wissenschaft* as a whole was being received and what its adherents imagined their role to be in the future of European Judaism. Taken together, these contexts reveal Jellinek's own understandings about the development of Jewish ideas and the historic interplay of Jewish and non-Jewish philosophical perspectives. His six-volume collection *Bet ha-Midrasch* and his larger philosophy concerning the place of rabbinic thought for informing contemporary German-Jewish life are key aspects of this history. Together with his groundbreaking research on the origins of the *Zohar*, they reveal a whole world of Jewish learning and theorization that proved not only influential in academic circles of the time, but that, with Jellinek's appointment as rabbi in Leipzig and his later move to Vienna, were foundational in his creation of a new form of rabbinic voice and persona within modern Central European Judaism.

Jellinek's later prominence in Vienna has had the tendency to obscure his years in Leipzig, where he contributed groundbreaking work on the philology and intellectual history of Jewish mysticism, with special attention to the authorship of the *Zohar*, the foundational text of Spanish Kabbalism.[54] Though Jellinek was a prolific and well-regarded scholar in

---

54. Jellinek's work on Kabbalism has not been entirely neglected in the modern scholarly literature. See Idel, "Al Aharon Jellinek ve haKabbalah"; Isaiah Tishby, *Wisdom of the Zohar: An Anthology of Texts*, 3 vols. (Oxford: Littman Library of Jewish Civilization, 1989), 1:47–49; and Ronald Kiener, "From *Ba'al ha-Zohar* to Prophetic to Ecstatic: The Vicissitudes of Abulafia in Contemporary Scholarship," in *Gershom Scholem's Major Trends in Jewish Mysticism 50 Years after: Proceedings of the Sixth International Conference on the History of Jewish Mysticism*, ed. Peter Schäfer and Joseph Dan (Tübingen: Mohr Siebeck, 1993), 145–62.

Leipzig, it was not until his years in Vienna that he became truly famous, renowned as German Jewry's most gifted orator. That the move to Vienna marked a sharp decline in Jellinek's contributions to *Wissenschaft* journals has for too long meant that his early publications were overlooked by historians.

3

Breakthroughs in Scholarship: Jellinek's Studies on Kabbalah

> We are of the opinion that Adolf Jellinek may feel called to explore the whole nature of Kabbalah, its full content in the various directions of its development, formation, and degeneration, and to vividly portray its history.
>
> —Isaak Markus Jost (1852)

Jellinek's Earliest Scholarship

Adolf Jellinek brought with him to Leipzig a traditional yeshiva education complemented by knowledge of classical and contemporary European languages (Latin, English, French, Italian) and history. Jellinek's first years at the university were taken up by courses in Oriental languages, philosophy, and philology, with over half his lectures given by Heinrich Leberecht Fleischer, a specialist in Arabic literature and philosophy whose reputation was respected across Europe.[1] (Fleischer was also one of the few professors who actively cultivated personal relationships with Jewish students, and one of the few non-Jewish scholars to regularly contributed to *Wissenschaft* journals.) It was in Leipzig that Jellinek learned to read Arabic, and from Fleischer that he gained a knowledge of the Islamic philosophy of the Middle Ages, two skills he would later rely on heavily for his work decoding the authorship and literary background of the *Zohar*. It was also in these first years at the university that Jellinek

---

1. The list of Jellinek's courses in Leipzig has been preserved; see National Library of Israel, Ms. collection ARC. 4* 1588. Series 2- Collegian-Buch. On Fleischer, see Hans-Georg Ebert and Thoralf Hanstein, eds., *Heinrich Leberecht Fleischer – Leben und Wirkung: Ein Leipziger Orientalist des 19. Jahrhunderts mit Internationaler Ausstrahlung* (Frankfurt am Main: Peter Lang, 2013).

befriended Julius Fürst, the institution's Hebrew lecturer and the editor of *Der Orient*, which printed scholarly articles, news from around the Jewish world, short critiques and analyses, and book reviews. The publication ran for just over a decade (from January 1840 to May 1851), during which time it was the most important periodical for *Wissenschaft* scholarship in the German language in Central Europe.[2]

Jellinek's first (credited) writing appeared in *Orient* in November 1842.[3] Printed under one of *Orient*'s recurring subject heading, "Literarische Nachrichten und Miscellen," it was a brief philological exercise on the possible Arabic origins of the Hebrew *laḥan* (meaning "melody"). More important than the substance of the piece itself is what it already revealed about Jellinek's course of scholarship. Given his future interest in the Arabic (and therefore Islamic) influences on post-Talmudic Hebrew and Judaic culture, it is interesting to note that even his very first article in *Orient* focused on a Hebrew–Arabic connection. Though Jellinek was not the only writer to quote in Arabic in *Orient* (which the publisher printed in its original script), he was one of the most consistent to do so, as if in a personal attempt to keep the nascent *Wissenschaft* movement from looking too much inside Judaism's own enormous Hebrew literary oeuvre. Further, Jellinek mentioned Fleischer by name in this article, calling him "the learned and affable Mr. Professor" (*der gelehrte und menschenfreundliche Hr. Prof.*), expressing in public a fondness for a man whose mentorship and guidance would result in a lasting friendship.

Over the course of *Orient*'s decade-long run, Jellinek published at least seventy-five articles in it, ranging in length from a single page to many dozens, on topics related to Hebrew–Arabic linguistic connections,[4] the cultural milieu of the Jewish Middle Ages,[5] Kabbalah and its theological perspectives,[6] and reviews of new religious and scholarly books.[7] During these years, Jellinek was also scouring libraries in Leipzig, and corresponding with friends in Munich and elsewhere, in search

---

2. Its complete title was *Der Orient: Berichte, Studien und Kritiken für jüdische Geschichte und Literatur.*

3. *Orient* 49 (1842): 780–81. *Orient* was divided into two sections. The first gathered news from around the Jewish world. The second, under the additional title *Literaturblatt des Orients*, was where all of Jellinek's writings appeared. It is to this literary supplement that all references in this chapter refer.

4. See *Orient* 4 (1843): 63–64; 6 (1843): 88–91; 9 (1843): 141–42; 23 (1843): 360–61; 30 (1843): 471–72; 2 (1844): 26–27; 45 (1844): 719–20.

5. See *Orient* 17 (1843): 270–72; 19 (1843): 296-97; 39 (1843): 615–17; 46 (1843): 728; 52 (1843): 817–21; 11 (1844): 167–69; 12 (1844) 187–90; 50 (1844): 793–94; 5 (1847): 78–79; 9 (1847):141–42; 17 (1847): 263–64; 18 (1847): 275–77; 19 (1847): 296–98.

6. See *Orient* 11 (1844): 167–69; 30 (1844): 470.

7. See *Orient* 1 (1843): 9–13; 12 (1843): 201–2; and 17 (1843): 265–68 and 18 (1843): 279–81; 22 (1844): 350–52; 26 (1844): 413–14; 27 (1844): 428–29; 29 (1844): 458–59; 36 (1844): 573–76; 38 (1844): 603–8.

of unknown Jewish manuscripts from the Spanish Middle Ages, parts of which he published, with commentary, in *Orient*.[8] Finally, through the middle and end of the 1840s, Jellinek wrote a series of biographical sketches for *Orient*, focused mainly on medieval and early modern rabbinic proponents of Kabbalah and mysticism.[9] These mini-biographies were brief forays into the theological and philological particularity of individuals, and they foreshadowed the intensive work Jellinek would later undertake in his search for (what he came to believe was) the medieval Spanish originator of the *Zohar*.

Jellinek's frequent contributions to *Orient*, and his early and continued relationship with Fürst, provided the up-and-coming scholar with a platform and testing ground for his ideas, especially when it came to mapping the linguistic and intellectual connections between Jewish and non-Jewish texts. Jellinek's voluminous short writings in *Orient* demonstrated an early affinity for two key scholarly methodologies, both of which would direct his later research: close philological analysis, on the one hand, and a keen awareness of overlapping social contexts, on the other. These two approaches were complemented by a third, what might even be called Jellinek's theoretical lens: Jellinek began every investigation with the assumption that Jewish history constituted a series of historical developments, of changes over time, that arose in response to shifting social factors taking place outside of the Jewish community. This idea was already a core element of *Wissenschaft* ideology, but Jellinek took it a step further. Major historical developments, he believed, ones like the creation of the Talmud or the advent of Spanish Kabbalism, were prompted almost entirely by external factors, by social and intellectual trends that originated in the worlds of Christian and Islamic learning.

Taken together, these two methods of reading and this sense of historical development in conversation with external traditions appear to have guided Jellinek's presentation of his research throughout the 1840s. In fact, as he studied at the university and focused on philology and manuscript collection, his original intention to write a large, synthetic treatment of the entire history of the Kabbalah devolved into a dedication to trace the Kabbalah's historical development through small, focused works. We can see this evolution in his thinking quite clearly in two statements made seven years apart. In May 1844, Jellinek wrote:

---

8. See *Orient* 20 (1843): 305–9; 24 (1843): 376–77; 35 (1843): 557–60;

9. Jellinek's biographies included: Samuel Balerio (sixteenth century) (36 [1845]: 566 and 38 [1845]: 606); Moshe Botarel (fourteenth–fifteenth century) (12 [1846]: 187–89); David ben Solomon Vital (called ha-Rofe) (d. 1589) (13 [1846]: 198–99); Jacob Luzzato (d. 1587) (14 [1846]: 221–22); Emanuel Recchi (15 [1846]: 232–33); Aaron ben David ha-Kohen (fourteenth century) (16 [1846]: 252–53); Yisachar Bähr (16 [1846]: 254); Isaac of Neustadt (seventeenth–eighteenth century) (16 [1846]: 254–56); Naftali Hirsch Goßlar of Halberstadt (eighteenth century) (17 [1846]: 260–61); and Josef Jabez (fifteenth–sixteenth century) (16 [1846]: 261–63).

> Bound up with the question of the origin and the age of the Kabbalah is another, that of the time and place of the composition of the *Zohar*. This question appears to us as not having been sufficiently answered. The *Zohar*, in its entirety, contains no less than a uniform system. One finds in it repetitions; there are passages which have been borrowed from the Talmud and Midrash; the language is variously colored. One finds progressions within it, since the system developed gradually. [Ultimately,] it now must be shown what doctrines make up its original elements: how it developed under the hands of various teachers and what elements of other writings are found in it. In short, we need to give a critique of the entire *Zohar* according to its individual passages. This [I] shall attempt in a future work, [to be called] "The Composition of the Zohar." [10]

Jellinek published these words at the age of twenty-three, after having been a student in Leipzig for less than two years. His ambitions were grand and his insights clear. Yet he never did write such a great synthetic work. Instead, as his many small articles from *Orient* illustrate, his youthful exuberance slowly transformed into a methodology of micro-histories. By 1851, at the start of four highly productive years, he wrote another statement of purpose, this time with a very different tone.

> I stayed mindful of my promise [from 1844, to write a book on the composition of the *Zohar*], and it was not Horace's *nonum prematur in annum* [let it be kept back until the ninth year] that detained me from fulfilling it so far, but [rather] the consciousness that my subject could not be sufficiently solved until, over time, something affirmative placed the origins and authorship of the *Zohar*.[11]

These are the opening lines to Jellinek's *Moses ben Schem-Tob de Leon und sein Verhältniß zum Sohar* (Moses ben Shem-Tov de León and his relationship to the *Zohar* [discussed in detail below]), his attempt at a definitive statement that the authorship of the *Zohar* dated not from the Mishnaic period (second century CE) but from the milieu of medieval Spain. *Moses ben Schem-Tob* was a short book, fifty-three pages in length, closer really to an extended article, but it exemplified the methodologies and preferences Jellinek had honed throughout the 1840s. Jellinek was never to become known as a grand theorist. Instead, his preferred style was argument through quotidian analysis, the piecemeal assemblage of trace data that, in the end, created enduring proofs and bedrocks of text on which to build a grounded account of the Jewish past.

---

10. Adolphe Franck, *Die Kabbala oder die Religions-Philosophie der hebräer*, trans. Adolf Jellinek (Leipzig: Hunger, 1844), x (from Jellinek's "Vorrede des Uebersetzers").

11. Adolf Jellinek, *Moses ben Schem-Tob de Leon und sein Verhältniß zum Sohar: Eine historisch-kritische Untersuchung über die Entstehung des Sohar* (Leipzig: Hunger, 1851), 5.

There is one final text that requires mention before we can turn to Jellinek's core discoveries in the history of Spanish Kabbalism. The passage quoted above from May 1844 originated in one of Jellinek's first major contributions to German-language scholarship on the history of the Kabbalah: a translation. In 1843, the French Jewish philosopher (and member of the Institut de France) Adolphe Franck (1810–1893) published *La Kabbale ou la philosophie religieuse des Hébreux*, an attempted synthesis of the various philosophical concepts that make up the canonical texts of the Kabbalah, especially those originating in *Sefer Yetsirah* and the *Zohar*.[12] Immediately, Jellinek set to work translating the text. But Jellinek's was to be more than just a German-language version of the French original. Though still a student, Jellinek took many liberties with Franck's text, including adding introductory remarks, correctional footnotes concerning manuscript variations and alternate translations, and his own set of appendices. These were audacious acts by a man not yet out of his early twenties. But they likewise demonstrated Jellinek's already deep knowledge of both the original sources and the extant scholarship on Kabbalism.[13]

Jellinek's extensive notes in the Franck translation set into writing his earliest thoughts on the overall history and development of the Kabbalah. First, Jellinek sided with Johann Karl Ludwig Gieseler (1792–1854), a Protestant German church historian then working in Göttingen, who had argued (in a series of essays in the 1820s and 1830s) that Jewish Kabbalah did not originate in Zoroastrianism, nor was it the source of Christian Gnosticism.[14] Such debates—about the relationship of the mystical strands of Judaism to the more esoteric traditions of the ancient Near East and Mediterranean—were the cause of much speculation in the first half of the nineteenth century. Though never rejecting the interaction of Gnostic thought with Judaism, Jellinek argued vehemently that the Kabbalah was much closer to the mainstream of Judaism than it was to other esoteric traditions that persisted mainly in small circles of acolytes.[15] Second, Jellinek

---

12. See Wouter J. Hanegraaff, "The Beginnings of Occultist Kabbalah: Adolphe Franck and Eliphas Lévy," in *Kabbalah and Modernity: Interpretations, Transformations, Adaptations*, ed. Boaz Huss, Marco Pasi, and Kocku von Stuckrad, Aries Book Series 10 (Leiden: Brill, 2010), 107–28, esp. 111–18; Paul Fenton, "Adolphe Franck's Contribution to the Historico-Critical Study of the Kabbalah," *Kabbalah: Journal for the Study of Jewish Mystical Texts* 40 (2018): 61–84.

13. Jellinek's translation appeared in May 1844 and was reviewed widely, including in *Orient* by Isaak Markus Jost, a leader of the *Wissenschaft* movement and an early advocate of Jellinek's researches.

14. Franck, *Die Kabbala*, vii. Giesler's works appeared in numerous journals, among them *Theologischen Studien und Kritiken*.

15. This belief explains many of Jellinek's mini-biographies in *Orient*. Those who participated in kabbalistic thought, whether fully or merely as one project alongside other Talmudic and philosophical devotions, were not, for Jellinek, adherents of a secret sect, encamped outside the mainstream of Judaism. Rather, Kabbalah represented a fully accepted strain of

supported Franck's assertions that any examination of the Kabbalah must involve "an investigation on the relationship of the Kabbalistic system to other systems of philosophy and religion."[16] Still, Jellinek differed with Franck, specially over the age of the *Zohar* and its relationship to other theological literatures. (Franck continued to place the *Zohar*'s origins in the Mishnaic period.) Following the publication of the translation, Jellinek spent over half a decade searching widely through medieval Arabic, and later Christian, texts in search of proofs about the close ties of Kabbalah to the non-Jewish framework of the medieval world. Further, Jellinek used this translation (and especially his added appendixes) to begin to correct what he understood (rightly) to be a deeply corrupted manuscript tradition and a weak philological understanding among scholars of key kabbalistic terms.[17]

The *Zohar*: Authorship and Lineage

Jellinek's translation of Franck, together with his subsequent years carefully learning the cultural context of Spanish Kabbalism, marked the first chapter in his scholarly contributions to the history of Jewish mysticism. But beginning in the first half of the 1850s, Jellinek sought to bring definitive answers to some of the field's core outstanding questions: the authorship of the *Zohar* and the intellectual networks in which it was created.[18] Jellinek's central works on the authorship and lineage of the *Zohar* were published between 1851 and 1854. Writing almost nothing in 1850, he spent the year preparing a string of short books that would fundamentally reshape the debate on the origins and ideas of Spanish Kabbalism. With each of these texts Jellinek sought to expand the scholarly conception of the intellectual world of Spanish Kabbalism and to create a foundation of critical editions on which future research could be based.

Jellinek began his spate of publications with the short previously-mentioned monograph, *Moses ben Schem-Tob de Leon und sein Verhältniß zum Sohar* [1851]), which was his attempt to definitively identify the authorship of the *Zohar*. From there, Jellinek began a systematic investigation of texts within the *Zohar*'s cultural milieu, which he parsed at length in the two-volume *Beiträge zur Geschichte der Kabbala* (Contributions to the history of the Kabbalah [1852]). In this same period, he also published critical editions of texts he felt to be important to the kabbalistic imagi-

---

Jewish theological investigation in continual concert with other forms of religious experience. Jellinek did write a long essay on Gnosticism; see *Orient* 27–30 (1849).

16. Franck, *Die Kabbala*, xi.
17. Franck, *Die Kabbala*, xii.
18. For a recent synthesis and expansion of scholarship on this topic, see Huss, *Zohar*.

nary: in 1852, the "Dialogue on the Soul" by the Greek philosopher Galen (second century CE), which was influential in Arabic philosophy and had been translated into Hebrew by Judah ben Solomon Alharizi (d. 1225); in 1853, *Auswahl kabbalistischer Mystic* (Selections of kabbalistic mysticism), which included the texts of *Masechet Atzilut* (Tractate on Emanations), *Sefer ha'Iyun* (Book of Intuitions) by Rabbi Hamai Gaon (school of Isaac the Blind, thirteenthcentury), the *Epistles* of Abraham Abulafia, and *On the Tetragrammaton* by Abraham of Cologne (thirteenth century); also in 1853, the text of *Ma'arich*, an explanatory dictionary of Talmudic, midrashic, and kabbalistic terms by Menahem ben Judah de Lonzano (d. early seventeenth century); in 1854, the *Sefer Olam HaKatan* (Microcosmos) by Josef ibn Tzaddik (d. 1149) on religious philosophy and ethics; and also in 1854, Abraham Abulafia's *Epistles on Philosophy and Kabbalah*. Finally, Jellinek sought to illuminate kabbalistic connections with the Christian world, publishing, in 1853 and 1854, two essays by Thomas Aquinas (1225–1274), Hebrew translations of *Quaestiones disputate, quaestio de anima* (Disputed Questions, the Question of the Soul) and *De animae facultatibus* (The Faculties of the Soul).[19] Jellinek's critical editions have had a much longer scholarly life than have his proofs of de León's authorship of the *Zohar*.[20] Yet *Moses ben Schem-Tob de Leon und sein Verhältniß zum Sohar* is the key to understanding Jellinek's larger intellectual project and is essential for explaining why he chose certain works to publish in new editions. Therefore, it is to this book that we now turn.

Moses ben Schem-Tob de Leon und sein Verhältniß zum Sohar appeared in 1851. Subtitled "Eine historisch-kritische Untersuchung" (A historical-critical investigation), the book exemplified the methodological paradigms that Jellinek had been perfecting throughout the 1840s. Structured around a series of close readings and text-parallels, and relying heavily on philological comparisons to other twelfth- and thirteenth-century manuscripts, Jellinek claimed that the *Zohar* was not written by its purported author, the tannaitic sage Simeon ben Yochai (second century CE), but rather was authored by the Spanish rabbi Moses ben Shem-Tov de León (d. 1305).[21] Citing mainly Hebrew, Aramaic, and Arabic sources, Jellinek

---

19. For an overview of Jewish engagements with Thomas Aquinas, see Norman Roth, "Thomas Aquinas," *Medieval Jewish Civilization: An Encyclopedia*, ed. Norman Roth (New York: Routledge, 2016), 27–31.

20. Much of the reason for this is Gershom Scholem's attribution of the insight about de León mainly to himself but somewhat also to Heinrich Graetz (1817–1891)—although Graetz cited Jellinek.

21. Jellinek's theory of the *Zohar*'s primary authorial origins was accepted by Heinrich Graetz (1817–1891) in his *Geschichte der Juden von den ältesten Zeiten bis auf die Gegenwart*, 11 vols. (Leipzig: Leiner, 1853–1875), but was not fully embraced by scholars until Gershom Scholem (1897–1982) gave it his imprimatur a century later. The fifth lecture of *Major Trends in Jewish Mysticism*, entitled "The Zohar I: The Book and Its Author," is in part devoted to

traced in careful detail the development of kabbalistic mystical philosophy through centuries of preceding texts.[22]

Jellinek's contention in *Moses ben Schem-Tob* concerning the *Zohar*'s more recent authorship built on already-extant theories, some dating from the 1840s, others much older. As both Jellinek and Heinrich Graetz openly acknowledged, the idea of the *Zohar*'s medieval origin was not an invention of the nineteenth century. Jellinek listed a number of Jewish authorities who had, over the years, come to the conclusion that Moses de León was, at the very least, involved with the *Zohar*, perhaps even as its primary redactor (*verfasser*). Such historical figures included the medieval Spanish Talmudist Solomon ben Aderet (1235–1310, called Rashba), the Portuguese court astronomer Abraham Zakuto (1452–1515), and the German rabbi and publisher Jacob Emden (1697–1776). Jellinek credited the writings of these men as being essential to his own early research.[23] (Graetz, in his *Geschichte der Juden*, likewise recorded Emden's widely discussed idea that the *Zohar* was of medieval origin.[24]) But, Jellinek further noted, in order to make a final proof, modern scholars ought to return to the primary sources themselves.[25]

As mentioned, Adolphe Franck, in his 1843 book, still believed the *Zohar* to be of classical origin, an idea that Jellinek was beginning to doubt but could not yet prove at the time of his 1844 translation. Throughout the 1830s, while there was increased question about this dating (both from within and without Jewish scholarly circles), little solid historical evidence was gathered to prove a different conclusion. In the mid-1840s, however, as Jellinek was contributing his short pieces to *Orient*, Julius Fürst received the unpublished writings of a young scholar whose theories (though ultimately proven wrong) would fully inaugurate the modern idea of the *Zohar*'s medieval origins. Throughout the 1830s, Meyer Heinrich Hirsch Landauer (1808–1841) had been working through the uncatalogued Hebrew materials housed in the State Library in Munich (Bayerische Staatsbibliothek).

---

explaining how Scholem forwent his initial belief in the *Zohar*'s multi-authorship for Jellinek's theory—which Scholem credits to Graetz—of Moses de Leon's sole authorship. See Scholem, *Major Trends in Jewish Mysticism*, 156–204; and Daniel C. Matt, *Zohar, the Book of Enlightenment*, Classics of Western Spirituality (New York: Paulist Press, 1983), 4–10. Also Moses de Leon, *The Book of the Pomegranate: Moses de Leon's Sefer Ha-Rimmon*, ed. and trans. Elliot R. Wolfson, Brown Judaic Studies 144 (Atlanta: Scholars Press, 1988).

22. For a longer account of Jellinek's work on Abraham Abulafia and Jellinek's importance to the field of Jewish mystical studies generally, see Kiener, "From *Ba'al ha-Zohar* to Prophetic to Ecstatic," 145–62

23. Jellinek, *Moses ben Schem-Tob*, 6.

24. Graetz contextualized Emden's insight as part of the latter's ongoing attempt to combat crypto-Sabbatianism and Frankism in the mid-eighteenth century. For an extended discussion of these debates, see Graetz, *Geschichte der Juden*, 10:349–406.)

25. Jellinek, *Moses ben Schem-Tob*, 6: "Meine Hauptquellen waren der Sohar und eine gedruckte Schrift Moses de Leon's."

After Landauer's untimely death in 1841, Fürst spent four years organizing the papers, which were serialized in *Orient* in 1845 and 1846. The writings in Landauer's estate were highly varied and of mixed quality, ranging from the scholarly to the more abstruse and theological. Yet, after years of reading in Munich, Landauer had concluded that the *Zohar* was indeed of medieval origin. But as to the identity of the author, Landauer settled on Abraham Abulafia (b. 1240), the Spanish mystic, influential teacher, and disseminator of a school of prophetic Kabbalah.[26]

Jellinek, we know, read these articles in *Orient* carefully (working as closely as he did with Fürst, it is also possible that he saw them before publication), and *Moses ben Schem-Tob* was in many ways structured as a fair-minded but categorical rebuttal to Landauer's conclusions. Jellinek's disagreements with Landauer centered on a series of interlocking contradictions in Landauer's findings, which Jellinek laid out in his book's preface:

> 1. One cannot find mention in any [medieval or early modern] Jewish writer of Abulafia's having written the *Zohar*, while there are such notes for Moses de León.
>
> 2. It is psychologically unlikely that a man [like Abulafia] who is so prominent in his personality, who thinks he is inspired, should write his works under a borrowed name.
>
> 3. One finds teachings that form a bridge between the *Zohar* and Abulafia, as well as with other Kabbalists.
>
> 4. Landauer has misunderstood the evidence of the *Zohar* [itself], as was partly proved by me (*Orient* 1851) and partly by [David] Joël (*Die Religionsphilosophie des Sohar und ihr Verhältnis zur allgemeinen jüdischen Theologie*, Religionsphilosophischen Werke des Judentums 7 [1923; repr., New York: Arno Press, 1980], 68ff.).
>
> 5. A single person did not write the entire *Zohar*, the *Zohar Hadash* [New Zohar] and the *Tikunei ha-Zohar* [Rectifications of the Zohar]; and Abulafia was not a man to associate with others. And where could he have found helpers in Italy? It is, however, possible that in Ávila [Spain, where de León lived] certain writings of Abulafia were employed in the editing of the *Zohar*.[27]

These arguments against Landauer point in a number of directions, yet all rely on Jellinek's two main forms of scholarly methodology—philological analysis (point 4) and historical-intellectual context (points 1, 3, and

---

26. For a brief discussion of Landauer and Jellinek on Abulafia, see Giulio Busi, "Beyond the Burden of Idealism: For a New Appreciation of the Visual Lore in the Kabbalah," in Huss, Pasi, and von Stuckrad, *Kabbalah and Modernity*, 29–46, esp. 36–38.

27. Jellinek, *Moses ben Schem-Tob*, 7–8.

5)—with what appears to be the addition of a new angle, that of personal psychology (points 2 and 5, a point we will return to below in discussion about Jellinek's work on Thomas Aquinas). Abulafia, Jellinek argued, was simply not the kind of person who writes a work like the *Zohar*. Yet how might one discover just who that sort of person could be? By focusing even more closely on the literary style and external influences of the *Zohar* text, Jellinek concluded. In *Moses ben Schem-Tob*, Jellinek sought to show that only by comparing across literary genres and styles could a definitive argument be made for the authorship of such a large and complex pseudepigraphic text. Jellinek based his conclusions on a close philological investigation of the entire corpus of known writings by de León, as well as by comparing the manuscript remains of de León's students to the *Zohar*'s vocabulary, structure, and thematic choices.

To further his claims, Jellinek sought to give historical context to de León's education and influences, as well as to argue that such texts could have been written only after a couple of generations of kabbalistic investigation.[28] "[Moses de León] studied poetry, the masterpieces of Salomon ibn Gabirol [eleventh century], knew the Aristotelian philosophy, and was an enthusiastic supporter and promoter of the [already extant though nascent] Kabbalah."[29] Still, if Jellinek was to prove that de León was the primary author of the *Zohar*, he had also to demonstrate that de León's other works were deeply rooted in the thirteenth century and not the second. So Jellinek turned to the debate between philosophy and mysticism: "the original tendency of the *Zohar* collection was to offer a counterbalance to rationalism and its consequences,"[30] he argued. Such a context fit well with Jellinek's larger understanding of the place of the Kabbalah in Jewish cultural and intellectual history. Mysticism was not an aberration or embarrassment; it was, instead, a legitimate form of theological inquiry, one tied to the deepest longings of the human soul. "Mysticism is such an essential moment in the spiritual development of humanity that it is found in all nations and all religions," he wrote in 1853.[31]

For Jellinek, mysticism's opposing (yet complementary) partner was philosophy, the rational investigation of the world. As many of his contemporary *Wissenschaft* scholars had begun to discern in the middle of the nineteenth century, the works of Maimonides (1135–1204), and especially the *Moreh Nevukim* (Guide to the Perplexed), had given rise, in the century after Maimonides's death, to a series of debates over the centrality of rationalist philosophy in Jewish theology.[32] Some rabbis sided with Maimon-

---

28. See Jellinek, *Moses ben Schem-Tob*, 37–38.
29. Jellinek, *Moses ben Schem-Tob*, 17–18.
30. Jellinek, *Moses ben Schem-Tob*, 21.
31. Adolf Jellinek, *Auswahl kabbalistischer Mystik* (Leipzig: Colditz, 1853), iii.
32. For an account of the reception of Maimonides in the nineteenth century, see

ides, but others objected to the more dogmatic claims. Spanish Kabbalism, Jellinek argued, was one of the more "romantic" responses to this new outpouring of philosophical rationalism, as well as a tradition of Jewish thought with its own independent genealogy. The urge to mysticism was coterminous with the human condition, but the particular varieties promoted in medieval Spain gained their emotional fervor from the disputes over philosophy.

> For the fire, which was fueled twice against the *Moreh* [*Nevukim*], found its sustenance not only in the materialistic groping after gross anthropomorphisms, but essentially in the unsatisfied longing for mystical intuition.... Thus, Kabbalah also developed, both as a speculation and a mystical law.... And our Moses ben Shem Tov de León now found the tracks of Kabbalah in [an already] rich literature.[33]

Both philosophy and mysticism had roots in the Torah and the classical rabbis, Jellinek noted. But the challenge of philosophy to the emotional core of human yearning provoked an outpouring of mystical investigation, drawing not only on much earlier Jewish texts but also, crucially, on newer Islamic ones.

It is worth noting here, parenthetically, that, four years after the publication of *Moses ben Schem-Tob*, Jellinek was still working to convince his fellow scholars of the medieval origins of the Zoharic corpus. In the final section of his introduction to the third volume of *Bet ha-Midrasch* (1855, discussed below), Jellinek appended a section entitled "Ein historisches Datum im Buche Sohar." He wrote:

> Since there are still many scholars who prove that this book is very old, I want to prove the date 22 August 1280 in the same. For we read in *Zohar* III, 212b: [Aramaic quotation, which he translates as:] "God is ready to build Jerusalem and make visible a wonderfully shining star that will shine for 70 days. Friday, the 25th of Elul, it will be seen and Saturday at the end of the 70 days it will go down. On the first day [i.e., on the 25th of Elul] he will show himself in Rome, and on the same day three high walls and a great temple will collapse in Rome, and his ruler will die." This passage is understood by the following calculation: In the year 1280 Rosh Chodesh Elul fell on Sunday and Monday or on the 29th of July. Consequently, the 25th of Elul = 22nd of August, a Thursday, on the evening of which the star began to shine, the seventy days of which ended Friday evening—which evening is counted to the following Saturday. And Thursday, the 25th of Elul, 1040 [sic, this was no doubt

---

George Y. Kohler, *Reading Maimonides' Philosophy in 19th Century Germany: The Guide to Religious Reform*, Amsterdam Studies in Jewish Philosophy 15 (Dordrecht: Springer, 2012).
33. Jellinek, *Moses ben Schem-Tob*, 14-15.

meant as 5040] Anno Mundi or the 22nd of August 1280 Pope Nicolaus III died in Rome! His successor was Martin IV, whom Abraham Abulafia wanted to convert the following year.[34]

There is much that is unique in this argument. First, it is what scholars now refer to as text-immanent, as opposed to philological and contextual, meaning Jellinek relied on oblique references in the text itself to reveal its own historical context. This is very much removed from Jellinek's usual argumentative style. But it does give us a sense of the overwhelming scholarly (and religious historical) consensus that Jellinek was seeking to overturn. As best as I can ascertain, Jellinek's dates are off by about a week. But the argument stands. Like the late biblical book of Daniel, or the Apocryphal books of Tobit and Esdras, the *Zohar* ascribes itself a past but comments on its own contemporary setting.

In the three years following the publication of *Moses ben Schem-Tob*, Jellinek published, in critical editions and often for the first time, the core treatises in the debate between rationalism and mysticism. Both schools of thought, he argued, had made enormous medieval innovations, which were possible only because of the close interaction of Jews with Arabic and Christian learning. In the two volumes of *Beiträge zur Geschichte der Kabbala* Jellinek expanded on some of the theological influences he had mentioned only briefly in *Moses ben Schem-Tob*.[35] *Beiträge* examined the extant scholarship and historical genealogy of the *Sefer Yetsirah* and gave additional accounts of the *Zohar*'s philosophy and epistemology.[36] It likewise traced the kabbalistic imagery and theology of pre-*Zohar* thinkers, especially that of Sa'adia ben Yosef Gaon (d. 942 CE), who lived in what is today Iraq. In the book, Jellinek strove to establish an account of the development and transmission of kabbalistic imagery and archetypes between

---

34. Jellinek, *Bet ha-Midrasch*, 3:xxxvii–xxxviii. These dates do not quite correspond to historical dating, which puts 22 August 1280 on the 18th of Elul. Jellinek's point, however, remains pertinent.

35. Adolph Jellinek, *Beiträge zur Geschichte der Kabbala*, 2 vols. (Leipzig: Fritzsche, 1852). For recent scholarship on the genealogy of Jewish mysticism, see Roni Weinstein, *Kabbalah and Jewish Modernity* (Oxford: Littman Library of Jewish Civilization, 2015) and Rachel Elior, *The Three Temples: On the Emergence of Jewish Mysticism in Late Antiquity* (Oxford: Littman Library of Jewish Civilization, 2005).

36. Commenting on the two volumes of *Beiträge*, Isaak Markus Jost wrote, "Jellinek's recent accomplishments in this field ... we must designate as a great advance, and which we recommend to investigators, not only because of the great circumspection which manifests itself in them, to the extent of small writings, but also because of the clarity and prudence of the author in his judgments and conclusions.... All these are, of course, only very fleeting hints, but they will undoubtedly lead to further discoveries" (*Adolph Jellinek und die Kabbala*, 8, 11). For an overview of the recent scholarship and history of *Sefer Yetsirah*, see Tzahi Weiss, "The Reception of Sefer Yetsira and Jewish Mysticism in the Early Middle Ages," *Jewish Quarterly Review* 103, no. 1 (2013): 26–46.

the Jewish and Arabic worlds. Citing "families," or interconnected webs of pre-*Zohar* literature, Jellinek posited a genealogy of mystical theology, linking the Mesopotamian context of men like Sa'adia Gaon with the Spanish one of Moses de León. In this way, Jellinek buttressed his theory of de León's authorship (i.e., only someone who had learned from these earlier treatises could have written the *Zohar*) while simultaneously opening to scholarship a whole theological relationship between Jews and Muslims then only partially understood.

In 1853 and 1854, Jellinek edited two more volumes of kabbalistic texts, *Auswahl kabbalistischer Mystik* and *Philosophie und Kabbala*, and republished Menahem de Lonzano's dictionary. For the works that appeared in the first two collections, Jellinek composed critical introductions, which included discussions of the identity and personality of each text's purported author, particular characteristics of the texts themselves, and comparisons of extant manuscripts. The second half of each volume was devoted to a critical Hebrew text. With *Ma'arich*, de Lonzano's lexicon, Jellinek's aim was clear, and it was in many ways the final appendix to his Franck translation from a decade earlier. As Jellinek remarked in his brief introduction, "Menachem's dictionary is not without significance for the history of the *Zohar*: partly because he shows the Greek, Latin, Spanish, and Arabic origin of many words in the *Zohar*, and partly because he, as a connoisseur of the Kabbalah, correctly explains many things."[37] Always mindful of philological accuracy, and aware that the vast majority of *Wissenschaft* scholars of Kabbalah had no direct experience of mystical communities or their linguistic interpretations, *Ma'arich* offered a way to mediate between divergent historical uses of Hebrew. It was a logical addition to Jellinek's close philological critiques from *Orient* in the 1840s: a single reference work that would aid future scholars not only with translations but with more accurately understanding the immense intellectual and semantic creativity contained in Kabbalism. (Bernhard Beer, a personal and scholarly friend of Jellinek's, noted this aspect of the dictionary in his review for the *Monatsschrift für Geschichte und Wissenschaft des Judentums*, writing, "The present derascha [Lonzano's dictionary] intends mainly to emphasize the value of the divine revelation, paying tribute also to the merit of Christianity and Islam for the spread of better custom and knowledge."[38]

In 1854 Jellinek made an interesting, and, on the surface, unexpected turn. Such a fecundity of mystical spirit as he had identified in the centuries surrounding the composition of the *Zohar* could not last, he came to think. Jellinek saw the later students of Spanish Kabbalism, from the

---

37. Menachem de Lonsano, *Ma'arich*, ed. Adolf Jellinek (Leipzig: Colditz, 1853), vi–vii.
38. Bernhard Beer, "Recensionen und Anzeigen," *Monatsschrift für Geschichte und Wissenschaft des Judentums* 2 (1853): 152–56, here 156.

fifteenth century onward, as mere imitators of what had been a great, but relatively brief, flowering of true mystical insight.

> In fact, Jewish spiritual development in Spain, with a wavering between philosophy, supernaturalism, and mysticism, also ends, analogous to all development proceeding from opposites and ending in syncretism (compare this to the process of Greek, Scholastic, and German philosophy) in the writings of the Spanish epigones: Isaac Arama [1420–1492], Isaac Caro [1458–1535], Isaac Abarbanel [1437–1508], Joseph Jabez [d. sixteenth century], Joel ibn Shu'eib [fifteenth century], Judah Chayat [fifteenth century], and Abraham Saba [1440–1508], to prove it clearly.[39]

Contemporary scholars should rightly differ with Jellinek's interpretation of the accomplishments of these men.[40] But their grouping is important, more for what it tells us about Jellinek than for anything else. These men all share a single characteristic: they lived at the end of Islamic rule in Spain, and most were expelled from the Iberian Peninsula in 1492. When the Jews of Spain scattered across Europe and the Mediterranean, they lost access to the unique cultural mélange that had allowed thirteenth and fourteenth century Kabbalists to access the intellectual and theological insights of Christianity and Islam. At a moment that called out for an alternative to Maimonidean rationalism, the earliest Spanish Kabbalists had recognized the possibilities of interreligious theological exchange and pursued it.

In contradistinction, then, it was not that the men of the era of the expulsion were intrinsically of weaker mind. They were simply more like the Jews of the rest of European history: itinerants, exiles, intellectually insular by force rather than capacity, and excluded from the linguistic encounters that had made books like the *Zohar* even imaginable, let alone possible. Jellinek's dismissal of the accomplishments of the "Spanish epigones" was as much (perhaps even more so) an opaque indictment of the destruction of Islamic Spain and the parochialization of Spanish Catholicism as it was of the Jews themselves. If we are to follow this explanation to its logical conclusion, Jellinek's words imply a hope and warning to his own generation of liberal, non-Jewish, leaders. Do not turn back the possibilities offered by 1848, he seemed to be saying. Great flowerings of insight come only with the intellectual intermingling of very different sorts of minds.

---

39. Joseph ibn Zadik, *Der Mikrokosmos: Ein Beitrag zur Religionsphilosophie und Ethik*, ed. Adolf Jelinek (Leipzig: Fischl, 1854), v–vi.

40. For one recent investigation of this group, see Brian Ogren, "Sefirotic Depictions, Divine Noesis, and Aristotelian Kabbalah: Abraham ben Meir de Balmes and Italian Renaissance Thought," *Jewish Quarterly Review* 104, no. 4 (2014): 573–99.

4

Attraction to Rabbinic Innovation: Jellinek and Midrash

Bet ha-Midrasch: *Context and Conception*

Adolf Jellinek's most enduring contribution to primary-source scholarship, and in many ways the summation of his vision of *Wissenschaft des Judentums*, was his six-volume collection *Bet ha-Midrasch*.[1] It remains unclear whether Jellinek originally envisioned a six-volume work. More likely, he thought of the project as somewhat open-ended, publishing the initial volumes as supplements to the research he had been conducting on the *Zohar* and its context and continuing it later as time and resources allowed. Jellinek seems to suggest as much in his 1873 preface to volume 5, in which he writes, "After a break of fifteen years, I am again presenting the public with a new fifth part of the *Bet ha-Midrash*.... But the work is not finished with this fifth part. Both in Leipzig—where the first four parts were published—and in Vienna, I have accumulated so much aggadic material that as soon as my official activity allows me leisure, I will publish a sixth part."[2] As Jellinek tell us here, long after his move from Leipzig to Vienna, when scholarship, once his "official activity," had become something he could do only during his hours of "leisure," he continued to collect midrashim and prepare them for publication. In many ways, then, *Bet ha-Midrasch*, alongside the work of Solomon Buber (1827–1906), another pioneering scholar of midrash with whom Jellinek corresponded and who sent Jellinek manuscripts for inclusion in volumes 5 and 6 of *Bet ha-Midrasch*, was an early model for the scholarly preparation and publication of primary sources, a task that would occupy pride of place among the next two or three generations of Jewish studies scholars.

Bet ha-Midrasch, subtitled "Collection of Minor Midrashim and Miscellaneous Treatises from the Older Jewish Literature," brought together

---

1. The volumes, which appeared originally in the years 1853–1877, were twice reprinted in Jerusalem by Bamberger and Wahrmann, 1938 and 1967.
2. Jellinek, *Adolf Jellinek, Bet ha-Midrasch: Sammlung kleiner Midraschim und vermischter Abhandlungen aus der ältern jüdischen Literature*, vol. 5 (Vienna: Winter, 1873), v.

previously uncollected rabbinical texts with a scholarly apparatus that contained explanations of manuscript variation, elucidations of theological and philosophical ideas, and clarifications of archaic or obscure linguistic references. In *Bet ha-Midrasch* and its associated works, Jellinek made a point of collecting early Jewish mystical manuscripts that had otherwise been overlooked or recently described in bibliographies but not yet thoroughly studied. What is clear is that Jellinek, thirty-two years old when he began the *Bet ha-Midrasch* project, hoped to make a serious contribution to *Wissenschaft*, one he fully expected would have a lasting impact. "I expect that everyone whose position or personality is influential will feel obliged to promote and support this undertaking for the good of science," he wrote in 1853.[3]

Gathering midrashim from a wide variety of rabbinic sources, Jellinek's editorial introductions pressed into service his broad linguistic knowledge and his critical-historical education. As he wrote at the beginning of the project,

> The present collection ... forms the first part of a largely literary enterprise, which was begun in the sacred interest of science and with the intention of making the literary products of distant centuries accessible to a large number of connoisseurs and disciples. Not merely small midrashim—unprinted or printed, but always rare—but also small scientific treatises of outstanding personalities of Jewish literature are to be collected in continuous volumes. In itself [these books are] the planned union of smaller, often rare writings, scattered in various volumes, for the history of important fragments is a service rendered to science.[4]

For each text, Jellinek listed manuscript sources, explicated contents, identified variant texts, and gave relevant philological and theological background. (He relied heavily on Zunz's *Die gottesdienstlichen Vorträge der Juden*, [Berlin: Asher, 1832], going so far as to call Zunz "the greatest master of Jewish literary research.") For words, leitmotifs, and philosophical concepts that originated in languages other than Hebrew, Jellinek provided translations and elucidations as well as original-language citations.

Scholarly Friendships and Theoretical Precursors

No scholarship is a work of independent genius, so it is important in any examination of the *Bet ha-Midrasch* to note the many friends and intel-

---

3. Adolph Jellinek, *Bet ha-Midrasch: Sammlung kleiner Midraschim und vermischter Abhandlungen aus der ältern jüdischen Literatur*, vol. 1 (Leipzig: Vollrath, 1853), viii.

4. Jellinek, *Bet ha-Midrasch* 1:vii–viii.

lectual correspondents with whom Jellinek maintained relationships and who helped to shape his studies of Jewish mysticism, medieval history, and rabbinic midrash. These names give us a sense of the boundaries and scope of the *Wissenschaft* community and its interaction with non-Jewish scholarship, helping to illuminate the growth and perseverance of the new discipline across the nineteenth century. Through social and political changes, beyond linguistic and cultural boundaries, and despite fundamental disagreements concerning the character and nature of Jewish religious life in European modernity, generations of scholars built a robust network of collaborations that facilitated the collection of sources and the diffusion of findings. As Jellinek noted in 1855, "through the liberality of [Samuel David] Luzzatto and [Zacharias] Frankel I hope to soon be able to enrich the knowledge of the exegetical literature of the Jews, and [this will also be helped by] the literary society which [Ludwig] Philippson has brought into being....[Only] promotion and support are [still] missing."[5] Jellinek's direct references here are to Luzzatto's efforts (described below) to secure sources from libraries in Italy; Frankel's mentorship of Jellinek as well as Frankel's own editorial projects, including the *Monatsschrift für Geschichte und Wissenschaft des Judentums* (hereafter *MGWJ*); and Philippson's editorship of the *Allgemeine Zeitung des Judentums* (hereafter *AZJ*) and his founding that year (with the help of Jellinek and Jost) of the Institut zur Förderung der israelitischen Literatur, a society promoting contemporary Jewish scholarship and literature. But the broader point remains as well. Money and time are always the devil for any large-scale enterprise, which *Wissenschaft des Judentums* surely was. As Jellinek hinted at with these words, time, good will, and hard work (nearly all the early *Wissenschaft* scholars, from Zunz and Fürst to Frankel and Philippson, spent much of their energies editing and promoting the work of fellow scholars) had made, in effect, something from nothing: a rigorously scientific discipline almost entirely outside the institutional and financial support of German academia.

The men with whom Jellinek collaborated all contributed in multiple capacities to the development of Jewish scholarly circles in Europe. Sometimes they acted as intellectual interlocutors, writing responses back and forth in the new journals, adding to and rebutting claims made about one or another aspect of Jewish history. Sometimes they acted as manuscript collectors, hunters, or editors, traveling between libraries to catalogue materials, petitioning friends and the increasing number of well-to-do families with personal collections for copies of original documents, and publishing editions of rare sources or newly redacted versions based on the examination of multiple extant texts. And sometimes they acted

---

5. Samuel ben Meir, *Perush al Kohelet v'Shir haShirim*, ed. Adolf Jellinek (Leipzig: Schnauss, 1855), xii.

merely as personal recommenders or friends, penning supportive book reviews or letters of introduction.

We have already noted one of Jellinek's earliest *Wissenschaft* supporters, the Leipzig University Hebrew tutor and *Orient* editor Julius Fürst. Another was Isaak Markus Jost, who, in 1852, following the publication of Jellinek's *Moses ben Schem-Tob* and the two volumes of *Beiträge zur Geschichte der Kabbala*, penned a brief essay on the accomplishments and importance of Jellinek's still-unfolding work in the history of Spanish mysticism and its context. Jost began by describing the history of Jewish mysticism as a narrative of continuity, stretching from the Bible to the present age. It depicted Jewish expressions of mystical intention as similar to, and in fact often bound up with, those in Christianity and Islam. This is something of an unexpected narration, for it explicitly supported the idea—only then becoming normative in scholarly circles—that mysticism was not an aberration or anomaly within Jewish religious experience. (Although in keeping with broader prejudices among German Jewry, Jellinek did display a somewhat dismissive—or at least Germano-centric—attitude toward contemporary mystical piety, writing in a note to his 1844 translation of Franck that "for contemporary Judaism, the Kabbalah is an entirely foreign element."[6]) Jost described the yearning for mystical experience as part of the organic, almost logical investigations of the religious mind. What was clearly conveyed in Jost's *Literatur-Bericht* was his support for the continuance of the study of the history of Kabbalah, especially as it pertained to investigations into the Arabic connections at both the philological and theological levels—aspects of the work that were Jellinek's strength. Jost ended his brief review: "We are of the opinion that Adolph Jellinek may feel called to explore the whole nature of Kabbalah, its full content in the various directions of its development, formation and degeneration, and to vividly portray its history."[7] There could be no more fitting support by a senior member of the *Wissenschaft* community for a younger scholar.

Jost's essay was an early and very public endorsement not only of Jellinek's research methods and findings but also of his choice of topic itself. This is worth considering. While Jellinek had been published early and often in all the major *Wissenschaft* journals (e.g., *Orient*, *MGWJ*, *Zeitschrift für die religiösen Interessen des Judenthums* [*ZRIJ*], etc.), and though they continued to publish him even as he questioned the conclusions of more established scholars of Jewish history, none specifically endorsed his position. In other words, the *Wissenschaft* journals were, for the most part, about the diffusion of new research and theories, and their editors avoided making conclusive statements (at least in their editorial capacities) about

---

6. Franck, *Die Kabbala*, 283 n. 1.
7. Jost, *Adolph Jellinek und die Kabbala*, 15.

historical questions. Jost's essay, which appeared as a stand-alone pamphlet, did not contribute any new research to the question of the origins or development of the Kabbalah. Instead, it simply endorsed Jellinek's current pursuits (and those by other scholars like him) in a public forum.

Jost's essay expressed sentiments toward Jellinek's research already clearly felt through the world of Jewish scholarship. Jost and Jellinek, along with Philippson, would go on to collaborate until Jost's death in 1860, and Jellinek and Philippson beyond that. But public endorsement by a respected individual is, in this case, also a sign of a larger network of collaborators and interlocutors cultivated by Jellinek during his years in Leipzig. The names of many scholars, Jewish and non-Jewish, appeared in print throughout Jellinek's writings. His public acknowledgment of his professor and mentor Heinrich Leberecht Fleischer in his first article for *Orient* was one example of many that would follow, as were the previously mentioned citations of the works of Johann Karl Ludwig Gieseler. In some instances, Jellinek's citations of Jewish scholars proves to be a traditional list: Zunz (to whom Jellinek dedicated the first volume of *Bet ha-Midrasch*: "to Leopold (Yom Tov Lipman) Zunz.... In honor of a great man, from his brother in knowledge and wisdom.... A salute before him and his wife that the heavens may keep them", Frankel, Fürst, Steinschneider, and Geiger. A few of the names, however, are somewhat more obscure, including those of Raphael Kirschheim (1804–1889), Frankfurt native and scholar of rabbinics, and Adolf Neubauer (1831–1907), sublibrarian at the Bodleian Library at Oxford and author of *La Géographie du Talmud* (1868).[8]

Three more names deserve greater amplification here—those of Salomon Munk, Samuel David Luzzatto, and Marco Mortara—for they exemplify the intercultural, trans-European aspect of mid-nineteenth-century *Wissenschaft*. The overwhelmingly German (linguistic and cultural) nature of *Wissenschaft* held across the century, though it was, however, merely the center of a wider orbit, with letters flowing toward Leipzig for Jellinek and outward from him to cities across the continent.

One of Jellinek's closest intellectual mentors (even while it is unclear if the two men ever met in person) during Jellinek's years in Leipzig was the German Jewish French Orientalist Salomon Munk (1803–1867). Citations to the Frenchman's works appear throughout Jellinek's books on Kabbalah and midrash, and Munk's spirit of scholarly inquiry, which combined a gift for languages with a keen interest in the relationship between

---

8. See Elliott S. Horowitz, "'A Jew of the Old Type': Neubauer as Cataloguer, Critic, and Necrologist," *Jewish Quarterly Review* 100, no. 4 (2010): 649–56; Herbert M. J. Loewe, *Adolf Neubauer, 1831–1931* (Oxford: Oxford University Press, 1931); and J. Morgenstern, *Die französische Academie und die "Geographie des Talmuds"* (Berlin: Schlesinger, 1870). One of Neubauer's most important contributions came at the end of his life when he acquired for Oxford fragments from the Cairo Geniza.

differing philosophical and theological traditions, deeply impacted Jellinek's mode of critical analysis. (Munk published fairly consistently in *Orient*, and those articles in the early and mid-1840s were likely Jellinek's first encounters with the elder scholar's work.) In 1865, in a retrospective on Munk's life and accomplishments, Jellinek wrote,

> Munk's personal work in [both] practical life and in literature deserve our liveliest attentions.... By drawing, as it were, a portrait of Munk's spirit, erudition, and literary activity, I merely want to prove that science is intimately connected with life, that the scholars who move in the world of books and who do laborious research—not quite so impractical as one usually assumes, especially in Jewish circles—is not doing scholarship merely on a grey scale lacking in golden fruits.[9]

Writing in the 1840s, Munk (somewhat ironically for a man later famous for his studies of Maimonides) promoted the idea that Jewish mystical literature was worthy of modern scholarly analysis. Indeed, Munk believed that the entirety of Jewish history was part of a forgotten (or we might say, purposefully neglected) history of European thought.[10] Both of these themes—mysticism as an essential part of the religious experience and Jewish philosophy and theology having developed over time through continual conversation with Christian and Arabic (Islamic and pre-Islamic) sources—were fundamental tenets of Jellinek's view of history and already quite apparent in his earliest writings in Leipzig.[11]

Like Munk, Samuel David Luzzatto (1800–1865, called Shadal) was a formative figure in the origins of modern Jewish thought, if not quite *Wissenschaft* proper.[12] A scion of the famed Luzzatto family (his great uncle was Rabbi Moses Hayim Luzzatto (1707–1746, called Ramchal, con-

---

9. Adolf Jellinek, *Salomon Munk, Professor am Collège de France: Vortrag im Wiener Bet ha-Midrash am 21. Januar 1865 gehalten* (Vienna: Herzfeld & Bauer, 1865), 9.

10. Alfred L. Ivry, writing about Munk's great work *Mélanges de philosophie juive et arabe* (Paris, 1857–1859) noted that, for Munk, "Jewish philosophy is integral ... to Western civilization, to the Jews being contributors and custodians of much the West holds dear" ("Salomon Munk and the *Mélanges de philosophie juive et arabe*," *Jewish Studies Quarterly* 7, no. 2 [2000]: 120-126, here 121.)

11. The like-mindedness between Munk and Jellinek never waned. As we will see in coming chapters, Jellinek drew heavily on their common interests during his weekly sermons and public writings in Leipzig and Vienna.

12. While Luzzatto lacked the sort of university training that defined the worldview of most *Wissenschaft* figures, and while his historical writings were more variable in their use of critical methodologies than those of some of his peers, his support for modern scholarship and its methods was without question. For recent scholarship on Samuel David Luzzatto, see Ephraim Chamiel, Asael Abelman, and Yaacov Jeffrey Green, *The Middle Way: The Emergence of Modern Religious Trends in Nineteenth-Century Judaism; Responses to Modernity in the Philosophy of Z. H. Chajes, S. R. Hirsch, and S. D. Luzzatto*, Studies in Orthodox Judaism (Brighton, MA: Academic Studies Press, 2014).

sidered by many to be among the founders of modern Hebrew literature and poetry and around whom developed a circle of mystical disciples), Samuel David was born and raised in Trieste, resettling permanently in Padua to pursue his education in both Judaic and secular subjects.[13] A student and then teacher at the Rabbinical College of Padua, established by Isaac Samuel Reggio (1784–1855, called Yashar) in 1829, the school was founded on *Wissenschaft* principles and organized as a fully modern institution dedicated to Jewish learning and contemporary philosophy.

Jellinek dedicated the second volume of *Beiträge zur Geschichte der Kabbala* to Luzzatto, and frequently cited Luzzatto's *Lezioni di storia giudaica* (Lessons of Jewish History [1852], which Jellinek read in the original Italian), an early treatise on the culture and literature of ancient and modern Judaism. A generation older than Jellinek, Luzzatto's knowledge and access were instrumental in securing for Jellinek copies of texts from libraries in northern Italy. (In the early 1850s, the whole region around Trieste and Padua was governed as the Habsburg province of Lombardy-Venetia, vastly simplifying communication and mail delivery.) Unlike Jellinek, however, Luzzatto had little interest in mysticism. Instead, Luzzatto studied Syriac and made some of the first contributions to biblical criticism, including offering emendations to the Masoretic Hebrew.[14] Nevertheless, Luzzatto supported Jellinek's research ventures, and Luzzatto's dedication to Talmudic learning and traditional Jewish practice seem to have endeared the two men and sustained a lasting friendship. (When Luzzatto died on Yom Kippur in 1865, the editor of *Das Abendland*, Daniel Ehrmann [1816–1882], wrote: "A star in Israel is extinct."[15])

One of the students who attended Padua's rabbinical college and who eventually became one of Luzzatto's closest disciples was Marco Mortara (1815–1894), a mostly forgotten *Wissenschaft* scholar.[16] After graduating from Padua, Mortara became the rabbi in Mantua, and it was from him that Jellinek acquired a number of the texts that later appeared in *Bet ha-Midrasch*, primarily in the third volume. Mortara, like Luzzatto, opposed the theological premises (although not the historical study) of

---

13. In 1797, Padua became part of the Habsburg Empire. It was briefly ruled by Napoleon at various times between 1806 and 1814, after which it was returned to Austria. It was annexed into the newly formed Kingdom of Italy in 1866.

14. Through philological analysis he also claimed that Ecclesiastes was a late First Temple text, and therefore not written by King Solomon, to whom it was traditionally attributed.

15. Daniel Ehrmann, "S.D. Luzzatto," *Das Abendland* 20 (October 12, 1865), 164. The newspaper *Ben Chananja* devoted its opening pages to his passing ("Samuel David Luzzatto," *Ben Chananja* 42 [October 18, 1865], 729–32).

16. For some context about Mortara's work, see Marco Mortara, *L'epistolario di Marco Mortara (1815–1894): Un rabbino italiano tra riforma e ortodossia*, ed. Asher Salah (Florence: Giuntina, 2012). These letters show the wide variety of Mortara's correspondents, including Luzzatto, Steinschneider, Sabato Morais, and Alexander von Humboldt.

the Kabbalah, seeing it as a heterodox outgrowth of the rabbinic system. Mortara spent his academic career collecting and editing rabbinic manuscripts and his contributions to Jellinek's volumes are representative of the immense body of unedited texts that confronted early *Wissenschaft* scholars. Because of the efforts of men like Mortara (and, contemporaneously, Steinschneider in Prussia and England), thousands of these works were catalogued, edited, and published. (Jellinek was also personally discovering manuscripts in Leipzig's Municipal Library [*Raths-Bibliothek*, today's *Stadtbibliothek*], and in the private collection of David ben Abraham Oppenheimer.)

Libraries were not the only places to find lost manuscripts, and Jews were not the only scholars with whom Jellinek was friendly as he pursued his research. Jellinek likewise read and corresponded widely with the non-Jewish German scholars of his era. He quoted or cited many of the major works of German biblical criticism and firmly grounded his work on medieval Jewish texts in the nascent academic disciplines of philology and Orientalism. Of the non-Jewish scholars with whom Jellinek maintained either a personal or professional relationship, a number deserve mention here, for they offer a portrait of the range of academic disciplines and texts that Jellinek consulted for his research.

Aside from Fleischer, one of the most important non-Jewish scholars with whom Jellinek cultivated a personal connection was the renowned Saxony-born explorer and New Testament literary critic Constantin von Tischendorf (1815–1874).[17] Tischendorf was a professor in Leipzig for the entirety of Jellinek's residence there, although Tischendorf spent most of the early 1840s away from Germany, first in Paris and then in Italy and Egypt. In Egypt, Tischendorf read and collected a wide variety of manuscripts (many of which he brought back to his home university), becoming

---

17. See Stanley E. Porter, *Constantine Tischendorf: The Life and Work of a 19th Century Bible Hunter, Including Constantine Tischendorf's When Were Our Gospels Written?* (London: Bloomsbury T&T Clark, 2015); and Kurt Aland, *Konstantin von Tischendorf (1815–1874): Neutestamentliche Textforschung damals und heute*, Sitzungsberichte der Sächsischen Akademie der Wissenschaften zu Leipzig, Philologisch-Historische Klasse 133.2 (Berlin: Akademie, 1993). In 1859, on a trip to the Middle East, Tischendorf found the Codex Sinaiticus, one of the world's oldest extant Greek Bibles. See Jürgen Gottschlich, *The Bible Hunter: The Quest for the Original New Testament*, trans. John Brownjohn (London: Haus, 2013); David C. Parker, *Textual Scholarship and the Making of the New Testament*, Lyell Lectures (Oxford: Oxford University Press, 2012); Parker, *Codex Sinaiticus: The Story of the World's Oldest Bible* (London: British Library, 2010); Scot McKendrick, *In a Monastery Library: Preserving Codex Sinaiticus and the Greek Written Heritage* (London: British Library, 2006); James Bentley, *Secrets of Mount Sinai: The Story of the World's Oldest Bible—Codex Sinaiticus* (Garden City, NY: Doubleday, 1986); Matthew Black and Robert Davidson, *Constantin von Tischendorf and the Greek New Testament* (Glasgow: University of Glasgow Press, 1981).

most famous for the discovery of the Codex Sinaiticus at Saint Catherine's Monastery in the Sinai Desert.[18]

Upon Tischendorf's return to Saxony, Jellinek was already deeply involved in research for his various studies on medieval Jewry and the Kabbalah, but it seems to have taken into the early 1850s for the two scholars to be formally introduced. Tischendorf is first mentioned by Jellinek in a set of related publications from 1853: the second volume of *Bet ha-Midrasch* and an article for *MGWJ*. Writing in *Bet ha-Midrasch*, Jellinek noted, "This latter volume offers more new than the first [volume], especially in the fact that, through the kindness of the famous New Testament literature editor Professor Herr Tischendorf in Leipzig, I was able to use some Arabic codices brought by him from Cairo."[19] And in *MGWJ*, Jellinek wrote, "Professor Herr Tischendorf has, on his most recent stay in Cairo, usefully purchased several rabbinic and Arabic-Karaite manuscripts, and thus did a great service to science in general and Jewish [scholarship] in particular. Following the invitation of the famous traveler and editor I have visited the various codices, about which I am now only going to give you a general report, so that the readers of your monthly Journal receive a message from this precious travel good."[20]

In both of these mentions, Jellinek's relationship with Tischendorf revolved mainly around their shared interest in the historical usefulness of manuscripts from the ancient Near East. Tischendorf, however, was primarily involved in New Testament textual criticism, so Jellinek drew from elsewhere to conceive of a broader theoretical apparatus by which to approach his work on medieval Jewish culture. In the same article for *MGWJ* in which he thanked Tischendorf, Jellinek pointed his readers toward a newly published book (in English), the first volume of Samuel Davidson's *A Treatise on Biblical Criticism* (1853). Davidson (1806–1898), an Irish-born biblicist, received his doctorate at Halle and became well known for his interest in the various forms of manuscript criticism then being developed in Europe. It is immediately clear what attracted Jellinek to this new monograph. Davidson wrote, "In every ancient book which has descended to our times through a number of centuries, various readings exist. It is utterly impossible for human caution and diligence to guard against the slightest departure from an author's original words. Hence it becomes necessary to judge between different readings, to weigh

---

18. Tischendorf recorded his years in the Near East in two volumes of travel writings, *Reise in den Orient* (Leipzig: Tauchnitz, 1845–1846).

19. Adolph Jellinek, *Bet ha-Midrasch: Sammlung kleiner Midraschim und vermischter Abhandlungen aus der ältern jüdischen Literatur*, vol. 2 (Leipzig: Vollrath, 1855), v.

20. Adolf Jellinek, "Literarische Berichte," *Monatsschrift für Geschichte und Wissenschaft des Judentums* 2, no. 6 (1853): 245–47, here 245.

the evidence by which they are respectively supported, and the claims they present to a favourable reception."[21] Though Davidson's words refer most directly to the biblical literary canon (just as did Tischendorf's personal efforts), in the more abstract sense the sentiments are entirely in accord with what we have already seen in Jellinek's methodologies. Whether they be texts written by Jews in the Middle Ages or early Christians in the late antique world, rigorous philological analysis, manuscript comparison, and the tracing of intellectual genealogies and intercultural influences remained the bedrock of the new scientific study of the past. About this, Davidson, Tischendorf, and Jellinek were all in agreement.[22]

One final branch of research, conducted almost entirely by non-Jewish Germans, requires discussion here, as it both complements and completes the vision of the intellectual world in which Jellinek was thinking and writing as he embarked on the *Bet ha-Midrasch*. This was the study of ancient mythology, where Jellinek read works that focused primarily on the mythological traditions of ancient Greece. In the decade before Jellinek's birth, Georg Friedrich Creuzer (1771–1856), a professor at the University of Heidelberg, had published a four-volume work entitled *Symbolism and Mythology of the Ancient Peoples, Especially the Greeks* (1810–1812). These books were a groundbreaking example of historical synthesis and exegesis (which Jellinek probably would have read in their expanded third edition of 1836–1842, printed in Leipzig, though he does not cite a specific version). Working with manuscripts in almost a dozen languages, *Symbolism and Mythology* sought to demonstrate that classical Greek ideas, especially those of a religious variety, were either adaptations or developments of stories and tales already extant in the pre-classical world. Dismissing the notion that Greek mythology was a wholly indigenous creation, Creuzer argued that not only the foundations but even the minutiae of the Greek imagination were already well developed and widely known to the pre-Hellenic peoples of the Mediterranean, the Levant, and Central Asia.

Creuzer's research was foundational for the scientific study of mythology, and it was to both Creuzer and the following generation of scholars that Jellinek turned as he developed some of his ideas concerning the intercultural encounters that created the flowering of medieval Kabbalah (specifically) and the rabbinic genre of midrash (generally). Joseph Hein-

---

21. Samuel Davidson, *A Treatise on Biblical Criticism Exhibiting a Systematic View of that Science*, vol. 1 (Boston: Gould & Lincoln, 1853), 1–2.

22. Jellinek knew and/or quoted many other non-Jewish scholars, including Friedrich Nies (1804/1808–1870), Leipzig typographer and book publisher, whose work on printing Egyptian hieroglyphics made possible the dissemination of scholarly work on the ancient Near East; Johann Christoph Wolf (1683–1739), Christian Hebraist and compiler of *Bibliotheca Hebraea*, 4 vols. (Hamburg, 1715–1733); Heinrich Ewald (1803–1875), professor of Oriental languages at the University of Göttingen; and August Dillmann (1823–1894), German Orientalist, professor, and bibliographer, best known for his work on Ethiopic manuscripts.

rich Friedlieb (1810–1900), a contemporary of Jellinek, likewise drew from Creuzer in his studies of the Greek influences on the Jewish and Christian cultures of late antiquity, and Jellinek directed his readers toward both Creuzer and Friedlieb when classical references appeared in the Jewish manuscripts under his consideration. Freidlieb, a professor at the University of Breslau, published, in 1852, a translation of the Sibylline Oracles, a collection of prophesies dating from late antiquity that recorded (in Greek hexameter verse) a collage of mythological themes from across the Mediterranean world. Friedlieb set out to demonstrate a centuries-long genealogy of Sibylline or Sibylline-like prophecies, full of intercultural and intertheological allusions that transcended specifically national traditions:

> If one goes through the testimonies of the ancients about the Sibyls and the fragments of Sibyllinian prophecy they soon lead to the conviction that paganism, the later period of Judaism, and the earliest [period] of Christianity, had their own and peculiar sibyls.... Since, however, a fluctuation in the use of the designation of these sibyls is not to be misunderstood ... the obvious assumption that early on a Hebrew sibyl was renamed—sometimes as Erythrean, sometimes as Cumaean—in pre-Christian paganism is not supported. However, the existence of a Hebrew, pre-Christian sibyl is beyond doubt.[23]

The theoretical similarities between Friedlieb and Jellinek are clear even from this brief citation. In Friedlieb's telling, there was a common trope among pre-Christian pagans, Jewish texts, and early Christian sources referring to prophecy via a Sibylline oracle. They are not, according to Friedlieb, all simply a single source renamed for particular readerships. They are, however, of a common currency, that is, ideas and doctrines exchanged among diverse groups culling narratives from a shared set of images and folktales. As Jellinek sought to demonstrate in his early work on the *Zohar* and in his expanded studies of medieval midrash, a similar pattern to what Friedlieb identified was still at work a thousand years later. Kabbalah, for Jellinek, was not merely the reinterpretation of other mystical traditions in a Jewish vocabulary. It was, rather, derived and expanded upon from a much older and more varied set of traditions, some of which originated within specifically Jewish circles, much of which, however, did not.[24]

---

23. Joseph Heinrich Friedlieb, *Die Sibyllinischen Weissagungen* [Oracula Sibyllina] (Leipzig: Wiegel, 1852), vii, ix.
24. See Joseph Dan, "Midrash and the Dawn of Kabbalah," in *Midrash and Literature*, ed. Geoffrey H. Hartman and Sanford Budick (New Haven: Yale University Press, 1986), 127–39.

Key Themes in *Bet ha-Midrasch*

A number of key themes emerge in an examination of the complete contents of *Bet ha-Midrasch*, all of which follow from those explored in the previous chapter but appear here with somewhat different emphasis. First, Jellinek expanded his interest in the ways the entire genre of midrashic texts mirrored or developed themes found in works associated with other ancient Mediterranean groups, such as the Essenes, the pre- and post-Islamic Arabs, and the Church Fathers. For example, in his introduction to text III of volume 2, "Midrasch Cônen," Jellinek described connections between the Neoplatonic philosophy of Alexandria and the apocryphal books of the late Second Temple:

> This [text] deals with the glorification of the Torah, which is identified with wisdom according to an Old Alexandrian view. This, by the influence of Platonism, was considered as pre-worldly and as the principle of value creation. [It is] also to be compared with the hexameter as described is the 4th Book of Ezra ... and is perhaps a] remnant of ancient Essene cosmogony.[25]

In his notes on text III of volume 1, "Erzählung von Abraham und Nimrod," Jellinek wrote, "[I]n fact, the narrative [here] is also to be found—in terms of its material aspects—in [Gustav] Weil's *Biblische Legenden der Muselmänner*, and has probably been worked in Mohammedan interest to convert idolatrous Arabia."[26] In these and other instances, Jellinek sought to convey the intermingling of theological typologies. Seeking not origins, precisely, but (as he did with the *Zohar*) families and lineages of thought, especially ones that lay somewhat adjacent to a specifically biblical heritage and that later became central within rabbinic discourse, Jellinek used the texts in these volumes to convey a sense of extreme theological intermingling, not only in the ancient world but up though the Middle Ages as well.

That such genealogical analyses were to be found in *Bet ha-Midrasch* is of course no surprise, as they naturally complemented Jellinek's interests in all forms of intercultural intellectual exchange. In this particular example, the world of antique Alexandria—with its Neoplatonic academies and Greek translations of the Bible and Apocrypha—was the natural precursor to Scholasticism, the medieval school that included Thomas Aquinas, in whom Jellinek formed something of an interest around 1853. In that year and the next, Jellinek published two edited volumes of Jewish texts

---

25. Jellinek, *Bet ha-Midrasch*, 2:xii–xiii.
26. Jellinek, *Bet ha-Midrasch*, 1:xvi. In a footnote to this text Jellinek quoted Fleischer's edition of the Arabic text where this source can be found.

related to Aquinas, *Thomas von Aquino in der jüdischen Literatur* (1853) and *Philosophie und Kabbala* (1854). Jellinek's studies of Aquinas are different not in kind but in purpose from nearly all his other work in this period. What are revealed in these two books are Jellinek's intuitions rather than his detailed critical scholarship. In the introduction to *Thomas von Aquino*, Jellinek wrote:

> We must assume that the rapprochement between Jewish and Christian scholars in the Middle Ages, especially in Spain and France, must have taken place much more frequently than is commonly believed. Is it coincidence that a mystical touch blew in both Judaism and Christianity in the 13th century? That the Franciscan Bonaventure [1224–1271, Italy] ... and Ramon Llull [1232–1316, Spain] ... were the contemporaries of Moses ben Nachman [called Nachmanides/Ramban, 1194–1270, Spain],... Abraham Abulafia [1240–1291, Spain], ... and Joseph [ben Abraham] Chiquitilla [also Gikatilla, 1248–ca.1305] ...? Where does it come from that the two famous 13th century Dominicans use the *Mekor Chayim* of [Solomon] ibn Gabirol [1021–1070]? Let us further consider that the frequent disputes between Jewish and Christian scholars (e.g., between Moses ben Nachman and Fra Pablo [Christiani, in 1263]) in this century brought both parties closer to each other—both the Jews and Christians compelled to get to know the literature of the other.[27]

In prior writings, especially concerning the *Zohar*, Jellinek had been reticent to make assumptions concerning influence and development when he lacked historic proof texts. Rather than an early and comprehensive book on the *Zohar* he spent a decade incrementally gathering data and, even once assembled, only made arguments where he could direct readers toward passages they themselves could interpret.

Such is not the case here. Instead, in both *Thomas von Aquino* and *Philosophie und Kabbala*, Jellinek posited instead of proved. He knew of the Nachmanides–Fra Pablo disputations. He knew that Jews were translating the works of Catholic theologians. He knew that both Jews and Catholics in Spain in the twelfth and thirteenth centuries were writing mystical treatises and drawing on earlier sources to do so. What he could not prove—at least with the extant texts accessible to him at the time—were the sorts of theological genealogies between Jews and Catholics based on ancient manuscripts that were so abundant in the case of early Christianity and Islam and that formed the basis of *Bet ha-Midrasch*. But because the sources were not quite there, he theorized connections instead. Similar to the way early twentieth-century chemists hypothesized the existence of elements on the periodic table without being able (yet they assumed correctly) to

---

27. Adolph Jellinek, *Thomas von Aquino in der jüdischen Literatur* (Leipzig: Colditz, 1853), 15–16.

prove their existence in the laboratory, Jellinek set medieval Jewish and Catholic texts side by side and then suggested (heavily) a cultural similarity (and thereby a culture of dialogue). As he wrote in *Philosophie und Kabbala*:

> We ... see the important position that Thomas Aquinas occupies in Jewish literature, and how many distinguished minds, without denominational prejudices and particularism, devote themselves to studying and treating his works.... Historical research seeks to recognize all the factors that influenced the development and culture of a people, and, if it wants to take its place in the cathedral of general science and not in the confined space of denominationalism, cannot be guided by sympathy or antipathy. The real science, like the good, is for its own sake![28]

These final lines revealed Jellinek's true intentions with these two books on Aquinas. (Note the final exclamation mark.) In *Bet ha-Midrash*, Jellinek could prove through generations of manuscripts the way themes and discourses migrated into and out of rabbinic narrative. But for the works of Aquinas, and more generally for the relationship between Jews and Catholics in medieval western Europe, Jellinek simply did not have the textual proofs. Instead, what he possessed was a deep knowledge of the period, of its major figures and theological movements, and of the writings that preceded it from the end of the Second Temple period onward. "Where does it come from that the two famous 13th century Dominicans use the *Mekor Chayim* of ibn Gabirol?" he asked, almost rhetorically. He could not prove the answer, most probably to his own annoyance, but he could suggest some informed conjecture. (This is not altogether dissimilar to what we saw in the previous chapter, when Jellinek dismissed the possibility of Abulafia as the writer of the *Zohar* because "it is psychologically unlikely" that Abulafia would write a pseudepigraphic text.) And, Jellinek concluded, to not do so would be scholarly malpractice. Assuming separate Jewish and Catholic intellectual silos was not only irresponsible history, it exemplified the "confined space of denominationalism," which would never contribute to the "cathedral of general science." We can hear in these remarks a sort of warning not just toward fellow *Wissenschaft* scholars but toward the wider German academic world, which still rarely interacted at the most advanced levels with Jewish research. As we have seen throughout this chapter, Jellinek was a firm believer in the dogmas practiced inside the cathedral of science. To him, "real science" was the goal not only of *Wissenschaft* but, in some ways, of modernity—and of religion in modernity—itself. These books on Thomas Aquinas allowed

---

28. Adolph Jellinek, *Philosophie und Kabbala* (Leipzig: Hunger, 1854), xvi.

Jellinek to investigate materials that could not find a place in the larger *Bet ha-Midrasch* project.

Just as the first way the *Bet ha-Midrasch* differed from many of Jellinek's previous writings was that it allowed him to expand his interests in rabbinic narratives clearly related to similar stories found throughout the ancient Near East, the second difference—and the theme most comprehensively covered in all six volumes—was that it provided Jellinek with the space to gather together Jewish mystical writings that were not (in his mind) in the direct lineage of the *Zohar* or Spanish Kabbalah. Whereas in his prior books and articles Jellinek had focused almost exclusively on tracing the particular strains of mystical thought that allowed for the conception and composition of the *Zohar*, in *Bet ha-Midrasch* Jellinek ranged more widely, including between its covers texts from the *Hekhalot* and *Ma'asei Merkava* literatures, as well as the book of Jubilees and other writings he considered of Essene or Essene-like origin. Such texts, Jellinek believed, regardless of their relationship to the *Zohar*, were important documents in the evolution of religious ideas. He wrote:

> *Bet ha-Midrasch* contain several pieces dealing with Messiah and Paradise legends.... These writings have, first, a value for the history of civilization, in that they let us see the desires and hopes of a time in perspective. They also have a poetic interest, in creating vivid descriptions and in imaginative embellishment. Finally, they are important for literary history, with many works referring to [already widespread] representations of Paradise and the Messianic Age.[29]

In Jellinek's conception, the writings collected in *Bet ha-Midrasch* were not merely the background to Kabbalah per se, though some of them certainly were that. Rather, they comprised a sample of the general framework of the midrashic inheritance of all normative rabbinic Judaism and indeed, to some extent, of all European literature. As Jellinek sought to demonstrate time and again, Jewish writing was never solely Jewish. What was preserved in Hebrew within the Jewish community was but one instantiation of a set of themes and ideas equally discussed and disputed throughout the ancient world. It was precisely this fact—that these texts were not wholly unique but rather emblematic—that Jellinek believed made them worthy of modern critical-historical scholarship. For Jellinek, the Jews had preserved in their literature fragments of lost cultures, and just as Tischendorf studied the earliest Gospel manuscripts and Creuzer the later Greek myths, so *Wissenschaft* scholars searched the ancient texts of the Jews, finding (Jellinek believed) heretofore missing elements in the theological genealogy of European religion.

---

29. Jellinek, *Bet ha-Midrasch*, 3:xvii–xviii.

As part of Jellinek's editorial choices, and likely related to his underlying notions concerning the formation of historical texts, he did not provide a precise date of final redaction for the majority of mystical works found in *Bet ha-Midrasch*. Rather, he traced the way each text was produced through an agglomerative process, presenting them in the framework of cultures of thought and chains of translation and addition. For example, about text VII in volume 2, "Das Buch Serubabel," Jellinek noted, "Our book *Zerubbabel* is old enough that Saadiah [ben Yosef Gaon, ca. 882–942, Egypt and Babylonia] already knew of the Armelus-saga [medieval Jewish anti-Messianic figure] and it is mentioned by Ibn Ezra [1089–ca. 1167, Spain]."[30] As with this text, none of the manuscripts included in *Bet ha-Midrasch* were presented as a unique work of creative genius. Jellinek instead focused his editorial notes on two overlapping areas of historical criticism: first, the way a specific text reflected material found in the classical corpus of rabbinic midrash; and, second, how the text complemented the known apocryphal and pseudepigraphic writings of the late Second Temple and early post-Temple periods, works like Jubilees, *Sefer ha-Yashar*, *Sefer ha-Bahir*, and the multifarious Enochic and *Merkavah* literatures. Jellinek did not explicitly elaborate on some of the background and implications of these connections, but that would have been clear to many of his readers, especially those following contemporary scholarly developments in German academia.

One of the ways Jellinek maintained the balance between normativity and divergence was to focus on commonalities among all three literatures—the classical rabbinic, the known apocryphal, and the uncategorized (or uncategorizable) midrashim he was collecting. For example, in a discussion in volume 3, Jellinek wrote:

> We have, therefore, remains of the Essene's *Ma'aseh Bereishit* and *Ma'asei Merkhva* in the 2nd chapter of both the Jerusalem and Babylonian [versions of the] Tractate *Chagiga*, in the Midrash Cônen (see *Bet ha-Midrasch*, vol. II) and in the *Hekhalot* [literature]. [But] the indicated [literary] remains cannot always be linked directly to the texts of the Essene tradition. For in fact it would be an enigmatic phenomenon if nothing of such an important sect had been preserved. The analogy to other secret orders also teaches us that the esoteric doctrines come to light as soon as the order's fixed structure is relaxed or when it passes into other societies.[31]

In other words, Jellinek was arguing that within known canonical works (e.g., the Jerusalem and Babylonian Talmuds, the *Hekhalot* literature) were extracts, remnants, and adaptations of earlier traditions of

---

30. Jellinek, *Bet ha-Midrasch*, 2:xxii.
31. Jellinek, *Bet ha-Midrasch*, 3:xxi.

theological inquiry. He went so far as to say that it was perhaps impossible that secret writings could remain secret for long, for at some point their doctrinal strictures would loosen, the groups they originated in would disband, and the texts would fall into the hands of outsiders, who would then take up the theological-narrative ideas and integrate them into their own cultural contexts. Such a vision of Jewish history as this that Jellinek forwarded in *Bet ha-Midrasch* was strikingly different from those then being made by other *Wissenschaft* historians, such as Jost, or that which was later canonized by Graetz. That Jellinek never wrote a multivolume history of the Jews accounts for some of the reason these insights were never widely attributed to him. The other is that, though he was working on this material at an early date and proposing many revolutionary reevaluations of Jewish history, he was in actuality most often simply embracing to the fullest extent the zeitgeist of his age. Some of Jellinek's specific insights were certainly innovative, but the vast majority of his project was designed to integrate *Wissenschaft* more fully into modern German critical scholarship.

The Values of Medieval Exegesis

As we conclude this analysis of Jellinek's scholarship in Leipzig, we must turn to one more text in order to complete our understanding of what Jellinek valued most in historical sources. In 1855, the same year he completed the third volume of *Bet ha-Midrasch*, Jellinek published an edition of Samuel ben Meir's *Commentary on Ecclesiastes and the Song of Songs*.[32] In this book, Jellinek offered the most direct assessment of what he believed to be the value of medieval exegesis. Samuel ben Meir (ca. 1085–ca. 1158, called Rashbam), who lived his entire life in the small village of Ramerupt, in north-central France, was a grandson of Rashi (Rabbi Shlomo Yitzchaki [1040–1105]). Samuel was also the primary teacher of his own younger brother, Jacob ben Meir (known as Rabbenu Tam), who would go on to be one of the most important French Tosafists, a group of rabbis whose commentary on the Talmud sit alongside that of Rashi's.

Jellinek's decision to publish a work of Samuel's instead of Jacob's

---

32. Part of Samuel Ben Meir's commentary was republished as *The Commentary of R. Samuel Ben Meir, Rashbam, on Qohelet* [Hebrew], ed. Sara Japhet and Robert B. Salters (Jerusalem: Magnes Press, 1985). Japhet and Salters base their work on the same Hamburg manuscript that was printed by Jellinek. Japhet and Salters question a number of Jellinek's attributions and altogether find the original Hamburg text unsatisfactory. That Jellinek's scholarship has been displaced would not have displeased him. That Japhet and Salters conducted their later study of the text in a critical-historical manner would have pleased him greatly.

offers a clear view into Jellinek's ultimate understanding of the responsibilities and possibilities of modern Jewish scholarship. Samuel ben Meir was certainly not a modern German academic, but, in Jellinek's telling, he had already discerned some of the fundamental attributes of critical, dispassionate inquiry.

> Free from the mysterious course and the playing peculiarity of Abraham Ibn-Ezra; free of the considerations which his grandfather [Rashi] paid to aggadic romanticism; free from the mystical gloom of Moses ben Nachman, the fluctuations of David Kimchi, the philosophical rationalism of Leon de Bañoles, the tiring breadth of the scholastic epic Don Isaac Abarbanel; our R. Samuel is clear, definite, simple, decisive, and sensible in his whole being.[33]

As we have seen before, Jellinek's discursive assessments certainly reveal more about his own interests than they do about later scholarly consensus. But in Jellinek's description ("clear, definite, simple, decisive, and sensible") Samuel ben Meir was a scholar of the modern sort, employing a text-critical vision of exegesis focused on *pshat*, the literal meaning of words and the clarification of ideas though rational argumentation. "In explaining the actual part of *Kohelet*, R. Samuel endeavors to illuminate every verse in terms of its content and attitude to the contexts, to solve grammatical and lexical difficulties, especially through the medium of analogy and parallelism. All his explanations are simple, concise, and succinct."[34]

Finally, what Jellinek saw in Samuel ben Meir was not just a similar affinity for close philological comparison and cultural contextualization but also a desire to feel the emotions of the text itself.

> [In his commentary on *Song of Songs*] the allegory is simple and unsung; the eroticism of the song is reproduced in the commentary in such a way that dark words are lightened by other, more familiar ones, and the pictures receive freshness and life. But the prudent exegete, whose gaze is directed to the whole, and the ambitious grammarian, to whom the form of every single word is important, are not missed. Across the entire commentary there is a fascination of the visible expression and the shimmering sensation which one will seek in vain in other Jewish exegetes.[35]

Jellinek's words describe two passions at once. First, a care about accuracy in the text. Second, that scholarship need not obscure the lucidity and beauty of a narrative. As he wrote about Salomon Munk (that his

---

33. Samuel ben Meir, *Perush*, ed. Jellinek, vii–viii.
34. Samuel ben Meir, *Perush*, ed. Jellinek, ix.
35. Samuel ben Meir, *Perush*, ed. Jellinek, ix–x.

scholarship was not "merely on a grey scale lacking in golden fruits") so too he wrote again about Samuel ben Meir (that he maintained a "fascination [with] the visible expression and the shimmering sensation" of the original words). In the following chapters we will see that the ability of ancient texts to inspire in modern readers a passion for religion would become one of the central motifs in Jellinek's writings. Already in 1853, at the height of his career as a *Wissenschaft* scholar, Jellinek was beginning to express these sentiments himself. In his early work on the *Zohar* in the late 1840s, what had interested him was mapping narrative genealogies and linguistic overlaps. That still held pride of place in the 1850s. But it was supplemented by something else as well, what for lack of a better description might be called the poetry of religious history, the ability to continue to feel—in one's own era—the inspiration that had originally motivated the writing of these great works of Jewish theology.

As Jellinek moved away from full-time scholarly endeavors, he left behind an unflinching dedication to truth in the text, to discovering every bit of history's subtlety and intercultural complexity. These were the values embodied in his work through the 1840s and 1850s. Even after he left for Vienna, Jellinek would continue to support the ideals of *Wissenschaft*. The medieval mystics and midrashists, with their unique insights into humanity and their remarkable desire to assimilate the ideas and languages of Christianity and Islam, were not an embarrassment or aberration in Jewish history, he always argued. Rather, they had given the world one of its most remarkable accomplishments. It was these lessons that Jellinek took with him into his new public role as community rabbi and public figure on the vanguard of Jewish urban acculturation.

5

Divided Loyalties: Jellinek between Scholarship and Communal Leadership

When Adolf Jellinek moved to Leipzig and began his studies at its university, he slowly began to realize that, in the age of emancipation, a new ritual practice might be necessary in order to keep Judaism relevant and connected with its long tradition of meaning-making and community. But he also believed it was not just a new liturgy and prayer service that would bring Judaism into this new age. Practice needed to be coupled with a language of theology and moral philosophy that was in conversation with the ideas and aspirations of the age. He would need to find new ways of speaking about Judaism, ones that made it relevant at a moment of liberalizing values and spreading beliefs in universal, individualistic humanism.

As we saw in chapters 1 and 2, the various strands that constitute Jewish religious modernity were all already present in the early decades of the nineteenth century. But what we also saw was that the religious leadership in Central Europe had no pressing sociological need to engage in a major religious transformation; Jewish daily life in the 1820s and 1830s remained roughly coterminous with its historical precedents. By Jellinek's move to Leipzig in the 1840s, however, that was changing, and by his final years in the Saxon city, in the early to mid-1850s, his generation has become part of a new sort of demographic and social tumult for the Jews of Central Europe. Families were moving in unprecedented numbers from rural towns to urban centers. It is this later period in Leipzig—the early 1850s—that corresponds with Jellinek's focused reformulation of the rabbinic ideal of communal leadership.

Jellinek's earliest ideas about Jewish modernity were clearly linked with his university studies. The academic disciplines of philology, Orientalism, and biblical criticism gave him access to a language that had previously been absent from Jewish religious debate. Yet, within half a decade of arriving in Leipzig, Jellinek seems to have known that he would not be content to spend his life entirely as a scholar of Jewish history, and he worried that there was no space in the new sciences for a commitment to religious values, traditions, narratives, and discourses. Therefore, he sought out roles in communal religious leadership and, in so doing, began to develop a rabbinic persona that was just beginning to emerge in his time but has since become commonplace among non-Haredi rabbis in the present day. The elements of that persona were twofold. First, building off his scholarly training and interests (discussed in the previous two chapters), Jellinek looked to the non-halakhic traditions in Judaism for theological narratives and vocabularies that could be translated into a modern Jewish-German religious idiom. He found them primarily in midrash, the folkloric, somewhat esoteric, deeply imaginative discussions of the classical and medieval rabbis. Second, he developed and honed a rhetorical style that interwove traditional religious narratives with the ideas of contemporary philosophy and politics. Throughout his life, Jellinek directed his words at an acculturating but not assimilated Jewish community. Instead of arguing for the religious legality of Jewish social life in a new urban world, Jellinek focused on the moral and philosophical outlook of Judaism and its historical narratives. Just as German intellectuals were at that very moment engaged in writing a romantic account of their nation's past, so too should the Jews, Jellinek believed. And the Jewish narrative, Jellinek provocatively argued, was both older and wiser, the essential moral precursor to the universalizing story propounded by modern historians and carried into politics by its liberal heirs.

Early Thoughts on the Future of European Judaism

By the opening years of the 1850s, Jellinek was moving away from an all-consuming focus on scholarship. His school days were behind him. The 1848 revolutions had come and gone. A series of emancipatory reforms made large-scale Jewish settlement in the city of Leipzig possible, and innovations in economics and transportation made the move desirable. Finally, in the very middle of the nineteenth century, the diverse elements of Jewish modernity that had been spreading across European Jewish culture for the better part of a century were finally arrayed together: intellectual revolutions stemming from a liberalizing intelligentsia; political reforms following the Napoleonic invasion and the 1848 revolutions; and economic and transportation innovations that opened the way for a rural to urban demographic transitions.

On the evening of December 13, 1846, at the Hoftheater in Dresden, a play premiered by the well-known dramatist, essayist, and novelist Karl Ferdinand Gutzkow (1811–1878). Entitled *Uriel Acosta: A Tragedy in Five*

Acts, the play received general acclaim and was widely interpreted as being sympathetic to the Jewish cause, and especially the idea of Jewish civil emancipation and legal equality.[1] Set in Amsterdam in 1640, *Uriel Acosta* was a historical adaptation based on the real life of Uriel da Costa (d. 1640, called in German "Acosta"), the son of a Portuguese Jewish convert to Catholicism who, to some extent, returned to the religion of his ancestry over the course of his life. Da Costa's writings, especially those on the Pharisees and the relationship of the later rabbis to the Bible, led to much controversy within the various Jewish communities in which he sought to reside. He was excommunicated by the rabbinical courts in Venice and Hamburg in 1616, and again by the Amsterdam community in 1623 (though the latter edict was revoked the following decade).

Gutzkow's adaptation of da Costa's story for the German stage recast this historical tale into a modern frame, one that most of those sitting that evening in the Hoftheater or reading it as a printed booklet would likely have understood. For Gutzkow, da Costa embodied liberty and freedom of thought, a freethinker confronted by the parochialism of philosophical and theological conformity. In late 1846, such questions were much discussed. In the play, da Costa loses a great deal for his convictions: the love of a woman (Judith); the honor that comes through a place in an established social order (the Jewish community); permanence in a city that he might ultimately call home (Amsterdam). But the importance of his convictions, of the "truth," or even merely the ability to express the truth as he understood it, outweighed such suffering. Says da Costa (Act I, scene 3):

> You believe that I would still banish you / into distant valleys, myself, for your sake? / Because I, once hesitatingly wanted to save / myself and Judith from a fight of the heart, / should I now also escape the struggle of the spirit? / That was wrong! Whoever wants to confess truth / must not deprive it of the highest glory, / the glory of courage that truth gives. / What else can speak in me about escape? / I must now return [to the pursuit of truth], even if my heart breaks.

Act 4 of this great personal drama is a court scene, where the chief prosecutor is none other than Rabbi Akiva himself, one of the foremost sages in the history of Judaism. Comparing da Costa to Elisha ben Abuya, the famous tannaitic scholar who is said to have forsaken Judaism ("cut down the plantings" [b. Hagigah 14b]), Akiva demands a recantation of da Costa's most heretical ideas. Do not abandon the way of your people, Akiva warns. You are not the first who has harbored such heterodox ideas and you will not be the last. But honoring your teachers and students

---

1. Karl Gutzkow, *Uriel Acosta: Trauerspiel in fünf Aufzügen* (Leipzig: Reclam, 1847).

is ultimately more important than expressing every passing fantasy at "truth" that you might believe today or tomorrow.

> In such doubters as you are, Acosta, / there is only the wild drive to search. / There have been many [like you] in the Talmud / who have been led astray by too much knowledge. / There was a great doubter, by the name / of Elisha ben Abuya, disciple of one of our wisest rabbis. / And Rabbi Meir was his disciple. / And because [Elisha] doubted, he was cursed. / Elisha ben Abuja was like you. / They [the redactors of the Talmud] were afraid to utter the name, / and [so he became] *Acher—Acher*, meaning the "other," / the other only, so the Talmud writes of him— / and [when he died] an eternal smoke rose darkly from the grave / —the tomb, it smoked— / until his disciple, Rabbi Meir, / eased the peace of his soul by prayer. / [Rabbi Meir] prayed, the disciple for the master, / and from the grave it no longer smoked. / You are such an *Acher*. (Act 4, scene 2)

Throughout Act 4, Gutzkow's portrayal of both Akiva and da Costa is deeply sympathetic. Rabbi Meir's pain at the loss of his teacher to heresy is shown to have affected him for the rest of his life. When Elisha ben Abuya dies, Gutzkow conjures for us the image of the disciple sitting near his master's grave, praying for Elisha's eternal peace, calming the flames of earthly acrimony that still resounded.

Ultimately, of course, Acosta persists in his lonely venture—in the play as in real life. The search for truth required that he sacrifice all else, he believed. A century into the philosophical revolution that began with Enlightenment and gave birth to modern critical scholarship, and less than two years before the outbreak of the 1848 revolutions, which would demand greater freedoms of religion, press, and expression across Europe, Gutzkow's da Costa cannot be allowed to be swayed even by the high ideals of a Rabbi Akiva. As Calvin N. Jones describes it, though the play was "a blank-verse tragedy set in seventeenth-century Holland, involving a theological controversy among Jews ... there are close parallels with the suppression of thought by the political and clerical authorities of nineteenth-century Germany."[2] Gutzkow was a founding member of Young Germany (*junge Deutschland*), a group of writers in the pre-1848 (*vormärtz*) generation who dedicated themselves to advancing the principles of democracy, socialism, and freedom of thought. Opposed to legislative autocracy (which became more vociferous following the 1830 revolution in France) and the reactionary doctrines of state religion, Gutzkow and his Young Germany compatriots sought a new sort of literary engagement with politics, one that embraced the high Enlightenment ideals of Kant and Hegel, trusting in individual freedom and liberty as the power that

---

2. Calvin N. Jones, "Authorial Intent and Public Response to *Uriel Acosta* and *Freiheit in Krahwinkel*," *South Atlantic Review* 47, no. 4 (1982): 17-26, here 19.

could forge a path toward a more equitable, rational, and progressive society. In such a context, Gutzkow's da Costa had no choice but to reject the warnings of Akiva and make his way toward truth, alone.

In the opinion of one young man—one who, it must be noted, was deeply sympathetic to many of the ideals of Young Germany—Gutzkow's synonymy between da Costa, the present struggle for individual liberty, and Elisha ben Abuya was not the only story that could be told. In late January 1847, a little over a month after the premier of *Uriel Acosta* in Dresden, the twenty-six-year-old Adolf Jellinek, still a student at the University of Leipzig, published an essay in response to Gutzkow's play. Entitled "Elisha ben Abuya, called Acher: An Explanation and Critique of Gutzkow's Tragedy *Uriel Acosta*,"[3] the essay used the court scene between da Costa and Akiva in Act 4 to explore at greater length Judaism's religious and historical understanding of Elisha ben Abuya, the concept of apostasy, and the tragic fate of those who believe they are forced to choose between competing philosophical and religious systems. While admiring Gutzkow's dramatic style, Jellinek fundamentally disagreed with Gutzkow's portrayal of Judaism's reception of Elisha. "One can legitimately assume that only the smallest part of the [play's] listeners understand either the historical document [the Talmud] or the philosophical myth [Elisha "cut down the plantings"] in the poetic sense.... [The] poet [Gutzkow] could have arranged this episode in a much more effective way had he mastered this dark subject in every respect."[4] For Jellinek, Elisha ben Abuya was not a beacon of self-liberating rationalism in an era of stifling dogmatic religiosity. He was not a singular genius who saw through the accumulated philosophical detritus of centuries toward a more progressive and redemptive future. Instead, Jellinek portrayed Elisha as a man caught between two philosophical worlds, a man of divided loyalties, who, instead of managing the tension, chose to forsake one people for another. Jellinek described how Elisha studied not only Jewish law but Greek learning as well, and that it was ultimately this combination that tore him apart and resulted in his apostasy. For Jellinek, it was not doctrinal Judaism that was at fault. Instead, it was Elisha's inability to find complementarity between the Greek and Jewish systems.[5]

In his essay, Jellinek described Elisha's descent into heresy as stemming from his insistence that the world provide a single, pure, uncomplicated truth. Elisha's failure, thought Jellinek, was that he lacked the ability to hold in tension the teachings of two distinct schools of thought. In this

---

3. Adolph Jellinek, *Elischa ben Abuja, genannt Acher. Zur Erkärung und Kritik der Gutzkow'schen Tragödie* Uriel Acosta (Leipzig: Hunger, 1847).

4. Jellinek, *Elischa ben Abuja*, 3.

5. This same story is told in Milton Steinberg's classic novel *As a Driven Leaf* (1939; repr., Springfield, NJ: Behrman House, 2015).

way, Jellinek presented Elisha as an incipient Spinoza, a brilliant mind whose investigations resulted in magnificent insights but who ultimately was unable to channel his learning back toward the received tradition, and thereby undermined his ability to live within the Jewish community in which he had been raised. Wrote Jellinek:

> Soon also that conflict between the naivety of faith and the unleashed speculation occurred. From the silent hut of faith [Elisha] threw himself into the flood of research on the highest problems of the philosophy of religion. One surge piled on the other, [and because] the bold thinker did not set up a dam, he ended up dissolving the whole Mosaic law.[6]

Such an inability to see two truths at once, thought Jellinek, was simply the wrong way to think about religion and theology, either in the ancient world or in the modern one. Jellinek was here speculating both historically and practically—about the scholarly implication of the play and about the very real theological and moral conundrums being presented to German Jewry in the middle decades of the nineteenth century: "Both Acosta and Elisha have nourished their minds in a foreign domain of knowledge; both have lost the belief in an immortality through their doubts. When Acosta draws poison from the flowers, Elisha has lost eternal being in the disharmony of life."[7]

In his review of the play, Jellinek was searching for an intermediate way between parochial insularity and "the cliff of faith." Such a division between adherence to one's intellectual principles and separation from one's community was unnecessary, Jellinek believed. (In later chapters, we will see Jellinek retaining this belief his whole life.) The tragedy was avoidable: "Acosta could have held up a mirror, in which he would have again recognized the features of his mind."[8] Certainly, Jellinek's discussion of the play was an apology for traditional rabbinic Judaism, or at least for a deep and sustained intellectual relationship with rabbinic texts. But it was also something more. It was a statement of faith, a doctrine of modernity, and a warning to his friends.

By the end of the 1840s, Jellinek began to think very critically about these subjects: both the intellectual developments taking place within the circles of modern Jewish leadership and the broader communal implications that were confronting Central European Jewry in the years after this play premiered. What had been for da Costa in 1640 a personal struggle between the moral demands and expectations of the Jewish community and his intellectual conscience became for the Jews of Central Europe in

---

6. Jellinek, *Elischa ben Abuja*, 7–8
7. Jellinek, *Elischa ben Abuja*, 10.
8. Jellinek, *Elischa ben Abuja*, 11.

the middle of the nineteenth century a community-wide discussion, with very real implications for the fate and experience of all Jews. The stories of Elisha and da Costa were not isolated incidents, past events pertaining to eccentric individuals. The play was, in Jellinek's reading, a parable deeply representative of modernity. Finding the middle ground was not simply more pleasant when living in community with others. It was an absolute imperative if Judaism was to remain a living tradition in modern times.

Divided Loyalties

In the middle of the 1850s, Jellinek began to devote far less of his time to scholarship. In 1848 he had accepted a paid position as rabbi of Leipzig, a new post created specifically for him, and one that symbolized the broader urban transformation occurring throughout the Jewish communities of Central Europe. With his acceptance of the rabbinate in Leipzig, Jellinek was signaling an expansion of his vision, joining a second, parallel set of Jewish pioneers—not just those for whom *Wissenschaft* was everything (like Steinschneider, Jost, and Graetz, who were librarians, teachers, and professors), but the scholar-rabbis of his age, who thought that *Wissenschaft* was the foundation of religious reform. In Jellinek's view, the nineteenth century was changing too rapidly for traditional assumptions and expectations to entirely define Judaism's future. Instead, he believed that a new role for the rabbi was needed, one still rooted in the classical texts but with an eye toward a future predicated on Jewish integration within European cultural life.

Jellinek's growing involvement in the religious affairs of Leipzig's Jews (ended by his acceptance of a rabbinical position in␣Vienna in late 1856) was coupled with an increasing estrangement from the values of *Wissenschaft* and with the society of scholars who composed it. In 1855, as a preface to the third volume of *Bet ha-Midrasch*, Jellinek penned a long statement expressing his concern about the future of the scholarly movement with which he had been closely associated for over a decade. Nowhere else in his voluminous writings is there contained anything quite like these two pages, which excoriated his fellow scholars for their pettiness and querulousness. Jellinek's words bear full transcription:

> I should have failed to preface this third part of my *Bet ha-Midrasch* at all if I had not felt urged to utter a serious word about the sad situation in which Jewish scholarship finds itself. I must mention the despicable meanness and smallness of spirit that prevails in the circle of Jewish scholars, and that complicates any cooperation or cooperative pursuits. By mastering the conceit of sitting enthroned in the clouds, we have a *corps d'élite* who ignore the others. This all-knowing few only teach, but

they do not want to learn, and mostly they slander by searching everywhere for literary errors in others. They lack true humility, which was already considered by the ancients essential to genuine research. Such are weaknesses and infirmities that remain even today. Indeed, Jewish scholars have revealed the same social evils that have already been active over so many different generations. But there are damages which disturb the progress of research, and which must be removed, or at least be made light of, if the efforts of the last years are not to be thwarted. Above all, such petty actions lack that free spirit which imbues scholarship for its own sake and leaves it up to time to fully investigate all of it. The meaning of scholarship is to feel and sense every little thing that is important for true research, for how often can a side path end up being the clearest view to the realm of knowledge? Only on such a sense of striving with certainty and security will one spare no effort to open a field of research anew. But we cannot know what investigations remain undone because this sense is missing, what works fail to address the design of practical life since there are those who outright accuse others about miniscule observations and surprise them by treating this or that literary theme. The lack of disinterested scientific research results in a contempt of the work itself, which begins early in life. Seeking to capture the big picture, each supports his own literary tower. His aversion to receiving a new article of research has caused there to be no common ground in the most important matters of Jewish literary history. —Further, often one finds that influential men lack the ability to be objective about that which lies outside his specialty. Anyone in Talmudic study—because he thinks this is most closely associated with life—cannot understand why one should set his sights on [academic] scholarship. The former calls with all his strength of spirit and matter to suppress the study of literary history as something merely *minorum gentium* [of the minor nations], having no idea that it tells us about how the mind and body relate, and is of the cultural moment in literary history. Others look on with tedious smiles as he lays out his work, and cannot set as their highest point a series of various booklets that run to a great length such that the seemingly separate parts relate and make up a great whole. —Finally, one often looks in vain for that love of truth which has the courage to give truth in the world of research, someone who does not cover up or make up, and is not full of prejudices when it comes time to fight. He who has not the courage in scholarship to sincerity and truth, of him we say: Stay away, enter not as an unauthorized priest to desecrate this sanctuary!

I must in conclusion indict, as in court, the modern study of Jewish literature. The scholarly treatment of this vast, comprehensive, and manifold subject, written down in various languages and hidden in remote libraries of Jewish literature, is still very young, and the resources for its pursuance still very few. It requires great and exhausting efforts to complete this work in a sure and reliable manner, for just as literature itself has changed, so too have the methods for its research. What time and what resources were utilized to bring to their present state our knowledge of Greek and Roman literature, and of Church history!

In earnest do I wish the men of Jewish Studies to pursue the cause of truth in their research, and be just in judgment, so that the field might thrive. (Leipzig, 26 July 1855.)[9]

There is much to see in this long passage. It is a remarkable defense of the type of scholarship discussed in the previous two chapters. It also, quite clearly, comes from a place of deep frustration. There is a lack of true fellowship in the *Wissenschaft* community, Jellinek is saying, which not only impedes research but results in skewed accounts, in work that fails to take in the whole realm of learning because individual scholars refuse to move beyond their own intellectual silos.

Jellinek's words are not the retrospective held by contemporary historians, who often marvel at the immense productivity of nineteenth-century scholars, but it does perhaps reveal something that contemporary historiography can overlook. In the 1850s, Leipzig was full of Jewish scholars frustrated by the lack of opportunities available to them in the German university system. They could be educated but not be employed. There seems little doubt that this might have led to an intense amount of unnecessary bickering. "Often one finds that influential men lack the ability to be objective about that which lies outside his specialty," Jellinek noted, in words that seem somewhat out of place based on his rapid acceptance into the circle of *Wissenschaft* scholars and his steady acclaim. But there is always more to the story. By 1854, Zacharias Frankel had decamped from Saxony to Breslau, in Prussian Silesia, there to assume leadership over the new Jewish Theological Seminary. Steinschneider was spending summers in Oxford. Zunz was in Berlin. For nearly a decade Leipzig and Halle had together hosted one of the greatest concentrations of scholars in the fields of *Wissenschaft des Judentums*, Orientalism, and biblical criticism anywhere in Europe. It seems more than likely, then, that the pressures and egos were too much. Thus, Jellinek penned his critique.

This introduction to volume 3 might likewise be understood as a sort of public declaration by Jellinek of his decision not to pursue a life devoted exclusively to professional scholarship. Instead, he began to focus his attentions and intellectual energies on the growth and perseverance of a Jewish community in modern Europe. As will be discussed in the coming chapters, the value "to pursue the cause of truth" was something Jellinek took with him from scholarship into the full-time rabbinate. But creating scholarship for its own sake was not the only task of the modern

---

9. Jellinek, *Bet ha-Midrasch*, 3:vii–viii.

Jew, Jellinek came to realize. There was other work to be done, and it was toward them that Jellinek devoted most of the last four decades of his life.

Taking Up Communal Leadership

Observing these historic confluences, Jellinek took the insights from his scholarship and sought to apply them to the religious needs of the community, beginning to create and implement practical reforms that would respond to the needs of this new urban Judaism. These migrants were displaced of almost everything. The paradigm of individualism, so often assumed by contemporary readers, makes it difficult for us to understand the jarring effects that this mass Jewish migration must have had on families and communities. Jewish life in the premodern period was defined to an extraordinary extent by social circumstances, and the continuity of historical norms dictated most personal interactions and decisions. The various economic and intellectual transformations that defined Jewish modernity were not equivalent to a mass secularization. Instead, many of the same diversities that had existed in premodern villages continued to permeate the modern period.[10] Jellinek's recognition that religious institutions and traditions would persist but require reform compelled him to assert both a new paradigm of historical consciousness and a traditionalist assumption that theology and ritual practice were essential parts of Jewish life.[11]

With the breakdown of long-established communities during the migration to cities, new religious structures had to be devised to replace them. In a place like Leipzig, with no historical Jewish community to speak of, this meant that, in many ways, a leader like Jellinek had a free hand in crafting a vision of the rabbinate that diverged greatly from the model of small-town rabbis of premodern Central Europe discussed in chapter 1. As we will see, Jellinek created for himself a new model of the rabbi, centered on public sermons and anchored by the central community synagogue. He was not alone in seeing the newfound importance for urban Jewry of preaching and the synagogue. Instead, Jellinek's historical importance arises from his rhetorical craft, his integration of *Wissenschaft* scholarship into his vision of modern Jewish life, and his eventual fame as head of the

---

10. See Shmuel Feiner, *The Origins of Jewish Secularization in Eighteenth-Century Europe*, trans. Chaya Naor (Philadelphia: University of Pennsylvania Press, 2010), esp. 180–250.

11. This is why calling Jewish modernity a "Protestantization" of Judaism is incorrect. Jews encountered modernity in many of the same ways as religious Christians, and at many of the same times. The transformations that swept through rabbinic Judaism were much more often innovative responses to a changing world than they were parodies of Christianity.

Viennese community. Yet already in Leipzig, his writings proved to be some of the most sophisticated and nuanced attempts to unite a particular vision of Jewish moral and universal history with the most contemporary and respected texts of German modernity. Designed for an educated but not an intellectual audience, his prose told a continuous and thoughtful story about the Jewish contribution to European history and about the biblical underpinning of modern society and its values. Jellinek's talents and growing fame gave his rabbinic practices a unique importance as a model for young rabbis across German-speaking Central Europe.

In 1845, Jellinek began to take an active role in Leipzig's Jewish religious community, preaching in the town's Leipzig-Berlin Synagogue.[12] In 1847 he was appointed teacher in the newly founded religious school and, by the early 1850s, had taken over as the community's chief rabbi, presiding from the Community Synagogue.[13] (When Frankel left Dresden in 1854, Leipzig officially ended its relationship with the Dresden rabbinate.) In 1855, with much of the political and social organizing orchestrated by Jellinek, the Leipzig community inaugurated its New Israelite Temple on Gottschedstraße. As community rabbi, Jellinek's religious ideology flowed naturally from his earlier education. He was at home in both Jewish and German texts. He could write in multiple genres—critical histories, academic reviews, homiletic sermons. His respect for the traditional Jewish canon was without question.

In the early 1850s, Jellinek began to view the position of community rabbi as being as much a public intellectual as an arbiter of religious law and custom. The rabbi, he believed, should be dedicated to interpreting Jewish texts for the modern era. Less concerned with law, the rabbi's new role was as the proponent of a particular philosophy or creed, one that sought to bring together Jewish wisdom, modern politics, and the Enlightenment's universalist ethic. A series of sermons Jellinek delivered in 1849 in Leipzig, and later published as separate pamphlets, illustrated this new philosophy of the modern rabbi. They revealed how Jellinek sought to weave together various threads of Jewish and secular learning as he began to create what we now think of as the modern rabbi.

Many of Jellinek's 1849 sermons began with philosophical quotations. In this way, right at the beginning, the young rabbi was showing his listeners and readers that Jewish content was at once relevant to the larger philosophical project of the German Enlightenment, as well as equal to it. One sermon, entitled "Jericho: An Image of Israel's Freedom," written for

---

12. See Kempter, *Die Jellineks 1820–1955*; and Siegel, "Facing Tradition."
13. On Jellinek's response as a preacher during 1848, see Klaus Kempter, "Adolf Jellinek und die jüdische Emanzipation: Der Prediger der Leipziger jüdischen Gemeinde in der Revolution 1848/49," *Aschkenas – Zeitschrift für Geschichte und Kultur der Juden* 8 (1998): 179–91.

the holiday of Passover, opened with four quotations, three from Goethe and one from Hegel.[14] Then, in eleven pages of florid prose, Jellinek described the transition of Israel from a tribe of wanderers in the desert to an established nation in the land of Canaan. He ended the sermon with a personal prayer, extolling the freedoms that Jews were allowed in the present age under King Friedrich August II of Saxony. In its Passover context, the sermon presented the conquering of the city of Jericho and the Hebrews' entry into the promised land as a metaphor for the attainment of freedom and the struggles of nationhood in the new post-1848 era of emancipation—that while the liberal revolutions had failed in a practical sense (as in Egypt, not all people are yet free), they had offered a vision (as had the exodus) that could no longer be contained in marginal intellectual or workman's circles. In Jellinek's sermon, Hegel, Goethe, and the Saxon king bookend the Jewish narrative, as if to prove that Judaism was integral to European self-identity and patriotism, and to provide a context for a new modern Jewish understanding of the Jews' role in a (semi-)liberal nation-state.

For Jellinek, the freedom gained by the Israelites after their departure from Egypt was not one of individual rights or civil emancipations, as we might suspect a man dedicated to political liberalism might promote. Instead, for Jellinek, Passover was about freedom from a human master so that Israel might assume the yoke of a divine one. "For it is to me that the Israelites are servants. They are my servants, whom I freed from the land of Egypt. I, the Lord your God" (Lev 25:55). Because Passover is designed as a liturgical reenactment of the exodus, its rituals assume the role of transferring memories. "When you enter the land which YHWH will give you, as he said, you shall observe this rite. And when your children say to you, what does this rite mean to you? you shall say, it is a Passover sacrifice to YHWH who passed over the houses of the children of Israel in Egypt when he struck the Egyptians but spared our homes" (Exod 12:25–27) Participation in the Passover celebration is, according to Jewish custom, what creates the bond between those who came out of Egypt and those alive today: "I am making this covenant, with its oath, not only with you who are standing here with us today in the presence of YHWH our God, but also with those who are not here today" (Deut 15:14–15)

For Jellinek, Passover was about a freedom to assume the status of nationhood. In this sermon, like many others, Jellinek sought to convey how the idea of nationhood was both a burden and a gift, and how it demanded a responsibility of one individual for another, and all those individuals for their God. The nation, in the biblical conception, was the primary means through which God becomes manifest in the world. Jell-

---

14. Adolf Jellinek, *Jericho: Ein Bild von Israel's Freiheit* (Leipzig: Fritzscher, 1849).

inek's was an understanding of divinity wherein God appeared mainly in the fellowship of humanity. He quoted Hegel at the sermon's opening: "World history is the process of the development of the actual idea, namely, the idea of freedom, and is the real Will of the Spirit under the changing play of its history. This is the true theodicy, the justification of God in history."[15] Jellinek was turning away from the politics of individual rights and liberties. Instead, he was invoking an older model of nationhood, one with its origins in the philosophy of the Bible, and one that squares the circle he saw growing larger every day: how to retain Judaism's unity when the offering of civil rights in the modern period came only at the level of the individual. Jellinek quoted Goethe: "Nobody can make judgments about history except those who have experienced it for themselves. This goes for whole nations."[16]

What Jellinek imagined as the promises of emancipation could be fully realized only if the continuity of Judaism remained unbroken. Emancipation existed only if there were Jews—and a Jewish nation—to be emancipated. Jericho, to Jellinek in 1849, was not a city to be conquered but a metaphor of unity in a time of transition and engagement. The Jews wandered alone in the desert; there were no other peoples around to entice them to abandon their identity. Canaan was full of other nations, each with its own tempting elixirs. Jericho, as a place to settle but also assimilate, was the challenge to be fought—not against armies but against disappearance; not against kings but against promises of equality that were dependent on cultural conformity.

In the end, the sermon suggested the beginning of a sort of negotiated interweaving that Jellinek would seek to formulate throughout the 1850s (and which contrasted with the form of revolutionary politics advocated by his brother Hermann). In placing these quotations on his opening page, Jellinek strove to connect biblical and rabbinic understandings of the festival of Passover to the words of the great sages of German culture, and to bring together the ritual aspects of Jewish life with the philosophical ideas of the Enlightenment.

The sort of rabbinic leader that Jellinek started to formulate in Leipzig, and the one that he became in Vienna and that defines his legacy and sets him at the forefront of Jewish modernity, was different in almost every respect from the models of the rabbinate he witnessed in his youth. By the close of his tenure in Leipzig in January 1857, Jellinek had begun to

---

15. This quotation appears slightly differently in Hegel's collected works: Georg Wilhelm Friedrich Hegel, *Werke in 20 Bände*, ed. Eva Moldenhauer and Karl Markus Michel (Frankfurt am Main: Suhrkamp, 1986), 12:540. The ultimate meaning is the same.

16. Johann Wolfgang Goethe, *Goethe's poetiche und prosaische Werke in Zwei Bänden*, ed. F. W. Riemer and J. P. Eckermann (Stuttgart: Cotta, 1836–1837).

formulate a vision of the rabbinate markedly different from the one he had experienced as a child in Ungarisch-Brod, or as a student in Proßnitz, or as a young man in Prague. Jellinek's turn away from scholarship appears to have been out of a deeply felt empathy toward the community of Jews newly migrated to Leipzig. *Wissenschaft* was not the place, Jellinek believed, that he could make his greatest contributions to the future of Jewish life in Central Europe. Instead, it was in developing a new form of rabbinic leadership, one that sought to unite the traditional values of Judaism with a language and philosophy that felt authentically contemporary. As we will come to see, Jellinek recast midrash as the moral and philosophical underpinning of Judaism, linking it in his writings with the enlightenment project in Germany and thereby framing the Jew's religious experience within the broader narrative of European history.

The next chapter is a history of the Jewish community of Vienna at Jellinek's arrival. As Jewish migration became a major demographic phenomenon, elements of traditional Judaism began to be adapted to meet new needs and answer new questions. The intellectual developments of Enlightenment and *Wissenschaft* that we have traced in the previous chapters preceded these demographic and economic transformations. To define Judaism in 1800 it would be almost enough to describe the life of a Jewish family or rural community. By 1860 or 1870, for the Jews of Vienna and their urban compatriots across Europe and America, Judaism was no longer reflected in every aspect of their family lives. Instead, much of their religious experience was contained in the synagogue, and their knowledge of Jewish history was told to them by the rabbi. Vienna under Jellinek was one of the earliest and clearest examples of this transition. A trend that Jellinek embodied quickly spread outward and has become, for the vast majority of Anglo-American Jews, the model for liberal religious Judaism today.

6

A New Synagogue for a New Suburb: Jellinek in Vienna's Leopoldstadt

As we follow Adolf Jellinek to Vienna, we turn to examine the pivotal moment in the transition of rabbi, sermon, and synagogue for nineteenth-century Central European Jewry. Jewish urban migration across the German and Habsburg lands increased rapidly after 1848. Not just a fortunate handful but suddenly scores of young men from every village in Central Europe were attending university and seeking access to the professional classes and its bourgeois lifestyle. With the 1848 revolutions suppressed and the government of Franz Joseph firmly in control of the empire's political hegemony, new forms of civil rights were rapidly promulgated to the various ethnic groups across the Habsburg kingdom. In the 1850s and 1860s, legal restrictions for Jews were lifted on property ownership, membership in professional guilds, and access to education at every level.

In just the nineteen years that separated 1848 and 1867—when Jews attained full legal equality following the treaty between the governments in Vienna and Budapest that created the dual monarchy of Austria-Hungary—Jewish life in Central Europe had changed fundamentally. As Jacob Katz notes, "When the framework of traditional society all over Europe disintegrated, the more traditional a society had been, the deeper was its transmutation."[1] No longer was Jewish society identifiable or coterminous with that of the small towns or rural byways Jews had inhabited for centuries. The newfound rights of Jews as citizens of the Austrian kingdom reduced their religious communal autonomy by placing them under the jurisdiction of political bureaucracies and nominally elected elites who made decisions for a legally determined community in coordination with city and federal councils. Such a transition in civic participation allowed Jews to become a deeply integrated thread within the fabric of the empire's urban and commercial life. The result of this mid-nineteenth-century urbanization for Jewish social activity and cultural affiliation has been

---

1. Katz, *Out of the Ghetto*, 6.

widely documented. Writes David Sorkin: "Against the background of embourgeoisement, the Jews' emancipation and encounter with German culture and society produced a new kind of Jew, the 'German Jew', who lived in a new kind of Jewish community, a primarily voluntary one."[2] By 1867, Jews were a sizable minority in most of the larger cities of the Austrian Empire. Jewish entrance into the bourgeois class proved rapid and trenchant: within a single generation after 1848, Jews had firmly established themselves in a diversity of professions, and by the end of the century—the grandchildren's generation—they were highly successful artists and writers as well.[3]

The City of Vienna and Its Jewish Migrants

Jellinek left Leipzig in the early months of 1857. Accepting the post of community preacher in the Viennese suburb of Leopoldstadt positioned him to become one of the foremost rabbis in the German-speaking lands.[4] The post, officially described as that of preacher, would be second in importance only to the one held by Isak Noa Mannheimer, who had presided over the Jewish community in Vienna, mainly from the Seitenstettengasse

---

2. David Sorkin, "The Impact of Emancipation on German Jewry: A Reconsideration," in Frankel and Zipperstein, *Assimilation and Community*, 177–98, here 177. He makes a similar argument in a slightly earlier article: David Sorkin, "Emancipation and Assimilation: Two Concepts and Their Application to German-Jewish History," *Leo Baeck Institute Year Book* 35 (1990): 17–33.

3. This was true nowhere more so than in Vienna and Budapest, a story wistfully told in Stefan Zweig, *Die Welt von Gestern: Erinnerungen eines Europäers* (Stockholm: Bermann-Fischer, 1942). For classic overviews of this period, see Carl E. Schorske, *Fin-de-siècle Vienna: Politics and Culture* (New York: Knopf, 1979); and Peter Gay, *Schnitzler's Century: The Making of Middle-Class Culture, 1815–1914* (New York: Norton, 2002) as well as Gay's five-volume series *The Bourgeois Experience* (New York: Norton, 1984–1998).

4. The issue of Jellinek's official beginning in Vienna is somewhat a matter of interpretation, and therefore involves some confusion about dating. As part of the official hiring process by the Viennese Jewish community (the *Gemeinde*), Jellinek gave a sermon in the Seitenstettengasse Tempel, originally scheduled for May 3, 1856. But the sermon was moved back to November 1, 1856. Because of this, Jellinek took up his duties in Vienna at the beginning of 1857, although the position had officially been awarded to him at the end of the 1856. Scholars, therefore, have variously dated the beginning of his tenure in Vienna to 1856 or 1857 (with one outlier dating it to 1858). For a history of these negotiations and the discussions between Jellinek and the Viennese *Gemeinde*, see Rosenmann, *Dr. Adolf Jellinek*, 68–69, 76–78. For further discussion and dating, see Siegel, "Facing Tradition," 323 n. 17; Holger Preißler, "Heinrich Leberecht Fleischer: Ein Leipziger Orientalist, seine jüdischen Studenten, Promovenden und Kollegen," in *Bausteine einer jüdischen Geschichte der Universität Leipzig*, ed. Stephan Wendehorst (Leipzig: Leipziger Universitätsverlag, 2006), 254; and Wistrich, *Jews of Vienna*, 111. For the outlier, see Rozenblit, "Jewish Identity and the Modern Rabbi," 103–31, here 110. I follow the 1857 date here and elsewhere.

synagogue in the center of town (also called the Stadttempel, built 1826), since 1825.[5] Though the Viennese community of 1856 was still comparatively small, with the relaxing of Jewish settlement laws after 1848 the community's governing body (the *Gemeinde*) was planning for major growth. In 1800, the city was home to about six hundred tax-paying Jews (the province of Lower Austria hosted about five thousand Jews in total). By 1848, the number of registered Jews in the Viennese municipality had risen to four thousand[6] And in the following five decades, tens of thousands of Jews moved to Vienna, such that on the eve of the Second World War there were as many as two-hundred thousand Jewish residents in the Austrian capital, fully 10 percent of the city's population.[7]

As Jellinek prepared to relocate from Leipzig to Vienna, his travel was made considerably easier by the numerous improvements in transportation that had occurred since his move to Saxony from Prague in 1841, a decade and a half before. By 1857, both railroads and horse-drawn coaches were carrying passengers through the vast rolling farmlands of central Europe.[8] As Jellinek would say in 1863,

> Let us just consider the freedoms painfully gained, about which our age [already] speaks so smugly and complacently.... A person can travel

---

5. Between the 1670 expulsion of the Jews from Vienna by Leopold I and the appointment of Moritz Güdemann to preside at the Leopoldstädter Tempel in 1869, the term *rabbi* was not used for leaders of the Jewish community in Vienna. Instead, the term *Prediger* (preacher) was employed, and was meant, first, as a sign of the Jews' second-class status (they were not allowed official religious representation—a "rabbi"—in the city) and later, as a sign of religious reform ("preacher" being more modern than "rabbi"). Jellinek never assumed the title of chief rabbi, though it was officially presented to him at the very end of his life. Mannheimer likewise remained *prediger* throughout his tenure in Vienna. Güdemann began to use the title of chief rabbi once he succeeded Jellinek as head of the Viennese community, though likely this was motivated as much by intra-Jewish politics as out of reverence for the title itself. See Wistrich, *Jews of Vienna*, 122.

6. See Jersch-Wenzel, "Population Shifts," 55, 57.

7. Rozenblit, *Jews of Vienna, 1867–1914*, 17–18; and Rozenblit, "Jewish Assimilation in Habsburg Vienna," in Frankel and Zipperstein, *Assimilation and Community*, 225–45.

8. For general histories of railroad development, see Patrick O'Brien, *Railways and the Economic Development of Western Europe, 1830–1914* (New York: St. Martin's Press, 1983); Micheline Nilsen, *Railways and the Western European Capitals: Studies of Implantation in London, Paris, Berlin, and Brussels* (New York: Palgrave Macmillan, 2008); Wolfgang Schivelbusch, *The Railway Journey: The Industrialization of Time and Space in the 19th Century* (Leamington Spa, UK: Berg, 1986); Allan Mitchell, *The Great Train Race: Railways and the Franco-German Rivalry, 1815–1914* (New York: Berghahn, 2000); and David F. Good, *The Economic Rise of the Habsburg Empire, 1750–1914* (Berkeley: University of California Press, 1984), 65–66. For the Prague–Vienna line specifically, see Alena Kubova, "Railway Stations and Planning Projects in Prague, 1845–1945," in *The City and the Railway in Europe*, ed. Ralf Roth and Marie-Noëlle Polino, Historical Urban Studies (Aldershot, UK: Ashgate, 2003), 155–68, esp. 157–58. In an interesting Jewish connection, the first major stretch of the route, Prague–Brno, was financed by the Rothschild family.

from one city to another, from one country to another, and can move his own residency without having to identify himself at the gates or barriers, [say] where or when he was born, who he is, or what compels him and of which religion he is of.[9]

The middle decades of the nineteenth century were bull years for infrastructure development and the opening of frontiers. City councils across the continent, including in the various German states, were approving the construction of rail stations, and governments and private investors were building hundreds of miles of track each year.[10] The continent wedded itself together to an unprecedented degree, while at the same time maintaining the traditionally minimal police and military presence at international frontiers—a situation that would change only after the First World War.

Whether one took coach or rail, these routes had been plied for centuries, often as not by Jewish merchants, and Vienna's importance was based on its geographic accessibility on the Danube as well as the relatively stable political history of the Habsburg kingdom and its frontier with Saxony.[11] The borders of Saxony and Habsburg Bohemia were no exception, and the political expressions of state rule were all the more important there, since the intellectual and linguistic connections between nineteenth-century Vienna and the various German cities along the frontier were numerous.[12]

As Jellinek headed south and east, no-doubt sharing the road with scores of other migrants, Jewish and gentile, he left the small kingdom of Saxony for the much larger and more powerful Austria—and perhaps something of a feeling of returning home. No one on the road would have noticed the shifting frontiers, dotted as they were with small towns, medieval church steeples, and unassuming synagogues. No major geographic

---

9. Jellinek, *Predigten*, 3:49.

10. See Keith Neilson and T. G. Otte, "'Railpolitik': An introduction," in *Railways and International Politics: Paths of Empire, 1848–1945*, ed. T. G. Otte and Keith Neilson, Cass Series: Military History and Policy 25 (New York: Routledge, 2006), 1–20, here 3: "The railway sector was the 'pace maker' of economic growth in [the late 1840s] of German industrialization, and surpassed all other sectors until the 1880s." Until the middle of the century, private corporations constructed the majority of German railroads, including the Leipzig–Dresden line. See Dieter Ziegler, *Eisenbahnen und Staat im Zeitalter der Industrialisierung: Die Eisenbahnpolitik der deutschen Staaten im Vergleich* (Stuttgart: Steiner, 1996), esp. 93; Lothar Gall and Manfred Pohl, eds., *Die Eisenbahn in Deutschland: Von den Anfängen bis zur Gegenwart* (Munich: Beck, 1999), 19–39; and Ralf Roth, *Das Jahrhundert der Eisenbahn: Die Herrschaft über Raum und Zeit, 1800–1914* (Stuttgart: Thorbecke, 2005).

11. Caitlin E. Murdoch, *Changing Places: Society, Culture, and Territory in the Saxon-Bohemian Borderlands, 1870–1946*, Social History, Popular Culture, and Politics in Germany (Ann Arbor: University of Michigan Press, 2010).

12. See Kieval, *Languages of Community*, 74–76.

marker separated Saxony from what was then the Habsburg crown land of Bohemia. Instead, the border passed over numerous tributaries of the Elbe River, which itself separates from the Moldau (Czech: Vltava) north of Prague at the town of Melnik (Czech: Mělník). After crossing the border Jellinek surely would have noticed the different uniforms on the guards, whose insignia of twin black eagles facing outward and wearing a single crown represented the House of Habsburg-Lorraine, his imperial sovereign once again. When Jellinek left Prague in 1841, Ferdinand I was emperor. After 1848, Ferdinand abdicated in favor of his nephew, Franz Joseph, who would reign until his death in 1916.[13]

Unfortunately, none of Jellinek's personal papers survive from this period, so we cannot be sure precisely how he traveled from Leipzig to Vienna, or what arrangements were made for him upon his arrival in the capital city. But based on common travel routes of the day, and his needs to spend the Sabbath in Jewish communities, we might be safe in assuming that from Leipzig he went first to Prague, whence he continued to Vienna. In the capital city, Jellinek's first permanent residence was in Leopoldstadt, a rapidly growing neighborhood just east of the city center, on land formerly part of the private estates of the emperor but which had been ceded to the city and was being settled by migrants from across the empire, though disproportionately by Jews. The Jews of Leopoldstadt came from a wide swath of central Europe and from milieus that varied greatly in religious observance, local custom, and interaction with non-Jewish culture. Arriving in Vienna, Jellinek was no longer the central rabbinic figure in a small commercial city. He was about to become a leader in what would soon be the largest, most dynamic, and most influential Jewish community in the heart of Europe.

Regarding urban migration, there are two categories of migrants that need to be kept separate. The first category stems from the long history of human movement. Humans are a migratory species, which means that, in every country, there are periods of increased and decreased migration, and growing and fading urbanism. With the spread of the Italian Renaissance northward, for example, artisans, artists, and merchants were attracted to towns and cities, interested in the latest innovations and ideas.[14] Port cities, too, have always had their ebbs and flows of economic migrants. Amsterdam grew rapidly in the sixteenth century only to shrink again in the eighteenth. The same was true for cities like Alexandria, Trieste, Marseille, Constantinople, Beirut, and Lisbon. This first category of

---

13. Karl, Franz Josef's grandnephew, became the last emperor of Austria-Hungary, reigning until the kingdom's dissolution in 1918.

14. For an example of this in Central Europe, see Jaroslav Miller, "Early Modern Urban Immigration in East Central Europe: A Macroanalysis," *Austrian History Yearbook* 36 (2005): 3–39.

migration is really about the attraction of one or another mercantile class or guild to a particularly flourishing city. It does not, however, involve major demographic shifts either in the overall population of the city itself or in the surrounding rural agricultural regions or the broader imperial provinces. From the fifth century to the nineteenth in Western and Central Europe there were important periods of population movement and transfer (including successive waves of migrants from the east), but the continent as a whole retained its predominantly rural character.

The second category of urban migration is what took place in the middle of the nineteenth century and constitutes one of the fundamental elements of European and Jewish modernity. The demographic shifts that occurred in the modern period occured on an unprecedented scale. Cities doubled and tripled in size in single decades. Towns and villages were emptied, and those near to larger urban centers were annexed as suburbs. Trains made it possible to bypass much of the landscape, sidelining the market junctions and rural roadside inns that had long been the social and economic meeting places of the European peasant classes. Economies transformed and expanded, and a professional class came to replace the landed gentry as the political elite. Those who occupied this new social stratum spent their time in offices and at cafés instead of in countryside manor homes and taverns. When we add the relaxation of voting laws and the dissociation of land ownership from political participation at the end of the nineteenth century, we see clearly how wealth—and therefore power—was concentrating in the urban sphere, sidelining the rural estates or manors that had been the heart of the premodern economy. A robust governmental and educational bureaucracy developed alongside these economic shifts, and the autonomy once extended to rural communities was greatly diminished.

No region epitomized the migratory patterns of modernity more than Habsburg Central Europe. Many different peoples moved to Vienna and its new suburbs in the middle of the nineteenth century.[15] At first, they came from the nearer provinces: upper and lower Austria, Slovakia, Bohemia, and Moravia. By the 1870s they were arriving from farther afield: Hungary, Croatia, Bosnia, Silesia. Christian peasants constituted the majority of these migrants, of course, divided among Lutheran Germans, Catholic Austrians and Hungarians, and Orthodox Slavs. Jews, though outsized in their influence and the discourse allotted them in Vienna's intellectual culture, remained a relatively minor percentage of total urban immigrants.[16]

---

15. Not all of them melded into the growing bourgeois culture of the city. See Matthew Rampley, "Peasants in Vienna: Ethnographic Display and the 1873 World's Fair," *Austrian History Yearbook* 42 (2011): 110–32.

16. See Steven Beller, *Vienna and the Jews, 1867–1938: A Cultural History* (Cambridge:

Still, in per capita terms, the number of Jewish migrants in nineteenth-century Central Europe is significant. Most of those who moved did so because of newly enacted emancipatory laws as well as the promises of "embourgeoisement" (as David Sorkin calls it) offered by transformations in all aspects of nineteenth century life.[17] Leopoldstadt, long a neglected outlying region, was one of the first areas to be heavily settled by immigrating provincials in the mid- nineteenth century. But the town already had an interesting early-modern Jewish history.[18] A medieval village located on the islands between the Danube Canal and the Danube River east of the city center, in the sixteenth and seventeenth centuries Leopoldstadt was the only area around Vienna in which Jews could legally reside. From as few as a hundred residents at the beginning of the seventeenth century, by the time of the Edict of Expulsion in 1670 the neighborhood contained as many as two thousand Jewish families.[19] Originally referred to simply as the *Unterer Werd* (roughly "the lower quarter"; in Middle High German: "lower island"), after the 1670 expulsion the town was renamed in honor of Holy Roman Emperor Leopold I (1640–1705), at whose order the Edict was promulgated.[20]

Leopoldstadt's geography—in a floodplain, outside Vienna's defensive fortifications—provides something of a metaphor for the relationship that the capital's poorer Jewish immigrants (as well as many of its other

---

Cambridge University Press, 1998); and Beller, "Patriotism and the National Identity of Habsburg Jewry, 1860–1914," *Leo Baeck Institute Year Book* 41 (1996): 215–38.

17. David Sorkin, *The Transformation of German Jewry, 1780–1840*, Studies in Jewish History (New York: Oxford University Press, 1987). For broader studies of this moment in Austrian and Austrian Jewish history, see Rozenblit, *Jews of Vienna*; Robert A. Kann, *A History of the Habsburg Empire, 1526–1918* (Berkeley: University of California Press, 1980), 318–42; and Simone Lässig, *Jüdische Wege ins Bürgertum: Kulturelles Kapital und sozialer Aufstieg im 19. Jahrhundert*, Bürgertum N.F. 1 (Göttingen: Vandenhoeck & Ruprecht, 2004). For a broad and wide-ranging analysis of transformations in nineteenth-century life generally, see Osterhammel, *Transformation of the World*.

18. For an overview of construction and ordinances in pre-1848 Leopoldstadt (including three re-created survey maps of the suburb and its Danube island region), see Robert Meßner, *Die Leopoldstadt im Vormärz: Historisch-topographische Darstellung der nordöstlichen Vorstädte und Vororte Wiens auf Grund der Katastralvermessung* (Vienna: Wissenschaftlichen Gesellschaften Österreich, 1962). For a general introduction, including a brief account of medieval Jewish settlement in the area before 1670, see Helga Gibs, *Leopoldstadt: Kleine Welt am großen Strom* (Vienna: Mohl, 1997).

19. Gerson Wolf, *Die Juden in der Leopoldstadt ("unterer Werd") im 17. Jahrhundert in Wien* (Vienna: Herzfeld & Bauer, 1864), 3; Wistrich, *Jews of Vienna*, 7. For another history of the Jewish community of pre-1670 Leopoldstadt, see Hans Rotter and Adolf Schmieger, *Das Ghetto in der Wiener Leopoldstadt* (Vienna: Burg, 1926).

20. Kann, *History of the Habsburg Empire*, 125, 189; Gibs, *Leopoldstadt*, 12–13. See John P. Spielman, *Leopold I of Austria* (London: Thames & Hudson, 1977). See also Museum für Naturkunde und Vorgeschichte Dessau, Museum für Stadtgeschichte Dessau, and Museum Schloss Mosigkau, eds., *Fürst Leopold I. von Anhalt-Dessau (1676–1747): "Der Alte Dessauer": Ausstellung Zum 250. Todestag* (Dessau: Die Museen, 1997).

working-class citizens) had with the city's traditional brokers of power. The first new (official) synagogue in Vienna since the Jewish expulsion of 1670 was constructed in 1826 on Seitenstettengasse, in the center of town. Seitenstettengasse was where the chief rabbi presided and the Jewish lay leadership kept its offices.[21] Yet Leopoldstadt was less a satellite of the city center than a unique urban fabric in its own right.[22] With a dense Jewish population by the late nineteenth century, Leopoldstadt remained the home of those Jews who desired to live around other Jews. Well into the latter decades of the nineteenth century, when more neighborhoods were made available for Jewish settlement, Leopoldstadt retained its distinctive mores and conventions. Indeed, while never being more than about 36 percent Jewish, by the turn of the twentieth century the area had gained the nickname *Mazzesinsel* (Matza Island) and remained until the Second World War the Viennese neighborhood with the highest density of Jewish inhabitants.[23]

The Jews in Leopoldstadt came from all across the empire, but in the 1850s and 1860s the largest numbers originated from the Habsburg crown lands of Bohemia and Moravia and rural Austria.[24] Contrary to some accounts, Galician Jews did not arrive in large numbers until the 1880s and 1890s.[25] As Helga Gibs records, the cultural life in Leopoldstadt reflected the desire of its population for upward mobility and entrance into the bourgeois classes. The neighborhood contained the largest dance hall in pre-1848 Vienna; its concert house hosted some of the most famous conductors in Europe; and it was the site of Vienna's Nordbahnhof, one of the city's most important rail terminals.[26] Nonetheless, for many of the

---

21. A history of the Seitenstettengasse Synagogue (or Stadttempel), as well of the slow Jewish migration back into Vienna after the 1670 expulsion, is recounted in Wistrich, *Jews of Vienna*, 3–61. A catalogue of religious objects and essays on the Jewish community of Vienna is Karl Albrecht-Weinberger and Felicitas Heimann-Jelinek, eds., *Judentum in Wien: "Heilige Gemeinde Wien"* (Vienna: Museen der Stadt Wien, 1987).

22. This was similarly true for places like Berlin. See Kristin Poling, "Shantytowns and Pioneers beyond the City Wall: Berlin's Urban Frontier in the Nineteenth Century," *Central European History* 47, no. 2 (2014): 245–74; and Eli Rubin, "From the Grünen Wiesen to Urban Space: Berlin, Expansion, and the Longue Durée," *Central European History* 47, no. 2 (2014): 221–44.

23. Rozenblit, *Jews of Vienna*, 78. See also Ruth Beckermann, ed., *Die Mazzesinsel: Juden in der Wiener Leopoldstadt, 1918–1938* (Vienna: Löcker, 1984).

24. Robert Waissenberger, "Judentum in Wien bis 1938," in Albrecht-Weinberger and Heimann-Jelinek, *Judentum in Wien*, 18–28.

25. See Israel Bartal and Antony Polonsky, "Introduction: The Jews of Galicia under the Habsburgs," in *Focusing on Galicia: Jews, Poles, and Ukrainians, 1772–1918*, ed. Israel Bartal and Antony Polonsky (London: Littman Library of Jewish Civilization, 1999), 3–24.

26. Gibs, *Leopoldstadt*, 30–44. See Klaus Hödl, *Als Bettler in die Leopoldstadt: Galizische Juden auf dem Weg nach Wien*, Böhlaus zeitgeschichtliche Bibliothek 27 (Vienna: Böhlau, 1994). Robert Wistrich argues that, before 1880, it seems unlikely that the largest percentage of Jews

Jews in Leopoldstadt, some form of traditionalism remained the more natural religious disposition.²⁷

The Idea and Aesthetics of the Monumental Synagogue

As remarkable as Jewish acculturation to the urban milieu in the middle decades of the nineteenth century were the religious reforms implemented and institutions established by the migrants. Within only a few years after 1848, Jews had created a functional communal bureaucracy that supported a vibrant religious and educational infrastructure.²⁸ Especially important were Jewish reforms of two of the main institutions of rabbinic Judaism: the rabbi and the synagogue. These changes sought to ensure the survival of a type of rabbinic Judaism that proved to be a fascinating and somewhat haphazard mixture of the traditional and the modern. In one way, the reforms of the mid-nineteenth century maintained the centuries-long habits and attitudes of Jews toward their traditional leadership and texts. In another, they fundamentally reshaped this inheritance in many and unique ways. Essential for this new sort of rabbinic Judaism were the construction of monumental communal synagogues and the formation of a clergy to specifically preside within them. Jewish religious communities in the 1850s were the first to experiment with this union of synagogue and rabbi, bringing together two historic institutions of Judaism that had formerly been quite separate, such that by the turn of the century, for most Jews in Central and Western Europe, it had become impossible to imagine the rabbi and the synagogue apart.

---

to migrate to Vienna were so-called "Ostjuden" from Galicia (*Jews of Vienna*, 43). The Nordbahnhof opened in 1838. It was rebuilt in 1865 in magnificent style. For a history of the terminal and its surrounding neighborhood, see Evelyn Klein and Gustav Glaser, *Peripherie in der Stadt: Das Wiener Nordbahnviertel – Einblicke, Erkundungen, Analysen* (Innsbruck: Studien, 2000). During the Second World War the Nordbahnhof became the main site for the deportation of Vienna's Jewish community. After receiving heavy damage during Allied bombing in the final months of the war, the station fell into disrepair and was torn down in 1965. The new Wien Nord station was built a few blocks south, on the Praterstern roundabout.

27. Waissenberger, "Judentum in Wien"; Hödl, *Als Bettler in die Leopoldstadt*, 147–65.

28. As Jonathan Hess has observed, "Religious reform was the avenue Jews often chose in which to seize political agency for themselves, reclaiming the Jewish tradition as their own in such a way as to issue fundamental challenges to Protestant Orientalism and the politics of civic improvement alike" (*Germans, Jews and the Claims of Modernity*, 17). For a similar discussion of the internal dialogue of the Jewish community toward questions of modernity, see Moshe Zimmermann, "Zukunftserwartungen der deutsch-jüdischen Gesellschaft im langen 19. Jahrhundert," *Aschkenas: Zeitschrift für Geschichte und Kultur der Juden* 18/19 (2008/2009): 25–39.

This shift in the rabbi's role in the 1850s and following was subtle but profound. As discussed in depth in the following chapter, the eighteenth and nineteenth centuries witnessed the reimagined definition of religion and the place of God, theology, and ritual practice in European culture. Adopting these definitions, urbanizing Jews in Central Europe reshaped the figure of the rabbi into that of public religious authority. No longer was the rabbi primarily an arbiter of civil law, concerned with such things as contracts between shopkeepers or monetary loans. In the modern city the rabbi became a minister and a preacher, the exemplar of theological virtue and traditional teaching, emphasizing religious practices based in the synagogue and focusing on the ritualization of events in the life cycles of individuals, families, and national communities. Through the new practice of the weekly sermon, the rabbi became both communal pedagogue and modern prophet, responsible for interpreting contemporary events through the lens of classical Jewish texts.

Likewise, in the new urban spaces of the nineteenth century, the synagogue was similarly reimagined, and urban Jewish communities created a new language about the value, authenticity, and sacredness of their synagogues.[29] No longer a small, local gathering place for men to pray, it became the central institution embodying the practices and beliefs of Jewish civilization. Often called a "Temple" by German Jews, the term drew upon the special relationship developed in the Bible between the Land of Israel, the Temple in Jerusalem, and the Jewish people. Reworking that formula, German and Habsburg Jews began to speak about their synagogues as permanent homes for the presence of God, rather than as mere prayer spaces looking toward an idealized future in the promised land. Projecting the bourgeois project of family and hearth onto the synagogue, middle-class Jews in Central Europe idealized their new synagogues as permanent dwelling places, the final stop on the Jews' two-millennia-long diasporic journey.

On the one hand, these new synagogue buildings were merely expressions of newfound wealth, a confidence in the long-term viability of liberal reforms and their protection of Jewish citizenship. On the other, the buildings invited (and dictated) a different sort of synagogue practice from that previously fostered by Jewish religious spaces.[30] By the end of the century, the synagogue was a centerpiece of communal religious experience, with the rabbi creating a tone and language about its meaning

---

29. See William G. Tachau, "The Architecture of the Synagogue," *American Jewish Year Book* 28 (1926–1927): 155–92, esp. 189–92.

30. As Saskia Coenen Snyder writes, "Before [the late nineteenth century], 'being Jewish' was not defined by attendance at a synagogue.... The synagogue building itself played only a marginal role in Jewish life" (*Building a Public Judaism: Synagogues and Jewish Identity in Nineteenth-Century Europe* [Cambridge: Harvard University Press, 2013], 3).

that differed dramatically from anything previously expressed in Jewish religious discourse. By looking closely at the architecture and discourse around the new synagogue in Vienna, we can get a sense of broader trends in Central European Judaism in the middle of the nineteenth century.

On May 18, 1858, a year and a half into Jellinek's rabbinic tenure, a new synagogue was dedicated in the Leopoldstadt neighborhood of Vienna.[31] Eponymously named the Leopoldstadt Temple (Leopoldstädter Tempel), the building was located on Wallisch Gasse (now called Tempelgasse) and was (until its destruction on November 9, 1938, *Kristallnacht*) one of the grandest of Vienna's Jewish houses of worship, representing the beginning of an era of wealth, affluence, and stability for the community.[32] The Leopoldstadt Temple was among the first of the great monumental urban synagogues in Europe, "mediating," writes Saskia Coenen Snyder, "Jewishness in a modern society, announcing the cultural sophistication, bourgeois affluence, and religious respectability of the Jewish community."[33] Commissioned by the Viennese community, the synagogue was designed by the non-Jewish German-born Viennese architect Ludwig von Förster (1797–1863), who, though now known mainly for his majestic synagogue designs, was at the time a familiar and respected architect to the non-Jewish Habsburg elite.[34] Förster contributed greatly to the plans for Vienna's mid-century reconstruction and was the father of Emil von Förster (1838–1909), who designed a number of important buildings on

---

31. See Siegel, "Temple in Leopoldstadt," 109–23.
32. For overviews of these new modern urban synagogues, see Bob Martens and Herbert Peter, *Die zerstörten Synagogen Wiens: Virtuelle Stadtspaziergänge* (Vienna: Mandelbaum, 2009), 21–30; Carol H. Krinsky, *Synagogues of Europe: Architecture, History, Meaning* (Cambridge: MIT Press, 1985), 191–95; and Snyder, *Building a Public Judaism*. Anthony Alofsin writes that, to correctly interpret the historical import of building forms, we must assume "that [the] social and political forces of architecture are transmitted through [a building's] physical form and that the two inseparably create a dialectical realism. In other words, the visual manifestation of architecture—its space, light, color, texture, pattern—and its social and historical context must be considered inseparable if we, as receptors, are to grasp the messages of buildings." He calls this sort of analysis "contextual formalism" (*When Buildings Speak. Architecture as Language in the Habsburg Empire and Its Aftermath, 1867–1933* [Chicago: University of Chicago Press, 2006], 11). For a history of the early modern urban synagogue, see Barry L. Stiefel, "The Architectural Origins of the Great Early Modern Urban Synagogue," *Leo Baeck Institute Year Book* 56 (2011): 105–34. For an account of architectural culture concerning synagogue construction during the nineteenth century, see Helen Rosenau, "Gottfried Semper and German Synagogue Architecture," *Leo Baeck Institute Year Book* 22 (1977): 237–44.
33. Snyder, *Building a Public Judaism*, 2.
34. Förster's best-known synagogues are the Leopoldstädter Tempel in Vienna (dedicated 1858); the Dohány Street Synagogue in Budapest (also called the Great Synagogue, dedicated 1859); and the Kazinczy Street Synagogue of Miskolc, Hungary (dedicated 1862). The latter two remain standing, and all three were constructed in neo-Byzantine/Moorish-revival style. See Kinga Frojimovics and Géza Komoróczy, *Jewish Budapest: Monuments, Rites, History* (Budapest: Central European University Press, 1999), 107–8.

the Ringstraße.[35] In commissioning so esteemed an architect (and by having the commission accepted), the Viennese community was signifying not only that its new synagogue was to be the equal of the other grand buildings of modern Vienna, but also that Jews could match the fine taste, elegance, and aesthetic sophistication of their gentile neighbors—and that they could afford to.[36]

With the push toward monumentality, a problem arose: except for the Bible's descriptions of Solomon's Jerusalem Temple (and the Talmudic rabbis' attempts to define its precise dimensions), Judaism possessed no overriding historical precedent for important communal architecture. This peculiar absence was an acute issue for the Jewish communities of Europe's nineteenth-century cities, especially at a time when governments across the continent were investing enormous sums in construction projects and architects were experimenting with new forms of design and material. The Leopoldstadt Temple was, therefore, part of a growing movement to define a distinctly Jewish style of synagogue architecture.

Searching for a model for their buildings beyond the borders of northern Europe—where the symbolic representation of religion came mainly in the form of Romanesque and Gothic cathedrals—these new bourgeois Jewish communities looked both outward and backward for inspiration.[37] Whereas Ismar Schorsch argues that the memory of Jewish Spain and its

---

35. Janine Burke gives a brief account of Ludwig Förster's role in the building of the Ringstraße as well as some common perceptions of Leopoldstadt (*The Sphinx on the Table: Sigmund Freud's Art Collection and the Development of Psychoanalysis* [New York: Walker, 2006], 28–30).

36. Vienna was one of the first cities in Europe to dedicate a monumental communal synagogue. Berlin's golden-domed Oranienburgerstraße Synagoge—perhaps the most famous example of this sort of grand Jewish architecture in Central Europe—was only completed in 1866. Often an even longer period elapsed between the dedication of the Leopoldstädter and similar edifices in other national capitals. Though Vienna was only one year ahead of Budapest (Dohány Street Synagogue, dedicated 1859 [they shared an architect]), it was fourteen years ahead of New York (Central Synagogue, 1872), sixteen years ahead of Paris (rue de la Victoire and rue des Tournelles, dedicated 1874 and 1876, respectively), nineteen years ahead of London (West End Synagogue, dedicated 1879), and forty-six years ahead of Rome (Tempio Maggiore di Roma, dedicated 1904). Despite their magnificence, Snyder warns against seeing monumental synagogues as the normative model for Jewish bourgeois self-expression: "Plurality and variability, rather than the monumental Moorish model, characterized the landscape of nineteenth-century synagogue building" (*Building a Public Judaism*, 3). For a more comprehensive review of synagogue architecture, see Harold Hammer-Schenk, *Synagogen in Deutschland: Geschichte einer Baugattung im 19. und 20. Jahrhundert (1780–1933)*, 2 vols. (Hamburg: Christians, 1981).

37. See John M. Efron, *German Jewry and the Allure of the Sephardic* (Princeton, NJ: Princeton University Press, 2016). The book jacket features an image of the then newly built synagogue on Gottschedstraße in Leipzig, presided over by Jellinek before he left for Vienna. See also Ivan D. Kalmar, "Moorish Style: Orientalism, the Jews, and Synagogue Architecture," *Jewish Social Studies* 7, no. 3 (2001): 68–100.

civilizational accomplishments could explain the new synagogue style that flourished in the mid- to late nineteenth century, Ivan Kalmar argues that the turn toward "Moorish" style was associated with German Jews' embrace of their Eastern heritage.[38] In what became an unusually common and widespread choice, Jewish communities in Europe and North America commissioned structures that invoked the memory of Moorish-dominated Spain. Kalmar writes, "Throughout much of the nineteenth century, many Jews confidently asserted their 'Oriental' origins and their 'Oriental' race."[39]

The memory of Sephardic Spain, with its amalgam of secular languages, biblical philosophy, and Jewish literary creativity, suggested that, inside the Moorish walls of the Leopoldstadt Temple and its siblings across the continent, Jewish communities could experience a type of Judaism new to Central Europe. Again, as Schorsch has noted, the turn toward Spain by Jewish intellectuals of the Haskalah and *Wissenschaft* was as much a rejection of yeshiva Judaism (centered on the memorization and practice of religious law) as an embrace of a historically accurate accounting of Judaism in Islamic Iberia.[40] In the case of synagogue architecture of the mid-nineteenth century, the design choice of neo-Islamic style might well have been as much about a critique of Eastern European Jews (with their makeshift synagogues and dark interiors) and Christians (whose Gothic masterpieces symbolized many centuries of anti-Jewish repression) as about a turn toward the embrace of a mythic Spanish renaissance.[41] Yet,

---

38. Ismar Schorsch writes, "The appeal of Moorish architecture for the emancipated synagogue derived from its Spanish connection. It answered the need for a distinctive style precisely because it dovetailed so completely with the overriding Spanish bias of German Jewry. There was nothing oriental about the Arabs; without them Greek philosophy would never have reached the West. One was fully entitled to draw on the inspiration of Spain to renovate both the interior and the exterior of the synagogue. What more powerful symbol of the rupture with [pre-emancipation] culture than to build synagogues in the spirit of Spain!" ("The Myth of Sephardic Supremacy," *Leo Baeck Institute Year Book* 34 [1989]: 47–66, here 57).

39. Kalmar, "Moorish Style," 70. See also Carsten Schapkow, *Vorbild und Gegenbild: Das ibirische Judentum in der deutsch-jüdischen Erinnerungkultur, 1779–1939* (Cologne: Böhlau, 2011). As an important corrective to Schapkow's work, see the book review by Florian Krobb, "Vorbild und Gegenbild: Das ibirische Judentum in der deutsch-jüdischen Erinnerungskultur 1779–1939 (review)," *Shofar: An Interdisciplinary Journal of Jewish Studies* 31, no. 4 (2013): 127–30.

40. "As construed by Ashkenazic intellectuals, the Sephardic image facilitated a religious posture marked by cultural openness, philosophic thinking, and an appreciation for the aesthetic. Like many an historical myth, it evoked a partial glimpse of a bygone age determined and colored by [contemporary] social need" (Schorsch, "Myth of Sephardic Supremacy," 47). He continues, "Advocacy of secular education, the curbing of talmudic exclusivity and the resumption of studies in Hebrew grammar, biblical exegesis, and Jewish philosophy, and the search for historical exemplars led to a quick rediscovery of Spanish models and achievements" (49–50).

41. According to Olga Bush, "The Jewish turn to neo-Islamic architecture ... identified

for someone like Jellinek, whose studies of Kabbalah already suggested a propensity for modeling contemporary problems on (a belief in) a more philosophically "open" Sephardic past, the Moorish aesthetic offered in bricks and mortar just such an example of a different sort of Jewish reform.

The building designed by Förster for the Leopoldstadt Temple fit the model of these new Sephardic-inspired imaginings and in part was meant to evoke the image of Solomon's Temple in Jerusalem. Förster's building had "[h]orseshoe arches and wiry cast-iron columns," an eastern wall "articulated with a monumental arch," and two minaret-like turrets framing the front entranceway.[42] If the Jews of Spain under the caliphate, and the exiled Sephardim of Amsterdam, Constantinople, London, and elsewhere, had remained true to the traditional threads of rabbinic Judaism, then it surely seemed plausible that the Ashkenazi Jews of Vienna could likewise retain a balance between secular culture and traditional religion.[43]

In attempting to explain why the 1850s, specifically, were witness to this turn toward monumentality in synagogue architecture, Olga Bush focuses on both the social and religious considerations of acculturating German Jews, writing that, by ceasing to imagine Jews as in exile, and excising traditional liturgical language calling for the return of the Jerusalem Temple service, the Reform movement "motivated the creation of synagogues as sumptuous spaces, where the worshipers did not have to mourn any longer, but rather could rejoice with music and singing."[44] Following a similar line of reasoning, Michael A. Meyer argued that the use of the word *Gotteshaus* by nineteenth-century Jewish communal leaders (instead of the word "synagogue") signaled a larger attempt by acculturating Jews to pair the social roles of the synagogue with that of the Christian church.[45] Indeed, both the words *Tempel* and *Gotteshaus* func-

---

the Jews themselves as 'oriental,' though the ideological values were thereby inverted: the implicit claim was that the Jews were in the 'Orient,' indeed were the 'Orient,' long before the arrival of British steamships, and that their continuing presence in Europe stood as a reminder that not only was the 'Orient' civilized before Europe, but also European civilization itself was built on that 'oriental' foundation." ("The Architecture of Jewish Identity: The Neo-Islamic Central Synagogue of New York," *Journal of the Society of Architectural Historians* 63, no. 2 [2004]: 193–94.) See also Ivan D. Kalmar and Derek J. Penslar, eds., *Orientalism and the Jews*, Tauber Institute Series for the Study of European Jewry (Waltham, MA: Brandeis University Press, 2005).

42. H. A. Meek, *The Synagogue* (London: Phaidon, 1995), 189.

43. An almost identical copy of the Leopoldstädter Tempel was constructed a few years later (1864–1866) in the Romanian capital of Bucharest (Romanian: *Bucureşti*). See Krinsky, *Synagogues of Europe*, 153–54.

44. Bush, "Architecture of Jewish Identity," 193.

45. Michael A. Meyer, "'How Awesome is this Place!' The Reconceptualization of the Synagogue in Nineteenth-Century Germany," *Leo Baeck Institute Year Book* 41 (1996): 51–63, here 56–57. As Meyer describes it, "For millennia the Jewish distinction had been temporal, not spatial, especially between the Sabbath and the rest of the week. In re-introducing

tioned to distinguish the modern synagogue from its historic precursors, the house of prayer (*beit* tefilla) or the house of study (*beit midrash*). This was a conscious theological move, made apparent in the various sermons and pamphlets published around the dedication of each new communal synagogue.

The link between the new Jewish houses of worship and the Jerusalem Temple was a way of solidifying and proclaiming Jewish gains in the realm of civil rights, a connection not, in fact, altogether misguided. Following 1848, and especially 1867, the social and civil status of Jews in Europe was more equal to that of non-Jews than it had ever been under Christian political domination. Not since Jewish autonomy during the century of Hasmonean rule in Judea had so many Jews possessed equivalent freedoms under law. Europe in the middle of the nineteenth century really did appear to be on the cusp of fundamental change.

Jellinek's Dedication of the Leopoldstadt Temple

The newfound centrality of the synagogue in congregational life made it all the more essential that the monumentality and physical experience of the synagogue convey something about the beliefs and attitudes of the community that inhabited it. We can observe the development of just such a language in Jellinek's dedication of the Leopoldstadt Temple in 1858, as well in some of his other dedicatory addresses.[46] In his dedicatory sermon in Leopoldstadt, Jellinek made the rhetorical distinction between the "*alten Bethaus*" (the old prayer house) and the new Temple. The latter, he said, was like the rebuilding of the destroyed Temple in Jerusalem.[47] In almost every way, this was a historically unprecedented connection. The Temple in Jerusalem had been more than just a space for communal prayer, more than just a sign of the relationship between God and Israel. As the biblical narrative recounts (see 1 Kings 8:12–13, 29–30), Jerusalem was a home for

---

spatial sanctity, the preachers were not simply following the cultural code of contemporary Christianity, they were returning to the paradigm of ancient Judaism and, consciously or not, describing their new houses of worship more on the model of the Temple than on that of Diaspora houses of prayer" (59). Snyder likewise comments on this transformation, see Snyder, *Building a Public Judaism*, 5-6, esp. n. 10.

46. See Adolf Jellinek, *Zwei Reden zur Schlußsteinlegung und zur Einweihung des neuen israelitischen Tempels in der Leopoldstadt am 18. Mai und 15. Juni 1858* (Vienna: Knöpflmacher, 1858). See also Jellinek, *Rede zur Einweihung des israelitischen Tempels in Iglau, am 9. September 1863 (25. Elul 5623)* (Vienna: Bendiner & Schloßberg, 1863); and Jellinek, *Zur Feier des fünfzigjährigen Jubiläums des israelitischen Tempels in der inner Stadt Wien. Zwei Reden am 26. März (1. Nisan 5636) und 9. April (1. Tage des Passah festes 1876)* (Vienna: Winter, 1876).

47. Jellinek, *Zwei Reden zur Schlußsteinlegung*, 10.

God, an abode on Earth where God's enduring presence could be sought day and night. For the Bible, Jerusalem is unique in the world. (The term *sanctuary*, often used in American synagogues to denote the prayer space, has some of the same theological connotations as the German *Tempel*.)

Yet, by resuscitating the term *temple* and by comparing the new synagogue in Vienna to its Solomonic predecessor in Jerusalem, Jellinek was doing much more than being rhetorically effusive. He was, instead, one of the early creators of an entirely new language of Jewish religious expression, one that imagined Jewish civil rights in a changing Europe as the harbinger of a new historical epoch. His words at the dedication were not mere German nationalism—Jews were not full citizens in Austria yet, and few of those who worshiped at these new synagogues had grown up in culturally German households. Instead, this theological rhetoric was aspirational, forward looking, and to some degree messianic. It was also self-justifying, reaching into the Jewish past for a language that would validate and rationalize Jewish desires in the present. A few years after Leopoldstadt, at the opening of the new Temple in Iglau (Moravia) in 1863, Jellinek would say, "From the nearby small towns the Jewish landowners gathered in the district, towns whose 'Palestine' counted twenty [families], ... and] under flute playing and Psalm singing raised themselves a Temple of Jerusalem."[48]

In his sermon for the Leopoldstadt Temple, Jellinek used the metaphor of a holy rock to describe the new building, a symbol of God's enduring presence in physical space, "Yes, this stone, which is to form the keystone of this House, has sprung from Zion's holy and consecrated ground," he proclaimed.[49] Jellinek called the new synagogue building a "Stein des göttlichen Beistandes," a stone of divine assistance, a somewhat poetic translation of a scene from 1 Samuel 7:12: "Then Samuel set up a stone ... and he called it by the name *even ha-azer* [stone of assistance], and he said, 'So far has God helped us.'" Indeed, the Bible is full of stone monuments signifying the eternal, benevolent presence of God in the life of Israel.[50] Following on these biblical examples, Jellinek's phrase "a stone of divine assistance" was not only a hope that the Jewish experience in a new liberal Austria was long and enduring. The biblical Samuel set his stone in the sacred ground of the Land of Israel, to stand for all time as a sign of God's enduring care for the People of Israel. So, too, the modern Jellinek was setting a stone into the ground, in a new Europe, a rebirthed Europe,

---

48. Jellinek, *Predigten*, 3:120.
49. Jellinek, *Zwei Reden zur Schlußsteinlegung*, 4.
50. Jacob at Beth El (Genesis 28); Jacob meeting Esau (Genesis 31); Moses at Sinai (Exodus 24); Moses's instructions for the conquest of Canaan (Deuteronomy 27) Joshua across the Jordan (Joshua 4); Samuel at Mizpah (1 Samuel 7); and Solomon at his Temple (1 Kings 7).

whose extension of liberty to the Jews was akin to the fulfillment of the biblical promise of a stable, prosperous homeland. It was a radical theological repositioning, an appropriation of a divine sacredness previously meant only for the Land of Israel but here placed on the soils of Central Europe. Not only were the Jews no longer in diaspora, Jellinek appeared to be saying, they were no longer even threatened as they had always been. The new synagogue was a monument to the continued protection of the Jews by God, one that extended well beyond the limits of the biblical lands and would endure forever.

The idea that a new synagogue was a holy space, something as profound as a stand-in for the ancient Temple in Jerusalem, expressed the liberal idea that the Jews were a separate yet equal people living peaceably among the various nations of Europe. The yearning for Zion remained liturgically important, but, just as God had followed Israel into exile in the sixth century BCE, so too, then, this language implied that God resided among the Jews in their European homeland. As Jellinek said:

> On this land a house of God rises, which—according to the saying of the ancients—is called like Benjamin: a friend, a favorite, and a chosen one of God. And so the annals of the Jews of Austria praise and glorify God as the favorite, and about their gracious sovereign it is now proven by scripture: *ha-'asiri yihje kodesch la-Adonai* (Lev. 27:32), 'the tenth year of his reign is holy to the Lord.'[51]

In this remarkable rhetorical display, Jellinek interwove the tenth year of Franz Joseph's reign over Austria (1848–1858) with the founding of the Leopoldstadt Temple and God's guidance of Israel in the desert. Jellinek was saying: just as the Jews built for themselves a home in Vienna, so too they built a home for their God; and just as the holy texts honor the Jewish nation, so too do they speak about the glory of the king who rules over the Jews—even though that king be not a Jew himself. If traditionally, then, God had only one house, and it was in Jerusalem, now, with the reimagining of the synagogue as a place for God's continued domestic presence, Judaism's distinct rituals could be reconciled with the Christian understanding of an ever-present and accessible God. With Europe's turn toward liberalism, and the promise of a lasting peace between the Christian nations and their Jewish minorities, the permanence of the Jewish presence in the lands outside Zion could, finally, be firmly established.

---

51. Jellinek, *Zwei Reden zur Schlußsteinlegung*, 12.

The Vienna Rite

Debate over what sort of Judaism would be practiced inside the new synagogue in Leopoldstadt offers a picture of ideological moderation in an age of increasingly caustic neo-denominational quarrels. In the opening decades of the nineteenth century, liturgical reforms became the focus of community disagreements across German-speaking Central Europe.[52] Reformers emphasized changes to the wording of prayers, often including numerous readings in the vernacular, and even excising long portions of the historic text.[53] A distinct yet similarly motived set of ritual modifications came in the realm of music, perhaps the most contentious of which were the introduction of the organ and formal choirs. But to a lesser degree also came changes in traditional melodies, the influence of classical and ecclesiastical traditions in solo and ensemble singing, and the increasing disregard for the halakhic problems of word repetition. Yet we must see liturgical reforms as part of a larger set of institutional and religious changes accompanying Jewish modernity. For example, in 1800 the prayer book was a vessel for religious expression. By 1900, it was often one of the few commonalities holding fractured communities together.

In Vienna, as noted, Jellinek arrived just as the community was growing from a small, cohesive group of families into a network of sprawling immigrant neighborhoods and divergent religious traditions. Carol Krinsky comments that the Leopoldstadt Temple was built with space for an organ but "the fact that the congregation did not use [it] ... showed that the more liberal Jews wanted to come to terms with the more orthodox."[54] The rabbi in charge of communal affairs in Vienna, Isak Noa Mannheimer, was thoroughly against inclusion of an organ, on the grounds that it was too Christian,[55] though he was not against music innovations altogether. In 1826 he invited Salomon Sulzer (1804–1890) to become chief cantor (*chazan*), a man widely known for his interest in modernizing the music aspects of prayer along the lines of moderate reform. Importantly, it was

---

52. See David Ellenson, "The *Israelitische Gebetbücher* of Abraham Geiger and Manuel Joël: A Study in Nineteenth-Century German-Jewish Communal Liturgy and Religion," *Leo Baeck Institute Year Book* 44 (1999): 143–64. See Jakob Josef Petuchowski, *Prayerbook Reform in Europe: The Liturgy of European Liberal and Reform Judaism* (New York: World Union for Progressive Judaism, 1968). See also Goldschmidt, "Studies on Jewish Liturgy," 119–35.

53. See, e.g., Daniel Frank and Matt Goldish, "Rabbinic Culture and Dissent: An Overview," in *Rabbinic Culture and Its Critics: Jewish Authority, Dissent, and Heresy in Medieval and Early Modern Times*, ed. Daniel Frank and Matt Goldish (Detroit: Wayne State University Press, 2008), 1–53, here 38.

54. Krinsky, *Synagogues of Europe*, 194. The other synagogues Förster designed also either included or had space for an organ.

55. For a further discussion of the controversy over organs in synagogues, see David Ellenson, "A Disputed Precedent: The Prague Organ in Nineteenth-Century Central-European Legal Literature and Polemics," *Leo Baeck Institute Year Book* 40 (1995): 251–64.

under Mannheimer's tenure that Vienna embarked in the 1830s and 1840s on a series of small but meaningful liturgical reforms (together called the "Vienna Rite"). Mannheimer preached weekly in the Stadttempel even before Jellinek's arrival. Yet both Nikolaus Vielmetti and Marsha Rozenblit note that reform came slowly to the Stadttempel.[56] While nearly all of the Jews who lived in the Habsburg capital before 1848 were from the more affluent professions, and generally more welcoming of religious change, they resisted the radical reforms being implemented in other German-speaking cities.[57]

The entire creation and evolution of the Vienna Rite itself represent a deeply conflicted view about the meaning and practice of modern Jewish religion. Mannheimer, whose education spanned both the religious and the secular, was hired in 1825 specifically for his interest in creating a synagogue ritual that could respond to the liberal urban cosmopolitanism that Vienna's Jews hoped to make their own.[58] What made Mannheimer attractive to the Viennese Jews was his knowledge not of theology or religious law but of contemporary non-Jewish learning.[59] As part of

---

56. Nikolaus Vielmetti, "Reform und Tradition im Neuen Stadttempel in der Seitenstettengasse zu Wien," in Albrecht-Weinberger and Heimann-Jelinek, *Judentum in Wien*, 30–34; Rozenblit, "Jewish Identity and the Modern Rabbi," 106.

57. For a history of the Reform movement in Germany, see Michael A. Meyer, *Response to Modernity: A History of the Reform Movement in Judaism* (Oxford: Oxford University Press, 1988). For a specific case study, see Andreas Brämer, "The Dialectics of Religious Reform: The *Hamburger Israelitische Tempel* in Its Local Context, 1817–1938," *Leo Baeck Institute Year Book* 48 (2003): 25–37; see also Brämer, "The Dilemmas of Moderate Reform: Some Reflections on the Development of Conservative Judaism in Germany, 1840–1880," *Jewish Studies Quarterly* 10 (2003): 73–87.

58. For a specific discussion of Mannheimer's debts to Christianity in his style of sermon, see Alexander Altmann, "The New Style of Preaching in Nineteenth-Century German Jewry," in *Studies in Nineteenth-Century Jewish Intellectual History*, ed. Alexander Altmann, Philip W. Lown Institute of Advanced Judaic Studies, Brandeis University: Studies and Texts 2 (1964; repr., Cambridge: Harvard University Press, 2013), 65–116, esp. 71–72 and 79–80. See also Rozenblit, "Jewish Assimilation in Habsburg Vienna," 225–45, esp. 228.

59. See Benjamin Maria Baader, *Gender, Judaism, and Bourgeois Culture in Germany, 1800–1870*, Modern Jewish Experience (Bloomington: Indiana University Press, 2006), 188: "Born in Copenhagen in 1793 and raised there, he had attended a university in Denmark at a time when his colleagues in Germany had only rarely received a formal secular education." The entire paragraph from which this is taken is also important: "Rabbis and preachers presided at the life-cycle events of the men, women, and children in their communities, overseeing confirmations, weddings, and funerals. For many, Talmudic study no longer played a central role. Isaac [sic] Noa Mannheimer in Vienna, for instance, readily admitted that his rabbinic learning was limited. Born in Copenhagen in 1793 and raised there, he had attended a university in Denmark at a time when his colleagues in Germany had only rarely received a formal secular education. Yet Mannheimer had no intention of standing out as a modern Jewish scholar. He did not understand himself primarily as a man of learning. From 1824 to 1865, he served the Jewish community in Vienna as a preacher, delivering sermons at the Vienna temple with passion and in a distinct personal style. Mannheimer took pride in the

Mannheimer's program of modernization, he made the German-language sermon a standard practice in the Vienna Rite. But he likewise published a prayer book in 1840 that contained no reform to the liturgy whatsoever. This was a typical (though ultimately short-term) religious compromise, adding German elements while retaining the older Hebrew traditions.[60] The Vienna Rite remained central to the Viennese community's sense of identity and cohesion well into the final decade of the nineteenth century.

There is a clear relationship between the writings of Isak Noa Mannheimer while he was head of the Viennese community and those of Jellinek upon his arrival in the Habsburg capital. But as we will see in the coming chapters, the sermons Jellinek delivered during his years in Leopoldstadt revealed him to be much interested in transformational ideas, in adapting tradition and arguing for its relevance, rather than in obsessing over the minutiae of ritual reform. Unlike Jellinek's contemporary Michael Sachs, who introduced Talmudic and rabbinic references into his sermons in "his desire to revive the true 'spirit' of Judaism, which he [saw as] throttled by a misconceived enlightenment,"[61] Jellinek embraced *Wissenschaft*-style discourse as the key to the continuation (or even rejuvenation) of rabbinic texts in the religious life of German Jewry. Jellinek's writings were deeply empathic toward those who sought a continuation with the more conservative past, yet likewise focused with intensity and nuance on the present. In Leopoldstadt, Jellinek became intimately concerned with finding a way to mediate between *Wissenschaft* ideas and the historical practices and ethics that he believed formed the core of traditional Judaism.

As we have seen, the nineteenth-century reconnection with the memory and meaning of Solomon's Jerusalem Temple was part of a larger intellectual transformation shaping modern German Judaism, one that fundamentally reoriented traditional religious practice away from the home and toward the built communal environment and the figure of the rabbi. In other words, just as the physical space of the synagogue was transforming in the nineteenth century, so too was the conception of the synagogue's role in ritual life. With the Enlightenment's growing influence in the intellectual world of Central Europe, a discourse of morality came to dominate discussions of religion, and Jews began to see something pedagogical in the beauty of the synagogue.[62] In the coming chapters we will analyze in

---

popularity he enjoyed as a public speaker, but even more than his preaching he prized being a *Seelsorger*, spiritual counselor, and intimate friend of his congregants."

60. See Rozenblit, "Jewish Identity and the Modern Rabbi," 105–6.
61. Altmann, "New Style of Preaching," 85.
62. See Meyer, "'How Awesome Is This Place!,'" 62: "The old synagogue had failed in this task, the beautiful new one, with its aesthetic appeal to the cultured tastes of the congregation, would succeed. But it was not only a matter of aesthetics, for in the eyes of at least

greater detail how, alongside the revival of the imagery and special holiness of the Solomonic Temple, there arose, in the writings and sermons of Jellinek, a moralization of history, an accentuation of ethics within the core narrative of religious development in the West. The new synagogue building expressed not only the economic and social security of the Jewish community but also the moral uprightness and wisdom of the Jewish people, its glorious philosophical and aesthetic past, and its ability to embrace and promote the deepest insights and cultural flowerings of the present.

---

one preacher the physical characteristics of the synagogue were themselves the transmitters of religious and moral messages. They were the external representation of internal qualities."

7

Tradition and Change in the Rabbinic Persona: Jellinek's Context and Innovations in Vienna

[W]hat concerns us most is the ideal that inspired Jellinek, that lay behind all his work, that guided and goaded him in all his diverse rabbinical activities. For an appreciation of Jellinek's ideal might well help us to answer a question, which is often asked today, namely, What should be the ideal of a modern rabbi?
—H. G. Enelow, *The Jew and the World* (1921)

A New Rabbinic Persona

Sometime between 1800 and 1900, the role of the rabbi changed dramatically. Scholars have long noted the shifting role of the rabbinate in Jewish society. The two major writers in the first half of the twentieth century who came to define the long history of modern Jewry—Simon Dubnow and Salo W. Baron—focused on economics, culture, and communal structure. Their narrative of the rabbinate traced its slow decline in the modern world, a movement from relevance to irrelevance. No comprehensive history of the modern rabbinate has been written with the nineteenth-century transformation at its forefront. Simon Schwarzfuchs gave a broad historical overview, but the causal mechanisms for rabbinical change remained unexamined.[1]

While the majority of Central European Jews openly embraced the promises of emancipation and integration, these same Jews on the whole remained devoted to many aspects of Jewish religious practice, albeit in new forms adapted to their new situations. No longer was Judaism

---

1. Schwarzfuchs, *Concise History of the Rabbinate*. See also Andrea Bieler, *Die Sehnsucht nach dem verlorenen Himmel: Jüdische und christliche Reflexionen zu Gottesdienstreform und Predigtkultur im 19. Jahrhundert*, Praktische Theologie heute 65 (Stuttgart: Kohlhammer, 2003).

primarily lived in the household through ritual and pattern. Suddenly, Judaism was lived mostly in the synagogue, a space newly inclusive of women, where larger numbers could listen to sermons that not only discussed the basic rules of practice and belief but offered a language of Jewish moral philosophy and historical grandeur that united Judaism with the broader rhetoric and affect of urban modernity. "What replaced [pre-modern] rabbinic Judaism," notes David Sorkin, "was not any one interpretation of Judaism, but an ideology of emancipation that determined cultural preferences and political assumptions."[2]

The core elements of the modern Jewish experience were already beginning to be widely felt by the time Jellinek assumed his position in Vienna in 1857. Jews were migrating to cities in record numbers. The Jewish intellectual embrace of European Enlightenment was more than half a century old. Liberal policies were allowing Jews to buy property and build new communal and private buildings. What makes Jellinek's first decades in Vienna exceptional were the numerous ways he addressed these communal and intellectual transformations, presenting himself as one who could bridge the world of religious texts with that of German culture.

Jellinek played a formative role in founding and solidifying the version of modern rabbinic leadership based in the synagogue and centered on the sermon. As we will see in this chapter and the following two, the politics of mid-nineteenth-century European liberalism—with its mixture of idealist philosophy and practical political accommodation to ruling imperial forces—framed the political climate for much of the Jewish urban cultural experience of that era. But alongside broader trends in European politics was the deeply intimate and personal experience of individual rabbinic leaders and their communities. Newly hired urban rabbis in the 1850s and 1860s were creating a version of rabbinic Judaism that differed greatly from what had been the only model of rabbinic practice across the whole of Europe just a couple of decades prior. These rabbis were thrust into a role based on speaking. They were hired as preachers (*Predigers*), and their central contractual obligations were to deliver a weekly sermon and preside over religious services inside the synagogue.[3] For someone like Jellinek, such a role was uniquely suited to his personality and intel-

---

2. Sorkin, "Impact of Emancipation," 178. There is certainly a historical debate worth having to ask the question: Is the Judaism ultimately described in this book still "rabbinic"? That is not, however, at its core a historian's debate. What we find in this post-emancipation moment is truly a reimagining of the rabbi and the synagogue. Whether that creates a Judaism that is not rabbinic I cannot here pass judgment. It is, though, right to say that— outside of certain insular communities constituting less than 10 percent of world Jewry—the functional purpose of the rabbi as understood in the twenty-first century is fundamentally different from that which was understood at any time in two millennia preceding the nineteenth century.

3. See Alexander Deeg, *Predigt und Derascha: Homiltische Textlektüre im Dialog mit dem*

lectual goals. That is no coincidence. A man who could not give weekly sermons or who had little appetite for political activism would not have been attracted to the rabbinate as it was being redefined in the nineteenth century.[4] Wrote Nahum Glatzer, "the preacher, or rabbi, though well acquainted with the subject of his particular sermon ... was, with some exceptions, no longer the scholar in the Hebrew tradition. What counted now was rhetoric."[5]

As seen in chapters 3 and 4, Jellinek was certainly still a "scholar in the Hebrew tradition." But he was not a pious, quiet man who spent most of his days bent over a book—the sort of disposition held up for esteem by the heads of the East European yeshivot. Neither was he a strict halakhist, whose decisions were based on an exacting reading of the Talmudic exegetes. Instead, Jellinek was a verbose, public personality. In Leipzig, starting at the age of twenty-two, he thrust himself into the center of scholarly discussions about Jewish history and textual origins, debating men of international reputation. At twenty-four he accepted communal leadership in Leipzig and initiated the community's formal break from Dresden. Now in Vienna, at the age of thirty-six, he stood before a crowd in a monumental hall and argued for an entirely new way of imagining Jewish history, as a moral, spiritual, and political tradition in every way older and wiser than the (Christian) Enlightenment being propounded in the intellectual circles of Europe. As the *Illustrirte Zeitung* wrote in a retrospective, "Jellinek almost always spoke in front of an audience which was thrown together from all parts of the world. Because of this, he sought from the beginning to dissociate himself in his sermons from local events and [instead] to treat cosmopolitan themes. This variety [of sermon] became his [trademark] characteristic."[6] In Vienna, Jellinek perfected his rhetorical talents, refining a language that could be understood and embraced by his community of Jewish migrants, whose lives were, in effect, building modern Judaism, even if they did not quite realize it.

The persona that Jellinek crafted for himself in Vienna, both through his public appearances and in his writings, was something like what we might now call a "public intellectual"—a learned scholar who has left the Ivory Tower to further a cultural and political agenda. In Jellinek's

---

Judentum, Arbeiten zur Pastoraltheologie, Liturgik und Hymnologie 48 (Göttingen: Vandenhoek & Ruprecht, 2006).

4. For example, the nineteenth-century Jewish historian Heinrich Graetz discusses his poor talent for sermonizing and, subsequently his difficulty finding a professional appointment in the Jewish community. See Heinrich Graetz, *Tagebuch und Briefe*, ed. Reuven Michael, Schriftenreihe wissenschaftlicher Abhandlungen des Leo Baeck Instituts 34 (Tübingen: Mohr, 1977).

5. Nahum N. Glatzer, "On an Unpublished Letter of Isaak Markus Jost," *Leo Baeck Institute Year Book* 22 (1977): 129–37, here 129–30.

6. *Illustrirte Zeitung*, no. 2637 (13 January 1894), 45-46, here 46.

case, that agenda was to establish Judaism as a "legitimate" ethical system, that is, a Jewish religion embraced with pride by acculturating Jews and treated with respect by non-Jewish intellectuals, and in whose accumulated wisdom could be found solutions to present and future social questions.[7] As Jellinek wrote in 1864, "The words of the Talmudic sages are as stepping stones, holding together the faith and the various types of human community through the teachings of justice, humanity, and morality [... and doing this] so the Heavens can be witness to the harmonious and peaceful interaction of the enlightenment of the universe!"[8] For Jellinek, telling the world about the universal nature of Judaism meant, in part, crafting a genealogical narrative in which Judaism was portrayed as an organic branch of the tree of European moral philosophy, rather than (at best) a grafted limb or (at worst) an invasive, unwanted hanging vine.

Jellinek's ideas and writings in Vienna were deeply shaped by contemporary events and political-philosophical trends. His audiences were men and women who had upended their lives in rural Central Europe for the economic possibilities offered by the capital city. In Vienna, these Jews aspired to a particular sort of urban bourgeois lifestyle—to speaking German, to sending their children to gymnasium and university (and eventually to having them join the professional classes), and to finding for themselves a degree of long-term stability that had eluded their ancestors. For this community, Jewish culture and tradition in rural Europe had been something that pervaded their lives without a great deal of self-reflection, and certainly without a personal, individual stake in something as grand as the historical veracity of Jewish moral truths. In the modern city, with the continual influence of modern ideas and new cultural norms—ethical universalism, individualism, hints of secularism—and without the inherited, site-specific ties to neighbors, synagogues, cemeteries, and family businesses, Jewish "affect"—the feel that one's life follows patterns of Jewish tradition and expectation—could not simply be assumed and were increasingly absent altogether. Jellinek came to believe that in an environment like mid-nineteenth-century Vienna, which was itself a site of almost total physical and demographic transformation, Jewish history and memory needed to be made overt, brought to the front of people's minds through rhetoric, narrative, encouragement, and repetition—lots and lots of repetition. Jellinek feared that without a language of, to put it crudely, Jewish importance, Judaism would be lost, not out of malice but out of distraction.

---

7. As Malachi Hacohen writes, "Jellinek's sermons had a political urgency.... The sermons were part of an ongoing struggle for emancipation and against antisemitism" (*Jacob & Esau*, 274).

8. Adolf Jellinek, *Der Talmud: Zwei Reden, am Hüttenfeste 5625 (am 16. und 22. October 1864)* (Vienna: Herzfeld & Bauer, 1865), 32.

The challenge of preaching in such a place and for such an audience pushed Jellinek to his intellectual limits. (Indeed, he all but gave up on scholarship the first two decades he lived in Vienna.) But it also resulted in his greatest rhetorical creativity and widespread lasting impact, an ingenuity and originality that were every bit the equal of the insights of his earlier career as a scholar of *Wissenschaft*. As we will see in the next section, for the vast majority of Jewish history, rabbis did not give frequent public sermons, limiting their communal addresses to a handful a year and spending most of their waking hours adjudicating matters of civil law. And when they did speak, they lectured on theological or exegetical topics internal to Judaism, seeking not the universalization of Judaism but instead the reaffirmation of Jewish narratives and ideas. In Vienna, Jellinek modeled a form of rhetorical Jewish traditionalism and moral universalism that was at that time just beginning to emerge but that eventually came to pervade Jewish communal language across the European world. In Central Europe, and later Anglo-America, in part due to Jellinek's influence, rabbis used their sermons in the synagogue to address questions and events of national importance. In fact, Jellinek's model was so dominant that, by the turn of the twentieth century, Jewish leadership in all the major cities of Central Europe, England, and the United States saw it as their responsibility to bring together Jewish tradition and secular culture, and to do so within a national narrative of shared liberal values.[9]

The Development and Transformation of the Rabbinic Sermon

The nineteenth-century idea that it was the responsibility of the community rabbi to give weekly sermons during Sabbath morning services marked a fundamental shift in the conception of the rabbi's role in public Jewish culture. What occurred was a radical change in the rabbinic persona—from that of halakhic decisor (*posek*) to one of preacher, public educator, and caretaker of synagogue ritual. Because of this evolution in the position and responsibility of the rabbi in public Jewish communal life, nineteenth-century rabbinic sermons—their content and rhetoric—tell us a great deal about the social context of Jewish religious practice in the early decades of urban modernity. Jewish religious culture in Europe went from being almost exclusively rural, and mainly reliant on local tradition and custom, to one that was primarily urban, dependent on the large communal synagogue, religious instruction by the rabbi, and the overall

---

9. See Marc Saperstein, "Rabbis as Preachers, 1800–1965: Regensburg Conference Lecture," in Homolka and Schöttler, *Rabbi – Pastor – Priest*, 111–28, esp. 120–21.

governance of centralized Jewish councils. Instead of marginalizing the synagogue and the rabbi, as might have been expected with increasing Jewish acculturation and decreasing religious observance and familial piety, nineteenth-century Jewish communities simply transformed these historic institutions to meet new needs.

The rabbi and his words have long figured centrally in both the mythology and the practice of Judaism.[10] The opening lines of the Mishnaic tractate "Sayings of the Fathers" (*Pirkei Avot*) trace an idealized genealogy for rabbinic Judaism: "Moses received the Torah from Sinai and gave it to Joshua. Joshua [gave it] to the Elders, the Elders to the Prophets, and the Prophets gave it to the men of the Great Assembly" (1:1). Though historically unverifiable as an account of the transmission of Jewish tradition, the Mishnah's statements are interesting for their sociological observation. For the Mishnah, the role of the rabbi (equated here with "the men of the Great Assembly") is multifaceted. At the core, the rabbi is an exegete of divine law. Just as Moses wrote and taught the Torah, so too the rabbi is to learn and teach Torah. But Joshua was the next to receive the tradition, and he is remembered not for his wisdom but for his military strength and political acumen—for his faith in God's word that the Jewish people would settle the Land of Israel, and for his will to see that project to completion. Finally, the prophets were neither scholars nor warriors. They were moral exemplars and interpreters, exhorting the people to desist from their unclean ways, warning of the dangers that arise from cultural complacency, ethical degeneracy, and religious apathy.

To a certain extent, these opening lines offer a portrait of the Mishnah's version of a well-rounded individual and of a successful leader of the Jewish people. "Simon the Righteous was among the last members of the Great Assembly. He would say: On three things does the world stand: on Torah, on the service of God, and on deeds of kindness" (*Pirkei Avot* 1:2). In other words, wholeness comes only through the unification of Moses (Torah), Joshua (service of God), and the Prophets (deeds of kindness). The rabbis who composed the Mishnah, and the generations of students who learned it after them, saw in it a moral lesson for rising leaders and made it an enduring part of the liturgy.[11] The Mishnah enumerates and instantiates this authority, while also providing a mechanism by which succeeding generations could account for and build upon the insights of their teachers.

---

10. See Alexander Deeg, *Preaching in Judaism and Christianity: Encounters and Developments from Biblical Times to Modernity*, Studia Judaica 41 (Berlin: de Gruyter, 2008).

11. "Rabbinic culture is founded upon a literature—its interpretation, the imperative to study it, and the authority of its leading interpreters" (Daniel Frank and Matt Goldish, "Rabbinic Culture and Dissent: An Overview," in Frank and Goldish, *Rabbinic Culture and Its Critics*, 1).

Importantly, of course, the Mishnah is neither a beginning nor an end in the history of rabbinic Judaism. It is merely a useful exemplar of rabbinical self-understanding, as well as a central authority for those who see themselves as part of the postbiblical Jewish exegetical experience.[12] Just as true, however, is that from classical times onward, the authority of the rabbi in Jewish religious life has been consistently debated, witnessing to ebbs and flows as Jewish society cycled through periods of lesser and greater autonomy and integration.[13] Plasticity is a fact of rabbinic history. It was also one of its greatest strengths.

Historically, the rabbi's public role was quite different from what we find today. Jewish communities were often highly autonomous, with Jewish texts acting as the civil law for the community. The rabbi presided mainly over the civic and ritual responsibilities and obligations (as well as disputes) of his people, something akin to a town's mayor.[14] He gave lessons to his students and an elucidation of that week's biblical reading (called a *shir*) on Sabbath afternoons in the study hall. But he was not likely to give a sermon during weekly Sabbath morning prayer, nor was he likely to make any formal speech (exegetical, theological, or otherwise) to the women of the community on the Sabbath at all. Instead, the rabbi would make a formal sermon outlining ritual actions and laws (*halakhot*) only a few times each year, traditionally on the Sabbath of the High Holidays (*Shabbat Shuva*) in the fall and on the Sabbath before Passover (*Shabbat HaGadol*) in the spring.[15] In fact, as it came to be understood in the early modern period, the rabbi's position outside of the study hall was primarily civil and interpersonal, dealing with the daily needs of the people while extensively educating only a few.

As for the synagogue itself, this term applied to whatever room was designated as the gathering place for men's prayer.[16] Synagogues might be sumptuously or modestly decorated, depending on the wealth of the community. In rural Central Europe, where communities were small, synagogues were often unassuming one-story buildings, with wooden

---

12. See Michael S. Berger, *Rabbinic Authority* (Oxford: Oxford University Press, 1998).

13. See Jack Wertheimer, *Jewish Religious Leadership: Image and Reality* (New York: Jewish Theological Seminary, 2004).

14. For the many-faceted role of the rabbi as community leader, see Marc Saperstein, *Leadership and Conflict: Tensions in Medieval and Early Modern Jewish History and Culture* (Oxford: Littman Library of Jewish Civilization, 2014); Shaul Stampfer, *Families, Rabbis and Education: Traditional Jewish Society in Nineteenth-Century Eastern Europe* (Oxford: Littman Library of Jewish Civilization, 2010); Frank and Goldish, *Rabbinic Culture and Its Critics*; and Schwarzfuchs, *Concise History of the Rabbinate*.

15. For an example of a rabbinic contract that specified days of preaching, see Schwarzfuchs, *Concise History of the Rabbinate*, 51–53.

16. See Barry L. Stiefel, *Jews and the Renaissance of Synagogue Architecture, 1450–1730*, Religious Cultures in the Early Modern World 14 (London: Routledge, 2014).

benches or desks, the most extravagant piece of furniture being a carved ark for the Torah scrolls or a decorated table on which the Torah was set for reading.[17] The women's gallery was behind a window or (if the building was large enough) in a balcony overhanging the main prayer space.[18] The services that occurred in these synagogues were organized and led by members of the community. The civil and political functions of the rabbi would have been conducted from his home or another communal space (such as a study hall), not the prayer space of the synagogue. Even on the Sabbath, the synagogue was not a meeting place for the community; that would have been a separate public structure or the private home of a wealthy family. The synagogue was an intimate and guarded space for the men of the community, and synagogues often lacked a permanent rabbinical figure, hosting traveling sages when they passed through or for special occasions or holidays.[19] Similarly, young children and women spent most of their time elsewhere.[20]

With such a gendered space as the synagogue and such a proscribed role for the rabbi in communal and religious life, Jewish tradition and values—the *affect* of Jewish experience—were primarily passed down within families and taught through participation in local communal gatherings, rituals, and celebrations.[21] In fact, the interactions of Jewish mothers and their children account for much of the continuity and change seen in Jewish culture and religious practice across the centuries, nearly all of which occurred inside the private family home.[22] In other words, though histories of Judaism have often traced the shifting role of men in the public sphere, much of the pattern of daily life for premodern Jewry was directed

---

17. See Thomas C. Hubka, *Resplendent Synagogue: Architecture and Worship in an Eighteenth-Century Polish Community*, Tauber Institute for the Study of European Jewry Series (Hanover, NH: Brandeis University Press, 2003); Krinsky, *Synagogues of Europe*; and Maria Piechotka and Kazimierz Piechotka, *Wooden Synagogues* (Warsaw: Arkady, 1959).

18. See Karla Goldman, *Beyond the Synagogue Gallery: Finding a Place for Women in American Judaism* (Cambridge: Harvard University Press, 2000), esp. 4–11 and 24–31; Susan Grossman and Rivka Haut, eds., *Daughters of the King: Women and the Synagogue; A Survey of History, Halakhah, and Contemporary Realities* (Philadephia: Jewish Publication Society, 1992); and Tachau, "Architecture of the Synagogue," 155–92.

19. See Jeffrey R. Woolf, *The Fabric of Religious Life in Medieval Ashkenaz (1000–1300): Creating Sacred Communities*, Études sur le judaïsme médiéval 30 (Leiden: Brill, 2015), esp. 81–130.

20. See Elisheva Baumgarten, *Practicing Piety in Medieval Ashkenaz: Men, Women and Everyday Observance*, Jewish Culture and Contexts (Philadelphia: University of Pennsylvania Press, 2014), esp. 21–50.

21. See Ivan G. Marcus, *Rituals of Childhood: Jewish Acculturation in Medieval Europe* (New Haven: Yale University Press, 1998).

22. See Elisheva Baumgarten, *Mothers and Children: Jewish Family Life in Medieval Europe*, Jews, Christians, and Muslims from the Ancient to the Modern World (Princeton, NJ: Princeton University Press, 2004).

by the internal affairs of nuclear and extended families.[23] Religious education rarely stretched past the age of ritual adulthood (twelve for girls, thirteen for boys), except for preparations related to marriage.[24] Because of this, Jewish aesthetics and customs in the premodern period in Europe were driven less by the rules of the study house and more by the norms and historical associations of Jewish individuals themselves.

In this premodern era, the rabbi played almost no role in fostering such a religious culture.[25] The rabbi was a resource for questions of practical law and an essential mediator for civil needs (disputes, contracts, loans). But rabbis did not *promote* Jewish culture. Only rarely did they lecture about the importance of Jewish history; only rarely did they attempt to inspire the community about the beauty of Jewish ritual or the sanctity of Jewish prayer or the divinity of the Hebrew language.[26] These things were lived assumptions, part and parcel of the very fabric of Jewish existence. And they did not come from the rabbi. Instead, the community of Jews, through their daily activities, their routines, desires, expectations, ideas, values, and creative expressions (poems, songs, paintings, ritual objects) created the milieu for Jewish cultural transmission down the generations. In a world in which most families had very few possessions, a house with Sabbath candlesticks, a ritual wine cup, a prayer shawl and phylacteries, and the practice of not working on the Sabbath expressed an intrinsically Jewish aesthetic that the rabbi played almost no role in creating or fostering.

The rabbinic sermon acquired a new and unprecedented significance as part of the major shift in European Jewish religious experience that occurred in the middle period of the nineteenth century. Though as we have just laid out, rabbis had distinctly important functions in Jewish life in the premodern period, it was not mainly in the public pronouncement

---

23. For works related to Jewish daily life in the premodern period in Europe, see Robert Chazan, *Reassessing Jewish Life in Medieval Europe* (New York: Cambridge University Press, 2010); David B. Ruderman, *Early Modern Jewry: A New Cultural History* (Princeton, NJ: Princeton University Press, 2010); Norman Roth, *Daily Life of the Jews in the Middle Ages* (Westport, CT: Greenwood, 2005); Avraham Grossman, *Pious and Rebellious: Jewish Women in Medieval Europe* (Waltham, MA: Brandeis University Press, 2004), esp. 174–97; and Chava Weissler, *Voices of the Matriarchs: Listening to the Prayers of Early Modern Jewish Women* (Boston: Beacon Press, 1998).

24. See Grossman, *Pious and Rebellious*, 154–73.

25. See Marion A. Kaplan, ed., *Jewish Daily Life in Germany, 1618–1845* (Oxford: Oxford University Press, 2005), esp. 70–83. See also Glikl von Hameln, *Glikl: Memoirs 1691–1719*, ed. Chava Turniansky, trans. Sara Friedman (Waltham, MA: Brandeis University Press, 2019.)

26. In many ways, the exceptions prove the rule. It is not just that we have records of some of the more famous sermons and disputations, but these were special events, one-time affairs that were recorded and published for posterity, not weekly events happening in each synagogue in every city and town. See Marc Saperstein, *Jewish Preaching, 1200–1800: An Anthology*, Yale Judaica Series 26 (New Haven: Yale University Press, 1989).

of religious philosophy, politics, or ethics. Still, the sermon did not arise *ex nihilo*. From ancient times, there were precedents for the rabbi to deliver a sermon, with special emphasis at least twice during the yearly festival cycle.[27] Further, premodern liturgical additions also foreshadowed the themes and roles the modern sermon has come to play. For example, the liturgical hymn has been a part of Jewish ritual practice from at least the late classical period.[28] Tracing the interplay between broader cultural developments and the composition of these hymns, Leon J. Weinberger has described the way rabbis encouraged their communities to write religious songs and poems that reflected their emotions and desires. "The immense volume of Jewish liturgical writing is undoubtedly related to its dialogic focus," he writes. "A constant feature of the Jewish experience emerged with the hymnic ritualization of the great events of human life."[29] In a sense, just as Jellinek would preach about the great cholera outbreak of 1866 following the Austro-Prussian War,[30] the hymns bewailing the suffering exile of Israel in the Middle Ages had fulfilled a similar function.[31] In the nineteenth century, the sermon took on this "hymnic ritualization," inscribing contemporary history into the language and rituals of Jewish life.

The Nineteenth-Century Sermon

Beginning in the first decades of the nineteenth century, the rabbi's sermon became one of the formative mechanisms by which Jewish religious

---

27. See Richard Hidary, *Rabbis and Classical Rhetoric: Sophistic Education and Oratory in the Talmud and Midrash* (Cambridge: Cambridge University Press, 2018), esp. 41–77.

28. See David Flusser, "Psalms, Hymns and Prayer," in *Jewish Writings of the Second Temple Period: Apocrypha, Pseudepigrapha, Qumran Sectarian Writings, Philo, Josephus*, ed. Michael E. Stone (Philadelphia: Fortress, 1984), 551–77.

29. Leon J. Weinberger, *Jewish Hymnography: A Literary History*, Littman Library of Jewish Civilization (London: Vallentine Mitchell, 1998), 4.

30. "But the disease cannot be banished and finished-off. It assails the house next door, infects people going and coming, pollutes the air, spreads anxiety and unease everywhere. It even makes its way to the dwellings of the well-off.... [But!] Seeing the Esrog goldenradiant and precious, the palm tree towering and fertile, the myrtle evergreen and fragrant— all images of modesty, secure possessions and wealth. These are joined together with the willow, which bends and swallows swiftly, like the poor and suffering, so that Israel may be remembered at the harvest festival; that rich and poor may meet; and that the bond of reciprocity may entwine them" (Adolf Jellinek, *Das Gesetz Gottes außer der Thora: Fünf Reden nebst einer Rede über die Cholera* [Vienna: Herzfeld & Bauer, 1867], 1–16, here 13–14).

31. As Rabbi Asher HaKohen (ca. fifteenth century) wrote, "Zion, lift your eyes heavenward, and see and eulogize and wait, for your Advocate has abandoned you.... Rachel and Leah, cry! Bilhah and Zilpah, also lament, and cry out loud, tear at your face! For God is eternal and will not forsake. There is hope; great peace will come for your children!" Quoted in Simon Posner, ed., *The Koren Mesorat Harav Kinot* (Jerusalem: Koren, 2011), 584.

leaders engaged with the problems and possibilities posed by Europe's intellectual, technological, and cultural modernity.[32] The reinvention of the sermon represented a profound revolution in the way Jewish history and belief were spoken about in the public sphere. This was a shift that fundamentally separated the experience of Judaism before and after the nineteenth century. Jewish life in premodernity was composed mostly of inherited customs, certainly in line with but rarely dictated by rabbinic decree. By the end of the nineteenth century the synagogue service and the rabbi's leadership represented much of the ritual content of urban Jewish life in Central Europe.

In an attempt to explain the sudden importance of the sermon in Jewish religious practice, David Sorkin describes it as part of an "ideology of emancipation" on the part of Jews in the German-speaking lands following the Napoleonic invasion.[33] Early maskilic texts, with a few exceptions (such as Mendelssohn's *Jerusalem*), were accessible only to Hebrew readers, which not only excluded almost all non-Jewish intellectuals but most Jews as well.[34] An "ideology of emancipation," in Sorkin's view, was the attempt to do away with all structural distinctions between the Jewish community and its gentile neighbors.[35] While in the latter decades of the eighteenth century the tone and substance of what Jewish maskilim wrote depended on their choice of language (German for polemics, Hebrew for philosophy), by the first decades of the nineteenth century that division no longer held.

This idea certainly accounts for some of the increased importance placed on the sermon. Given in German, the weekly sermon began the process of translating Jewish concepts into the vernacular. Relatedly, the similar structural form of Jewish sermons and their Christian counterparts proved essential for the acculturation of migrating Jews in the middle decades of the nineteenth century. By adopting some of the Christian models, the sermon itself became a site of Jewish modernity. As Alexander Altmann notes, "the sermon had evolved into a type of pulpit oratory decidedly different from the genre of the homily. It was not to be an exegetical discourse on Scriptural verses loosely strung together but was to be a disquisition on some definite theme based on a text and presented according to a well-defined pattern of component parts."[36] Sorkin calls these "edification sermons" (*Erbauungspredigt*), describing their

---

32. See Altmann, "New Style of Preaching," 65–116.
33. David Sorkin, "The Genesis of the Ideology of Emancipation: 1806–1840," *Leo Baeck Institute Year Book* 32 (1987): 11–40.
34. Moses Mendelssohn, *Jerusalem, or, On Religious Power and Judaism*, trans. Allan Arkush (Hanover, NH: University Press of New England, 1983).
35. Sorkin, "Genesis of the Ideology of Emancipation," 16.
36. Altmann, "New Style of Preaching," 68.

model as similar to that developed among German Protestants. Still, nineteenth-century rabbinical sermons were not merely derivative of the Protestant model; rather, both styles evolved in tandem, responding to needs and developments within both Christian and Jewish religious milieus. The rabbinical sermon, therefore, became an important theological tool for identifying and amplifying the moral message of traditional religious texts for newly urban Jewish communities.

Importantly, as the physical space of the synagogue changed, so too did the communities calling it home, including the many women who began to participate in its life in historically unprecedented ways.[37] The shift in gender roles, and especially the place of women in Jewish ritual and intellectual life, was one of the most important developments brought about by changes in synagogue culture. As Benjamin Maria Baader has written about, throughout the mid-nineteenth century religious leaders noted a steep decline in domestic piety, that is, in the religious life of Jewish families inside their private homes.[38] In response, rabbis began incorporating women more deeply into the lives of the wider community, something most easily done inside the new urban synagogues and at the community schools.[39] There was, indeed, a profoundly egalitarian undercurrent in many of these ritual reforms.[40] One might say that the sermon became the first means of widespread Torah education for both men and women, fulfilling the Talmudic wish that every Jew learn Torah from a sage. Jellinek wrote sermons both specifically about women and specifically for them.[41] Though women and men continued to sit separately, as they had always done, Jellinek made a point of noting the increased presence of women in the synagogue spaces, preaching about the role of women in Jewish history and practice, using sermons on Sabbaths and festivals to highlight the importance of the feminine within Jewish history and tradition.

---

37. See Maria Benjamin Baader, "When Judaism Turned Bourgeois: Gender in Jewish Associational Life and in the Synagogue, 1750–1850," *Leo Baeck Institute Year Book* 46 (2001): 113–23.

38. Baader, *Gender, Judaism, and Bourgeois Culture*, 74–75. Michael A. Meyer also notes that in the mid-nineteenth century, women began attending religious services more often, which resulted in an increased size in the women's section of new synagogue buildings (Meyer, "'How Awesome Is This Place!,'" 62).

39. For example, Abraham Meyer Goldschmidt (1812–1889), who succeeded Jellinek as rabbi in Leipzig, and his wife, Henriette (1825–1920) (née Benas) were pioneers in women's education. Goldschmidt Straße in Leipzig is named for Henriette, not her husband.

40. Julius Carlebach, "The Forgotten Connection: Women and Jews in the Conflict between Enlightenment and Romanticism," *Leo Baeck Institute Year Book* 24 (1979): 107–38.

41. For example, see Adolf Jellinek, *Die Psyche des Weibes: Vortrage im Saale des Academischen Gymnasium in Wien* (Vienna: Hölder, 1872); "Rut," in *Predigten*, 1:1–12; "Die religiöse Erziehung des israelitischen Weibes (Wochen-Fest, 1864)," in *Predigten*, 3:65–78; "Der Mutterherz (Hütten-Fest, 1854)," in *Predigten*, 3:79–90; and "Israel's Familiensinn (am 1. Tage des Hütten-Festes, 1865)," in *Predigten*, 3:215–28.

Jellinek the Preacher

Titles carry a great deal of meaning, and Adolf Jellinek had three: rabbi, doctor, and preacher (*prediger*). When and where he chose to use them—or they were applied to him—offer insight concerning his expected role in the Viennese Jewish community after taking up his position in 1857. Officially, Jellinek was hired from Leipzig to be a preacher, and he was referred to that way in communal publications.[42] In private correspondence, however, he was addressed most often as "Rabbi."[43] For his published books he added "Dr." before his name. The varying usages of these titles symbolized the transforming role of the rabbi in the public sphere of mid-nineteenth-century Central European Judaism. The word "rabbi" retained its strong connection with the traditional lifestyle and role held over from the early modern period. By the 1840s, community rabbis were also legally obligated to earn a doctorate at a university, and many, like Jellinek, did so with degrees in Oriental languages or Near Eastern history. But, for German Jews, it was the title of "preacher" that signaled the most decisive shift away from the old models of communal structure and religious practice. With it, they described their new expectation of rabbinic leaders, with its focus on speech and rhetoric above legal guidance.

As still today, in the nineteenth century, *preacher* was a gentile term. By its adoption, the German-speaking Jewish community signaled a desire to move their practices toward a style more broadly similar to that of the German-speaking Christian elite. As these Jews established residence in cities, the modern sermon took on the duty of promulgating a coherent religious ideology, one that could answer many of the questions arising in modernizing, liberalizing Europe. Jellinek's preaching touched on all the facets of modern life: "his greatest speeches were on God, religion, Judaism, Torah, Talmud, Hebrew language, about Israel, its life, home and family, about love, humanity, fraternity, truth, freedom and justice," wrote one of his admiring students, Adolf Kurrein.[44] Jews adapted the sermon for the purposes of communal cohesion and theological pedagogy. For urban German-speaking Jews, *prediger* symbolized the newfound centrality of

---

42. For just a few examples, see the announcement for Jellinek's *Predigten* from the publisher Carl Gerold's Son (Vienna, 1863); Jellinek's Letter to the Editor, *Neue Freie Presse* (January 21, 1868); his Statement in *Die Neuzeit* 4 (January 24, 1868); the review of Jellinek's *Der jüdische Stamm* in the *Neue Freie Presse* (May 31, 1869); and Jellinek's essay in *Social-Reform: Ein Central-Organ für Volkserziehung, Fortbildung und National-Oekonomie* 8 (5), no. 135 (1871): 65–67.

43. See Jellinek's correspondence at the National Library of Israel in Jerusalem (ARC 4* 1589) and at the Zentralarchiv zur Erforschung der Geschichte der Juden in Deutschland in Heidelberg (Jellinek B.2/4).

44. Adolf Kurrein, ed., *Dr. Adolf Jellinek: Lichtstrahlen aus den Reden Dr. Adolf Jellinek's* (Vienna: Bermann & Altmann, 1891), vii–viii.

the act of public speaking, over and above the traditional roles of the rabbi as master of the intricacies of legal arbitration.

For Jellinek in Vienna, the majority of his public speaking took place in either the Leopoldstadt Temple or the Stadttempel, whose grand sanctuaries became the forum where he delivered, week after week, his discourses on the past and future of Judaism. In Vienna, Jellinek channeled his energies into communal education and outreach. He experimented with ways of making his knowledge and love of texts accessible to a wide public who were generally only rudimentarily educated concerning Jewish religious texts and philosophical traditions. He began to reinterpret the classical rabbinic canon with an eye toward the future of the Jewish people. In a way, Jellinek became less insular than he had ever been. Whereas the scholar educated in Prague and Leipzig had previously written for a select crowd of fellow academics, in Vienna, by turning to the traditional sources and using them to explain contemporary intellectual theories and political affairs, Jellinek broadened his notion of what it meant to be a religious reformer and teacher in modernity. As Kurrein, who also edited a collection of Jellinek's most inspiring writings, wrote in 1891, "he is always an orator who draws from the rich depths of Jewish knowledge, from the inexhaustible source of the Jewish heart and mind. [He does so] with Jewish spirit and wit, with Oriental imagination, yet at the same time tempered in artistry, and while rich in images he comes down from the heights ... speaking to his people and to humanity."[45]

Kurrein was not simply extolling his favorite teacher and mentor. Jellinek was a brilliant rhetorician, often referred to as the greatest Jewish preacher of nineteenth-century Europe, and he gave hundreds of sermons over the course of his long career.[46] For Jellinek, the sermon represented the very best of modernity, allowing ancient texts and ideas to be heard in new spaces and under new conditions. Much of the wisdom of Judaism is contained in deeply esoteric compendia, organized as much associatively as topically, in various dialects of Hebrew and Aramaic. It takes years to master the traditional sources, and decades to cultivate a life structured around its wisdom, a luxury few Jewish men (and almost no women) have ever had. Jellinek, by virtue of a kindly father, a peaceful childhood, and personal interest (his two brothers were offered the same training but took different paths), had received this classical education, gaining a fluency in Jewish learning that defined his outlook and persona. But the yeshiva is a cloistered estate, unsuited to popularization. What Jellinek realized, first as a young man in Leipzig, then in Vienna, was that the sermon had

---

45. Kurrein, *Dr. Adolf Jellinek*, viii.

46. Jellinek published his sermons in different ways, as single-pamphlets, in newspapers, as well as in multivolume collections. The largest collection are the three-volumes of *Predigten*, which appeared from 1862 to 1866.

the capacity both to convey the nuance of Jewish traditional thinking (the ins and outs of dialectical argumentation) and to deliver in cogent, lucid terms gems of Jewish wisdom about God, humanity, and the construction of an ethical society.

Jellinek always spoke out of the classical sources. This is one of the key and decisive ways in which his sermons are distinct from most nineteenth-century Jewish preachers. Jellinek structured his sermons around the interplay of texts and ideas, the way a biblical passage could give life to a Talmudic or midrashic conversation, which then bore fruit in medieval philosophy, which in turn spoke to a central question of modern times. He rejoiced in the rhetorical grace of the sermon, the big ideas, the sweeping narratives, the piercing summations. He loved that sermons gave him a way to speak about Jewish texts, because exactly what Jellinek loved about modernity—new ideas concerning justice, citizenship, universal ethics—also brought with it everything he most feared, especially the loss of traditional forms of religious knowledge and study. He feared that the ways in which Judaism had accumulated its wisdom over centuries—abstruse, veiled, beguiling, labyrinthine, associative—would be replaced wholesale by encyclopedias and scientific journals. He loved encyclopedias and scientific journals. But he also loved Talmud and midrash. He wanted an intellectual modernity that was agile enough for them both.

Jellinek found this agility, at least for himself, in the sermon. He invested much of his twenties and early thirties in the methods and discourses of *Wissenschaft*. But after publishing many books and articles, including groundbreaking work on the historical authorship and context of the *Zohar*, he mostly abandoned this form of writing and thinking, turning instead to community formation and popular education. By his late thirties, the sermon became his main intellectual outlet.

Jellinek's sermons were as much about education or edification as about religious pride and heritage. They were meant to instill in listeners and readers a sense of wonder at the power and majesty of God and an awe in the moral wisdom and judiciousness of Judaism and its sages. When so much of modern culture expected the abandonment of old ideas, and when Christian Europe offered entrée to Jews as Jews but not to Judaism as a real and true faith, Jellinek sought through his sermons to give his community innumerable proofs to the contrary. Judaism, old in practice and ritual, was the true wellspring of Western morality, he said, an eternal commitment to the fundamental ethical notion that all humanity was created in the image of God.

There was little that religious leaders could do, however, to alter the increasing acculturation of the Jewish home from the middle of the century onward. Rabbis spent less and less of their time in the personal spaces of their community members and more hours of the day in institutional settings like schools, synagogues, and hospitals. With these trends, the rabbi and the synagogue came to be seen as interlocking institutions, each intimately bound up with the other. Such a link gave liberal rabbis newfound freedoms—like the increasing inclusion of women in prayer spaces—but it also limited the rabbi's broader communal importance. When Jews went home from the synagogue, the rabbi and Jewish ritual played a less prominent role than it had just a few decades previously. But when Jews went to the synagogue, the rabbi and his voice took on far greater prominence than ever before. In the new urban culture, as the need for the rabbi's halakhic knowledge declined, his moral and oratorical leadership took on newfound importance.

8

Major Themes in Jellinek's Sermons

> [Jellinek] excelled in the art of weaving an abundance of quotations from biblical and rabbinic sources into the texture of his sermons. His associative memory and the skillfulness of his interpretations, wedded to his oratorical brilliance, single him out as the most fascinating preacher of the period.
> —Alexander Altmann, "The New Style of Preaching in Nineteenth-Century Germany"

As the role of the rabbi and synagogue radically transformed in the middle of the nineteenth century—with the rabbi's sermon becoming an integral part of the Sabbath morning religious experience in synagogues across Central Europe—the form and content of these sermons shifted as well. Each rabbi brought something different to his role as a communal preacher. Adolf Jellinek was among the first of the modern rabbis to make his religious role almost entirely about the values and aesthetics of the sermon, rather than about those of halakhic authority. Each Sabbath and festival, Jellinek stood at the front of the synagogue and preached to a culturally diverse (in matters of tradition, language, observance, economic status, and education) and mixed-gender community about the relevance of Jewish history in the modern era. His voice filled the sanctuary, first at the new Leopoldstädter Tempel, later at the Stadttempel, and many more read his words when they appeared in pamphlets, newspapers, and collected volumes. Though now almost entirely forgotten, Jellinek's sermons exemplified and solidified the new role of the rabbi in Jewish modernity, and they offer a unique window into the various philosophic and political elements that propelled religious change in the middle of the nineteenth century.

Jellinek's sermons revolved around a handful of key themes—those ideas, concepts, and values to which he returned time and again. One was universal morality, the idea that human society was stitched together with a shared common core of ethical norms and divinely revealed truths. Another was care of the stranger. Jellinek believed that many of the universal values of liberalism were embodied in the textual and, more importantly, the ritual and dialogical history of Judaism's relation to the stranger. A third was a set of interrelated concepts—truth, freedom, justice (*Wahrheit, Freiheit, Gerechtigkeit*)—through which Jellinek characterized the positive developments of modern liberal society. In Jellinek's search for a language undergirding both Judaism and the broader human experience, he relied heavily on these core themes and returned to them repeatedly, finding their referent in nearly every classic Jewish text, folktale, and ritual. Jellinek cared deeply about defining (or redefining) a sense of Jewish community and nationhood within the modern European state. He did not think it wise to displace a community dedicated to morality with a code built on the sovereign rights of the individual, no matter how moral that individual was supposed to be. Fearing the total breakdown of the traditional Jewish community, as well as the irreversible separation of the newly founded denominations, he sought a language that would value the rights of individuals while maintaining the focus on Judaism and its common religious and ethnic heritage.

Jellinek's Vienna sermons are some of the best examples of an early rabbinic attempt to wed traditional Jewish narratives, commandments, and practices to modern liberal philosophy. Quoting from the wide range of biblical and rabbinic literature, Jellinek sought to demonstrate that the values of European liberal modernity were already deeply entrenched in the theology and textual history of the Jewish people. Jellinek's faith in the rabbinic tradition arose from his deeply held belief in the alliance between historical Jewish thought and progressive modern values. Some of his writing was undoubtedly motivated by a fear that the traditions he cherished would be lost to the new generation of acculturating Jews.[1] Yet never does one find fear to be his overriding concern. Instead, Jellinek's abiding interests were in the discourses of universalism, nation, community, and progress.

> It is not modern education—with its good tone and its dainty manners—which make the Jews into loyal and selfless citizens, honest and loving member of the whole. Rather, it is Judaism, our confession, which inspires truth, justice, love, and fidelity toward every human being without distinction. [Further,] we can show our devotion to the Throne and Fatherland not with our own success and beneficence, but rather by ensuring that the training of teachers and preachers, who, filled with the divine spirit of Judaism, have the course and the power of conviction.[2]

---

1. See Todd H. Weir, "The Specter of 'Godless Jewry': Secularism and the 'Jewish Question' in Late Nineteenth-Century Germany," *Central European History* 46, no. 4 (2014): 815–49.
2. Jellinek, *Predigten*, 2:137.

Jellinek's belief that Judaism was the moral core of life formed the foundation for all his writings. But Jellinek's was a distinctly modern sort of morality, defined by principles that would have felt very comfortable to any liberal political activists of his era. His ideals—"truth, justice, love, and fidelity toward every human being without distinction"—remain the quest of liberal Judaism to this day, though the challenges of modernity have proven themselves to be far more overwhelming than initially imagined. But as the leader of a community that was, for the first time, experiencing vastly expanded legal equality, new forms of social inclusion, and the promises of bourgeois living, Jellinek earnestly strove to create a marriage between Judaism and European culture.

Judaism Plus Liberalism in a Viennese Setting

Jellinek was fascinated by modern political liberalism and its impact on Jewish life and practice. In many ways, understanding, navigating, and embracing liberalism was one of Jellinek's greatest intellectual challenges throughout the many years he lived in Vienna. European liberalism in the middle of the nineteenth century brought with it an entirely new vocabulary, one by which politicians and intellectuals sought to express their satisfactions and frustrations with a rapidly changing world. As we will explore in this chapter and the next, liberalism explains Jellinek's rhetorical focus on the treatment of strangers and foreigners, and the centrality of morality and justice in his writing.

To understand at greater depth the model of liberalism to which Jellinek adhered, the term must suggest three separate, though interrelated, nineteenth-century phenomena.[3] First, the liberal project aimed to modify and alter traditional Jewish practices, especially as they were developed and fostered by scholars and rabbis in the *Wissenschaft* tradition. Such changes could affect anything from liturgy (what was included in the prayer book),[4] to pedagogy (who attended and what was taught in Jewish schools),[5] to the physical experience of religious practice (what rabbis

---

3. For Jellinek, the idea of liberalism never became divorced from that of theology. The Jewish cosmopolitan intelligentsia, both during the fin-de-siècle and after, took an altogether different path, disposing of the religious content of their Jewish heritage almost entirely. See Malachi Hacohen, "From Empire to Cosmopolitanism: The Central European Jewish Intelligentsia, 1867–1968," *Simon Dubnow Institute Yearbook* 5 (2006): 117–133.

4. See Ferziger, *Exclusion and Hierarchy*, 1–17; and Breuer, *Modernity within Tradition*, 173–84.

5. See Simone Lässig, "Bildung als *kulturelles Kapital*? Jüdische Schulprojekte in der Frühphase der Emanzipation," in *Juden, Bürger, Deutsche: Zur Geschichte von Vielfalt und Differenz, 1800–1933*, ed. Andreas Gotzmann, Rainer Liedtke, and Till van Rahden, Schriftenreihe wissenschaftlicher Abhandlungen des Leo Baeck Instituts 63 (Tübingen: Mohr, 2001),

wore and how synagogues were built).⁶ Second, liberalism involved vast shifts within non-Jewish philosophy and intellectual life as an outgrowth of the eighteenth-century Enlightenment and is most often associated with universalizing ethical and cultural assumptions.⁷ Third, liberalism manifested as a political platform, expressed in the French Revolution of 1789, in the 1848 revolutions, and then intermittently by governments and political parties until the First World War.⁸

Jellinek employed the weekly Sabbath sermon as an essential tool for creating and fostering a liberal Jewish ethos in this new burgeoning urban community. The sermon was a public forum through which Jellinek could actively speak about the impact of contemporary political and philosophical ideas and their relation to traditional Judaism. Jellinek used his sermons to discuss grand ideas—truth, freedom, justice—grounded, so he argued, in Jewish texts. Beginning in the 1850s he settled on a series of themes and narratives that articulated the ways Judaism as a philosophical and religious system was compatible with, and reliant on, the new liberal order. "Judaism and hierarchy are like day and night. When one rises, the other must retreat," he wrote in 1862.⁹ Hierarchy was the chosen regime of despots, he said, and the opposite of liberalism. It was fit only for those who sought power at the expense of the will and benefit of the people. Judaism in its truest incarnation could abide no despotic regime. The Torah was given to all Israel; its commandments applied to all Israel; and all Israel suffered when some among its people brought shame on the name of God. Therefore, Jellinek urged, the Jews had a moral obligation to support a system of governance that devolved upon every nation an equal set of rights and responsibilities.¹⁰ In many ways, Jellinek wholeheartedly

---

263–98; Lässig, *Jüdische Wege ins Bürgertum*; Wilke, "Den Talmud und den Kant," esp. 191–254 and 401–16; and Schwarzfuchs, *Concise History of the Rabbinate*, 97–109.

6. See Eric Kline Silverman, *A Cultural History of Jewish Dress*, Dress, Body, Culture (London: Bloomsbury, 2013); and Krinsky, *Synagogues of Europe*.

7. See Hans-Joachim Salecker, *Der Liberalismus und die Erfahrung der Differenz: Über die Bedingungen der Integration der Juden in Deutschland* (Berlin: Philo, 1999), 65–97.

8. For Jellinek, the practice of liberal democracy was not a fundamental part of liberal politics. His belief in the project of the Habsburg Empire—its polyglot assemblage of nations kept at peace by a benevolent sovereign—hints at a conservatism concerning the full democratic impulse, with its focus on the rights and responsibilities of the individual over and above those of the collective. See David Weinstein, "Nineteenth- and Twentieth-Century Liberalism," in *The Oxford Handbook of the History of Political Philosophy*, ed. George Klosko (Oxford: Oxford University Press, 2011), 414–35; and Baader, *Gender, Judaism, and Bourgeois Culture*.

9. Jellinek, *Predigten*, 2:115.

10. Similarly, Immanuel Wolf, one of the founders of *Wissenschaft*, wrote, "[T]he spiritual content, the idea of Judaism, has communicated itself to the most varied peoples of the world. What is this idea that has existed throughout so much of world history and has so successfully influenced the culture of the human race? It is of the most simple kind and its content can be expressed in a few words. It is the idea of unlimited unity in the all. It is

embraced the new liberal lexicon. But he did so by always finding its corollary somewhere in the Jewish past.

Just below the surface of Jellinek's professed liberalism, however, was the inevitable tension between individual self-expression and what he understood to be the needs and demands of the historic Jewish community and its sense of unified peoplehood. The belief that Jews had a moral responsibility to support the rights of the non-Jewish groups that existed within their same political framework was a central motif in Jellinek's interpretation of Jewish texts. Jellinek's idea of modern Judaism always centered on the idea of the "tribe" (*Stamm*). In Jellinek's mind, *Stamm* signified an identifiable, unified, and culturally distinct people, with rights and responsibilities equal with but never subservient to either the state or other nationalities living inside the state.[11] In the context of the Habsburg Empire, *Stamm* meant something like peoplehood, so the Jewish *Stamm* was like a corporate body in which every individual Jew participated. There was, of course, no one universal *Stamm*. That was fulfilled by the concept of "humanity." But every individual was part of a *Stamm*, be it defined by religion, nationality, or race. In Jellinek's conception, the *Stamm* was a historic, linguistic, and cultural identity; not quite a priori—but almost.

In this vein, Jellinek's sermons praised the autonomous Jewish past while looking toward a mutually shared, respectful, but still separate German *and* Jewish future. His language was proud and complimentary, polemical and poetic. He sought a strong Jewish communal identity within the concert of Habsburg nations: the Jewish *Stamm*, a German cultural affinity, and a Habsburg loyalty.[12]

> Jews have emerged from a wonderful mixture of the primitive elements of the Semitic, Yaphetite, and Hamite, alongside the Europeans of the Orient, [forming] connections and mediating between the Orient and the Occident.... The Jewish *Stamm* consists of nothing but opposites.... Part of this great set of opposites is the particularism and universalism of the Jewish *Stamm*. The German is at home in the universal.... He enthuses for all the oppressed nationalities ... thinking of himself only at the very last ... The Magyar is thoroughly particularistic: he has a Magyar god, a holy Magyar country, a solemn Magyar language.... That Hungarian

---

contained in the one word [YHWH] which signifies indeed the living unity of all being in eternity, the absolute being outside defined time and space" ("On the Concept of a Science of Judaism," 194)

11. Nationalism, of course, can be both the dark side of liberalism or its happy companion. For a discussion of Habsburg nationalism after 1867, see Gary B. Cohen, "Nationalist Politics and the Dynamics of State and Civil Society in the Habsburg Monarchy, 1867–1914," *Central European History* 40, no. 2 (2007): 1–38.

12. See Rozenblit, "Jewish Assimilation in Habsburg Vienna," 238.

peasant who demanded a Hungarian globe in an art trade is the natural representative of a people who want the world to assimilate [to them] and not to assimilate to the world. The Jew unites in himself Germanic universalism and Magyar particularism, Occident and Orient. Therefore, in future times, [the Jew] will have to fulfill a great mission, when these two worlds [German and Magyar] will require the Oriental to mediate questions, [just as] in the Middle Ages the Jew was the mediator between Arabic and European education.[13]

In every case, Jellinek's embrace of liberalism was based primarily on its proven ability to make non-Jews accept Judaism as part of the patrimony of Europe. Look again at the above-quoted passage. Judaism, in Jellinek's vision, forever remains distinct, neither German nor Magyar. But it fulfills an essential role, empathizing with all, assimilating to none. (German and Magyar are not random choices; they were the two dominant ethnicities in the Habsburg Empire of the time.) For Jellinek, the Jewish people were forever in the middle, at home everywhere, and in possession of a literary, theological, and moral tradition that had brought wisdom to Europe in the past and was destined to do so again.

In framing Jewish history and the Jewish contribution to Europe in these terms, Jellinek was seeking two ends, one religious, one political. In terms of religion, he hoped that Jews would increasingly seek out their ancient texts as sources of modern wisdom, and thereby keep alive (or rekindle) their relationship with Jewish religious practice.[14] In terms of politics, Jellinek wanted to inscribe (literally, in the books of scholars) Jewish history into European history, to write the Jews into the European story.[15] In his vari-

---

13. Adolf Jellinek, *Der jüdische Stamm: Ethnographische Studien* (Vienna: Herzfeld & Bauer, 1869), vii, 8–9.

14. For example: "Blessed, blessed be this hour, my dear listeners, if I should succeed in inspiring the love of our language, the language of the Bible, the language of our tribe in the heart of this great, excellent, and generous community, the will to honor and strengthen them and their representatives by esteem and encouragement." (Jellinek, *Predigten*, 2:266.)

15. For example: "'Love the stranger, for you were strangers in the land of Egypt.' What a sublime, blessed law! What a triumph here celebrating the Jewish spirit, which lovingly gathers all strangers around it! Strike out the law books of the ancient peoples; inquire of Egypt, Assyria, Babylon, Greece, and Rome; inquire of the Middle Ages, with their blood fanaticism; inquire of the present age, with its clever statecraft: see if [any of their law codes] contain the three words: 'Love the stranger!'" (Jellinek, *Predigten*, 1:104–5.) Though not directly confrontational with Christianity, Jellinek's comments here suggest a willingness to combat the growing liberal view that moralities across (or even without) religion are equivalent. In a similar vein to Jellinek, Joseph Herman Hertz used his position as chief rabbi in Britain to argue for Judaism's unique moral insights. Benjamin J. Elton writes, "[Hertz's commentary in his edition of the] Pentateuch also took aim at the idea that Greek and Roman civilizations are to be admired, and that Christianity had made an important moral contribution to the world. These were ideas promoted by Claude Montefiore of the Liberal Jewish Synagogue and Hertz thought they would lead Jews into Christianity. He therefore argued that

ous writings and sermons, Jellinek consistently made a claim for Judaism's moral centrality and honorable heritage at a moment when the intellectuals of Europe were rewriting European history by solidifying their Western heritage in Greece and Rome.[16] "Has not the Hebrew tribe, through its Bible, more deeply impacted the freedom and morality of the nations than Greece through its artistic and literary creations?" he asked.[17]

In a way both audacious for its time and almost entirely normative in ours, Jellinek argued that the God of the Jews could genuinely be claimed to have invented the ideals of universal freedom and morality. Therefore, Jellinek said, seeing as the Hebrew Bible was the first document to espouse a belief in universal human ethics, then its creators and caretakes, the modern Jews, were deserving of honor alongside—nay, ahead of—Greece and Rome as progenitors of modern liberal philosophy.

> Mordechai, say our sages, was a *yehudi*, known as a Jew, because while resident in Shushan he was known as an adherent of the one-and-only God above all others, and no man on earth had the right to deny a Jew his belief, so long as with unswerving truth he upheld the banner of the one-and-only God. And what is learnt from the history of Judaism? It tells us that the appearance of Judaism was acted upon by many designs and marks: by the destruction of the Jerusalem Temples, by the dissolution of the Jewish state, by the dispersal of the Jewish nation, by new times, new relationships, and new conditions, by bondage and persecution, by outside influences and internal moods. It [also] tells us of a new epoch in the development of humanity, of the gradual victory of freedom over slavery, love over hate, justice over oppression, recognition over persecution, equality over class strife, humanity over barbarism—a [new] epoch molded from a new form, carried on new blood, and requiring new formative elements.[18]

In this passage, which is typical of Jellinek's rhetorical style, he opens with a distinctly Jewish scene, an interaction or event only available or comprehensible to Jews. In this case, the imagery revolves around an

---

classical civilization was barely disguised barbarism, and Christianity was its bastard child. Anything positive in Christianity came, according to Hertz, from its Jewish roots" (Benjamin J. Elton, "A Bridge across the Tigris: Chief Rabbi Joseph Herman Hertz," in *Conversations: The Journal of the Institute for Jewish Ideas and Ideals* 21 [Spring 2015], https://www.jewishideas.org/articles/bridge-across-tigris-chief-rabbi-joseph-herman-hert).

16. In *Der jüdische Stamm*, Jellinek references Wilhelm von Humboldt (1767–1835), Heinrich Ewald (1803–1875), Ernest Renan (1823–1892), and Gustav Baur (1816–1889), among others. See Suzanne L. Marchand, *Down from Olympus: Archaeology and Philhellenism in Germany, 1750–1970* (Princeton, NJ: Princeton University Press, 1996); and William S. Davis, *Romanticism, Hellenism, and the Philosophy of Nature* (Cham, Switzerland: Palgrave Macmillan, 2018).

17. Jellinek, *Predigten*, 1:69.

18. Jellinek, *Predigten*, 2:235–36.

aspect of Mordecai from the book of Esther: that he was true to the God of Abraham despite his circumstances and the enticements of life in the Persian capital. Dwelling on this religious fidelity, Jellinek makes Mordecai's experience into a metaphor for Jews and Judaism throughout history. Much has changed about the face of Judaism, surely, but appearances were not essences. Even after all their hardships the Jewish people retained their belief in the God of Israel, the one-and-only God. It was for this reason, Jellinek argues, that Judaism survived.

That conclusion should have been the end of the passage. Judaism survived in modernity because it had faith in God and God's commandments. Such a message would have been enough for the millennia of rabbis preceding Jellinek's own. But it was not enough for Jellinek's new milieu— and he knew it. So, in an additional rhetorical move, Jellinek makes the Jews into ethical pioneers for all the world's peoples. Jellinek deeply felt what Martin Luther King Jr. articulated almost exactly a century later, that "the arc of the moral universe is long but it bends toward justice."[19] The adversities faced by the Jews were at the same time like the razing of great oppressive walls; one after another the evils of the world were faced by the Jews, and as the Jews overcame them, the terrible things fell away: "freedom over slavery, love over hate, justice over oppression, recognition over persecution, equality over class strife, humanity over barbarism." Even if, at the time of their overcoming, the world had not recognized that a new moral era had begun, the text of the Bible and the commentaries of the rabbis recorded the transition for them. As *The Jewish Chronicle* would later comment, Jellinek "maintained that Judaism never hints at hoping for a temporal sway over mankind; its hope is for a 'God-rule,' a heavenly kingdom of universal love and universal peace. Indeed, from Jellinek's sermons might be culled some of the finest flowers of eloquent insistence on the claims of humanity."[20] In the middle of the nineteenth century, as the European world began to embrace for the first time and on a universal basis a set of moral principles already (for Jellinek) deeply woven into the fabric of Judaism, Jellinek was there to show his community the source of all these new values, and to extol and rally the people who had kept them alive across all those many centuries.

The Possibilities of Midrash

Jellinek had been interested in midrash since his student days, when he understood it as the spiritual essence of Judaism, almost like a national

---

19. Martin Luther King Jr., *A Testament of Hope: The Essential Writings and Speeches of Martin Luther King, Jr.*, ed. James Melvin Washington (San Francisco: Harper & Row, 1991), 52.

20. *The Jewish Chronicle* (January 5, 1894), 7–8, here 7.

soul, the creative energy and motivating passion that made adaptation across the millennia possible for the Jewish religion and its adherents. Jellinek adapted this idea when he turned to preaching, describing midrash as one of the world's greatest philosophical innovations, the antidote to inflexible dogmatism and scholastic rigidity. "Freedom of spirit is the source of midrash," he wrote, "and we can invent freely and without coercion, without all having to repeat the same creed. In general, it is the midrash that is the lovely fruit of a magnificent tree."[21]

Midrash, in Jellinek's conception, was the Jewish pathway to freedom of thought. It was not simply the Jewish version of non-Jewish liberalism but actually a mode of thinking all its own, one that had continually freed Judaism from the constraints of dogma and doctrine—constraints that had bedeviled other religious traditions. In a jab at the self-satisfaction of Protestant rationalism, which conceived of itself as having been the first to shed the garb of Catholic scholasticism and medieval sentiment and folklore, Jellinek, through the language of midrash, sought to declare that Judaism had always been thusly free. As Jonathan Hess comments, "Typically cast as a clannish and coercive form of legalism irreconcilable with the Enlightenment's insistence on individual autonomy, freedom of conscience and the very power of reason itself, Judaism seemed to provide the perfect point of contrast for [Christian] intellectuals wishing to imagine a secular political order grounded in the principles of rationalism and universalism."[22] Jellinek rejected just this sort of anti-Judaism in liberal modernity. Having studied with some of Germany's most eminent Orientalists in Leipzig, Jellinek, not unremarkably, was decidedly opposed to those who singled out Judaism for unique theological or ritual disdain. His defenses of midrash were, to continue quoting Hess, an example of the fact that "[f]rom Mendelssohn on, Jews also offered up Jewish critiques of modernity. Repeatedly calling attention to those elements of Judaism that Enlightenment culture typically viewed as most antithetical to the spirit of the modern age, Jews reformulated and reclaimed dominant visions of universalism by grounding them in Judaism's own normative tradition."[23] Midrash, for Jellinek, was an essential part of Judaism's "normative tradition," and its remarkable variety and intellectual elegance provided for him an argumentative bulwark against Christian opinions of Judaism that portrayed it as legalistic and spiritually deadened.

In every way, Jellinek's employment of the theme and idea of midrash was unique in his time. No other Jewish preacher of his era did anything similar. Jellinek believed that through midrash he could convince his community of urbanizing and acculturating Jews that the resources

---

21. Jellinek, *Der Talmud: Zwei Reden*, 10–11.
22. Hess, *Germans, Jews and the Claims of Modernity*, 6.
23. Hess, *Germans, Jews and the Claims of Modernity*, 8–9.

for adapting and understanding a changing and conflicted modernity already existed within the Jewish tradition itself.[24] He wrote, "We want today to restore to ourselves the hope of renewal. That, from the confusion and contradictions of modern times—from the battle against external foes who slander [Judaism], and against its blind friends, for whom its essence remains locked[25]—Judaism will emerge radiant in splendor through the divinely blessed weapons of spirit [midrash] and truth [law and ritual]."[26] By Jellinek's own conception, the rabbinic system, which had negotiated the problems of the Jewish world for nearly two thousand years, could continue to function in the present age. In midrash he found a key that could make Jewish texts applicable to the questions of contemporary human life.[27]

The Hebrew Language

While in many ways willing to liberalize aspects of Jewish religious practice, Jellinek was not entirely willing to forgo some aspects of Judaism that he believed both essential to its historic distinctiveness and necessary for its continuation. One of these was praying in Hebrew and teaching Hebrew to children. Hebrew, Jellinek wrote, "which to anyone would be venerable, is most especially thus to the Jewish people.... In it our ancestors felt, thought and talked, and their echoes sound, [for when it was spoken] Israel was independent and respected among the peoples."[28]

As part of Jellinek's dedication to the persistence of Hebrew in modern German Jewish learning, and what set Jellinek's sermons apart from a vast majority of those by his rabbinic colleagues in German pulpits, was his continuous advocacy for Hebrew education, as well as his use of Hebrew in the published versions of his texts. Michael A. Meyer writes of how Jellinek's "elegantly crafted sermons were lavishly embellished

---

24. Interestingly, Jay M. Harris argues that much of modern Jewish denominationalism can be traced to differing ideas about midrash (*How Do We Know This? Midrash and the Fragmentation of Modern Judaism*, SUNY Series in Judaica [Albany: State University of New York Press, 1995], esp. chs. 6–8).

25. This is probably a remark about philo-Semitic Christians, who saw Jews as living remnants of the Old Testament and culture of Jesus. Jellinek's point here (and of any deeper or more nuanced account of rabbinic Judaism itself) is that modern Judaism (Judaism after the destruction of the Second Temple) is both heir to its ancient texts and entirely transformed since (and by) them.

26. Jellinek, *Der Talmud: Zwei Reden*, 18.

27. This belief that midrash is a key to the modern Jewish experience has become one of the central motifs of postmodern Jewry. So-called midrashic writing abounds in contemporary Jewish literature, but almost entirely within nonreligious or nontraditional segments of the community.

28. Jellinek, *Predigten*, 2:259 and 262.

with appropriate [Hebrew] texts from Midrash and Talmud. Their dominant purpose, it seems, was to make his listeners proud of their particular Jewish heritage, to make them 'feel good' about being Jewish."[29] Meyer's understanding of Jellinek's sermons is to see them as motivational: Judaism not only contained essential moral truths, but it had proven throughout the centuries that it could sustain and enhance them, creating a unique society that embodied and advanced both an ethical and a divine mission. "The Hebrew language," Jellinek wrote, "is already venerable because of its old age, since its beginnings reach into the gravest antiquity."[30] One's Jewish ancestors, Jellinek wanted his listeners to believe, were the equal of any modern person in their enlightenment. In the same ways that German writers and philosophers freely quoted the Greek classics, Jews could cite Bible, Mishnah, and Talmud. And when they did, instead of just finding law—as the Christian polemic insisted—they would find a universal moral code as sophisticated and thoughtfully designed as anything being taught in the university.

We can also understand Jellinek's German sermons and their Hebrew footnotes as being pedagogical as well as motivational.

> We must, above all, inspire our children—the heirs of our historical name of honor, the bearers of humanity's religious future—with love for this ancient language. For if Judaism is not to be decomposed, or at least trivialized, by the influences of time, the knowledge of Hebrew must remain at home in Israel. We must ... assist all persons who are anxious to study and fathom the Hebrew language, its construction and formation, its twists and its turns.[31]

Though Germany had produced some exceptionally poetic translations of the Bible (not least of which was Martin Luther's), modern rabbis needed to reiterate that the God of Israel did not speak from Sinai in German.[32] As the liturgical service in non-Orthodox congregations increasingly adopted German-language elements, and as German (rather than Yiddish, which intrinsically reminds its speakers and readers of its Hebrew roots) became the communal language of Habsburg Jewry, Jellinek's consistent references and gestures to the ur-language of Jewish theology and philosophy aimed to reinforce its illustrious status.[33]

---

29. Meyer, *Response to Modernity*, 192.
30. Jellinek, *Predigten*, 2:259.
31. Jellinek, *Predigten*, 2:265.
32. See Simone Lässig, "Systeme des Wissens und Praktiken der Erziehung: Transfers und Überzetzungen im deutschen Judentum des 19. Jahrhunderts," in *Kommunikationsräume des Europäischen: Jüdische Wissenskulturen jenseits des Nationalen*, ed. Hans-Joachim Hahn et al. (Leipzig: Leipziger Universitätsverlag, 2014), 15–42. See also Abigail Gillman, *A History of German Jewish Bible Translation* (Chicago: University of Chicago Press, 2018).
33. See Yaacov Shavit and Mordechai Eran, *The Hebrew Bible Reborn: From Holy Scripture*

Keeping Hebrew central to Jewish ritual and cultural experience was a task not only for progressive rabbis and their communities, however. As Mordechai Breuer has noted, by the middle of the nineteenth century, even among self-identified (and self-selecting) Orthodox communities, such as the one in Frankfurt, Hebrew fluency was rapidly decreasing.[34] Seemingly, then, an audience for Jellinek's ideas remained abundant: both the Orthodox and the less observant were struggling to find the balance between modern European culture and historic Jewish sources.

To solve this problem, Jellinek hoped to prove (to both Jews and non-Jews) that Judaism not only already embodied the tenets of German Enlightenment but that it had done so at least since the time of the early rabbis—if not since Sinai. If they believed this, then studying Hebrew would not be an extracurricular activity—a distraction from modernity—but would actually become (or remain) essential to any complete understanding of liberal values. Just as there was little doubt about the usefulness of reading Plato in the original Greek, so too the Hebrew of the rabbis should bring philosophical insight and cultural honor (and thereby hopefully acceptance and equality) to modern Jewry. In 1857, Jellinek gave a sermon in which he devoted a long, lyrical, passionate description to all the beautiful religious emotion that had been expressed using the Hebrew tongue down the long history of Judaism.

> [Hebrew] is called Holy because it has preserved the most sacred inheritance of humanity.... [It is the] language in which Moses proclaimed the faith in a single, living, eternal, and unchangeable God, the blessing, salvation and bliss of all peoples in the most sublime simplicity. [It is the] language of which Isaiah with a fiery speaker's tongue, Hosea with incomparable pictorial richness, Joel with lively creative power, Amos with rural freshness, Micha with throbbing lips, Nahum with picturesque vividness, Habakkuk with majestic splendor, Jeremiah with shattering tones, Ezekiel with sky-storming imagination—[the language in which they all] delivered immortal speeches, unsurpassed doctrines of righteousness and love, of gentleness and mercy, recited the commandments of the highest and purest morality, the future of humanity, [and in which]

---

to the *Book of Books; A History of Biblical Culture and the Battles over the Bible in Modern Judaism*, Studia Judaica (Berlin: de Gruyter, 2007); and Ran HaCohen, *Reclaiming the Hebrew Bible: German-Jewish Reception of Biblical Criticism*, Studia Judaica (Berlin: de Gruyter, 2010).

34. According to Breuer, "The bookshelves ... were likely to hold incomparably more German books than books in Hebrew. Familiarity with German literature was generally more thorough than familiarity with Hebrew literature, not to mention the Talmud. The Orthodox press admonished its readers on occasion that it was their duty to revive the study of Torah in their families, pointing out that true enthusiasm for the heritage of Judaism could be sparked only through study and knowledge. But Torah study remained confined to a minimum even in many families who regarded themselves as strictly observant and faithful to tradition" (*Modernity within Tradition*, 11).

Major Themes in Jellinek's Sermons   153

the peaceful and friendly times of the Messiah [were] portrayed in the loveliest words. [It is a] language in which the psalmists have composed those marvelous poems which today still elevate and encourage, comfort and console, millions of hearts in synagogues, churches, and mosques all over the earth, which here represent man in his truthfulness and decrepitude, there in his sovereignty and dignity. [It is a language] from which war and victory sound in powerful chords and counter-tones. [It is] a language in which Solomon and his comrades left behind the most glorious and reliable words of wisdom, in which Job and his friends wrote profound speeches spanning God and humanity. [Does] such a language not deserve to be called venerable?[35]

Jellinek's focus on Hebrew was part of a larger program of modernizing Jewish values. Judaism's long history, Jellinek argued, was part of its great strength. For Jellinek, Judaism was a continual act of overcoming, an assimilating of the ideas and opinions of the past by absorbing them into new commentaries, which at once allowed Jewish culture to live inside a tradition while feeling perpetually contemporary. His writings during this period were deeply concerned with Jewish history and the continuing relevance of religious ritual for life in the modern era. "I want to introduce [Judaism] in the midst of the grappling and contentions of our moment," he wrote, "[so that we may] know how it responds to the important questions of our time; I want today to speak to and judge [Judaism] on some of the principle tasks with whose solution our age is occupied."[36] Such words appeal to a "soul" of Judaism, looking not only at ritual strictures but even more so at ethical wisdom and history.

> Language is the soul of a people, a pure and loud source, from which we can draw the knowledge of a tribe. [It is] a bright and clear mirror, in which we see its peculiarities unmixed and unadulterated, the primal history of its spirit, its heart, its character, its inclinations, its light and shadow sides. As we raise the language of the Torah—the language of our prayer houses, the Hebrew language—to their depths and expose their roots to meet the people that once formed and spoke them, it provides a glorious testimony of the Jewish spirit that must shame our adversaries and persecutors.[37]

In Jellinek's formulation, the preservation of Hebrew across so many centuries distinctly followed the language theories of German philosopher Johann Gottfried von Herder (1744–1803). Hebrew expressed, for Jellinek, the continuous development of the national soul that allowed Judaism to

---

35. Jellinek, *Predigten*, 2:260–61.
36. Jellinek, *Der Talmud: Zwei Reden*, 21.
37. Adolf Jellinek, *Die Hebräische Sprache: Ein Ehrenzeugnis des jüdischen Geistes; Dritte Rede über die Hebräische Sprache; Am Sabbat Wajiggasch 5641* (Vienna: Schlossberg, 1881), 5.

remain ever perceptive to new trends in cultural and moral thought. This final act—the ability to accommodate new ethical ideas—was what Jellinek believed made the heart of the rabbinic project not just modern but its continuance also a moral imperative.

Between Orthodoxy and Reform

Jellinek's commitment to traditional Jewish sources placed him in the middle of the liturgical and theological disagreements that were dividing the Central European Jewish community in unprecedented ways. Unlike many of his fellow rabbis, whose reformist agendas put them at odds with the core values of historic Jewish practice, Jellinek could speak to the more conservative immigrants whose numbers were growing every year. On the one hand, Robert Wistrich is correct to note that "[Jellinek's] sermons of the 1860s can be seen as a faithful mirror of the aspirations and ideas of liberal Austrian Jewry,"[38] as is Björn Siegel when he writes that "[Jellinek's] view was similar to Mannheimer's concept of moderate Reform."[39] But, on the other hand, much of what later came to be associated with German-style liberal religion (a repudiation of the Talmud; the excision of large numbers of traditional prayers; the use of instrumentation and discouragement of communal participation during Sabbath services) was anathema to Jellinek.[40]

Both Wistrich and Siegel underestimate the unique rabbinic epistemology that runs through Jellinek's writings. The Reform movement, epitomized by such figures as Abraham Geiger (1810–1874), Samuel Holdheim (1806–1860), and Ludwig Philippson (1811–1889), represented its own unique strand of Jewish intellectual innovation, one that Jellinek recognized and studied but did not adopt.[41] Similarly, the forerunners of the Conservative movement, the rabbis of Zacharias Frankel's Jewish Theological Seminary in Breslau, also developed a set of critical methodologies and theological assumptions that likewise fail to capture either the spirit or the purpose of Jellinek's commitments.[42]

---

38. Wistrich, *Jews of Vienna*, 120.
39. Siegel, "Facing Tradition," 325.
40. Still, we must acknowledge the immense debt Jellinek owed to Mannheimer. See Adolf Jellinek, *Festrede am LXX. Geburtstage Seiner Ehrwürden des Predigers Herrn Isaak Noa Mannheimer (17. October 1863) im alten israelitische Bethause gehalten* (Vienna: Schloßberg, 1863); and Jellinek, *Rede bei der Gedächtnissfeier für den verewigten Prediger Herrn Isak Noa Mannheimer, am 26. März 1865 im Tempel in der Leopoldstadt* (Vienna: Herzfeld & Bauer, 1865).
41. See Christian Wiese, ed., *Redefining Judaism in an Age of Emancipation: Comparative Perspectives on Samuel Holdheim, 1806–1860*, Studies in European Judaism 13 (Leiden: Brill, 2007); and Wilke, "Den Talmud und den Kant," esp. 295–302.
42. Interestingly, the rabbi who followed Jellinek at Leopoldstadt, Moritz Güdemann (1835–1918), was a product of the Seminary in Breslau, suggesting affinity—but not neces-

Though not aligned with a particular movement, these various visions of Jewish reform were expressions of political and theological innovation and represented a desire to face modernity with the full arsenal of Jewish tradition. Jellinek was by no means unique in this regard. Where he differed was that instead of just forwarding a distinct ideology he also experimented with a new ritual-liturgical practice. Eventually, even as the ideological battles continued into the twentieth century, Jellinek's model of urban rabbinical practice gained widespread acceptance. Reformers and those from the Breslau Seminary, and later adherents of neo- and modern Orthodoxy, would all disagree with Jellinek over politics, but each group adopted some version of his template of modern rabbinic practice.

Among the many things that made Jellinek unique among the early generation of urban rabbinic reformers was his use of classic rabbinic sources. Unlike many of his more reform-minded counterparts, Jellinek believed that the Jewish answer to modernity lay within the Jewish texts themselves. For his entire life, Jellinek's faith in the ongoing relevance of the whole history of the Jewish textual tradition was unwavering. He felt free to quote Kant and Hegel, but he also wanted it known that, in many cases, he thought that the Bible and the rabbis had already grappled with the same principles or philosophical ideas centuries beforehand. (We will see numerous instances of this in the next chapter.) At the end of the day, Jellinek was passionately committed to the rabbinic story line and to the quest to help Jews find answers using particularistic Jewish sources, languages, and philosophical methodologies.

Many of the urban rabbis of the mid-nineteenth century cultivated some form of this same view concerning the relation between traditional texts and modern society. Jellinek's innovation was in how he found and shaped a view of contemporary philosophical questions in the language and tonality of classical texts, and of rewriting the history of liberalism, placing Jews at the forerunners of German (and even more so of European) culture. Jews, in Jellinek's vision, were both progenitors and recipients. He sought to make the ancient Israelites into what the Germans had made the ancient Greeks: forebears whose legacy modern peoples were reconstructing toward a more moral and universalist future.

Jellinek's Rhetorical Method

By 1865 Jellinek was one of the most celebrated Jewish communal leaders in the German-speaking world and was renowned for his rhetorical gifts.

---

sarily coterminous intent—between Jellinek's thought and that of the Breslau school. See Schorsch, "Zacharias Frankel and the European Origins of Conservative Judaism," 344–54; Brämer, *Rabbiner Zacharias Frankel*; and Brämer, "Dilemmas of Moderate Reform," 73–87.

His fame derived from more than just his capacity to turn a stirring phrase. His writings captured a particular zeitgeist then motivating Jewish urban culture. More than the writings of his peers, Jellinek's sermons became a model for a sort of progressive traditionalism, a middle way between the Reform and Orthodox positions. Not dedicated to a particular theology or denomination, every word he spoke was nonetheless carefully tailored to the present social and political moment. His sermons were infused with a love of Jewish learning and of ancient texts—of the writings that had captivated him as a young student in the yeshivas of Bohemia and Moravia. As he wrote in 1861, "Love and loyalty molded ancient Judaism; one ties it around one's neck [like a scarf] or hangs it over one's heart."[43]

Those same traditional virtues, Jellinek felt, should be present in the German Judaism of his day. What he valued were ethics and morality, not the revitalization of ancient law. His sermons proposed a spirit of Judaism, a philosophy of Judaism, something that could be used to interpret and mold the present era but that would not reimpose (this time from the Jewish side) the Jewish–gentile separation that had long defined the Jews' experience in Central Europe. "The true dictator has at all times and in all religions placed the sacrifice higher than the ethos; set the visible forms over the spirit; and preferred the flames of the altar to those of the intimate heart."[44]

Jellinek's most influential sermons were written during his first decade in Vienna, 1857–1867. Those same years witnessed the greatest economic and demographic shifts in the empire's history, a fact with which Jellinek was both deeply acquainted and intimately a part. Indeed, for the almost twenty years after his arrival in Vienna Jellinek wrote nothing but articles and sermons aimed at the new Jewish urban migrant community. His focus was singular and pointed: to find a language that would mediate the Jews' transition from rural religious traditionalism to the throes of a theologically confused modernity. Jellinek's work, like that of many of his peers, was, in the words of Mordechai Breuer, "rooted in the desire and the ability to respond to the challenge of tradition by the new, the modern. [His was] not a stubborn and purely passive rejection [of all things contemporary] but a response to them through activity and imagination."[45]

Mining the classic Jewish sources week after week, Jellinek proposed ways of seeing that couched the new in a language of the old. His writings mediated the crosscurrents of German intellectual discourse and Jewish ritual, narrative, and historical consciousness. As Björn Siegel writes, "For

---

43. Jellinek, *Predigten*, 2:105.
44. Jellinek, *Predigten*, 2:112.
45. Mordechai Breuer, "Kreativität und Traditionsgebundenheit," in *Schöpferische Momente des europäischen Judentums in der frühen Neuzeit*, ed. Michael Graetz (Heidelberg: Winter, 2000), 113–20, here 113.

Jellinek, the focus was not on the blind observance of religious rules, but rather centered on the preservation of religious, ethical and social ideals embodied in the Jewish scriptures and texts."[46] Jellinek sought to bring together, on equal terms, the languages of Judaism and German modernity, writing in a way that clearly demonstrated the importance of Judaism for a full and thoughtful life.

By the close of the 1860s, the world of rural Central European Jewry had mostly vanished. Residency laws for Jews had been lifted across the region, and economic conditions attracted tens of thousands of Jewish families to the continent's thriving and expanding cities. Jewish students attended gymnasiums, trade schools, and universities in growing numbers, and increasingly sought professional advancement through careers in industry and the civil service. Religious institutions had been set on a new track as well. The German-language sermon was already a widely accepted addition to the Sabbath prayer service. The synagogue had been reimagined as a communal space with a modern architectural style, creating a public monument to a newfound urban Jewish presence. By the late 1860s, modernity, in all its definitions, had thoroughly pervaded Central European Jewish life.

Jellinek's sermons were all written in this moment of immense change and possibility. Perhaps we might call it the moment of the supremacy of the modern, or the moment of the solidification of the modern. Either way, the transformations wrought by the various threads mapped out in the preceding chapters had finally come together and flowered into a new sort of European society (Jewish and gentile), one pervaded by the past but entirely barred from returning to it. No catastrophe or political agenda could send European social life back to what it had been before Napoleon; or before the mill, or the train, or the telegraph; or before the idea of full Jewish emancipation—or, in fact, before the idea of full emancipation more generally, of a world without human subservience, bondage, or slavery altogether. That is the moment in which Jellinek's sermons were set and in which they must be understood. The past was decisively cut off. The future promised an endless string of progress. But what of morality, tradition, ritual; what of God? Toward those questions Jellinek focused his attention. Philosophers of all types were proposing answers. Jellinek wanted his community, and thereby all Jews, to have a voice in that conversation, to be representatives of a modern and thriving religious tradition.

---

46. Siegel, "Facing Tradition," 325.

9

Jellinek's Sermons: Justice, Care of the Stranger, and Ethical Universalism

> It is with design that Jellinek has been described by us as a preacher rather than as a student. Scholar as he was, though his learned works were widely read and dearly prized, yet Jellinek himself always regarded his other studies as accessories to his sermons.... All the stories of his learning, all his eloquence, his wealth of varied knowledge, were turned to the service of the pulpit.... He was probably the greatest Jewish preacher of the century.
>
> —*The Jewish Chronicle*, January 5, 1894

The sermons discussed in this chapter are generally typical of Jellinek's broader style and outlook. They are at once defensive of Judaism, bordering often on the apologetic, yet also supremely generous and fraternal toward other faiths and ideas, seeing in them different but equal paths to a world expressive of God's laws and lived in God's ways. These sermons engage in the grand exercise of biblical exegesis and argument from commentary at which Jellinek greatly excelled. And they contain many of Jellinek's most common rhetorical tropes: the long historical view, the energetically flowing prose, and the axial assumption that the human pursuit of justice and righteousness is the purest instantiation of God's divine authority over the world.

As discussed in preceding chapters, the enormous intellectual shifts brought about in the second half of the eighteenth and first part of the nineteenth centuries overturned centuries of tradition, belief, and social practice. The need for Jellinek to interpret and address German-speaking liberal culture for Jewish immigrants was acute from the 1840s onward. His impassioned defenses of Judaism, alongside his obvious learning and ability to engender respect in non-Jewish scholarly and theological circles, represented for the Jews of Vienna the quintessence of modernity.¹ Unlike what the French had offered in 1789, which was for the Jew as Jew to be a full emancipated individual but not to be part of a communal Judaism, it appeared to many that the potentials of the German Enlightenment did not require the same total individualization and loss of community. In Vienna, it was believed by some that perhaps the Jews could integrate and gain rights while remaining Jews identifiable as such and part of a historic people.²

For Jellinek, as well as for many of his rabbinic peers, modern political liberalism required the same sort of theological work as was done by the writers of the Talmud, who themselves took nearly five centuries to construct an edifice solid enough to see the Jews through a millennium and a half of diaspora. Jellinek recognized the perceived gap between Jewish traditional discourse and liberal discourse and sought to bring about a harmony between them. The weekly Sabbath sermon was not merely a vessel for this project. It was the new way that Jews in modernity could be enfolded into the process of religious transformation itself. Jewish society was changing fundamentally. Much that had previously been taken for granted was lost, probably forever. The urban synagogue brought Jews together and gave them a space in which to express their inherited tradition, with a rabbi who could offer them hope for the future in a language culled from the vast resources of Jewish literature and history. In this way, a new Jewish community was formed, one based on rabbis and public teaching, vastly different from the provincial, custom-based Judaism of premodernity. But it was something. And Jellinek believed it could be everything.

---

1. See Meyer, *Response to Modernity*, 192–93: "To the Viennese Jewish leadership [Jellinek] must have seemed just the right man for their Jewish milieu: a religious leader who did not create ideological division, an accomplished preacher who provided his listeners with memorable artistic experiences, and a man who expressed their own feelings, reconfirming both Jewish loyalties and universal convictions."

2. Samson Raphael Hirsch, too, to a surprising degree, sought in his writings to balance the language of human individuality and personal freedom with the needs and role of a sacred community: "The community sought to be the individual's sole master. This was an attack on the inalienable worth of the individual, which does not depend on the glory of the community, and which can never be reckoned in terms of mere bricks, not even bricks used in building the glory of the community. It was also a denial of *shem ha'shem* [the name of God]. [God] summons every individual directly to His service and thereby makes every man, be he prince or slave, *free* and *equal*. The Name *hashem* [God] tolerates no slavery! The moment the community says *na'aseh lanu shem* [make for ourselves a name] and does not summon each individual *b'shem hashem* [in the name of God], then *vayered hashem*, God descends and does not forsake His world; he descends to see the edifice the community has been building and to assess the intent of the builders" (*The Hirsch Chumash: The Five Books of the Torah: Sefer Bereshis*, ed. and trans. Daniel Haberman [New York: Feldheim, 2006], 270).

Truth, Freedom, and Justice

For Jellinek, the themes of truth, freedom, and justice were the bedrock of his definition of the promises of modernity, transcending any specific political event or historical moment. They stood for him as the pillars of the liberalizing program, the essential ideas whose fruition would eventually allow Jews and Judaism a place in the general progress of Europe. "Has not the Hebrew tribe, through its Bible, more deeply impacted the freedom and morality of the nations than Greece through its artistic and literary creations?,"[3] he asked. With such words, Jellinek directly confronted those intellectuals of the German Enlightenment who retained their anti-Jewish prejudices, even as they quoted freely from the ancient Greek and Latin classics on the idealized notions of freedom and morality.

In his sermons, Jellinek often found subtle links between traditional religious practices and modern notions of truth and justice. In one such example, Jellinek wrote, "The palm [used during the Jewish festival of Sukkot, the Feast of Booths] is the image of the righteous, of the right, the strictly, impartially right. Over everything the standpoint of the right is the most excellent mark of halakhah."[4] The closed palm frond, straight and narrow, sharp at the edges but sturdy, was the central metaphor of halakhah and Jellinek's idea of the moral. Jellinek heard the enemies of Judaism crying out, Where was the moral among the legal jargon? It was there, in the halakhah, he responded. By rhetorically associating morals with the sturdy and straight, invoking along the way the literal definition of the Hebrew word *halakhah* as "way, road, or path," physical forms often associated with straightness (like the English expression, "the straight and narrow"), Jellinek interwove apologetics with traditional rabbinic interpretation. The place of morality, and therefore of justice, he argued, was in the tall and strong center, in the traditional laws and practices.

Jellinek's is an argument reminiscent of Moses Mendelssohn. In *Jerusalem*, Mendelssohn argued that Judaism received "revealed legislation," which was not a unique form of revealed truth but simply a mechanism for solidifying a code of ethics within the people. Because humanity is flawed and full of moral errors, "the lawgiver of [Israel] gave the *ceremonial laws.... Men must be impelled to perform actions and only induced to engage in reflection.*"[5] But Mendelssohn was at pains to say, these cere-

---

3. Jellinek, *Predigten*, 1:69. Abraham Joshua Heschel makes a similar argument in his essay "No Religion Is an Island" (1965), arguing that the values of contemporary Christianity necessitate the protection of the Jewish people, who are the original keepers of the Hebrew Bible (*Moral Grandeur and Spiritual Audacity: Essays*, ed. Susannah Heschel [New York: Farrar, Straus & Giroux, 1996], 235–50).
4. Jellinek, *Der Talmud: Zwei Reden*, 12.
5. Mendelssohn, *Jerusalem*, 118–19 (emphasis original).

monial laws were merely to ensure a form of morality among the Jews equivalent to that which is practiced and preached in the other nations of the world. "Judaism," he says, "boasts of no *exclusive* revelation of eternal truths that are indispensable to salvation."[6] Judaism, expressing its ethical heritage through laws and ritual, is neither more nor less moral than the other nations of the world. It simply codified an already existing universal morality through different mechanisms.

But Jellinek took Mendelssohn's argument one step further. The historical record of Judaism's revealed legislation, Jellinek argued, suggested that Judaism was not only in full concert with the Enlightenment but was quite obviously its progenitor. Whereas European thinkers came to understand the separation of universal and particular moral systems only recently, Judaism had recognized just such a bifurcation for the better part of two millennia. Israel, Jellinek argued, had always enlisted people to fight for a just and universal moral code.

> [The sages] were to be the speaking-conscience of Israel, the blaring trumpet of God's court. When arrogance, violence, tyranny, hypocrisy, pretense, and bigotry roam, they should teach, advise, admonish, warn, threaten, punish, fight with the strength of the word, and make war upon anything wrong, mendacious, mean, and low—[upon] all that weakens the truth, undermines liberty, or paralyzes justice.[7]

The moral codes God gave to the non-Jewish nations could not be in conflict with the moral codes of Israel, which meant that there must be a universal system underlying the particularity of Judaism. This is why Jellinek wrote, "'Love the stranger' ... [for] every human being ... is loved by God."[8] For Jellinek, the Bible and its rabbinic interpreters gave Judaism a central role in the historical arc toward Enlightenment's recognition of universal justice.

Described another way, Jellinek imagined the rabbinic corpus as functioning like a prism, taking the non-Jewish elements of the world and refracting them into a Jewish idiom and practice. What that new post-prismatic idiom might look like varied across time and geography, but what Jellinek desired was for the Talmud's method of meaning-making to open Judaism outward, helping it become a part of the conversation of modernity.

> The words of the Talmudic sages are at the same time as stepping stones, whilst also holding together the faith and the various types of human

---

6. Mendelssohn, *Jerusalem*, 97 (emphasis original).
7. Jellinek, *Predigten*, 2:115.
8. Jellinek, *Predigten*, 1:105–106.

community through the teachings of justice, humanity, and morality, which, they note, are instilled in every nation and every state through the principles of religious toleration, and by exhortations to peacefulness, which they preach aloud to the glory of God—who makes peace in His heights—so the Heavens can be witness to the harmonious and peaceful interaction of the enlightenment of the universe![9]

Jellinek hoped his community might believe that the resources of the Jewish past could speak to the Jewish present. He wanted to convince them that rabbinic literature would be able to positively engage with whatever modernity created. The Talmud, you can almost hear him say, was fundamentally a system of Enlightenment, motivated by the same philosophical questions and searching for the same political ends. Jellinek's version of Enlightenment, it should be noted, applied not just to people but to governments as well. He wrote, "Justice, humanity, and morality ... are instilled in every nation and every state through the practice of religious toleration."[10] Civil order and religious toleration are synonymous, he argued. He set the Talmudic sages as the originators of the idea of universal justice and humanity, which meant that Jews, long hated for their purported insularity, were really incubators of a broader world vision. Only through the Enlightenment had non-Jews come to recognize what Judaism had understood and practiced all along.

In arguing for the greatness of Judaism because it had long incorporated the new liberal philosophies, Jellinek embodied the novel role being created for the rabbi and for Jewish texts in modernity, one that sought to place Judaism overtly into the lineage of European history and ideas. In his biblical exegesis, Jellinek continuously looked not toward law and history but toward goodness, righteousness, and lawfulness.

> [God] is our God, we pronounce. This is the same loving being who includes all families of the earth. And on the basis of written statements, the Babylonian Talmud raises as unbreakable law that of cheating, deceiv-

---

9. Jellinek, *Der Talmud: Zwei Reden*, 32.
10. Jellinek, *Predigten*, 1:105. Compare these words to those from Immanuel Kant's famous essay *What Is Enlightenment?*: "When even a people may not decide for itself [the sort of freedom it wants,] can even less be decided for it by a monarch; for his lawgiving authority consists in his uniting the collective will of the people in his own. If only he sees to it that all true or alleged improvements are consistent with civil order, he can allow his subjects to do what they find necessary for the wellbeing of their souls" ("An Answer to the Question: What Is Enlightenment?," trans. James Schmidt, in *What Is Enlightenment? Eighteenth-Century Answers and Twentieth-Century Questions*, ed. James Schmidt, Philosophical Traditions 7 [Berkeley: University of California Press, 1996], 58–64, here 62). Kant's opinion of Jews and Judaism remains a subject of some question and concern. See Sidney Axinn, "Kant on Judaism," *Jewish Quarterly Review* 59, no. 1 (1968): 9–23; and Emil L. Fackenheim, "Kant and the Jews," *Commentary*, December 1, 1963.

ing, betraying, insulting, and offending ... and that loyalty, truthfulness, peacefulness, and justice should necessarily be used against them.[11]

Jellinek was interested in the cultivation of a certain type of moral life, one that Judaism embodied but that ultimately transcended the particularities of Judaism. He wrote, "And only in free realms of spirit [does one meet] arbitrariness and randomness, distance and alienation, from the path of the original human nature, from the way of law and justice."[12] Jellinek did not want a fully liberalized Jewish religion. He did not want a Jewish philosophy of life, which could mean a way of being moral without ritual or practice. A "free realm of spirit" meant a lonely and isolated world, where people look inside themselves for moral truth rather than to the texts and rituals of the tradition. Jellinek believed that the ancient Jewish sources embodied the universalizing spirit of his age, but he also believed that, without the ancient sources, their commentaries, and their ritual practices, the ethical wisdom could be easily discarded. In the view of Judaism, a morality created in one's own era has almost no weight when compared to a system undergirded by centuries of tradition, discussion, and practice.

Loving the Stranger

Across all his writings, Jellinek argued repeatedly that religion, and even more so the Bible, is the ground upon which all ethical values stand. The Bible, Jellinek said, gives the world the idea of social welfare, with its love of the widow and the orphan. The Bible orders respect of the foreigner, rather than her conversion. The Bible suggests the separation of civil and religious law, rather than the theological monarchies of Europe. For Jellinek, there could be no universal values, no sense of the individual, no notion of justice, without the grounding of revealed religion.

Jewish thought has a long history of devoting special moral attention to the treatment of the "stranger."[13] In the Hebrew Bible the stranger is called a *ger*, and when used in the phrase *ger toshav* means something like

---

11. Jellinek, *Predigten*, 2:134.
12. Jellinek, *Predigten*, 1:39.
13. This notion remains liturgically present as well. In the Sabbath blessing on wine, it is recited that the stranger who lives in one's midst must be allowed to rest as well. See David Novak, *The Image of the Non-Jew in Judaism: The Idea of Noahide Law*, ed. Matthew Lagrone (Oxford: Littman Library of Jewish Civilization, 2011); David L. Lieber, "Strangers and Gentiles," in *Encyclopaedia Judaica*, 2nd ed., ed. Michael Berenbaum and Fred Skolnik, 22 vols. (Detroit: Macmillan Reference, 2007), 19:241–42; and Daniel Sperber and Theodore Friedman, "Gentile," in Berenbaum and Skolnik, *Encyclopaedia Judaica*, 2nd ed., 7:485–87.

the modern legal phrase "resident alien."[14] In a long discourse near the end of his life on the wisdom and beauty of the Hebrew language, Jellinek discussed the Bible's language around the foreigner and stranger.

> The stranger? What is he called in Hebrew? *Ger*. Does this monosyllabic word really mean to be 'foreign'? No! He will say that he is by your side, in the midst of your people, under the protection of your law. He has not sprung from your tribe, does not belong to your race, does not speak your language, does not confess your religion, does not look like your fellow countrymen—but he sojourns and resides on your national soil, lives peacefully in your environment, nourishes himself and his people in intercourse with you. You should not have in mind—and should not repeat [to others in your group]—that it is his strangeness that separates him from you.... Whoever lives outside your territory is a foreigner, a stranger, a '*nochri*'. But whoever settles near you, in the Holy Land, under the roof of the Torah, you must call him something else, which you should call *ger*.[15]

The word *ger* appears dozens of times in all five books of the Torah, throughout the prophetic writings, and across rabbinic literature.[16] These biblical and rabbinic texts formed the core materials for Jellinek's various discussions of the Jews' moral obligations to the other and the stranger. Drawing heavily on the language of Exodus ("You shall not wrong or oppress a stranger, for you were strangers in the land of Egypt"), Jellinek sought to resuscitate a native language of universalism from within the heart of biblical Judaism. His sermons concerning the treatment of strangers were meant for both his Jewish community and a broader circle of modern readers. Jews remained both a community that must accept

---

14. "Resident alien" is the translation of *ger* used most often by the New Revised Standard Version (NRSV) and sometimes by JPS.

15. Jellinek, *Die Hebräische Sprache*, 8.

16. See the entry "*ger*" in Avraham Evan-Shoshan, *Konkordenziyah hadashah le-Torah Nevi'im u'Khtuvim: ozar leshom ha-Mikre, Ivrit ve'Aramit; shorashim, milim, shemot peretiyim zerufim venirdafim, ba'arikhat Avraham Evan-Shoshan* (Jerusalem: Miryst Sefer, 1978). As an ethical injunction, the Bible employs the word as a reminder of Israel's sojourn in the land of Egypt ("You shall not wrong or oppress a stranger [*ger*], for you were strangers [*ger'im*] in the land of Egypt" [Exodus 22:21]), though the first usage of the word in Genesis is actually by Abraham describing himself ("I am a stranger among you. Give me a burial place among you, so that I may bury my dead from before me" [Genesis 23:4].) The vast majority of references occur in the latter four books of the Pentateuch, after the Israelites have left Egypt and are receiving the laws that are to govern them in the land of Canaan. The essential paradigm for the Bible is that Egypt's oppression of Israel is the dialogical model for every subsequent moral system: through Egypt's sins we learn the proper conduct for our own society. In classical rabbinic literature, one of the most quoted references to the treatment of the stranger occurs at the conclusion of, or as the coda to, one of the Talmud's most famous stories, referred to in shorthand as the "Oven of 'Aknai" (b. Baba Metzia 59b).

strangers among them, and they themselves remained strangers in a predominantly Christian empire.

Jellinek's writings balance these two, sometimes conflicting, circumstances. The Jews would always remain a minority, and for that they would be perpetual foreigners, though the liberal tradition Jellinek sought to transmit guaranteed them certain rights and privileges. But the urbanization of European Jewry had also confronted them with a new sort of challenge. The liberal model meant that Jewish choices now impacted the lives and prosperity of many peoples quite different from themselves. A growing Jewish presence in the civil service, the intelligentsia, and the professional classes gave every Jewish action an added importance. The Bible's moral language concerning the stranger, Jellinek believed, was essential for the creation of a new Jewish ethics in the modern liberal city.

Supporting this point, the very first chapter in Jellinek's three-volume collected sermons is entitled "Ruth" (delivered in 1861) and is an exegesis on the importance of treating the stranger with fairness and equity. Responding to the age-old slur that Jews cared only for themselves, and that Judaism was a religion of laws without loving kindness, Jellinek described the legal obligation to care for those who are different: "But is Judaism so indifferent to the healing of other people? Is it really so narrow-minded and selfish that is does not care about its progress and the spreading of its truth? Certainly not! Forty-five times ... God focuses the Israelites on justice, love, and mercy toward the stranger." [17] We read the book of Ruth on Shavuot (The Feast of Weeks), the holiday commemorating and celebrating the giving of the Torah on Mt. Sinai and which is traditionally marked by all-night religious study, as a reminder, Jellinek said, that the values inherent in Judaism are universal and accepting.[18] Though the Torah was given specifically to the Jewish people, its moral strength arises out of a sense of creating universal order and goodness. Over forty times the Jews are called in the Torah to remember that they were once strangers in a strange land, yet upon each reading Ruth's story leaves one breathless and fearful. How will she be treated in a land not her own? Being a Moabite, is she condemned to remain outside the community of Israel?[19]

In the end Ruth is treated fairly, and for her commitment to Israel she is abundantly rewarded, becoming the great-grandmother of King David, the greatest of the biblical monarchs and progenitor himself of the line of

---

17. Jellinek, *Predigten*, 1:7. Jellinek's forty-five times is perhaps a misremembering of Eliezer's forty-six times from the story recounted in b. Bava Metzia 59b.

18. Jellinek, *Predigten*, 1:4.

19. Deuteronomy 23:3: "No Ammonite or Moabite shall be admitted to the assembly of the Lord. Even to the tenth generation none of their descendants shall be admitted to the assembly of the Lord."

the Messiah. What does Jellinek say one should learn from this story? That the Jews have shown to the world forbearance to history, love of stranger, and loyalty to those who share their values. Not insular, parochial values, but universal ones: welcoming the stranger, feeding and housing the poor, and trusting in the piety and benevolence of those who ask for assistance. For Jellinek, the book of Ruth is about the practice of civic virtues. It is a biblical argument that the Jewish presence in non-Jewish lands could be something to value and not to fear. The Jews were kind to Ruth—even after an ancient hostility, which could have bred resentment and suspicion—because that is what the Bible enjoined upon them. You were once foreigners in a new land, like Ruth. Be now like Boaz, Jellinek said, and make for others a home in your community.

The Torah's use of *ger toshav*, a resident alien, does not, however, always refer to a proselyte like Ruth. If the stranger wishes to partake in the rituals of the community, then yes, he or she must convert. But if the foreigner is merely someone who lives in the community, then she has no obligations to take on the commandments of the Jewish people. She must simply be treated fairly and allowed to practice her own customs. A mandate of kindness toward this sort of stranger, Jellinek argued in "Ruth," was unique to the Bible, and from this far more difficult moral imperative he derived some of his most insightful and deeply powerful ideas.

In an earlier sermon, "Love the Stranger!" (1858), Jellinek had noted that, instead of care for the stranger being a commandment simply about justice, the Bible was also mandating a particular emotion. Citing the verse "Love the stranger [*v'ahavtem et ha-ger*], for you yourselves were strangers in the land of Egypt" (Deut 10:19), Jellinek translated the opening phrase as an imperative: Love! Through this he argued two points: that the commandment to the Jews to love the stranger was unique among the nations; and that the communal legacy within the Jewish nation to uphold this commandment had remained strong throughout the centuries. Jellinek said,

> "Love the stranger, for you were strangers in the land of Egypt." What a sublime, blessed law! What a triumph here celebrating the Jewish spirit, which lovingly gathers all strangers around it! Throw out the law books of the ancient peoples; inquire of Egypt, Assyria, Babylon, Greece, and Rome; inquire of the Middle Ages, with its blood fanaticism; inquire of the present age, with its clever statecraft: see if [any of these law codes] contain the three words: "Love the stranger!"[20]

---

20. Jellinek, *Predigten*, 1:104-5. Though not directly confrontational with Christianity, Jellinek's comments here suggest a willingness to combat the growing liberal view that moralities across (or even without religion) are equivalent.

Jellinek believed that one should love the stranger, that is, that one could be implored through law to reach out and be kind to the stranger. God is not the state; since the demise of political theology one is not imprisoned for ignoring God's laws. (Mendelssohn called this the "non-coercive" nature of religious law.) But divine laws are still meant to show a person the moral way to act. Jellinek thought that the Bible had, in fact, created the potential for "positive liberty" among the Jewish people, an impetus for responsible and thoughtful decision-making.[21] One would not be stoned for disrespecting the stranger. Instead, one could be taught to choose to love the stranger. In this sense, God was taking a gamble on humanity. Jellinek, full of optimism, wanted to be part of that bet.

Jellinek concluded that to fully internalize the imperative "love the stranger" humanity must remember the second part of the biblical command, "for you yourselves were strangers in the land of Egypt." Strangers might not be individuals. Even Mendelssohn missed the gravity of the latter half of the phrase. Israel was a stranger in the land of Egypt for four hundred years. Not individual Hebrews but the Children of Jacob in its entirety. Therefore, even if the Jews were to be strangers in Europe for a thousand years, such a thing could only make this commandment more essential. Not only, thought Jellinek, did the nations of Europe need to respect the right of individual Jews to practice their traditions. The Europeans needed to love the presence of the Jewish people—as a separate people—in their midst, in order for true liberalism to find root on Habsburg soil.

Jews and Christians

In the fall of 1859, Jellinek gave a sermon entitled "Israel's Teachings on the Relationship of Jews and Non-Jews."[22] The sermon was written for *Shabbat Vayera*, the selection from Genesis (18:1–22:24) as designated by the annual Jewish cycle for reading the complete Pentateuch. As it opens, the sermon is a passionate discourse on the relationship between Jews and non-Jews; by its end, it is a pointed and searing call to reimagine the entire relationship between Judaism and Christianity writ large. There had been mutual animosity between the two religions for so long, Jellinek said, a bitterness that dated back centuries and echoed in the writings of both

---

21. I am adopting this term from Isaiah Berlin (its opposition being "negative liberty"); see Isaiah Berlin, *Four Essays on Liberty* (New York: Oxford University Press, 1969). Berlin is particularly appropriate here, since he believed that "political theory was a branch of moral philosophy" (120) just as Jellinek did.

22. Jellinek, *Predigten*, 2:122–39.

sides.²³ Do we not now, he asked, inhabit a century and society in which mutual respect—indeed, even friendship—between Jews and Christians was possible? Have we not had enough of hatred and bloodshed, of antipathy and malice, that we should not strive for a new beginning? Can we not now recognize that we share reverence for the same God, creator of Heaven and Earth, in a Europe that has space for us all? "Love generates love and hatred generates hatred, or, in concert with the great poet [Friedrich Schiller] who is celebrated these days in all parts of Germany: 'Love is love's price.'"²⁴

In the sermon, Jellinek's answer as to how Jews and Christians could forge mutual trust and charitable goodwill in modernity followed on ideas developed in the eighteenth century, that of both religions as children of Abraham.²⁵ But Jellinek's idea was to imagine Judaism and Christianity not as siblings but as parent and child, and therefore to prompt emotions not of fraternity but of filial piety and maternal love. Christianity is, Jellinek wrote, one of Judaism's "daughter religions" (*Tochterreligionen*), and is this not why, he asked, "[the great Jewish authorities of the early modern period] recognize in their legal provision that the followers of the oldest daughter religion of Judaism invoke the same God of Heaven and Earth as Israel, and that only through their conception and organization of the idea of God do they differ and are separate [from us]?"²⁶ Just as children are an intrinsic part of their parents' story, embodying their parents' values but forging their own lives, so too Judaism and Christianity were engaged in the same great earthly endeavor—love of God and pursuit of justice.

Still, in the middle of the nineteenth century, to assert (in positive tones) a familial bond between Judaism and Christianity, and to have it be meaningfully believed, required more than rhetorical flourish. Rather than a meditation on holiness or a heartfelt plea for justice, this sermon was structured as almost an academic argument in the mode of an article in a *Wissenschaft* journal: analytical in its methods, comprehensive in its scope, brimming with citations and references. Using Abraham as his model and starting point, Jellinek's sermon took listeners from the actions of their forefather as recorded in *Vayera*, through the positive relations between Israelites and non-Israelites chronicled in later biblical texts, and up to the classical and medieval codifications of the rules and ethics of Jewish–gentile relations. In the end, said Jellinek, the great pagan civili-

---

23. Jellinek, *Predigten*, 2:138: "For every drop of ink which the Jews used to write these outbursts [against Christians] ... streams of Jewish blood had flown before!"
24. Jellinek, *Predigten*, 2:137–38.
25. This idea was made famous in Gotthold Ephraim Lessing's play *Nathan der Weise* (1779).
26. Jellinek, *Predigten*, 2:136–37.

zations of the past about whom the rabbis often wrote had long ceased to exist; therefore, the words of Judaism that once applied to them must now be understood as guiding Israel's relationship with Christianity. And if the Bible and Talmud could find words of respect for the pagan peoples of history, should not—all the more so—Jews of the present find happy communion with their Christian neighbors, whose beliefs were not alien but actually derive from Judaism itself?

As in all his sermons, Jellinek opened with a framing passage from the week's biblical text, in this case Genesis 18:25: "Far be it from You to do such a thing, to bring death upon the righteous as well as the wicked, so that righteous and wicked fare alike." These words are spoken in a famous scene in the cycle of stories concerning Abraham, forefather of the major monotheistic faiths. Abraham and God are standing on a hilltop, overlooking the plain which contains the cities of Sodom and Gomorrah. God has decided to destroy the two cities and all their inhabitants because of their sinfulness, but does not want to keep such a momentous decision from Abraham, whom, God thinks, "I have singled ... out, that he may instruct his children and his posterity to keep the way of the LORD by doing what is just and right [*tz'dakah u'mishpat*]" (Gen 18:19). But when God tells Abraham what he is about to do, Abraham does not think such an action is *tz'dakah u'mishpat*. Instead, Abraham strenuously objects, asking, "Will You sweep away the righteous [*tzadik*] along with the wicked?" (Gen 18:23) after which begins Abraham's famous negotiation with God concerning the number of righteous necessary to save the two cities. This is the passage from which Jellinek takes his opening quotation: "Far be it from You to do such a thing, to bring death upon the righteous [German *Gerechten*/Hebrew *tzadik*] as well as the wicked, so that righteous and wicked fare alike. Far be it from You! Shall not the judge of all the earth deal justly [*Recht/mishpat*]?"

The reading for *Vayera* actually does not begin with this conversation overlooking the cities of the plain. Instead, it opens with a tableau of Abraham sitting at the entrance to his tent, greeting three unknown travelers. Jellinek identifies the men—following midrashic tradition (Genesis Rabbah 40:8)—as a Saracen, a Nabatean, and an Arab. "As soon as he [Abraham] saw them, he ran from the entrance of the tent to greet them and, bowing to the ground, he said, 'My lords, if it please you, do not go on past your servant'" (Gen 18:2–3). The biblical scene is meant to highlight Abraham's immediate and unconditional kindness, as well as the men's thankfulness and their bestowal of a blessing (the birth of a future son, Isaac) on Abraham in return for Abraham's hospitality. Abraham's unreserved generosity is all the more striking because he is a foreigner in this land and among this people (see Gen 12:1, 23:4). He is a resident alien, a sojourner, yet still he welcomes in strangers and offers them food and rest.

By opening his sermon with these accounts of Abraham's doings, Jellinek frames Israel's forefather not as a Knight of Faith but as a Knight of Justice (*Gerechtichkeit*). There is justice in Abraham's treatment of the three strangers and justice in Abraham's argument with God over the fate of the two wicked cities. The Hebrew word *tzedek/tz'daka* captures these two sides of Abraham's actions. Whereas in English, "justice" is often associated with law,[27] in Hebrew, "just law" is *mishpat* whereas tz'*daka* is a combination of legal and ethical righteousness, the act of full humane treatment one person to another, be it juridical or philanthropic. In this case, Abraham is "just" (*tzedek*) not only in the legal sense (arguing for the lives of those about to die) but also in the humanitarian one (feeding weary travels).[28] From the very beginning, Jellinek argued, the Jewish model has been that of openness to strangers, welcoming to those who are different from oneself, cognizant that only in a world in which there is justice for everyone is there justice for anyone.[29] (For a more comprehensive discussion of Jellinek on the treatment of foreigner and strangers, see the previous section.)

For Jellinek, Abraham's righteous actions toward strangers became the foundation on which to build an argument for how Judaism has always understood its relationship to non-Jews: as one based on the principle of mutual justice (*tz'daka*).[30] "Already in Israel's founding father, true human-

---

27. The German *Gerechtigkeit* has somewhat more nuance, including not only "justice" but also "justness" and "fairness." Jellinek will often link *Gerechtigkeit* with *Wahrhaftigkeit* (truthfulness) and *Friedfertigkeit* (peacefulness), making from them a single idea, "justice-that-is-true-and-full-of-peace," an awkward but approximate definition of *tz'daka*.

28. Indeed, Abraham's phrase "shall not the judge of all the Earth deal justly" (*hashofet kol ha'aretz lo ya'aseh mishpat*) brings out this distinction between *mishpat* and *tzedek* cogently. Abraham is asking God: should not the judge (the *shofet*) in the courtroom make a law (*mishpat*) that is just across all the world? (Actually, one really cannot say "a law that is just" and translate only half the sentence [a law] as *mishpat*; *mishpat* means "a law that is just," which is Abraham's entire argument: if God is going to issue a *mishpat*, it cannot be unjust, or it is not a *mishpat* and God is not a judge [*shofet*].) And when Abraham describes the good people in Sodom upon whom a just law (*mishpat*)—in this case, not being destroyed—should be enacted, he calls them *tzadikim*: "What if there should be fifty *tzadikim* within the city walls ...? Far be it from You to do such a thing, to bring death upon the *tzadik* as well as the wicked, so that the *tzadik* and the wicked fare alike." Thus, when Abraham calls those who are "innocent" (the standard translation; rendered here as "righteous") in Sodom and Gomorrah by the term *tzadik*, and then says that God must issue a "just decree" (*mishpat*), he is already separating the two terms. Jellinek capitalizes on this philological distinction, which lends credence to Jellinek's identity of Abraham as the originator of the Jewish notion that *tzedek* is justice that is humanitarian plus legal. (This example does not work in German translation, where the "righteous" of Sodom are called *Gerechten*, the "judge" of the Earth is *der ... Erde richte*, and to "deal justly" is *Recht üben*, all of which is based on the root word *Recht* [right-law, closer to *mishpat*] and fails to capture the distinction between *tzedek* and *mishpat*.)

29. E.g., "There shall be one law [*torah akhad*] for the citizen [*ezrach*] and for the stranger [*ger*] who resides among you" (Exod 12:49) and "You shall have one law [*mishpat ekhad*] for stranger [*ger*] and citizen [*ezrach*] alike, for I the Lord am your God" (Lev 24:22).

30. Jellinek, *Predigten*, 2:126. One should hear echoes of the core ideals of nineteenth-century liberalism, not only justice itself but also equality, liberty, fraternity, and universalism.

ity toward every human being without distinction was embodied and pronounced, and Jewish history from its very beginning represented the noblest love of the human being."³¹ By focusing on justice, Jellinek shifted the conversation away from theological and ritual differences between Jews and non-Jews and toward moral continuities among individuals. What the stories of Abraham offered Jellinek was biblical evidence that, from its very foundation, Judaism had always understood the ethical ideas espoused by its God as universalist in their outlook. "Justice [*Gerechtigkeit/tzedek*], justice [*Gerechtigkeit/tzedek*] shall you pursue" (Deut 16:20), which, Jellinek says, "a writer in the spirit of the Talmud explains [thus]: the doubling of the word 'justice' here indicates that one should make no difference in this point [i.e., in pursuit of justice] between Jews and Gentiles."³²

Expounding on the deeds of Abraham was, for Jellinek, an argument meant to combat Christian anti-Judaism as much as to educate his own Jewish congregation about their ethical responsibilities toward non-Jews. For Jellinek, one of the most disturbing claims made against Jews and Judaism by Christians was that Judaism is clannish and insular, and that its vision of God's ethical commandments barely extends beyond the borders of the Jewish community. Such a view of Judaism by Christians represented a deep problem for Jellinek, who believed that the flourishing of Judaism in modern Europe depended on the continued familial separation of Jews from non-Jews (i.e., no intermarriage) but also on Jewish legal emancipation and social integration based on a shared notion of universal ethics. As Jellinek wrote, "Judaism, by virtue of its fundamental truths about God and Man, must determine—and has determined—and [must] establish at all times and in all its writings the relations of Jews to Gentiles according to the principles of love and justice [*Gerechtigkeit*]. [As it says in the Talmud:] "He who has no love of his fellow man is a stranger to his forefather Abraham."³³

In a point that Jellinek adopts from the rabbinic tradition, he notes that the Hebrew Bible begins not with the Jewish people, nor even with Abraham, but with creation itself, and therefore with the origin of all humanity.

> [Could it be that the God of Creation] would really be [only] a Jewish God, an Idea in which all humanity would find no room, a Prince who, as it were, would have to content Himself with the little country of Palestine [as His kingdom] and with a few millions of Judeans [as His subjects]?³⁴

---

31. Jellinek, *Predigten*, 2:126.
32. Jellinek, *Predigten*, 2:134. The reference is to Rabbeinu Bahya, *Kad ha-Kemah*.
33. Jellinek, *Predigten*, 2:130. The reference is to b. Betzah 32b.
34. Jellinek, *Predigten*, 2:127.

An affirmative answer to that question is patently absurd, for it not only contradicts the soaring vision of Psalm 24 ("The Earth is the LORD's and the fullness thereof") and Isaiah 66 ("The heaven is My throne and the Earth is My footstool") but more profoundly the simple but powerful description of human Creation itself: "And God created man in His image" (Gen 1:27). Not Jewish Man. Not Abrahamic Man. But Man, person, human being, Everyman, what the rabbis call simply *adam ha'rishon*, "First Man."

> [The Biblical story of Creation] considers every man—wherever he is born, wherever he dwells, however he looks, however he can speak and dress—as a child of the One Creator God. This doctrine knows only one human family, whose members may well have different forms, voices, inclinations, abilities, and talents, but who in God, like children in their father, must know and empathize one with another.[35]

Would the God who is credited with creating humanity then content himself merely with the ethical cultivation of one nation, especially one so small? Why go to the trouble of making the universal point of human equality at creation if only to settle on adjudicating a particularistic ethics among a small number of people for the rest of history? Jellinek forcefully rejected such an idea of God's parochial moral governance, as did the rabbis before him, who wrote, "Therefore, was Adam created singular ... for the sake of peace among creation, that one should not say to another, 'My father was greater than your father'" (m. Sanhedrin 4:5).

For Jellinek, making ethical distinctions between Jews and gentiles was simply not how the Hebrew Bible understands God's ethical commandments. (Abraham's argument for saving the *tzadikim* of Sodom—who were decidedly not Jewish—being a case-in-point.) At its core, Jellinek argued, the Bible teaches that the Jewish people have always been in relationship with non-Jews, and that the God of Israel has always also been the God of the world.

> [Need I argue] that the biblical rules relating to stealing, robbery, murder, measures, weights, labor, wages, hatred, resentment, vengeance, widows, orphans, and the poor ... all make no distinction between Jews and Gentiles?[36]

Of course not, is the obvious answer, not just for Jellinek and his community but for every biblical commentator, Jewish and gentile alike.[37]

---

35. Jellinek, *Predigten*, 2:128–29.
36. Jellinek, *Predigten*, 2:133.
37. It is important to point out that Jellinek believes that these moral laws comprise much more than what some might call "natural law." He would likely admit that laws

These laws all apply as much to Jews as to non-Jews, and as much by Jews *toward* non-Jews as vice versa. Which is why Abraham's argument "shall not the judge of all the Earth deal justly" is convincing to God, and also why there is theological import to the fact that it is said by the man who will become the forefather of the Jewish people: even at the beginning, Abraham's God is *already* the God of the world.[38]

But Jellinek was not content to prove that the Hebrew Bible is universal. More or less, the Christians believe that on their own. Indeed, the problem was that Christians did not believe that Jews believed that on their own. Therefore, for much of the sermon, through quotations and rhetorical questions and impassioned pleas for moral common sense, Jellinek sought to argue that postbiblical Jewish tradition *had* understood God's ethical commands as being universal, while simultaneously threading a very delicate line between Jewish particularism and God's ethical universalism. For Jellinek,[39] the Jewish people's *ritualistic* and *covenantal* expectations are unique, but their practice and adjudication of *justice* is universal. He noted, "The Israelite should not mock and blaspheme the gods worshiped by foreign peoples. As the Mishnah says, 'Despise no person.'"[40] For Jellinek, Jewish tradition had been in constant internal dialogue concerning its ethical relationship with non-Jews and had continually reinforced the position that Judaism seeks and expects justice both toward and from gentiles.

To prove this thesis, Jellinek outlined the various ways non-Jews have been understood by Jewish texts and history. It is true, he admitted, that none of the major works of Temple or post-Temple Judaism—his list included Bible, Apocrypha, Philo, Josephus, Mishnah, Tosefta, Mekhilta, Sifra, Sifre, or the Talmuds—commented much on the Christians or Muslims, for (he believed) these canons were all but complete by the time Judaism's "daughter religions" became theological rivals.[41] Nevertheless, Jellinek provided numerous sources against the idea that Jews ever

---

against stealing, robbery, and murder are "natural," that is, in a Lockean sense, intrinsic to the very essence of human society itself. But, Jellinek would say, ethical presumptions such as those concerning labor relations, honest weights and measures, and treatment of orphans and widows, are far from being "natural" but exist and are incumbent upon us because of God's mandate, as human acts of justice that are in *imitatio dei*.

38. Abraham's God stands in stark contrast to many of the other gods of Abraham's time, which were specific to cities and nations. For instance, of Marduk, god of Babylonia, it would not make sense to ask "shall not the judge of all the Earth deal justly," for Markuk was neither judge of all the world nor inclined to weigh the needs of non-Babylonians as equal to those of his own people.

39. As, notably, for Mendelssohn (*Jerusalem*) before him.

40. Jellinek, *Predigten*, 2:133. The reference is to *Pirkei Avot* 4:3.

41. Since Jellinek's day, scholarship has both pushed back the closing of the rabbinic canons by many centuries as well as greatly expanded what we think were the extent of interactions between rabbinic communities and early Christians; see, e.g., Daniel Boyarin,

believed they were above or worthier than non-Jews writ large, or that the God of Israel had not also always been understood as the God of the whole world, who loves the whole world, and brings truth, freedom, justice, and peace to the whole world.[42]

But it was not until Jellinek's discussion of the great Jewish philosophers of the Middle Ages that he focused specifically on Christianity (and, to a lesser extent, on Islam). It was here that he began to more deeply develop his idea of Christianity and Islam as Judaism's "daughter religions." There is a clear reason for this. In Jewish–Christian relations, the long centuries of church domination prior to the onset of modernity and the Enlightenment witnessed some of the most horrifying and bloody events in Jewish European history: the Crusader massacres of the Rhineland; the burning of the Talmud in France; the exile of the Jews from Great Britain; the exile of the Jews from Iberia; the curtailment of Jewish civil rights, including land ownership, choice of profession, and freedom of movement; and the earliest blood libels and pogroms. As Jellinek would write a few years later, "The opponents of Judaism [in the Middle Ages], the usual enemies of freedom of conscience, belief, and thought, created fires of [flaming volumes of Talmud] in France and Italy ... or searched for the ridiculous [within Jewish religion] to make it hateful to their supporters."[43] If there were any centuries in which the conception that God's justice is not universal, or that the Jews hold a uniquely superior ethical position in the hierarchy of humanity vis-à-vis their Christian brethren, it would have been those of the Middle Ages.

Yet, Jellinek argued, that never happened. Jewish law and philosophy continued to understand God's ways as true and God's actions as just, and to imagine the Jewish people as merely one among the nations of the world.[44] The great insight of medieval Jewish philosophy, Jellinek argued, was to conceive of the Christians not as scions of the great pagan empires of the past but as in some ways descended from Judaism itself, or at least as part of the monotheistic family of theologies. Whereas the enemies of Israel's past—Assyria, Babylonia, Greece, and Rome—had been polytheist, by the Middle Ages both the church and Islam were exceedingly powerful monotheistic forces, and, in the eyes of Jewish philosophers, in some recognizable ways working on behalf of the same God and contributing to the same divine historical plan as were the Jews.

In this way, Jellinek said, in the Middle Ages there was a philosophi-

---

Border Lines: The Partition of Judaeo-Christianity, Divinations (Philadelphia: University of Pennsylvania Press, 2004).

42. See Jellinek, *Predigten*, 2:134. It is in this context that Jellinek mentions the Noahide laws, the basic moral code set out by the rabbis for non-Jews to follow; see b. Sanhedrin 56a.

43. Jellinek, *Der Talmud: Zweie Reden*, 1.

44. Traditionally numbered at seventy; see Genesis Rabbah 37.

cal reevaluation of the place of Christianity and Islam in the eyes of Judaism, one that began to conceive of them both in some way as, like Judaism, adjutants of God's will on Earth.

> Do we not have two famous teachers of the Middle Ages, Rabbi Yehuda Halevi [ca. 1075–1141] and Rabbi Moses ben Maimon [ca. 1135–1204, called Rambam], one in Spain and the other in Egypt, who have openly stated that both daughter religions of Judaism were, according to the counsel of Providence, given a great world-historical mission to the Gentile world? And that they both play a mighty role in the gradual realization of the kingdom of God on Earth?[45]

It is through arguments such as this that Jellinek refined his concept of the "daughter religion." Children were both part of oneself and yet entirely separate, recognizable as one's own through physical appearance, mannerism, strengths and weaknesses, and interests, yet also separate, individual, unique, a combination that had heretofore never existed; something new.[46] For Jellinek, Christianity and Islam were such daughters: familial yet separate, recognizable yet distinct. And daughters—not sons. Daughters because (so Jellinek wanted to argue) Christianity has no need for rebellion against Judaism, no desire to strike out at great distance against the paternal model and prove itself in the world. A daughter can, without acrimony, remain close to her parents and warmly tied to her childhood home—in this case, Jellinek meant the Hebrew Bible and its Jewish adherents.

Jellinek's description here of the relationship between Judaism and Christianity was not merely a metaphor; in his historical moment it could almost have been called a fantastical daydream. In the view of history from the mid-nineteenth century, had not the nearly two-millennia saga of discord between Judaism and Christianity proven beyond doubt that these two religions were, at the very least, antagonistic, destined forever to suspect and mistrust one another? But of course, that was precisely the point Jellinek was arguing against. The purpose of all these biblical and rabbinic examples of acceptance toward strangers was to demonstrate that both Judaism and Christianity had been basing their assumptions of one another on a centuries-long misunderstanding. Judaism has always been open to strangers, Jellinek argued, so the Christian attack of parochialism was moot (the thesis of the first half of the sermon). Christianity is not really a stranger to Judaism at all, but a child, a daughter, and one destined to play a leading role in God's divine plan (the thesis of the sec-

---

45. Jellinek, *Predigten*, 2:135–36.
46. The Oedipal paradox highlights this struggle: love of a person who is both deeply of oneself and yet entirely separate and distinct.

ond half of the sermon). And, undergirding it all, was Jellinek's enduring belief in modernity—that the nineteenth century was an era not of summary verdicts but of radical new beginnings, birthed by the promises of political and social liberalism.

Jellinek ended the sermon on this grand new vision, where Christianity and Judaism recognize their ancestral ties and together seek a more just world in the image of God.

> O, let but there be for once a century of love, of humanity, of freedom, and of tranquility, after a millennium of hatred, bigotry, slavery, and of contention in the relations between the religions. The Jews, with Abraham their forefather, say: "Let there be no strife between me and you, and between my herdsmen and your herdsmen, for we are relatives" [Gen 13:8]. On the ruins of the old, bloody hatred [let there] arise a new, wonderful, glorious temple of religious peace, in which any good, noble, and pious person is recognized as a true priest of the Lord. For as the proverb of our Sages says, He who lives the practices and follows the divine commandments with love is a high priest of humanity![47]

Such words were not simply utopic rhetoric, the naïve desires of a man who believed that the situation for the Jews in Europe is indisputably improving. Rather, they were the plea of someone who sought an enduring place for Jewry in European modernity.

Jellinek's return to Abraham at the end of the sermon is revealing, because what he quoted this time was not a conversation between Abraham and God. Instead, it is a conversation between Abraham and a member of his own family, his nephew Lot, who until the birth of Isaac is like a son to Abraham. In context, the herdsmen of Abraham and Lot are quarreling. But instead of bickering (as siblings might do), Abraham proposes an amicable solution: Lot should take his household in one direction, and Abraham should take his in another. The land is capacious and fertile; they can live harmoniously, side by side yet not intertwined. The world is big enough for them both. The solution worked in Genesis. Why, Jellinek hinted here at the end, should it not work with Judaism and Christianity as well?

Judaism in Modern Times

Jellinek's sermons suggested something different from a wholehearted commitment to progress for the sake of progress. What Jellinek desired, what he wanted to impart to his community, was a commitment to moral

---

47. Jellinek, *Predigten*, 2:138–39; the reference is to Sifra, *Acharei Mot* 13.

and theological advancement not only informed by but actually in the mold of historic Jewish answers and practices. While he wished to impart to his listeners that the past was full of wisdom, Judaism was, he ultimately believed, a religion about the future. Those who imagined that the First and Second Temples had achieved a greater holiness and spirituality than Jewry would ever again experience were simply wrong. Instead, Judaism was intimately a part of the great evolution of human society, living not outside of culture but right in the center of it. Just as Jellinek had argued that Judaism lay at the core of the European story, so again he claimed that Judaism would lead the way toward ultimate redemption.

In a sermon given in the fall holiday season of 1862 with the suggestive title (taken from Eccl 7:10) "Say Not: That the Earlier Times Were Better," Jellinek takes up the challenge of describing the present age, with all its upheavals, as the preliminary era for a better world in the making, even as something bordering on the messianic. Beginning with a long meditation on Ecclesiastes (the book traditionally read on the holiday of Sukkot and attributed to a writer named Kohelet), Jellinek focuses on the Hebrew word *ra'iti*, "I have seen," and its root *lirot*, "to see," conjugations of which occur over two dozen times in the biblical book. Kohelet, Jellinek explains, is a man who looks at the world continuously, a "man of cold observation,"[48] always discerning, always judging: a man who has "seen, observed, experienced."[49] And what he sees is that the world can forever be improved. That though the earth is beautiful and fertile, and though humans are creative and adventurous, somehow the world remains broken.

Yet there were, in his time as in ours, says Jellinek, those who insist that, while today it is broken, in the past the world was whole: "So in the days of Kohelet, there were those who looked longingly at the past, which appeared in ideal splendor." But Kohelet knows better. The golden age is a myth. The past is full of the same missed opportunities and failed utopias as the present. Jellinek implores his listeners to understand that unbridled veneration of the past is anything but wise—and is, indeed, warned against by Jewish thinkers across the ages. Then the sermon, through a series of fanciful set-pieces, takes listeners on an almost folkloric journey of imagination, where Jellinek introduces his listeners to a handful of different contemporary Jews, all of whom are complaining about the present and yearning for the past. But after introducing them, and telling us of their longings, he quotes a Jewish sage who urges against such unscrupulous desire over that which is gone and never really was, or a Jewish authority mimicking the same yearnings but of a time even farther in the past.

---

48. Jellinek, *Predigten*, 2:58.
49. Jellinek, *Predigten*, 2:56.

First, we enter the mind of a *ba'al teshuva*, one who has returned to the observant life, whose immodest love of the past becomes an embarrassment to piety rather than a humbling before God. This *ba'al teshuva*, whom Jellinek calls a "thoughtless eulogist of the past,"[50] is therefore reminded of the Maharsha, R. Samuel Edels (1555–1631), who, four hundred years earlier, was already complaining about how few Jews really strictly observe the sabbath, and how "the adolescent children in the community learn nothing."[51] If the Maharsha can complain about a lack of piety in his town, Jellinek asks, when in the past was there such a thing as a completely religious Jewish world?

From the *ba'al teshuva*, Jellinek takes his listeners to a public meeting of Jews, who sit around discussing the fallen state of prayer leaders, the boisterous insolence of those in the synagogue ("although, to be honest, it's hard for me to sit quietly for two hours and not chat," one of Jellinek's characters delightfully admits), and the intellectual poverty of today's rabbis and teachers. "I, too … have to complain about the present," Jellinek has the synagogue *shamash* chime in. "I'm supposed to keep order in a big temple, but people run back and forth during the sermon and push forward when they're late." To all these disputants, Jellinek responds, "'Say not: that the earlier times were better,' for there was never a lack of controversy in Israel, and no evidence from our literature is required [to prove] this, since every collection of reports tells only too much about it"[52]—though he does bring reports, including from the Mabit, R. Moses ben Joseph di Trani (1505–1585), who tells of the Jews of neighboring cities, some of whom agreed on which rabbinic authorities to follow, and some of whom did not, and of R. Kalonymus ben Kalonymus (1286–ca. 1328), who wrote, "The worst thing is that in this great city of Rome, whose example still has a decisive effect on other communities, the scholars are divided among themselves. What one says freely and openly, the other tries to cover up; what the one permits, the other forbids."[53]

Even a poor street beggar does not escape Jellinek's gallery of those who yearn ignorantly for the past, for Jellinek has him cry out, "The national economy has regrettably undermined the old Jewish charity."[54] To which Jellinek responds that the great R. Chayim ben Samuel of Tudela (fourteenth century) said, "work is domination," a phrase that sounds to Jellinek a great deal like nineteenth-century capitalism—or, perhaps to us,

---

50. Jellinek, *Predigten*, 2:60.
51. Jellinek, *Predigten*, 2:60.
52. Jellinek, *Predigten*, 2:65.
53. Jellinek, *Predigten*, 2:66, quoting Kalonymous's *Even Bochan*. (Jellinek assumes that the city is Rome; he writes Rome in German, but in the Hebrew footnote he quotes the original, which says simply *ir gedolah*, large city.)
54. Jellinek, *Predigten*, 2:66.

as Weberian Protestantism. Look, says Jellinek, even those in the Middle Ages, remembered as being centuries of the deepest piety, were careless of the poor and enamored of work. What hoary past of sinless religiosity could one possibly be in search of?

Still, we are moved to ask: Why count this theater of the golden age absurd? Why call those who believe in this fanciful past—in an age when all religion was pure and every heart was noble—as "the little folk who take such fairytales for literal truth"?[55] Why not let others have their beliefs, cling to their imagined memories? What harm does it do?

Very great harm, indeed, Jellinek believes—which is an argument intertwined with polemic. True, Judaism is inexorably tied to its past. Every law, every interpretation, must be based on previous sources. Nothing can arise out of whole cloth. Yet, at the same time, Judaism is messianic, forward looking (*olam ha-bah*). Its basic language speaks of law as a road followed (*halakha*) and observance as a way to God (*derekh haShem*). "For Judaism is not just a religion of the gray antiquity," he writes, "but even more a religion of the future."[56] It is a problem of religious philosophy. To honor the past without worshiping it. To acknowledge its precedent without ceding the present's authority. In Judaism, Jellinek thinks, this is a delicate balance. The tradition is so long and so beautiful that it can be like a seductress, its warm embrace encouraging an easy piety and escape from the trials of history. Such urgings must be softly, gently resisted. But, on the reverse, messianism is a powerful theological ideal, a force like pure magnetism, all consuming, alluring in its total escape from the self. It is arguably the single motivation powering all of Christianity. So while it guides Judaism into the future, it too must be resisted, the focus kept on today, on the living.

That is the argument.

The polemic proposes another view entirely. Alongside philosophy of religion, Jellinek takes a darker view of the past. Based on his scholarship, the vision he proceeds to put forth here is surprising, almost antithetical. But sermons are not scholarship; homiletics is not history. As Jellinek tells it, the past was a place where religion was practiced mainly out of fear and out of social convention, as much as or more so than out of love of God.

> Now I ask, in the recent past, wasn't the much-vaunted, general observance of religious forms very often the result of fear? Our ancestors lived separate from the [other] peoples, a world apart, in which there existed a tyrannical Jewish public opinion which compelled almost everyone to

---

55. Jellinek, *Predigten*, 2:67.
56. Jellinek, *Predigten*, 2:70.

follow the general trend and arrange their external life according to its meaning.[57]

These are harsh words. Too harsh, certainly, to be fully true. But they make a strong point. Yes, Judaism has never had a formal religious authority, an Inquisition. But it does have social convention. And the closed world of small town, pre-emancipation life possessed its own sort of insularity, replete with its own forms of enforcement: a social law quite separate from the religious one.

The move to cities changed all that. Social conventions and cultural cues and norms of everyday life and intercourse were all upended. As Jellinek tells it, in the cities, there is no longer an enforced cultural Judaism: "This has changed, and we are glad that it has changed, that the compulsion that creates a purely external religiosity has stopped."[58] Cities offer a reprieve from the social policing of small-town Jewish life. And while he does not directly say it—as he very rarely ever would—there is more than the whiff of a critique of contemporary neo-Orthodox thinkers in his words. While Jellinek always formally and publicly distances himself from the Reform, he equally opposed Jewish leaders who saw modernity as anything but the most recent challenge and opportunity in the long history of Judaism. Perhaps this is the trait that allowed him to be so open-minded to Jewish mysticism and Jewish midrash: he reveled in the ideas and experiences of Jews as they faced their moment, whatever and whenever that moment might be. His approach to life and religious leadership, perhaps as much about personality as it was a formal philosophical position, was not just that Judaism could meet, but that Judaism could thrive, in every moment. Judaism, Jellinek believed, in a way that could perhaps be best described as attitudinally existential, was like a small ship in an enormous sea: strong enough to be sustained across the gale force winds of history's ocean, yet supple enough to navigate shoals, land in ports, and discover new worlds.

But in this sermon, Jellinek did not not stop there. This sermon was not just a defense of Judaism's forward-facing inclinations against critics of modernity. It was also a radical vision for the promise of urban Judaism itself.

Urban Judaism is not just free from coercion, Jellinek says. The move to cities has allowed Jews to express their true selves, which is to believe and practice out of love of God, from one's own volition, rather than out of the pressures of social conformity. There is no one in the city who can look in the window of your flat, two or three stories up, and check on your Shabbos candles or see that you are hosting a holiday meal, as there was in your little house just off the road. There is no city *shamash* to wake you

---

57. Jellinek, *Predigten*, 2:68.
58. Jellinek, *Predigten*, 2:69.

in the morning for prayers, or to check that you left work early on Friday afternoon to return home before dusk. Everything in the city must be done out of love of religion, love of Judaism, love of God.

> What is observed in our time [in the cities] is done out of conviction, it comes from the heart; it is rooted in love for the God of Israel, in unshakable loyalty to Judaism. And surely this is more pleasing to God: one who, out of pure love for Him, fulfills one commandment with all his heart, than one who observed a hundred religious ordinances out of fear of man.[59]

This is certainly a harder task, Jellinek knows well. And there is clearly a sense about it of the making of lemonade from lemons, since the freedoms of urban modernity pulled Jews away from tradition as much as it buttressed any sort of renewed individual religiosity. It does not seem inappropriate to imagine—and from all we know about Jellinek, certainly seems likely to have been the case—that the sermon really is conflicted: one the one hand, part of it is just homiletics, taking a difficult situation and making it into a religious opportunity, the classic role of any preacher; but, on the other hand, Jellinek really did believe that every new development in history was an opportunity to see a different face of Judaism, to employ one of its hidden strengths (what he calls "after time has proven its teachings durable, able everywhere to pave the way to be explored and heeded")[60] and, in this case specifically, to call upon what he (and all other rabbis past and present, and the Bible itself) hold most true, that the Jewish people themselves, the nation that is Israel, are the backbone of Judaism, and on the shoulders of their individual choices rides the whole project of Judaism in historical and messianic times.

Still, the harshness of Jellinek's tone, his ahistorical, almost cruel, dismissal of historic piety, suggests that the sermon is all homiletics. The preacher must carry his flock in the place in which he finds them. If that means dismissing the past, even in a way shameful for a scholar, so be it. But the underlying message, the use of traditional sources, and the way he ends (discussed below), all moderate this interpretation. In this sermon, we see Jellinek negotiating, all at once, like a juggler with his many balls, the various aspects of a changing Jewish life in urban modernity. Here we see him pleading for his community to not turn away from the present, to not recede into a nostalgia for a past that either never existed or can never be regained. The polemical aspect of this writing—of course there have always been Jews who loved Judaism without the regulations of social pressure—is in fact a reversal of the *ba'al teshuva*'s piety. For while the

---
59. Jellinek, *Predigten*, 2:69.
60. Jellinek, *Predigten*, 2:71.

ba'al teshuva thinks that real religion lies in the past, Jellinek polemicizes that it actually awaits us in the future. And, whereas the public meeting of Jews bemoaned the state of the modern synagogue, Jellinek asks his listeners to look out around them, to the majesty of their surroundings in the Leopoldstadt Temple, to the vibrant, growing Jewish neighborhoods of Vienna, and, beyond that, to the liberalizing of European laws and the increasing social acceptance of Jews across the continent. The choice to be Jewish, to observe God's laws out of love and desire, rather than out of legal coercion or social pretense—is that not a better form of religion? "For the fulfillment of one commandment permeates one's whole being, elevates one's spirit, and warms one's soul, while a hundred religious precepts obeyed out of fear and anxiety leave no ennobling traces in one's inner world."[61] For Jellinek, the freedom Jews are beginning to enjoy in civil life is codeterminate with that in their religious life. The time when Jews are separated from their gentile neighbors is coming to an end, he says, and that leaves us with two choices: nostalgia and longing on the one side, hope and optimism on the other. Part of this is polemic and homiletic, but most of it is classic Jellinek, the champion of the dual promises of urbanism and liberalism.

To end the sermon on this hopeful, indeed almost messianic, theme ("the spirit of Judaism ... demands that we profess the principle that history progresses for the better, and that therefore the earlier times were not more beautiful"[62]) nonetheless requires Jellinek to move some distance away from his original source text in Ecclesiastes. Jellinek might have taught Kohelet's lessons against the admiration of things long gone, but he carefully elides Kohelet's message about the ultimate fruitlessness of wisdom itself. Instead of returning to Kohelet's *hevel* (vanity, breath), the merest trifle of things, Jellinek invokes Isaiah, that is to say, a vision of a world made whole and pure through the triumph of God's word and the veneration of God's oneness.

> [In times to come,] a new world epoch must be entered, in which, from the historical heights of progress will be inaugurated a new Temple of the Peoples, a new King of Peace, a new shoot from the House of David. And in its Holy of Holies all nations on the earth will cry out from the depths of conviction: "[God] alone is God and there is no other!"[63]

Jellinek's imagery and metaphors are at once fantastically idealistic and deeply traditional. The image of the Temple remains, but, from its unique place as the center of Judaism and Israel's relationship with its God, a metaphorical Temple of the People was to be erected, a *Völkertem-*

---

61. Jellinek, *Predigten*, 2:69.
62. Jellinek, *Predigten*, 2:70.
63. Jellinek, *Predigten*, 2:71.

pel, not overseen by priests and high officials but accessible to the masses, who would come to proclaim the holiness and oneness of God. This "new shoot from the house of David" was an idea, a vision, a system of being; it was a collective action, not a messianic individual. The phrase, taken from Isaiah 11, points toward a messianic dream of a rebuilt Zion and a universal peace. But it is more than just a geographical Zion. Jellinek long looked to Jewish history to make prescriptions and set a tone for a general European future. Here, in line with the ancient and medieval rabbis (see b. Sanhedrin 42a), he lays out a vision in which it was not Jesus and Christianity that began the messianic redemption. Rather, the promise always existed; the Jerusalem Temple was imagined from the start not as the cultic shrine of a single people in one location but as the model for a universal vision. How could all the nations of the earth fit into the Holy of Holies in Jerusalem? Only if their voices are together reflected entirely in the single prayer of the high priest on the one day when he is allowed to enter that sacred space. In Isaiah's piquant words (14:18), though the Christians might have said to the Jews "you are cast out from your grave like a detestable branch" (a phrase the Talmud puts back on the disciples of Christ [see b. Sanhedrin 42a]), that has always been wrong. There was never a detestable branch. Jews and Christians have always been part of the same tree. This will be a new shoot from the same trunk, a continuation and renewal, not a grafting or replanting. It will be a recognition of eternal truths, a solidifying of the fundamental theological and moral order, that God alone is God and God's will alone is good.

But as we have seen, modernity, too, has its many difficulties, its fractures and fault lines. Just as there was no past golden age, so too there is no utopian present. In a sermon from 1860, two years before he laid out his vision of a messianic restoration, Jellinek turned his criticism on the leadership of the Jews themselves, which he saw as undermining the very fragile consensus that had existed during the early years of Jewish urbanization. Criticism of this sort was not something he often did in his Sabbath sermons. A man deeply attuned to the qualities and expectations of different sorts of religious and social spaces, Jellinek usually reserved his political opinions for the popular press, community meetings, or rabbinic gatherings. In this case, however, he appears to have felt that the need was too great to be ignored.

In the sermon, Jellinek uses the image of Israel's greatest foe, Amalek, as a metaphor for the infighting that was tearing the modern Jewish community apart. ("Jellinek," notes Malachi Hacohen, "walked casually where others treaded lightly."[64])

---

64. Hacohen, *Jacob & Esau*, 275.

How does Amalek fight in our day? The Jews are divided into two classes: Orthodox and Reform. The former, they say, represent the true and real carrier of ancient Judaism, and should, mercifully and as witness of the curse that weighs upon Israel, be tolerated completely and exclusively. The latter no more find Jews than find dangerous their community, undermining, destabilizing, and rotting all the foundations of state and religion. Let us be honest! From whom does one experience Amalek? From the Jews themselves![65]

Remarkable words. For his entire tenure in the Vienna rabbinate, Jellinek wanted little more than to keep the Jewish community united as a single entity, working together for the religious and political betterment of all the city's Jews. While the community fractured, he found every possible way to stall and delay, stonewall and obstruct, anything he believed would make a fundamental rupture in Viennese Jewish unity.

Ritual and theological differences aside, Jellinek believed that it was the evangelicals of both left and right who placed the community at greatest risk. It was no accident, therefore, that Jellinek invoked the name of Amalek in his warning about the disasters that arise from infighting. Amalek is condemned in the Bible beyond all the other nations, not because it made war on Israel but because of what sort of war it made. "Remember what Amalek did to you on the road out of Egypt, how he surprised you on the road when you were faint and weary, and cut down all who lagged behind. He did not fear God" (Deut 25:17–18). Amalek took aim at those who were exhausted by the journey and could not defend themselves and never would have taken part in a formal battle. It was a tactic done out of malice, for the sake of bloodshed. The Jewish people were again weak and in danger, Jellinek was warning. Again, they were on the road, leaving what they knew behind and settling in a new land they barely understood. This was not the time for Jewish leaders to be hurtling ideological stones at one another, to be, on the one hand, separating themselves from the larger community as so-called keepers of the true tradition, or on the other, rejecting out of hand so many beliefs and practices that had sustained the nation through its many long centuries of exile.

Amalek was Jellinek's warning. In times of transition, he believed, there will always be an enemy motivated by cruelty. Only when the community remained together could they stand against the common foe, each in his or her own way. For the Bible, that was Joshua with the troops and Moses, Aaron, and Hur with hands raised to heaven. For the Jews of Vienna, it meant the traditionalists and the reformers remaining united. Jellinek did not believe it was predetermined that Judaism would survive the transformations of urban modernity. Instead, for him it was Judaism

---

65. Jellinek, *Predigten*, 2:235.

itself that needed to supply the solutions to its most recent challenges—Judaism in concert with non-Jewish Europe. Internal struggles distracted from the more important project of making Judaism an essential element of the European future.

Conclusion

Making Twentieth-Century Connections: From Central Europe to Anglo-America

> It must be left to another hand to offer a personal estimate of Jellinek. It must be left to others to indicate his friendliness to the poor, his generosity to students, his wit in conversation, his marvelous readiness in argument, his courtliness of demeaner, his unique personality. He was undoubtedly the most remarkable figure among the Jews of his age. But even one who never saw him, who never came under the glamour of his oratory, who has known him only by his works, the secret of his immense influence is clear. He earned his place in nineteenth century Judaism by two gifts often found separate, irresistible when combined in one man. These gifts were genius and sincerity.
> —Jellinek's Obituary, *The Jewish Chronicle*, January 5, 1894[1]

This book has addressed two major questions at the heart of Jewish religious modernity: In what ways did liberal Jewish practice change in these last two hundred years? And why is its current form the one that it took? To answer these questions, we have followed the transformation of three key aspects of the modern Jewish religious experience—the urbanization of European Jewry and the construction of monumental synagogues; the transformation of the rabbi's role and persona in Jewish ritual life; and the development and content of the modern liberal rabbi's weekly sermon—in the middle decades of the nineteenth century in Central Europe. We have focused on one of the seminal figures in this reconstruction of religious Judaism, the Austro-German rabbi and scholar Adolf Jellinek, whose leadership of the Jewish communities in Leipzig and Vienna was important for solidifying the new rabbinical norms and practices. Jellinek was born into a small Jewish community in Habsburg

---

1. *The Jewish Chronicle* (January 5, 1894): 7-8.

Moravia and died in the midst of Vienna's *belle époque*. Over the course of the nineteenth century, he was instrumental in shaping the new style of urban rabbi, whose scholarly training, weekly sermons, advocacy for Judaism's embodiment of universal ethics, and synagogue-based leadership replaced the traditional communal functions of the rabbinate in premodern Jewish society.

In telling this story, I have sought to historicize many of the places and strategies that were decisive for religious Judaism's transition into its modern form. Following the demographic changes that resulted from Jewish emancipation and Europe's economic modernization in the first half of the nineteenth century, a new generation of Jewish leaders in Central Europe began to fundamentally reconstruct the role and importance of the communal rabbi. These young men realized that the rabbi was no longer the chief civil authority in the Jewish community and recognized that the composition of Jewish communal structure itself was transforming radically, transitioning from a rural-based semi-autonomous civil and familial unit to a religious and cultural affiliation within a broader liberal, bourgeois body politic. As Jonathan Hess observes, "Whether conceived of as a distinct period or a more general process, modernity inevitably meant a life for Jews where Jewish identity emerged as a problem, something they needed to define and redefine in relation to themselves, their history and their non-Jewish environment."[2] Believing that the rabbi still had a part to play in this new form of Jewish social and religious experience, these men sought to make the rabbinic role into one of communal teacher and chief ideologue of modernity. Jellinek himself was a main proponent of the connection between Judaism and Enlightenment liberalism, arguing for Judaism's foundational role in the creation of a universal moral system.

Seizing on the structure of the sermon—historically a rare rhetorical device in Judaism—the young rabbis of nineteenth-century Central Europe adopted it into their practice of religious Judaism, placing onto it the burdens of educating and steering the theological and moral beliefs of a new urban Jewry, and demonstrating the connection between traditional Judaism and Enlightenment universalism. The modern sermon focused on negotiating the intellectual borderland and underpinnings of Jewish and non-Jewish culture and, in this way, became a chief site of theological innovation and intellectual exchange for modern Jews. By the *fin-de-siècle* in Central Europe, the rabbi's sermon had become the central channel through which most Jews received their education in Jewish religious values and principles.

In the history of modern rabbinic Judaism, Vienna was more than merely one among a handful of possible locations, and Adolf Jellinek was more than just a single exemplary figure. In the middle decades of the

---

2. Hess, *Germans, Jews and the Claims of Modernity*, 19.

nineteenth century, the Habsburg capital was growing rapidly, attracting migrants from across the empire's vast territories. Owing to the nature of its imperial acquisitions, by the end of the 1850s Vienna had become one of the continent's most ethnically diverse cities. Municipal authorities constructed new neighborhoods and expanded the capital's metropolitan area in ways that would become the model for urban projects across the continent in the following decades. Though royal troops defeated an attempted liberal revolution in 1848, the insurgents succeeded in forcing the abdication of Austria's monarch, Ferdinand I, inaugurating (after a period of reactionary absolutism) the long and relatively moderate reign of Franz Joseph. While now a mostly forgotten ghost on the map of Europe, the nineteenth-century Habsburg Empire, with Vienna as its crown, cultivated a social and intellectual world that has indelibly defined the contours of Western modernity.

After Jellinek moved to Vienna in 1857, his career grew to outsized influence, and he used his weekly Sabbath sermons as a means of expounding upon a distinct (and ultimately influential) philosophy of modern Judaism. His intellectual choices concerning the connection between Jewish texts and contemporary philosophical values made his works highly original and later provided a model for generations of rabbis. Over many pages and many Sabbaths, Jellinek asked his congregation to see the relationship between the Jewish and non-Jewish worlds as one of fluidity and dynamism, as an interaction without a requisite antagonism, and of Judaism's origin as the place for much of the moral code that liberal modernity held dear. Despite increasing political fractiousness within the Jewish community and continued attacks on Jewish practice and theology, Jellinek used his intellectual training and rhetorical skills to forcefully define a moderate center. His sermons are the foundational examples of what modern rabbinic rhetoric eventually came to be.

By focusing on the rabbi, the rabbi's sermon, and the synagogue, I have maintained religion (identified as both theology and social structure) as a key lens through which to describe and understand the Jewish experience in modernity. Jellinek's entire world was infused with God. Yet his was a God who depended on a human community to imbue the world with divinity. Jellinek never put any distance between himself and the language of divine closeness or divine plan. Jellinek's understanding of the world was one in which God played an active role, and in which the hand of God could be seen in the actions and choices of human beings.

> The cornerstone of family life is God; without Him it crashes. The ground of the Community is God; without Him "it floats in the air," as the Talmud expresses itself. The cornerstone of the state is God; without Him it becomes the seat of tyranny and lawlessness. The main pillar of humanity is God; without Him, it lacks gravity and sustaining vigor.... God

forms the largest and last circle.... God, in all circumstances of life, will be a model of love, goodness, and justice.³

Though modern Jewish history is often recounted through the prisms of culture, economics, or politics, a great deal of Jewish social space remains inextricably linked with, and defined by, historic religious structures, beliefs, and institutions. Immanuel Wolf wrote similarly in 1822: "In the diverse unfolding of the whole life of a people there do of course exist aspects and tendencies which are remote from the sphere of religion; but in Judaism, more than anywhere else, the influence of the basic religious idea is visible in all the circumstances of human life."⁴ What remained so fascinating in modern Jewish history is the extraordinary creativity of Jewish religious life itself, which is why this book has been concerned with the shifts, creations, apologies, innovations, accentuations, dissociations, and leaps of theological imagination exhibited by Central European Jewish religious leaders, and most especially of Jellinek, as they confronted a rapidly changing world. Faced with new philosophical ideologies, internal demographic shifts, and immense pressure from their Christian counterparts to justify the continuation of religious Judaism in an enlightened and rational age, these leaders forged the foundational elements that continue to sustain and organize the vast majority of Jewish religious practice in the present day. This is a story that needed to be told.

Genealogical Connection: Jellinek, Hertz, Sacks

Despite the fact that the rabbinical transformation in the mid-nineteenth century occurred in such a swift and profound way, restructuring the very foundational assumptions about the role of the rabbi and synagogue in liberal Jewish religious life, the practices and assumptions that resulted have had a profoundly deep and long-lasting effect on Jews from that time to the present day. I therefore want to take these final pages to discuss the ways that the nineteenth-century transformation of rabbinic practice has impacted the traditions and experiences of modern Anglo-American Judaism. The historical period represented by this book encompassed the creation of most of the core elements that now define liberal Jewish religious life in the United States, Britain, and the British Commonwealth. The rabbi, rabbi's sermon, and the large centralized, urban synagogue are arguably the primary loci of religious experience for all but a few Jews in

---

3. Adolf Jellinek, *Die Bürgschaft: Kohelet, Sohn David's* (Leipzig: Fritzsche, 1850), 13.
4. Wolf, "On the Concept of a Science of Judaism," 194.

these places. That is a truly remarkable transformation. In 1815, Jewish religious continuity was based on local communal custom, spread across vast, mostly rural districts, and religious expression was tied deeply to family and intergenerational practice. Today it is based on a formal religious infrastructure, centered on the rabbi and the synagogue in overwhelming urban and suburban spaces.

Comprising almost half of extant world Jewry (around eight million people), simply the number and importance of Anglo-American Jewry seem to be justification enough for pursuing this connection. But numbers alone do not reflect the overwhelming influence that European, and especially German and Habsburg, Jewish modernity has had on the practices and beliefs of contemporary Anglo-American Judaism. Vast numbers of German or German-educated rabbis migrated to England and the United States in the second half of the nineteenth century. The institutions they built and the customs they established greeted the later arriving migrants from the Russian Empire. Though often of Hassidic background, these eastern migrants quickly discarded their old traditions and embraced an Anglo-American form of German Judaism. Almost all Anglo-American Jews (except arguably the ultra-Orthodox or Haredim) express sentiments about Judaism—its history and theology—that more closely resemble the views of other Jews alive today than ideas thought or written by their classical, medieval, or early modern forebears. It is my contention that, more than any other, Anglo-American Jewry is the clearest inheritor of Central European modernity. It reflects a continuation of the German tradition more or less uninterrupted by the vast upheavals (fascist occupation and liquidation, Soviet social engineering, Israeli nation building, expulsion from Islamic lands) experienced by the other half of their coreligionists.[5]

The relationship between the new type of rabbinic Judaism described in this book and twentieth- and twenty-first-century Anglo-American religious belief and practice is made compellingly when one reads the statements of three chief rabbis side by side. First, Jellinek:

> When we built [the first new synagogue in Vienna in 1825] ... we wanted a place to extoll the religious teachings of Israel, its great truths, and the great ideas of Judaism concerning clemency and humanity, concerning justice and freedom.... On Sabbaths and holidays, when from our

---

5. Of course, any project that seeks to draw even the weakest link between the world of Franz Joseph, on the one hand, and the present day, on the other, must do so with care. As Imre Kertész said, "Which writer today is not a writer of the Holocaust? One does not have to choose the Holocaust as one's subject to detect the broken voice that has dominated modern European art for decades" ("Nobel Lecture," December 2, 2002). For an interesting thought experiment about a world without the dissolution of the Habsburg Empire in 1918, see Robert A. Kann, "Should the Habsburg Empire Have Been Saved? An Exercise in Speculative History," *Austrian History Yearbook* 42 (2011): 203–10.

ancient scriptures law, history, and the prophets are read publicly in the old sacred language, evidence can be made in the German language that from our laws emanate wisdom and goodness. They are a source of love and justice at a time when the current alphabet of civilized humanity has hardly been able to stammer [such moral truths]. Our law, with bright and clear voice, unequivocally proclaims: "Love your neighbor as yourself," whoever he is and whoever you may be.... Come down to him and recognize in him your human brother.[6]

Second, Joseph Hertz (1872–1946), chief rabbi of the British Empire from 1913 to 1946:

What is true of the child, is true of the nation as well, and is true of humanity at large. Through the Ten Commandments ... Israel planted Duty and Holiness into the heart of humanity. No religious document has exercised as great an influence on the moral and social life of man.... Israel must be conscious of itself, of what it has done, of what it is still capable of doing. Israel is ... a great, eternal, indomitable people, that has fought and suffered on every battlefield of human thought—to whom the present moment should appear not as the end, but only as the center, of its career.[7]

Third, Jonathan Sacks (1948–2020), chief rabbi of the United Hebrew Congregations of the Commonwealth from 1991 to 2013:

---

6. Jellinek, *Zur Feier des fünfzigjährigen Jubiläums des israelitischen Tempels*, 8.

7. Joseph H. Hertz, *Sermons, Addresses and Studies*, 3 vols. (London: Soncino, 1938), 1:230–31. See also Hertz, *A Book of Jewish Thoughts* (London: Office of the Chief Rabbi, 1940). For a shorter introduction to the life and works of Hertz, see Elton, "Bridge across the Tigris." The overlaps between Hertz and Jellinek are remarkable. Elton writes, "Hertz had not emerged [in the position of chief rabbi] simply because other candidates fell away or because of a quiet chat between Milner and Rothschild. He provided something which the community had sensed it lacked under the Adlers [the father Nathan (1845–1890) and son Hermann (1891–1911)]. When Nathan Adler became Chief Rabbi, British Jewry was essentially a German community and increasingly acculturated. This began to change in the 1880s and by 1911 traditionalists from Eastern Europe were becoming powerful. Hermann Adler lacked a natural affinity for them and in some cases was outright unsympathetic to their situation. Hertz was from the East; Yiddish was a natural tongue for him and he had grown up in the old-world culture of the Lower East Side. His Seminary and university training made him suitable as the leader of Anglicized Jewry and as religious representative of Jews to the outside world. His innate traditionalism made him acceptable to the Jews of the East End of London and comparable communities around the country. The very qualities which made him unemployable in [increasingly assimilating] 1890s America made him ideal for the greatest rabbinic position in the world." This article condenses some of the work done in Elton's book, *Britain's Chief Rabbis and the Religious Character of Anglo-Jewry, 1880–1970* (Manchester: Manchester University Press, 2009). See also Derek Taylor, *Chief Rabbi Hertz: The Wars of the Lord* (London: Vallentine Mitchell, 2014).

If there is one shared feature of [my sermons], it is that I have tried to set the biblical text in the wider context of ideas. Many traditional commentaries look at the Torah through a microscope: the detail, the fragmentation of text in isolation. I have tried to look at it through a telescope: the larger picture and its place in the constellation of concepts that make Judaism so compelling a picture of the universe and our place within it.[8]

What we see running through these texts, separated as they each are by three-quarters of a century, is a shared theory of the rabbi's role in a new world order.[9] All speak of Judaism as if it were an obvious part of the narrative of Western intellectual development, even when such a naturalization of Judaism into the broader history of European ideas was a unique creation of the mid-nineteenth century (and of Jellinek in particular). Just as we see the turn toward a language of universal morality among Christian theological tracts in the early decades of the nineteenth century, so we see it in Jewish texts as well. These three leaders (somewhat more than implicitly) claim that the rabbi is a negotiator and integrator of Jewish morality within a broader universal framework of moral universalism, and that the rabbi is a forger of links between the long and deep Jewish past and the complex, somewhat inscrutable multicultural present. The fact that not only is this an entirely new innovation devised by Jewish leaders in Central Europe at the dawn of modernity, but that it has now become such a dominant part of the rabbi's role within Jewish religious experience suggests that the past one hundred and fifty years constitute a new cultural event in the history of rabbinic Judaism, a recognizable break and transfiguration from the premodern Jewish experience that came before it; in other words, a new shoot from the House of David.

To begin to trace more carefully the lineage of the rabbi, the rabbi's sermon, and the urban synagogue from Central Europe to modern Anglo-American Jewry, we must examine the various ideologies of Judaism present in contemporary Jewish life in the English-speaking West. For many of these Jews, Judaism represents a social category (as opposed to a race or nationality) that most easily encompasses a cross-section of human diversity—albeit a "Western" form tied exclusively to the idea of individual self-expression (and increasingly to identity politics). An interesting corollary to the individual diversity expressed by Anglo-American Jewry is the extremely limited physical and mental space allotted to its

---

8. Jonathan Sacks, *Covenant & Conversation: Genesis, The Book of Beginnings* (New Milford, CT: Maggid, 2009), 3.

9. Commenting on Hertz, but capturing a critique that can be made about Jellinek as well, Elton writes, "If Hertz's reputation during his lifetime derived from his actions as a religious leader, since his death it has rested on his writings. He was not primarily an original scholar, but he was extremely well-read and a great popularizer" ("Bridge across the Tigris.")

religious observance. Outside specific Orthodox enclaves in a handful of cities, rarely is a whole street or neighborhood considered an area of dense Jewish presence.[10] The following is a description of a contemporary Anglo-American Jewish religious service, which should be familiar to everyone who has encountered it: A rabbi stands at the pulpit of a synagogue located in an urban (or suburban) environment and preaches about the universal ethics and the historical importance of Jewish texts and practices. The community is composed of many congregants born elsewhere, or with local roots only two or three generations old. Few of those sitting quietly in the pews know how to read or understand much Hebrew or consider themselves religiously observant (followers of mitzvot or halakhah) or keepers of Jewish dietary restrictions (kashrut). They expect the rabbi to connect Jewish texts to a current event, a social mission, or a public policy, and for the rabbi's secular politics (about which they care very deeply) to align mostly with their own.

Such scenes predominate on Sabbath mornings in cities and towns across Anglo-America. Its familiarity has made it banal. Certainly, Jewish ethnographers strive to classify and explain the myriad small differences between communities, especially as we see them in the United States.[11] And new religious factions attempt to gain supporters by accentuating ever-narrower disparities.[12] But the core components of Anglo-American Jewish life today (large synagogues, a reliance on urban spaces to create Jewish density, pulpit rabbis, diverse congregant backgrounds, a belief that Judaism embodies universal ethics) remain consistent across the denominational spectrum.[13]

---

10. This is made clear by the relative dearth of eruvs—symbolic markers of Jewish neighborhoods—in the United States. Few exist in cities with total populations below half a million, even when many smaller cities host Jewish communities of a few thousand families or more. (The contributors to Wikipedia maintain a fairly comprehensive list of American and international eruvim. See "List of Places with Eruvim," Wikipedia, https://en.wikipedia.org/wiki/List_of_eruvin#United_States. In looking at this list, and then realizing that the United States is home to some six million Jews, the number of Jews who live inside these eruvim is miniscule.)

11. See Jonathan D. Sarna, *American Judaism: A History* (New Haven: Yale University Press, 2004); Samuel C. Heilman, *Portrait of American Jews: The Last Half of the 20th Century*, Samuel and Althea Stroum Lectures in Jewish Studies (Seattle: University of Washington, 1995); and Jack Wertheimer, *A People Divided: Judaism in Contemporary America* (New York: Basic Books, 1993).

12. This is happening now, for example, between Yeshivat Chovevei Torah (YCT), the Hadar Insitute, the Jewish Theological Seminary, and Drisha, all in New York. See the article by Rabbi Avi Weiss, founder of (YCT) proclaiming a new "Open Orthodoxy" ("Defining 'Open Orthodoxy' Within Judaism," *Tablet Magazine* [June 29, 2015]).

13. There is much talk, however, that we might we living through some sort of paradigm shift, as "independent minyanim"—prayer groups organized without rabbis—are finding larger numbers of young adherents than traditional synagogues. See Elie Kaunfer,

In contemporary Anglo-American Judaism, religion and religious expression are often limited to a synagogue, a school, or a community center. A private home might witness religious blessings on special holidays or when family is present, but would otherwise lack daily ritual activity. Judaism is often an intellectual exercise, being the idea of the Sabbath (which is itself probably not observed for its full twenty-five hours) or a small library of Jewish history, philosophy, and Zionism. Judaism might be a Hebrew name, a family story, a vacation to Israel or a pilgrimage to Poland, a devotion to a homeless shelter, a food bank, a halfway house, or a civil rights rally (with a commitment to these social goods perhaps attributed in some way to the Jewish concept of *tikkun olam*, repairing the world).

In all these cases, being Jewish and participating in Judaism are often entirely devoid of their historic theological content. Today, Anglo-American Jews *go* to Jewish places, *make* time for Jewish practice, *seek* out Jewish learning, and *create* Jewish space, which means that to be religiously Jewish they must *do* things that are in some way opposed to any number of larger cultural forces compelling them otherwise. It also means that living in Jewish space can be justified only when Jewish purposes align with reigning social and intellectual norms—when Judaism's unique theological demands are not being undercut by the ostensibly more important (and more moral) assumptions of individual liberty and personal freedom.

Yet as scarce and disjointed as twenty-first century Anglo-American Judaism might appear, it is also intellectually creative and socially vibrant. Seemingly full of contradictions, Anglo-American Judaism today reflects a continually transforming response to the immense pressures of historical continuity, economic and political evolution, and intellectual acculturation. At a time when Jewish religious practice has ceased to be an organizing factor in the daily lives of most Anglo-American Jews, synagogues continue to be built and funded, more than half of self-identifying Jews still celebrate major religious holidays, and books continue to be written proclaiming the moral and ethical insights of the Jewish tradition. All the contradictory and affirmative aspects of present-day Anglo-American Jewish experience are reflections of what might be seen as the major transformations within religious Judaism fashioned by nineteenth-century Central European Jewish religious leaders in their attempt to create a religious practice applicable to modern Western life. That these elements of contemporary Judaism are so vastly different from the ideas and experiences of Jews who lived before 1800 is certainly underappreciated. But what is truly astonishing is that, less than two centuries ago, a relative

---

Empowered Judaism: What Independent Minyanim Can Teach Us about Building Vibrant Jewish Communities (Woodstock, VT: Jewish Lights, 2010).

handful of people created the institutions and theologies that continue to influence the lives of millions of Jews well into the twenty-first century.

In the end, it is not from simple historical interest that we should draw lines of connection between the religious challenges and constructions of the 1850s and the lives of Jews in the 2020s. Modernity created a set of assumptions that set the European world on a particular course. Those values and normative ethics appear to be, in many quarters, breaking down. Knowing that the modern synagogue was formed and reimagined based on a unique set of historical trends and demands offers us a perspective on its possibilities and limitations unavailable to those who view the institutional arrangements of Judaism as much longer, older, and more stable than they really are. The rabbi has always been a part of Judaism, but who he or she has been, what has been expected of him, where she resides, and what her religious purpose is continue to present challenges for religious Judaism. Finally, listened to or ignored, the sermon remains a central component of Jewish religious practice in our era.

Each of these aspects of Jewish religious life had its origins in the cities and synagogues of Central Europe a century and a half ago. Studies like this one are not designed to pass judgments on the decisions of the past. But knowing why particular societies formed as they did should provide a measure of honesty in discussions about the present and future. The powers of the liberal tradition, with its universalistic ethic, are still loudly promoted across the Jewish community. It is not just to a historical era that one should look for future guidance. But it is certainly through past experiences that one can gain a measure of perspective concerning the great range of Jewish religious possibilities in the centuries to come.

Selected Bibliography of the Works of Adolf Jellinek

1844
Franck, Adolphe. *Die Kabbala oder die Religions-Philosophie der hebräer.* Translated by Adolf Jellinek. Leipzig: Hunger.

1847
Elischa ben Abuja, genannt Acher: Zur Erkärung und Kritik der Gutzkow'schen Tragödie Uriel Acosta. Leipzig: Hunger.

1849
Drei Gräber. Leipzig: Fritsche.
Jericho: Ein Bild von Israel's Freiheit. Leipzig: Fritzsche.

1850
Die Bürgschaft: Kohelet, Sohn David's. Leipzig: Fritzsche.

1851
Moses ben Schem-Tob de Leon und sein Verhältniß zum Sohar: Eine historisch-kritische Untersuchung über die Entstehung des Sohar. Leipzig: Hunger.

1852
Beiträge zur Geschichte der Kabbala. 2 volumes. Leipzig: Fritzsche.

1853
Thomas von Aquino in der jüdischen Literatur. Leipzig: Colditz.
Auswahl kabbalistischer Mystik. Leipzig: Colditz.
Menachem de Lonsano. *Ma'arich.* Edited by Adolf Jellinek. Leipzig: Colditz.
Bet ha-Midrasch: Sammlung kleiner Midraschim und vermischter Abhandlungen aus der ältern jüdischen Literature. Volume 1. Leipzig: Vollrath.

1854
Joseph ibn Zadik. *Der Mikrokosmos: Ein Beitrag zur Religionsphilosophie und Ethik.* Edited by Adolf Jelinek. Leipzig: Fischl.
Philosophie und Kabbala. Leipzig: Hunger.

1855
Samuel ben Meir, *Perush al Kohelet v'Shir haShirim*. Edited by Adolf Jellinek. Leipzig: Schnauss.
Bet ha-Midrasch: Sammlung kleiner Midraschim und vermischter Abhandlungen aus der ältern jüdischen Literature. Volume 2. Leipzig: Vollrath.
Bet ha-Midrasch: Sammlung kleiner Midraschim und vermischter Abhandlungen aus der ältern jüdischen Literature. Volume 3. Leipzig: Vollrath.

1857
Bet ha-Midrasch: Sammlung kleiner Midraschim und vermischter Abhandlungen aus der ältern jüdischen Literature. Volume 4. Leipzig: Vollrath.

1858
Zwei Reden zur Schlußsteinlegung und zur Einweihung des neuen israelitischen Tempels in der Leopoldstadt am 18. Mai und 15. Juni 1858. Vienna: Knöpflmacher.

1862
Predigten. Volume 1. Vienna: Carl Gerold's Sohn.

1863
Predigten. Volume 2. Vienna: Carl Gerold's Sohn.
Festrede am LXX. Geburtstage seiner Ehrwürden des Predigers Herrn Isaak Noa Mannheimer (17. October 1863) im alten israelitische Bethause gehalten. Vienna: Schloßberg.
Rede zur Einweihung des israelitischen Tempels in Iglau, am 9. September 1863 (25. Elul 5623). Vienna: Bendiner & Schloßberg.

1865
Der Talmud: Zwei Reden, am Hüttenfeste 5625 (am 16. und 22. October 1864). Vienna: Herzfeld & Bauer.
Rede bei der Gedächtnissfeier für den verewigten Prediger Herrn Isak Noa Mannheimer, am 26. März 1865 im Tempel in der Leopoldstadt. Vienna: Herzfeld & Bauer.
Salomon Munk, Professor am Collège de France: Vortrag im Wiener Bet ha-Midrash am 21. Januar 1865 gehalten. Vienna: Herzfeld & Bauer.

1866
Predigten. Volume 3. Vienna: Herzfeld & Bauer.

1867
"Oberrabb. Sal. J. Rappoport." *Die Neuzeit*, October 25, 1867, 498.
Das Gesetz Gottes außer der Thora: Fünf Reden nebst einer Rede über die Cholera. Vienna: Herzfeld & Bauer.
"Erinnerungen an den verewigten Oberrabb. S. J. Rappaport." *Die Neuzeit*, November 15, 1867, 531–33.

Selected Bibliography of Adolf Jellinek   199

1869
Studien und Skizzen: Erster Teil: Der jüdische Stamm: Ethnografische Studie. Vienna: Herzfeld & Bauer.

1872
Die Psyche des Weibes: Vortrage im Saale des Academischen Gymnasium in Wien. Vienna: Hölder.

1873
Bet ha-Midrasch: Sammlung kleiner Midraschim und vermischter Abhandlungen aus der ältern jüdischen Literature. Volume 5. Vienna: Winter, 1873.

1876
Zur Feier des fünfzigjährigen Jubiläums des israelitischen Tempels in der inner Stadt Wien: Zwei Reden am 26. März (1. Nisan 5636) und 9. April (1. Tage des Passah festes 1876). Vienna: Winter.

1877
Bet ha-Midrasch: Sammlung kleiner Midraschim und vermischter Abhandlungen aus der ältern jüdischen Literature. Volume 6. Vienna: Winter.
Jellinek, Adolph, and S. J. Halberstam. *Ḳontres ha-mefaresh.* Vienna: Winter.

1880
Franzosen über Juden. Vienna: Gottlieb.

1881
Die Hebräische Sprache: Ein Ehrenzeugnis des jüdischen Geistes. Dritte Rede über die Hebräische Sprache. Am Sabbat Wajiggasch 5641. Vienna: Schlossberg.
Der jüdische Stamm in nichtjüdischen Sprichwörtern. Vienna. Waizner.

1882
Der jüdische Stamm in nichjüdischen Sprichwörtern. Zweite Serie. Vienna: Waizner.
Organisation gegen Organisation. Vienna: Waizner.

1885
Der jüdische Stamm in nichjüdischen Sprichwörtern. Dritte Serie. Vienna: Waizner.

1938
Bet ha-Midrasch: Sammlung kleiner Midraschim und vermischter Abhandlungen aus der ältern jüdischen Literature. 6 volumes. Jerusalem: Bamberger and Wahrmann, 1938. Reprinted, 1967.

Bibliography

Aland, Kurt. *Konstantin von Tischendorf (1815–1874): Neutestamentliche Textforschung damals und Heute*. Sitzungsberichte der Sächsischen Akademie der Wissenschaften zu Leipzig, Philologisch-Historische Klasse 133.2. Berlin: Akademie, 1993.

Albrecht-Weinberger, Karl, and Felicitas Heimann-Jelinek, eds. *Judentum in Wien: "Heilige Gemeinde Wien."* Vienna: Museen der Stadt Wien, 1987.

Alofsin, Anthony. *When Buildings Speak: Architecture as Language in the Habsburg Empire and Its Aftermath, 1867–1933*. Chicago: University of Chicago Press, 2006.

Altmann, Alexander. "The New Style of Preaching in Nineteenth-Century German Jewry." In *Studies in Nineteenth-Century Jewish Intellectual History*, edited by Alexander Altmann, 65–116. Philip W. Lown Institute of Advanced Judaic Studies, Brandeis University: Studies and Texts 2. Cambridge: Harvard University Press, 2013.

———. "Zur Frühgeschichte der jüdischen Predigt in Deutschland: Leopold Zunz als Prediger." *Leo Baeck Institute Year Book* 6 (1961): 3–59.

Axinn, Sidney. "Kant on Judaism." *Jewish Quarterly Review* 59, no. 1 (1968): 9–23.

Baader, Benjamin Maria. *Gender, Judaism, and Bourgeois Culture in Germany, 1800–1870*. Modern Jewish Experience. Bloomington: Indiana University Press, 2006.

———. "When Judaism Turned Bourgeois: Gender in Jewish Associational Life and in the Synagogue, 1750–1850." *Leo Baeck Institute Year Book* 46 (2001): 113–23.

Baader, Benjamin Maria, Sharon Gillerman, and Paul Lerner, eds. *Jewish Masculinities: German Jews, Gender, and History*. Bloomington: Indiana University Press, 2012.

Bamberger, Fritz. "Zunz's Conception of History: A Study of the Philosophic Elements in Early Science of Judaism." *Proceedings of the American Academy for Jewish Research* 11 (1941): 1–25.

Baron, Salo W. "The Impact of the Revolution of 1848 on Jewish Emancipation." *Jewish Social Studies* 11, no. 3 (1949): 195–248.

Bartal, Israel. *The Jews of Eastern Europe, 1772–1881*. Translated by Chaya Naor. Philadelphia: University of Pennsylvania Press, 2005.

Bartal, Israel, and Antony Polonsky. "Introduction: The Jews of Galicia under the Habsburgs." In *Focusing on Galicia: Jews, Poles, and Ukrainians 1772-1918*, edited by Israel Bartal and Antony Polonsky, 3–24. Portland, OR: Littman Library of Jewish Civilization, 1999.

Bartoš, Josef. *Uherský Brod: Minulost i současnost slováckého města*. Brno: Blok, 1971.

Baumgarten, Elisheva. *Mothers and Children: Jewish Family Life in Medieval Europe*. Jews, Christians, and Muslims from the Ancient to the Modern World. Princeton, NJ: Princeton University Press, 2004.

———. *Practicing Piety in Medieval Ashkenaz: Men, Women and Everyday Observance*. Jewish Culture and Contexts. Philadelphia: University of Pennsylvania Press, 2014.

Bayer, Rolf. *Die bayerische Bahnhof in Leipzig: Entstehung, Entwicklung und Zukunft des ältesten Kopfbahnhofs der Welt*. Berlin: Transpress, 1895.

Bayly, Christopher. *The Birth of the Modern World, 1780–1914: Global Connections and Comparisons*. Malden, MA: Blackwell, 2004.

Beachy, Robert. "Reforming Interregional Commerce: The Leipzig Trade Fairs and Saxony's Recovery from the Thirty Years' War." *Central European History* 32, no. 4 (1999): 431–52.

———. *The Soul of Commerce: Credit, Property, and Politics in Leipzig, 1750–1840*. Studies in Central European Histories 34. Leiden: Brill, 2005.

Beckermann, Ruth, ed. *Die Mazzesinsel: Juden in der Wiener Leopoldstadt 1918–1938*. Vienna: Löcker, 1984.

Beer, Bernhard. "Recensionen und Anzeigen." *Monatsschrift für Geschichte und Wissenschaft des Judentums* 2 (1853): 152–56.

Beller, Steven. "Patriotism and the National Identity of Habsburg Jewry, 1860–1914." *Leo Baeck Institute Year Book* 41 (1996): 215–38.

———. *Vienna and the Jews, 1867–1938: A Cultural History*. Cambridge: Cambridge University Press, 1989.

Ben Meir, Samuel. *The Commentary of R. Samuel Ben Meir, Rashbam, on Qohelet*. Edited by Sara Japhet and Robert B. Salters. Jerusalem: Magnes Press, 1985. (Hebrew.)

Bentley, James. *Secrets of Mount Sinai: The Story of the World's Oldest Bible—Codex Sinaiticus*. Garden City, NY: Doubleday, 1986.

Berger, Michael S. *Rabbinic Authority*. New York: Oxford University Press, 1998.

Berlin, Isaiah. *Four Essays on Liberty*. New York: Oxford University Press, 1969.

Bieler, Andrea. *Die Sehnsucht nach dem verlorenen Himmel: Jüdische und christliche Reflexionen zu Gottesdienstreform und Predigtkultur im 19. Jahrhundert*. Praktische Theologie heute 65. Stuttgart: Kohlhammer, 2003.

Black, Matthew, and Robert Davidson. *Constantin von Tischendorf and the Greek New Testament*. Glasgow: University of Glasgow Press, 1981.

Boyarin, Daniel. *Border Lines: The Partition of Judaeo-Christianity*. Divinations. Philadelphia: University of Pennsylvania Press, 2004.
Brämer, Andreas. "The Dialectics of Religious Reform: The *Hamburger Israelitische Tempel* in its Local Context, 1817–1938." *Leo Baeck Institute Year Book* 48 (2003): 25–37.
———. "The Dilemmas of Moderate Reform: Some Reflections on the Development of Conservative Judaism in Germany, 1840–1880." *Jewish Studies Quarterly* 10 (2003): 73–87.
———. *Rabbiner Zacharias Frankel: Wissenschaft des Judentums und konservative Reform im 19. Jahrhundert*. Netiva 3. Hildesheim: Olms, 2000.
Brenner, Michael. *Propheten des Vergangenen: Jüdische Geschichtsschreibung im 19. und 20. Jahrhundert*. Munich: Beck, 2006.
Brenner, Michael, Vicki Caron, and Uri R. Kaufmann, eds. *Jewish Emancipation Reconsidered: The French and German Models*. Schriftenreihe Wissenschaftlicher Abhandlungen des Leo Baeck Instituts 66. Tübingen: Mohr Siebeck, 2003.
Brenner, Michael, Stefi Jersch-Wenzel, and Michael A. Meyer, eds. *German-Jewish History in Modern Times*. Volume 2: *Emancipation and Acculturation, 1780–1871*. New York: Columbia University Press, 1996.
Breuer, Mordechai. "Kreativität und Traditionsgebundenheit." In *Schöpferische Momente des europäischen Judentums in der frühen Neuzeit*, edited by Michael Graetz, 113–20. Heidelberg: Winter, 2000.
———. *Modernity within Tradition: The Social History of Orthodox Jewry in Imperial Germany*. Translated by Elizabeth Petuchowski. New York: Columbia University Press, 1992.
Brocke, Michael, Julius Carlebach, and Carsten Wilke, eds. *Biographisches Handbuch der Rabbiner*. Teil 1: *Die Rabbiner der Emanzipationszeit in den deutschen, böhmischen und großpolnischen Ländern, 1781–1871*. Munich: Sauer, 2004.
Burke, Janine. *The Sphinx on the Table: Sigmund Freud's Art Collection and the Development of Psychoanalysis*. New York: Walker, 2006.
Bush, Olga. "The Architecture of Jewish Identity: The Neo-Islamic Central Synagogue of New York." *Journal of the Society of Architectural Historians* 63, no. 2 (2004): 180–201.
Busi, Giulio. "Beyond the Burden of Idealism: For a New Appreciation of the Visual Lore in the Kabbalah," in *Kabbalah and Modernity: Interpretations, Transformations, Adaptations*, edited by Boaz Huss, Marco Pasi, and Kocku von Stuckrad, 29–46. Leiden: Brill, 2010.
Carlebach, Elisheva, John M. Efron, and David N. Myers, eds. *Jewish History and Jewish Memory: Essays in Honor of Yosef Hayim Yerushalmi*. Hanover, NH: University Press of New England, 1998.
Carlebach, Julius. "The Forgotten Connection: Women and Jews in the Conflict between Enlightenment and Romanticism." *Leo Baeck Institute Year Book* 24 (1979): 107–38.

Carmilly-Weinberger, Moshe. "The Similarities and Relationship between the Jüdisch-Theologisches Seminar (Breslau) and the Rabbinical Seminary (Budapest)." *Leo Baeck Institute Year Book* 44 (1999): 3–22.

Chamiel, Ephraim. *The Middle Way: The Emergence of Modern Religious Trends in Nineteenth-Century Judaism: Responses to Modernity in the Philosophy of Z. H. Chajes, S. R. Hirsch, and S. D. Luzzatto*, 2 vols. Studies in Orthodox Judaism. Brighton, MA: Academic Studies Press, 2014.

Chazan, Robert. *Reassessing Jewish Life in Medieval Europe*. New York: Cambridge University Press, 2010.

Cohen, Gary B. "Nationalist Politics and the Dynamics of State and Civil Society in the Habsburg Monarchy, 1867–1914." *Central European History* 40, no. 2 (2007): 1–38.

Cohen, Naomi W. *What the Rabbis Said: The Public Discourse of Nineteenth-Century American Rabbis*. New York: New York University Press, 2008.

Cohon, Samuel Solomon. "Zunz and Reform Judaism." *Hebrew Union College Annual* 31 (1960): 251–76.

Dan, Joseph. "Midrash and the Dawn of Kabbalah." In *Midrash and Literature*, edited by Geoffrey H. Hartman and Sanford Budick, 127–39. New Haven: Yale University Press, 1986.

———, ed. *Binah: Studies in Jewish History*, vol. 1. New York: Praeger, 1989.

Davidson, Samuel. *A Treatise on Biblical Criticism Exhibiting a Systematic View of that Science*, vol. 1. Boston: Gould & Lincoln, 1853.

Davis, William S. *Romanticism, Hellenism, and the Philosophy of Nature*. Cham, Switzerland: Palgrave Macmillan, 2018.

Deeg, Alexander. *Preaching in Judaism and Christianity: Encounters and Developments from Biblical Times to Modernity*. Studia Judaica 41. Berlin: de Gruyter, 2008.

———. *Predigt und Derascha: Homiletische Textlektüre im Dialog mit dem Judentum*. Arbeiten zur Pastoraltheologie, Liturgik und Hymnologie 48. Göttingen: Vandenhoek & Ruprecht, 2006.

de Leon, Moses. *The Book of the Pomegranate: Moses De Leon's Sefer Ha-Rimmon*. Edited and translated by Elliot R. Wolfson. Brown Judaic Studies 144. Atlanta: Scholars Press, 1988.

Dupré, Louis. *Passage to Modernity: An Essay in the Hermeneutics of Nature and Culture*. New Haven: Yale University Press, 1993.

Ebert, Hans-Georg, and Thoralf Hanstein, eds. *Heinrich Leberecht Fleischer – Leben und Wirkung: Ein Leipziger Orientalist des 19. Jahrhunderts mit Internationaler Ausstrahlung*. Leipziger Beiträge zur Orientforschung 30. Frankfurt am Main: Peter Lang, 2013.

Efron, John M., *German Jewry and the Allure of the Sephardic*. Princeton, NJ: Princeton University Press, 2016.

Ehrmann, Daniel. "S.D. Luzzatto." *Das Abendland* 20, October 12, 1865, 164.

Eisler, Moritz. "Feuilleton: R. Moses Katz Wanefried: Eine Reminiscenz aus dem Leben des Herrn Dr. Adolf Jellinek von einem Jugendgenossen." *Die Neuzeit*, May 22, 1891, 205–7.
Eliáš, Bohuslav. "Zur Geschichte der Israelitengemeinde von Prostějov (Proßnitz)." *Husserl Studies* 10 (1994): 237–48.
Elior, Rachel. *The Three Temples: On the Emergence of Jewish Mysticism in Late Antiquity*. Portland, OR: Littman Library of Jewish Civilization, 2005.
Ellenson, David H. "A Disputed Precedent: The Prague Organ in Nineteenth-Century Central-European Legal Literature and Polemics." *Leo Baeck Institute Year Book* 40 (1995): 251–64.
———. "The *Israelitische Gebetbücher* of Abraham Geiger and Manuel Joël: A Study in Nineteenth-Century German-Jewish Communal Liturgy and Religion." *Leo Baeck Institute Year Book* 44 (1999): 143–64.
———. *Rabbi Esriel Hildesheimer and the Creation of a Modern Jewish Orthodoxy*. Tuscaloosa: University of Alabama Press, 1990.
Elton, Benjamin J. "A Bridge across the Tigris: Chief Rabbi Joseph Herman Hertz." *Conversations: The Journal of the Institute for Jewish Ideas and Ideals* 21 (February 3, 2015).
———. *Britain's Chief Rabbis and the Religious Character of Anglo-Jewry, 1880–1970*. Manchester: Manchester University Press, 2009.
Enelow, H. G., *The Jew and the World*. New York: Bloch, 1921.
Ephraim Carlebach Stiftung. *Judaica Lipsiensia: Zur Geschichte der Juden in Leipzig*. Leipzig: Edition Leipzig, 1994.
Evans, R. J. W., and Hartmut Pogge von Strandmann, eds. *The Revolutions in Europe, 1848–1849: From Reform to Reaction*. Oxford: Oxford University Press, 2000.
Evan-Shoshan, Avraham. *Konkordenziyah hadashah le-Torah Nevi'im u'Khtuvim: ozar leshom ha-Mikre, Ivrit ve'Aramit; shorashim, milim, shemot peretiyim zerufim venirdafim, ba'arikhat Avraham Evan-Shoshan*. Jerusalem: Miryst Sefer, 1978.
Exhibition Committee of the Textile Industry. *The Textile Industry of Saxony and Its Importance. Appendix: List of Exhibitors Interested in the Textile Industry of Saxony*. Leipzig: Leipziger Monatschrift für Textil-Industrie, 1893.
Fackenheim, Emil L. "Kant and Judaism," *Commentary* (December 1, 1963).
Feiner, Shmuel. *Haskalah and History: The Emergence of a Modern Jewish Historical Consciousness*. Translated by Chaya Naor and Sondra Silverston. Portland, OR: Littman Library of Jewish Civilization, 2002.
———. *The Origins of Jewish Secularization in Eighteenth-Century Europe*. Translated by Chaya Naor. Philadelphia: University of Pennsylvania Press, 2010.
Feiner, Shmuel, and Natalie Naimark-Goldberg. *Cultural Revolution in Berlin: Jews in the Age of Enlightenment*. Oxford: Bodleian Library, 2011.

Fenton, Paul. "Adolphe Franck's Contribution to the Historico-Critical Study of the Kabbalah." *Kabbalah: Journal for the Study of Jewish Mystical Texts* 40 (2018): 61–84.

Ferziger, Adam S. *Exclusion and Hierarchy: Orthodoxy, Nonobservance, and the Emergence of Modern Jewish Identity*. Jewish Culture and Contexts. Philadelphia: University of Pennsylvania Press, 2005.

Figeac, Petra. *Moritz Steinschneider, 1816–1907: Begründer der wissenschaftlichen hebräischen Bibliographie*. Jüdische Miniaturen. Berlin: Hentrich & Hentrich, 2007.

Flatto, Sharon. *The Kabbalistic Culture of Eighteenth-Century Prague: Ezekiel Landau (the "Noda Biyehudah") and His Contemporaries*. Portland, OR: Littman Library of Jewish Civilization, 2010.

Flusser, David. "Psalms, Hymns and Prayer." In *Jewish Writings of the Second Temple Period: Apocrypha, Pseudepigrapha, Qumran Sectarian Writings, Philo, Josephus*, edited by Michael E. Stone, 551–77. Philadelphia: Fortress Press, 1984.

Formstecher, Salomon. *Die Religion des Geistes: Eine wissenschaftliche Darstellung des Judenthums nach seinem Charakter, Entwicklungsgange, und Berufe in der Menschheit*. Frankfurt am Main: Hermann, 1841.

Franck, Adolphe. *Die Kabbala oder die Religions-Philosophie der hebräer*. Translated by Adolf Jellinek. Leipzig: Hunger, 1844.

Frank, Daniel and Matt Goldish. "Rabbinic Culture and Dissent: An Overview." In *Rabbinic Culture and Its Critics: Jewish Authority, Dissent, and Heresy in Medieval and Early Modern Times*, edited by Daniel Frank and Matt Goldish, 1–53. Detroit: Wayne State University Press, 2008.

Frank, Daniel, and Matt Goldish, eds. *Rabbinic Culture and Its Critics: Jewish Authority, Dissent, and Heresy in Medieval and Early Modern Times*. Detroit: Wayne State University Press, 2008.

Frankel, Jonathan. "Assimilation and the Jews in Nineteenth-Century Europe: Towards a New Historiography." In *Assimilation and Community: The Jews in Nineteenth-Century Europe*, edited by Jonathan Frankel and Steven J. Zipperstein, 1–37. Cambridge: Cambridge University Press, 1992.

Frankel, Jonathan, and Steven J. Zipperstein, eds. *Assimilation and Community: The Jews in Nineteenth-Century Europe*. Cambridge: Cambridge University Press, 1992.

Frankl-Grün, Adolf. *Geschichte der Juden in Ungarisch-Brod: Nebst Biographien von R. Moses Perls, P. Singer, Ad. Jellinek, P.F. Frankl &c. Nach Archivalien Dargestellt*. Vienna: Waizner, 1905.

Fremdling, Rainer, et al., eds. *Statistik der Eisenbahnen in Deutschland, 1835–1989*. Quellen und Forschungen zur historischen Statistik von Deutschland 17. St. Katherinen: Scripta Mercaturae, 1995.

Friedlieb, Joseph Heinrich. *Die Sibyllinischen Weissagungen [Oracula Sibyllina]*. Leipzig: Wiegel, 1852.

Friedrichs, Christopher R. "Leisure and Acculturation in the Jewish Community of Dresden, 1833–1837." *Leo Baeck Institute Year Book* 56 (2011): 137–62.
Friesel, Evyatar. "Abraham Geiger in 1848: His Views on the Revolution, German Culture, and the Jews." *Leo Baeck Institute Year Book* 56 (2011): 163–73.
———. "The German-Jewish Encounter as a Historical Problem: A Reconsideration." *Leo Baeck Institute Year Book* 41 (1996): 263–74.
———. "The *Oesterreichisches Central-Organ*, Vienna 1848: A Radical Jewish Periodical." *Leo Baeck Institute Year Book* 47 (2002): 117–49.
———. Frojimovics, Kinga, and Géza Komoróczy, *Jewish Budapest: Monuments, Rites, History*. Budapest: Central European University Press, 1999.
Funkenstein, Amos. *Perceptions of Jewish History* (Berkeley: University of California Press, 1993).
Galas, Michał. *Rabbi Marcus Jastrow and His Vision for the Reform of Judaism: A Study in the History of Judaism in the Nineteenth Century*. Jews of Poland. Boston: Academic Studies Press, 2013.
Gall, Lothar, and Manfred Pohl, eds, *Die Eisenbahn in Deutschland: Von den Anfängen bis zur Gegenwart*. Munich: Beck, 1999.
Gay, Peter. *The Bourgeois Experience*. New York: Norton, 1984–1998.
———. *Schnitzler's Century: The Making of Middle-Class Culture, 1815–1914*. New York: Norton, 2002.
Gibs, Helga. *Leopoldstadt: Kleine Welt am großen Strom*. Vienna: Mohl, 1997.
Gillman, Abigail. *A History of German Jewish Bible Translation*. Chicago: University of Chicago Press, 2018.
Glatzer, Nahum N. *Leopold and Adelheid Zunz: An Account in Letters, 1815–1885*. London: East and West Library, 1958.
———. *Leopold Zunz: Jude, Deutscher, Europäer; Ein jüdisches Gelehrtenschicksal des 19. Jahrhunderts in Briefen an Freunde*. Schriftenreihe Wissenschaftlichen Abhandlungen des Leo Baeck Instituts 11. Tübingen: Mohr Siebeck, 1964.
———. "On an Unpublished Letter of Isaak Markus Jost." *Leo Baeck Institute Year Book* 22 (1977): 129–37.
Goethe, Johann Wolfgang. *Goethe's poetische und prosaische Werke in Zwei Bänden*. Edited by Friedrich Wilhelm Riemer and J. P. Eckermann. Stuttgart: Cotta, 1836–1837.
Goldman, Karla. *Beyond the Synagogue Gallery: Finding a Place for Women in American Judaism*. Cambridge: Harvard University Press, 2000.
Goldschmidt, E. D. "Studies on Jewish Liturgy by German-Jewish Scholars." *Leo Baeck Institute Year Book* 2 (1957): 119–35.
Goldstücker, Eduard. "Jews between Czechs and Germans around 1848." *Leo Baeck Institute Year Book* 17 (1972): 61–71.

Good, David F. *The Economic Rise of the Habsburg Empire, 1750–1914*. Berkeley: University of California Press, 1984.

Gottschlich, Jürgen. *The Bible Hunter: The Quest for the Original New Testament*. Translated by John Brownjohn. London: Haus, 2013.

Gotzmann, Andreas, Rainer Liedtke, and Till van Rahden. *Juden, Bürger, Deutsche: Zur Geschichte von Vielfalt und Differenz, 1800–1933*. Tübingen: Mohr Siebeck, 2001.

Graetz, Heinrich. *Geschichte der Juden von den ältesten Zeiten bis auf die Gegenwart*. 11 volumes. Leipzig: Leiner, 1853–1875.

———. *Tagebuch und Briefe*. Edited by Reuven Michael. Tübingen: Mohr, 1977.

Graetz, Michael. "From Corporate Community to Ethnic-Religious Minority, 1750–1830." *Leo Baeck Institute Year Book* 37 (1992): 71–82.

———, ed. *Schöpferische Momente des europäischen Judentums: In der frühen Neuzeit*. Heidelberg: Winter, 2000.

Grafton, Anthony. *Defenders of the Text: The Traditions of Scholarship in an Age of Science, 1450–1800*. Cambridge: Harvard University Press, 1991.

———. "Juden und Griechen bei Friedrich August Wolf." In *Friedrich August Wolf: Studien, Dokumente, Bibliographie*, edited by Reinhard Markner and Giuseppe Veltri, 9–31. Palingenesia 67. Stuttgart: Steiner, 1999.

Grossman, Avraham. *Pious and Rebellious: Jewish Women in Medieval Europe*. Waltham, MA: Brandeis University Press, 2004.

Grossman, Susan, and Rivka Haut, eds. *Daughters of the King: Women and the Synagogue; A Survey of History, Halakhah, and Contemporary Realities*. Philadelphia: Jewish Publication Society, 1992.

Grote, Simon. "Review-Essay: Religion and Enlightenment." *Journal of the History of Ideas* 75, no. 1 (2014): 137–60.

Gruenewald, Max. "The Modern Rabbi." *Leo Baeck Institute Year Book* 2 (1957): 85–97.

Gutzkow, Karl. *Uriel Acosta: Trauerspiel in fünf Aufzügen*. Leipzig: Reclam, 1847.

Hacohen, Malachi. "From Empire to Cosmopolitanism: The Central European Jewish Intelligentsia, 1867–1968." *Simon Dubnow Institute Yearbook* 5 (2006): 117–33.

———. *Jacob & Esau: Jewish European History between Nation and Empire*. New York: Cambridge University Press, 2019.

HaCohen, Ran. *Reclaiming the Hebrew Bible: German-Jewish Reception of Biblical Criticism*. Studia Judaica. New York: de Gruyter, 2010.

Hahn, Barbara. *The Jewess Pallas Athena: This Too a Theory of Modernity*. Translated by James McFarland. Princeton, NJ: Princeton University Press, 2005.

Hahn, Hans-Joachim. *The 1848 Revolutions in German-Speaking Europe*. Themes in Modern German History. Harlow, UK: Longman, 2001.
Hahn, Hans-Joachim, et al. *Kommunikationsräume des Europäischen–Jüdische Wissenskulturen jenseits des Nationalen*. Leipzig: Leipziger Universitätsverlag, 2014.
Hameln, Glikl von. *Glikl: Memoirs 1691–1719*. Edited by Chava Turniansky. Translated by Sara Friedman. Waltham, MA: Brandeis University Press, 2019.
Hammer-Schenk, Harold. *Synagogen in Deutschland: Geschichte einer Baugattung im 19. und 20. Jahrhundert (1780–1933)*. Hamburg: Christians, 1981.
Hanegraaff, Woulter J. "The Beginnings of Occultist Kabbalah: Adolphe Franck and Eliphas Lévy." In *Kabbalah and Modernity: Interpretations, Transformations, Adaptations*, edited by Boaz Huss, Marco Pasi, and Kocku von Stuckrad, 107–28. Leiden: Brill, 2010.
Harmelin, Wilhelm. "Jews in the Leipzig Fur Industry." *Leo Baeck Institute Year Book* 9 (1964): 239–66.
Harris, Jay M. *How Do We Know This? Midrash and the Fragmentation of Modern Judaism*. Albany: State University of New York Press, 1995.
Hartman, Geoffrey H., and Sanford Budick, eds. *Midrash and Literature*. New Haven: Yale University Press, 1986.
Hartwig, Dirk. "Die 'Wissenschaft des Judentums' und die Anfänge der kritischen Koranforschung: Perspektiven einer modernen Koranhermeneutik." *Zeitschrift für Religions- und Geistesgeschichte* 61, no. 3 (2009): 234–56.
Hegel, Georg Wilhelm Friedrich. *Werke in 20 Bände*. Edited by Eva Moldenhauer and Karl Markus Michel. Frankfurt am Main: Suhrkamp, 1986.
Heilman, Samuel C. *Portrait of American Jews: The Last Half of the 20th Century*. Samuel and Althea Stroum Lectures in Jewish Studies. Seattle: University of Washington Press, 1995.
Hertz, Deborah Sadie. *Jewish High Society in Old Regime Berlin*. Syracuse, NY: Syracuse University Press, 2005.
Hertz, Joseph H. *Book of Jewish Thoughts*. London: Office of the Chief Rabbi, 1940.
———. *Sermons, Addresses and Studies*, 3 vols. London: Soncino, 1938.
Herzig, Arno. "The Process of Emancipation: From the Congress of Vienna to the Revolution of 1848/1849." *Leo Baeck Institute Year Book* 37 (1992): 61–69.
Herzog, Dagmar. "Anti-Judaism in Intra-Christian Conflict: Catholics and Liberals in Baden in the 1840s." *Central European History* 27, no. 3 (1994): 267–81.
Heschel, Abraham Joshua. *Moral Grandeur and Spiritual Audacity: Essays*.

Edited by Susannah Heschel. New York: Farrar, Straus & Giroux, 1996.
Heschel, Susannah. *Abraham Geiger and the Jewish Jesus*. Chicago Studies in the History of Judaism. Chicago: University of Chicago Press, 1998.
Hess, Jonathan. *Germans, Jews and the Claims of Modernity*. New Haven: Yale University Press, 2002.
Hidary, Richard. *Rabbis and Classical Rhetoric: Sophistic Education and Oratory in the Talmud and Midrash*. New York: Cambridge University Press, 2018.
Hirsch, Samson Raphael. *The Hirsch Chumash: The Five Books of the Torah: Sefer Bereshis*. Edited and translated by Daniel Haberman. New York: Feldheim, 2006.
Hobsbawm, Eric. *The Age of Capital, 1848–1875*. 1962. Reprint, New York: Vintage, 1996.
———. *The Age of Empire, 1875–1914*. New York: Pantheon Books, 1987.
———. *The Age of Revolution, 1789–1848*. 1962. Reprint, New York: Vintage, 1996.
Hödl, Klaus. *Als Bettler in die Leopoldstadt: Galizische Juden auf dem Weg nach Wien*. Böhlaus zeitgeschichtliche Bibliothek 27. Vienna: Böhlau, 1994.
———. "The Turning to History of Viennese Jewry." *Journal of Modern Jewish Studies* 3, no. 1 (2004): 17–32.
Hojda, Zdeněk, Lubomir Pořízka, and Jiří Pešek. *The Palaces of Prague*. New York: Rizzoli, 1994.
Homolka, Walter, and Heinz-Günther Schöttler, eds. *Rabbi – Pastor – Priest: Their Roles and Profiles through the Ages*. Berlin: de Gruyter, 2013.
Horowitz, Elliott S. "'A Jew of the Old Type': Neubauer as Cataloguer, Critic, and Necrologist." *Jewish Quarterly Review* 100, no. 4 (2010): 649–56.
Hubka, Thomas C. *Resplendent Synagogue: Architecture and Worship in an Eighteenth-Century Polish Community*. Tauber Institute for the Study of European Jewry Series. Waltham, MA: Brandeis University Press, 2003.
Huss, Boaz. *Ke-Zohar ha-rakiʿa: perakim be-hitkablut ha-Zohar uve-havnayat ʿerko ha-simli*. Jerusalem: Ben-Zvi Institute, Bialik Institute, 2008.
———. *The Zohar: Reception and Impact*. Translated by Yudith Nave. Portland, OR: Littman Library of Jewish Civilization, 2016.
Huss, Boaz, Marco Pasi, and Kocku von Stuckrad, eds. *Kabbalah and Modernity: Interpretations, Transformations, Adaptations*. Aries Book Series 10. Leiden: Brill, 2010.
Idel, Moshe. "Al Aharon Jellinek ve haKabbalah." *Peʿamim* 100 (2004): 16–21 (Hebrew).
Iggers, Georg G. "Historicism: The History and Meaning of the Term." *Journal of the History of Ideas* 56, no. 1 (1995): 129–52.

Iggers, Wilma Abeles, ed. *The Jews of Bohemia and Moravia: A Historical Reader*. Detroit: Wayne State University Press, 1992.
Illustrirte Zeitung, no. 2637 (13 January 1894), 45–46.
Ivry, Alfred L. "Salomon Munk and the *Mélanges de philosophie juive et arabe*." *Jewish Studies Quarterly* 7, no. 2 (2000): 120–26.
Jellinek, Herrmann. *Kritische Geschichte der Wiener Revolution vom 13. März bis zum constituirenden Reichstag*. Vienna: Sommer, 1848.

———. *Uriel Acosta's leben und lehre: Ein beitrag zur kenntniss seiner moral, wie zur berichtigung der Gutzkow'schen fiktionen über Acosta, und zur charakteristik der damaligen Juden*. Zerbst: Kummer, 1847.
Jersch-Wenzel, Stefi. "Legal Status and Emancipation." In *German-Jewish History in Modern Times. Volume 2: Emancipation and Acculturation, 1780–1871*, edited by Michael Brenner, Stefi Jersch-Wenzel, and Michael A. Meyer, 7–49. New York: Columbia University Press, 1996.

———. "Population Shifts and Occupational Structures." In *German-Jewish History in Modern Times. Volume 2: Emancipation and Acculturation, 1780–1871*, edited by Michael Brenner, Stefi Jersch-Wenzel, and Michael A Meyer, 50–89. New York: Columbia University Press, 1996.
The Jewish Chronicle, January 5, 1894, 7–8,
Jewish Publication Society. *JPS Hebrew-English Tanakh: The Traditional Hebrew Text and the New JPS translation*. 2nd ed. Philadelphia: Jewish Publication Society, 1999.
Jones, Calvin N. "Authorial Intent and Public Response to *Uriel Acosta* and *Freiheit in Krahwinkel*." *South Atlantic Review* 47, no. 4 (1982): 17–26.
Jost, Isaak Markus. *Adolph Jellinek und die Kabbala ein Literatur-Bericht*. Leipzig: Colditz, 1852.

———. *Geschichte der Israeliten seit der Zeit der Maccabäer bis auf unsre Tage*. 10 volumes. Berlin: Schlesinger, 1821–1847.

———. *Geschichte des Judenthums und seiner Secten*, 3 vols. Leipzig: Dörffling & Franke, 1857–1859.
Judson, Pieter M. *The Habsburg Empire: A New History*. Cambridge: BelknapPress of Harvard University Press, 2016.
Kalmar, Ivan D. "Moorish Style: Orientalism, the Jews, and Synagogue Architecture." *Jewish Social Studies* 7, no. 3 (2001): 68–100.
Kalmar Ivan D., and Derek J. Penslar, eds. *Orientalism and the Jews*. Waltham, MA: Brandeis University Press, 2005.
Kanarfogel, Ephraim. *The Intellectual History and Rabbinic Culture of Medieval Ashkenaz*. Detroit: Wayne State University Press, 2013.
Kann, Robert A. *A History of the Habsburg Empire, 1526–1918*. Berkeley: University of California Press, 1974.

———. "Should the Habsburg Empire Have Been Saved? An Exercise in Speculative History." *Austrian History Yearbook* 42 (2011): 203–10.

Kann, Robert A., and Zdeněk V. David. *The Peoples of the Eastern Habsburg Lands, 1526–1918*. Seattle: University of Washington Press, 1984.

Kant, Immanuel. "An Answer to the Question: What Is Enlightenment?" In *What Is Enlightenment? Eighteenth-Century Answers and Twentieth-Century Questions*, edited by James Schmidt, 58–64. Philosophical Traditions 7. Berkeley: University of California Press, 1996.

———. *Der Streit der Facultäten: In drey Abschnitten*. Königsberg: Nicolovius, 1798.

Kaplan, Marion A. *Jewish Daily Life in Germany, 1618–1945*. Oxford: Oxford University Press, 2005.

Katz, Jacob. *Out of the Ghetto: The Social Background of Jewish Emancipation, 1770–1870*. Cambridge: Harvard University Press, 1973.

Kaufmann, Uri R. "The Jewish Fight for Emancipation in France and Germany." In *Jewish Emancipation Reconsidered: The French and German Models*, edited by Michael Brenner, Vicki Caron, and Uri R. Kaufmann, 79–92. Tübingen: Mohr Siebeck, 2003.

Kaunfer, Elie. *Empowered Judaism: What Independent Minyanim Can Teach Us about Building Vibrant Jewish Communities*. Woodstock, VT: Jewish Lights, 2010.

Kempter, Klaus. "Adolf Jellinek und die jüdische Emanzipation: Der Prediger der Leipziger jüdischen Gemeinde in der Revolution 1848/49." *Aschkenas – Zeitschrift für Geschichte und Kultur der Juden* 8 (1998): 179–91.

———. *Die Jellineks 1820–1955: Eine Familienbiographische Studie zum deutschjüdischen Bildungsbürgertum*. Schriften des Bundesarchivs 52. Düsseldorf: Droste, 1998.

Kertész, Imre. "Nobel Lecture." December 2, 2002. NobelPrize.org.

Kestenberg-Gladstein, Ruth. *Neuere Geschichte der Juden in den böhmischen Ländern. Erster Teil: Das Zeitalter der Aufklärung, 1780–1830*. Schriftenreihe wissenschaftlicher Abhandlungen des Leo Baeck Instituts 18. Tübingen: Mohr Siebeck, 1969.

———. "A Voice from the Prague Enlightenment." *Leo Baeck Institute Year Book* 9 (1964): 295–304.

Kiener, Ronald. "From Ba'al ha-Zohar to Prophetic to Ecstatic: The Vicissitudes of Abulafia in Contemporary Scholarship." In *Gershom Scholem's Major Trends in Jewish Mysticism 50 Years after: Proceedings of the Sixth International Conference on the History of Jewish Mysticism*, edited by Peter Schäfer and Joseph Dan, 145–162 (Tübingen: Mohr Siebeck, 1993).

Kieval, Hillel J. "Autonomy and Interdependence: The Historical Legacy of Czech Jewry." In *The Precious Legacy: Judaic Treasures from the Czechoslovak State Collections*, edited by David Altshuler. New York: Summit, 1983.

———. "Choosing to Bridge: Revisiting the Phenomenon of Cultural

Mediation." *Bohemia: A Journal of History and Civilization in Central Europe* 46 (2005): 15–27.

———. "Imperial Embraces and Ethnic Challenges: The Politics of Jewish Identity in the Bohemian Lands." *Shofar: An Interdisciplinary Journal of Jewish Studies* 30, no. 4 (2013): 1–17.

———. "Jewish Prague, Christian Prague, and the Castle in the City's Golden Age." *Jewish Studies Quarterly* 18 (2011): 202–15.

———. *Languages of Community: The Jewish Experience in the Czech Lands*. Berkeley: University of California Press, 2000.

———. *The Making of Czech Jewry: National Conflict and Jewish Society in Bohemia, 1870–1918*. Studies in Jewish History. New York: Oxford University Press, 1988.

———. "The Social Vision of Bohemian Jews: Intellectuals and Community in the 1840s." In *Assimilation and Community: The Jews in Nineteenth-Century Europe*, edited by Jonathan Frankel and Steven J. Zipperstein, 246–83. Cambridge: Cambridge University Press, 1992.

———. "Texts and Contest: Myths of Origin and Myths of Belonging in Nineteenth-Century Bohemia." In *Jewish History and Jewish Memory: Essays in Honor of Yosef Hayim Yerushalmi*, edited by Elisheva Carlebach, John M. Efron, and David N. Myers, 348–68. Hanover, NH: University Press of New England, 1998.

———. "The Unforeseen Consequences of Cultural Resistance: Haskalah and State-Mandated Reform in the Bohemian Lands." *Jewish Culture and History* 13, no. 2 (2012): 1–16.

King, Martin Luther, Jr. *A Testament of Hope: The Essential Writings and Speeches of Martin Luther King, Jr.* Edited by James Melvin Washington. San Francisco: HarperSanFrancisco, 1991.

Klein, Evelyn, and Gustav Glaser. *Peripherie in der Stadt: Das Wiener Nordbahnviertel – Einblicke, Erkundungen, Analysen*. Innsbruck: Studien, 2000.

Kohler, George Y. *Kabbalah Research in the Wissenschaft des Judentums, 1820–1880: The Foundations of an Academic Discipline*. Berlin: de Gruyter, 2019.

———. *Reading Maimonides' Philosophy in 19th Century Germany: The Guide to Religious Reform*. Amsterdam Studies in Jewish Philosophy 15. Dordrecht: Springer, 2012.

Krinsky, Carol H. *Synagogues of Europe: Architecture, History, Meaning*. Cambridge: MIT Press, 1985.

Krobb, Florian. "Vorbild und Gegenbild: Das ibirische Judentum in der deutsch-jüdischen Erinnerungskultur 1779–1939 (review)." *Shofar: An Interdisciplinary Journal of Jewish Studies* 31, no. 4 (2013): 127–30.

Krone, Kerstin von der, and Mirjam Thulin. "*Wissenschaft* in Context: A Research Essay on the *Wissenschaft des Judentums*." *Leo Baeck Institute Year Book* 58 (2013): 249–80.

Kubova, Alena. "Railway Stations and Planning Projects in Prague, 1845–1945." In *The City and the Railway in Europe*, edited by Ralf Roth and Marie-Noëlle Polino, 155–68. Aldershot: Ashgate, 2003.

Kurländer, Adolf. *Biografi S. L. Rapoport's*. Pest: [Self-published,] 1869.

Kurrein, Adolf, ed. *Dr. Adolf Jellinek: Lichtstrahlen aus den Reden Dr. Adolf Jellinek's*. Vienna: Bermann & Altmann, 1891.

Lässig, Simone. "Bildung als *kulturelles Kapital*? Jüdische Schulprojekte in der Frühphase der Emanzipation." In *Juden, Bürger, Deutsche: Zur Geschichte von Vielfalt und Differenz, 1800–1933*, edited by Andreas Gotzmann, Rainer Liedtke, and Till van Rahden, 263–98. Schriftenreihe wissenschaftlicher Abhandlungen des Leo Baeck Instituts 63. Tübingen: Mohr Siebeck, 2001.

———. *Jüdische Wege ins Bürgertum: Kulturelles Kapital und sozialer Aufstieg im 19. Jahrhundert*. Bürgertum N.F. 1. Göttingen: Vandenhoeck & Ruprecht, 2004.

———. "Systeme des Wissens und Praktiken der Erziehung: Transfers und Übersetzungen im deutschen Judentum des 19. Jahrhunderts." In *Kommunikationsräume des Europäischen: Jüdische Wissenskulturen jenseits des Nationalen*, edited by Hans-Joachim Hahn et al., 15–42. Leipzig: Leipziger Universitätsverlag, 2014.

Leicht, Reimund, and Gad Freudenthal, eds. *Studies on Steinschneider: Moritz Steinschneider and the Emergence of the Science of Judaism in Nineteenth-Century Germany*. Studies in Jewish History and Culture 33. Leiden: Brill, 2012.

Lenger, Friedrich. *European Cities in the Modern Era, 1850–1914*. Translated by Joel Golb. Studies in Central European Histories 57. Leiden: Brill, 2012.

Levi, Franz. "The Jews of Sachsen-Meiningen and the Edict of 1811." *Leo Baeck Institute Year Book* 38 (1993): 15–32.

Levitt, Peggy. *God Needs No Passport: Immigrants and the Changing American Religious Landscape*. New York: New Press, 2007.

———. "'You Know, Abraham Was Really the First Immigrant': Religion and Transnational Migration." *International Migration Review* 37, no. 3 (2003): 847–73.

Liberles, Robert. *Jews Welcome Coffee: Tradition and Innovation in Early Modern Germany*. Tauber Institute for the Study of European Jewry. Waltham, MA: Brandeis University Press, 2012.

Lieber, David L. "Strangers and Gentiles." In *Encyclopaedia Judaica*, volume 19. 2nd ed., edited by Michael Berenbaum and Fred Skolnik, 241–42. Detroit: Macmillan Reference, 2007.

List, Friedrich. *Ueber ein sächsisches Eisenbahn-System als Grundlage eines allgemeinen deutschen Eisenbahn-Systems und insbesondere über die Anlegung einer Eisenbahn von Leipzig nach Dresden*. Leipzig: Liebeskind, 1833.

Loewe, Herbert M. J. *Adolf Neubauer, 1831–1931*. Oxford: Oxford University Press, 1931.
Lowenstein, Steven M. "Was Urbanization Harmful to Jewish Tradition and Identity in Germany?" *Studies in Contemporary Jewry* 15 (1999): 80–110.
Manekin, Rachel. "Praying at Home in Lemberg: The *Minyan* Laws of the Habsburg Empire, 1776–1848." In *Jews and Their Neighbors in Eastern Europe since 1750*, edited by Israel Bartal, Antony Polonsky, and Scott Ury, 49–69. Polin: Studies in Polish Jewry 24. Portland, OR: Littman Library of Jewish Civilization, 2012.
Marchand, Suzanne L. *Down from Olympus: Archaeology and Philhellenism in Germany, 1750–1970*. Princeton, NJ: Princeton University Press, 1996.
Marcus, Ivan G. *Rituals of Childhood: Jewish Acculturation in Medieval Europe*. New Haven: Yale University Press, 1998.
Martens, Bob, and Herbert Peter, *Die zerstörten Synagogen Wiens: Virtuelle Stadtspaziergänge*. Vienna: Mandelbaum, 2009.
Matt, Daniel C. *Zohar, the Book of Enlightenment*. Classics of Western Spirituality. New York: Paulist Press, 1983.
Mayhew, Henry. *German Life and Manners as Seen in Saxony at the Present Day with an Account of Village Life, Town Life, Fashionable Life, Domestic Life, Married Life, School and University Life, &c., of Germany at the Present Time*. London: Allen, 1864.
McKendrick, Scot. *In a Monastery Library: Preserving Codex Sinaiticus and the Greek Written Heritage*. London: British Library, 2006.
Meek, H. A. *The Synagogue*. London: Phaidon, 1995.
Mellor, Roy E. H. *German Railways: A Study in the Historical Geography of Transport*. Aberdeen: University of Aberdeen, Department of Geography, 1979.
Mendelssohn, Moses. *Jerusalem, or, On Religious Power and Judaism*. Translated by Allan Arkush. Hanover, NH: University Press of New England, 1983.
Meßner, Robert. *Die Leopoldstadt im Vormärz: Historisch-topographische Darstellung der nordöstlichen Vorstädte und Vororte Wiens auf Grund der Katastralvermessung*. Vienna: Wissenschaftlichen Gesellschaften Österreich, 1962.
Mevorah, Barouh. "Jewish Diplomatic Activities to Prevent Expulsion of the Jews from Bohemia and Moravia in 1744–45." In *Studies in Jewish History*, vol. 1, edited by Joseph Dan, 143–58. New York: Praeger, 1989.
Meyer, Michael A. "'How Awesome Is This Place!' The Reconceptualization of the Synagogue in Nineteenth-Century Germany." *Leo Baeck Institute Year Book* 41 (1996): 51–63.
———. "Jewish Religious Reform and Wissenschaft des Judentums: The

Positions of Zunz, Geiger and Frankel." *Leo Baeck Institute Year Book* 16 (1971): 19–41.

———. *The Origins of the Modern Jew: Jewish Identity and European Culture in Germany, 1749–1824*. Detroit: Wayne State University Press, 1967.

———. "Reflections on Jewish Modernization." In *Jewish History and Jewish Memory: Essays in Honor of Yosef Hayim Yerushalmi*, edited by Elisheva Carlebach, John M. Efron, and David N. Myers, 369–77. Hanover, NH: University Press of New England, 1998.

———. *Response to Modernity: A History of the Reform Movement in Judaism*. New York: Oxford University Press, 1988.

Miller, Jaroslav. "Early Modern Urban Immigration in East Central Europe: A Macroanalysis." *Austrian History Yearbook* 36 (2005): 3–39.

Miller, Michael L. "Going Native: Moritz Jellinek and the Modernization of the Hungarian Economy." In *The Economy in Jewish History: New Perspectives on the Interrelationship between Ethnicity and Economic Life*, edited by Gideon Reuveni and Sarah Wobick-Segev, 157–72. New York: Berghahn Books, 2011.

———. *Rabbis and Revolution: The Jews of Moravia in the Age of Emancipation*. Stanford Studies in Jewish History and Culture. Stanford: Stanford University Press, 2011.

Mitchell, Allan. *The Great Train Race: Railways and the Franco-German Rivalry, 1815–1914*. New York: Berghahn, 2000.

Morgenstern, J. *Die französische Academie und die "Geographie des Talmuds."* Berlin: Schlesinger, 1870.

Mortara, Marco. *L'epistolario di Marco Mortara (1815–1894): Un rabbino italiano tra riforma e ortodossia*. Edited by Asher Salah. Florence: Giuntina, 2012.

Munk, Salomon. *Mélanges de philosophie juive et arabe*. Paris: Franck, 1857.

———. *La philosophie chez les juifs*. Paris: Bureau des Archives Israelites, 1848.

Murdoch, Caitlin E. *Changing Places: Society, Culture, and Territory in the Saxon-Bohemian Borderlands, 1870–1946*. Ann Arbor: University of Michigan Press, 2010.

Museum für Naturkunde und Vorgeschichte Dessau, Museum für Stadtgeschichte Dessau, and Museum Schloss Mosigkau, eds. *Fürst Leopold I. von Anhalt-Dessau (1676–1747): "Der Alte Dessauer": Ausstellung zum 250. Todestag*. Dessau: Die Museen, 1997.

Myers, David. "Philosophy and Kabbalah in Wissenschaft des Judentums: Rethinking the Narrative of Neglect." *Studia Judaica* 16 (2008): 56–71.

Neilson, Keith, and T. G. Otte, "'Railpolitik': An introduction." In *Railways and International Politics: Paths of Empire, 1848–1945*, edited by T. G. Otte and Keith Neilson, 1–20. New York: Routledge, 2006.

Neusner, Jacob, ed. *The Rabbinate in America: Reshaping an Ancient Calling*. New York: Garland, 1993.

Nilsen, Micheline. *Railways and the Western European Capitals: Studies of Implantation in London, Paris, Berlin, and Brussels*. New York: Palgrave Macmillan, 2008.
Novak, David. *The Image of the Non-Jew in Judaism: The Idea of Noahide Law*. Edited by Matthew Lagrone. Portland, OR: Littman Library of Jewish Civilization, 2011.
O'Brien, Patrick. *Railways and the Economic Development of Western Europe, 1830–1914*. New York: St. Martin's Press, 1983.
Ogren, Brian. "Sefirotic Depictions, Divine Noesis, and Aristotelian Kabbalah: Abraham ben Meir de Balmes and Italian Renaissance Thought." *Jewish Quarterly Review* 104, no. 4 (2014): 573–99.
Osterhammel, Jürgen. *The Transformation of the World: A Global History of the Nineteenth Century*. Translated by Patrick Camiller. America in the World. Princeton, NJ: Princeton University Press, 2014.
Otte, T. G., and Keith Neilson, eds. *Railways and International Politics: Paths of Empire, 1848–1945*. New York: Routledge, 2006.
Pánek, Jaroslav, and Oldřich Tůma. *A History of the Czech Lands*. Prague: Charles University Karolinum Press, 2009.
Pařík, Arno, et al., eds. *Symbols of Emancipation: Nineteenth-Century Synagogues in the Czech Lands*. Prague: Jewish Museum in Prague, 2013.
Parker, David C. *Codex Sinaiticus: The Story of the World's Oldest Bible*. London: British Library, 2010.
———. *Textual Scholarship and the Making of the New Testament*. Lyell Lectures. Oxford: Oxford University Press, 2012.
Pelger, Gregor. *Wissenschaft des Judentums und englische Bibliotheken: Zur Geschichte historischer Philologie im 19. Jahrhundert*. Minima Judaica. Berlin: Metropol, 2010.
Perl, Gil S. *The Pillar of Volozhin: Rabbi Naftali Zvi Yehuda Berlin and the World of Nineteenth-Century Lithuanian Torah Scholarship*. Boston: Academic Studies Press, 2012.
Petrovsky-Shtern, Yohanan. *The Golden Age Shtetl: A New History of Jewish Life in East Europe*. Princeton, NJ: Princeton University Press, 2014.
Petuchowski, Jakob Josef. *Prayerbook Reform in Europe: The Liturgy of European Liberal and Reform Judaism*. New York: World Union for Progressive Judaism, 1968.
Piechotka, Maria, and Kazimierz Piechotka. *Wooden Synagogues*. Warsaw: Arkady, 1959.
Plowinski, Kerstin. "Die jüdische Bevölkerung Leipzigs 1853, 1925, 1933: Sozialgeschichtliche Fallstudien zur Mitgliedschaft einer Grossgemeinde." Diss., University of Leipzig, 1991.
Poling, Kristin. "Shantytowns and Pioneers beyond the City Wall: Berlin's Urban Frontier in the Nineteenth Century." *Central European History* 47, no. 2 (2014): 245–74.
Porter, Stanley E. *Constantine Tischendorf: The Life and Work of a 19th*

Century Bible Hunter, Including Constantine Tischendorf's When Were Our Gospels Written? London: Bloomsbury, 2015.
Posner, Simon, ed., *The Koren Mesorat Harav Kinot*. Jerusalem: Koren, 2011.
Preißler, Holger. "Heinrich Leberecht Fleischer: Ein Leipziger Orientalist, seine jüdischen Studenten, Promovenden und Kollegen." In *Bausteine einer jüdischen Geschichte der Universität Leipzig*, edited by Stephan Wendehorst, 245–68. Leipzig: Leipziger Universitätsverlag, 2006.
Rabault-Feuerhahn, Pascale. *Archives of Origins: Sanskrit, Philology, Anthropology in 19th Century Germany*. Translated by Dominique Bach and Richard Willet. Kultur- und sozialwissenschaftliche Studien 9. Wiesbaden: Harrassowitz, 2013.
Rampley, Matthew. "Peasants in Vienna: Ethnographic Display and the 1873 World's Fair." *Austrian History Yearbook* 42 (2011): 110–32.
Rapport, Mike. *1848: Year of Revolution*. London: Little, Brown, 2008.
Reill, Peter Hanns. *The German Enlightenment and the Rise of Historicism*. Berkeley: University of California Press, 1975.
Retallack, James N., ed. *Saxony in German History: Culture, Society, and Politics, 1830–1933*. Social History, Popular Culture, and Politics in Germany. Ann Arbor: University of Michigan Press, 2000.
Riff, Michael Anthony. "Assimilation and Conversion in Bohemia: Secession from the Jewish Community in Prague, 1868–1917." *Leo Baeck Institute Year Book* 26 (1981): 73–88.
Roemer, Nils H. *Jewish Scholarship and Culture in Nineteenth-Century Germany: Between History and Faith*. Studies in German Jewish Cultural History and Literature. Madison: University of Wisconsin Press, 2005.
Rosenau, Helen. "Gottfried Semper and German Synagogue Architecture." *Leo Baeck Institute Year Book* 22 (1977): 237–44.
Rosenbloom, Noah H. *Tradition in an Age of Reform: The Religious Philosophy of Samson Raphael Hirsch*. Philadelphia: Jewish Publication Society of America, 1976.
Rosenmann, Moses. *Dr. Adolf Jellinek: Sein Leben und Schaffen*. Vienna: Schlesinger, 1931.
Roth, Norman. *Daily Life of the Jews in the Middle Ages*. Westport, CT: Greenwood, 2005.
———. "Thomas Aquinas." In *Medieval Jewish Civilization: An Encyclopedia*, edited by Norman Roth, 27–31. New York: Routledge, 2016.
Roth, Ralf. *Das Jahrhundert der Eisenbahn: Die Herrschaft über Raum und Zeit, 1800–1914*. Stuttgart: Thorbecke, 2005.
Rotter, Hans, and Adolf Schmieger. *Das Ghetto in der Wiener Leopoldstadt*. Vienna: Burg, 1926.
Rozenblit, Marsha L. "Creating Jewish Space: German-Jewish Schools in Moravia." *Austrian History Yearbook* 44 (2013): 108–47.

———. "Jewish Assimilation in Habsburg Vienna." In *Assimilation and Community: The Jews in Nineteenth-Century Europe*, edited by Jonathan Frankel and Steven J. Zipperstein, 225–45. Cambridge: Cambridge University Press, 1992.

———. "Jewish Identity and the Modern Rabbi: The Cases of Isak Noa Mannheimer, Adolf Jellinek, and Moritz Güdemann in Nineteenth-Century Vienna." *Leo Baeck Institute Year Book* 35 (1990): 103–31.

———. *The Jews of Vienna, 1867–1914: Assimilation and Identity*. SUNY Series in Modern Jewish Literature and Culture. Albany: State University of New York Press, 1983.

Rubin, Eli. "From the Grünen Wiesen to Urban Space: Berlin, Expansion, and the Longue Durée." *Central European History* 47, no. 2 (2014): 221–44.

Rudavsky, David. "The Historical School of Zacharia Frankel." *Jewish Journal of Sociology* 5, no. 2 (1963): 224–44.

Ruderman, David B. *Early Modern Jewry: A New Cultural History*. Princeton, NJ: Princeton University Press, 2010.

Rudolph, Susanne Hoeber. "Introduction: Religion, States, and Transnational Civil Society." In *Transnational Religion and Fading States*, edited by Susanne Hoeber Rudolph and James Piscatori, 1–24. Boulder, CO: Westview Press, 1997.

Rürup, Reinhard. "German Liberalism and the Emancipation of the Jews." *Leo Baeck Institute Year Book* 20 (1975): 59–68.

Sacks, Jonathan. *Covenant & Conversation: A Weekly Reading of the Jewish Bible: Genesis, the Book of Beginnings*. New Milford, CT: Maggid Books, 2009.

Salecker, Hans-Joachim. *Der Liberalismus und die Erfahrung der Differenz: Über die Bedingungen der Integration der Juden in Deutschland*. Berlin: Philo, 1999.

Saperstein, Marc. *Jewish Preaching, 1200–1800: An Anthology*. Yale Judaica Series 26. New Haven: Yale University Press, 1989.

———. *Leadership and Conflict: Tensions in Medieval and Early Modern Jewish History and Culture*. Oxford: Littman Library of Jewish Civilization, 2014.

———. "Rabbis as Preachers, 1800–1965: Regensburg Conference Lecture." In *Rabbi – Pastor – Priest: Their Roles and Profiles through the Ages*, edited by Walter Homolka and Heinz-Günther Schöttler, 111–28. Berlin: de Gruyter, 2013.

Sarna, Jonathan D. *American Judaism: A History*. New Haven: Yale University Press, 2004.

Schad, Margit. *Rabbiner Michael Sachs: Judentum als höhere Lebensanschauung*. Netiva 7. Hildesheim: Olms, 2007.

Schäfer, Peter, and Joseph Dan, eds. *Gershom Scholem's Major Trends in*

Jewish Mysticism 50 Years After: Proceedings of the Sixth International Conference on the History of Jewish Mysticism. Tübingen: Mohr Siebeck, 1993.

Schapkow, Carsten. *Vorbild und Gegenbild: Das ibirische Judentum in der deutsch-jüdischen Erinnerungskultur, 1779–1939.* Cologne: Böhlau, 2011.

Schechter, Ronald. *Obstinate Hebrews: Representations of Jews in France, 1715–1815.* Studies on the History of Society and Culture 49. Berkeley: University of California Press, 2003.

Schivelbusch, Wolfgang. *The Railway Journey: The Industrialization of Time and Space in the 19th Century.* Leamington Spa, UK: Berg, 1986.

Scholem, Gershom. *Major Trends in Jewish Mysticism.* New York: Schocken, 1995.

———. *Ursprung und Anfänge der Kabbala.* Berlin: de Gruyter, 1962.

Schorsch, Ismar. "Beyond the Classroom: The Enduring Relationship between Heinrich L. Fleischer and Ignaz Goldziher." In *Modern Jewish Scholarship in Hungary: The 'Science of Judaism' between East and West*, edited by Tamás Turán and Carsten Wilke, 119–56. Europäisch-Jüdische Studien: Beiträge 14. Berlin: de Gruyter, 2016.

———. "Converging Cognates: The Intersection of Jewish and Islamic Studies in Nineteenth Century Germany." *Leo Baeck Institute Year Book* 55 (2010): 3–36.

———. "Emancipation and the Crisis of Religious Authority: The Emergence of the Modern Rabbinate." In *Revolution and Evolution: 1848 in German-Jewish History*, edited by Werner E. Mosse, Arnold Paucker, and Reinhard Rürup. Tübingen: Mohr, 1981.

———. *From Text to Context: The Turn to History in Modern Judaism.* Waltham, MA: Brandeis University Press, 1994.

———. "From Wolfenbüttel to Wissenschaft: The Divergent Paths of Isaak Markus Jost and Leopold Zunz." *Leo Baeck Institute Year Book* 22 (1977): 109–28.

———. "The Last Jewish Generalist." *AJS Review* 18, no. 1 (1993): 39–50.

———. *Leopold Zunz: Creativity in Adversity.* Jewish Culture and Contexts. Philadelphia: University of Pennsylvania Press, 2016.

———. "The Myth of Sephardic Supremacy." *Leo Baeck Institute Year Book* 34 (1989): 47–66.

———. "Zacharias Frankel and the European Origins of Conservative Judaism." *Judaism* 30, no. 3 (1981): 344–54.

Schorske, Carl E. *Fin-de-Siècle Vienna: Politics and Culture.* New York: Knopf, 1979.

Schwarzfuchs, Simon. *A Concise History of the Rabbinate.* Jewish Society and Culture. Oxford: Blackwell, 1993.

Seidel, Esther. *Zacharias Frankel und das Jüdisch-Theologische Seminar / Zacharias Frankel and the Jewish Theological Seminary.* Jüdische Miniaturen. Berlin: Hentrich & Hentrich, 2013.

Seligmann, Caesar. "Breslau Seminary 1881." *Leo Baeck Institute Year Book* 5 (1960): 346–50.
Shavit, Yaakov, and Mordechai Eran. *The Hebrew Bible Reborn: From Holy Scripture to the Book of Books; A History of Biblical Culture and the Battles over the Bible in Modern Judaism*. Studia Judaica. Berlin: de Gruyter, 2007.
Sheehan, Jonathan. *The Enlightenment Bible: Translation, Scholarship, Culture*. Princeton, NJ: Princeton University Press, 2005.
Sherwin, Byron L. *Mystical Theology and Social Dissent: The Life and Works of Judah Loew of Prague*. Portland OR: Littman Library of Jewish Civilization, 2006.
Siegel, Björn. "Facing Tradition: Adolf Jellinek and the Emergence of Modern Habsburg Jewry." *Simon Dubnow Institute Yearbook* 8 (2009): 319–44.
———. "The Temple in Leopoldstadt and Its Function in Habsburg Vienna: The Role of History in Fashioning Jewish Modernity." *Austrian Studies* 24 (2016): 109–23.
Silverman, Eric Kline. *A Cultural History of Jewish Dress*. London: Bloomsbury, 2013.
Simons, Thomas W., Jr. "The Prague Origins of the Güntherian Converts (1800–1850)." *Leo Baeck Institute Year Book* 22 (1977): 245–56.
Simonson, Otto. *Der Neue Tempel in Leipzig: Entworfen und Ausgeführt*. Berlin: Riegel, 1858.
Sládek, Pavel. "Judah Löw ben Betsalel – The Maharal of Prague: A Theologian with Humanist Bias." In *Jewish Studies in the 21st Century: Prague – Europe – World*, edited by Marcela Zoufalá, 59–83. Wiesbaden: Harrassowitz, 2014.
Snyder, Saskia Coenen. *Building a Public Judaism: Synagogues and Jewish Identity in Nineteenth-Century Europe*. Cambridge: Harvard University Press, 2013.
Sorkin, David. "Emancipation and Assimilation: Two Concepts and Their Application to German-Jewish History." *Leo Baeck Institute Year Book* 35 (1990): 17–33.
———. "The Genesis of the Ideology of Emancipation: 1806–1840." *Leo Baeck Institute Year Book* 32 (1987): 11–40.
———. "The Impact of Emancipation on German Jewry: A Reconsideration." In *Assimilation and Community: The Jews in Nineteenth-Century Europe*, edited by Jonathan Frankel and Steven J. Zipperstein, 177–98. Cambridge: Cambridge University Press, 1992.
———. *Jewish Emancipation: A History across Five Centuries*. Princeton, NJ: Princeton University Press, 2019.
———. *The Transformation of German Jewry, 1780–1840*. Studies in Jewish History. New York: Oxford University Press, 1987.

Soussan, Henri. *The Science of Judaism: From Leopold Zunz to Leopold Lucas*. Brighton: University of Sussex, 1999.
Sperber, Daniel, and Theodore Friedman. "Gentile." In *Encyclopaedia Judaica*, vol. 19, 2nd ed., edited by Michael Berenbaum and Fred Skolnik, 485–87. Detroit: Macmillan Reference, 2007.
Sperber, Jonathan, ed. *The European Revolutions, 1848–1851*. 2nd ed. New Approaches to European History 29. New York: Cambridge University Press, 2005.
Spielman, John P. *Leopold I of Austria*. London: Thames & Hudson, 1977.
Stampfer, Shaul. *Families, Rabbis and Education: Traditional Jewish Society in Nineteenth-Century Eastern Europe*. Portland, OR: Littman Library of Jewish Civilization, 2010.
———. *Lithuanian Yeshivas of the Nineteenth Century: Creating a Tradition of Learning*. Portland, OR: Littman Library of Jewish Civilization, 2012.
Steinberg, Milton. *As a Driven Leaf*. Springfield, NJ: Behrman House, 2015.
Steinschneider, Moritz. *Catalogus librorum hebraeorum in Bibliotheca Bodleiana [Bibliotheca Hebraica Bodleiana]*. Berlin: Friedländer, 1852–1860.
Stern, Eliyahu. *The Genius: Elijah of Vilna and the Making of Modern Judaism*. New Haven: Yale University Press, 2013.
Stiefel, Barry L. "The Architectural Origins of the Great Early Modern Urban Synagogue." *Leo Baeck Institute Year Book* 56 (2011): 105–34.
———. *Jews and the Renaissance of Synagogue Architecture, 1450–1730*. Religious Cultures in the Early Modern World 14. London: Routledge, 2014.
Tachau, William G. "The Architecture of the Synagogue." *American Jewish Year Book* 28 (1926–1927): 155–92.
Tasch, Roland. *Samson Raphael Hirsch: Jüdische Erfahrungswelten im Historischen Kontext*. Berlin: de Gruyter, 2011.
Taylor, Charles. *A Secular Age*. Cambridge: Belknap Press of Harvard University Press, 2007.
Taylor, Derek. *Chief Rabbi Hertz: The Wars of the Lord*. London: Vallentine Mitchell, 2014.
Temkin, Sefton. *Creating American Reform Judaism: The Life and Times of Isaac Mayer Wise*. Portland, OR: Littman Library of Jewish Civilization, 1998.
Tischendorf, Konstantin von. *Reise in den Orient*. 2 vols. Leipzig: Tauchnitz, 1845–1846.
Tishby, Isaiah. *Wisdom of the Zohar: An Anthology of Texts*, vol. 1. Portland, OR: Littman Library of Jewish Civilization, 1989.
Tramer, Hans. "Prague – City of Three Peoples." *Leo Baeck Institute Year Book* 9 (1964): 305–39.
Vielmetti, Nikolaus. "Reform und Tradition im Neuen Stadttempel in der Seitenstettengasse zu Wien." In *Judentum in Wien: "Heilige Gemeinde Wien."* Edited by Karl Albrecht-Weinberger and Felicitas Heimann-Jelinek, 30–34. Vienna: Museen der Stadt Wien, 1987.

Waissenberger, Robert. "Judentum in Wien bis 1938." In *Judentum in Wien: "Heilige Gemeinde Wien,"* edited by Karl Albrecht-Weinberger and Felicitas Heimann-Jelinek, 18–28. Vienna: Museen der Stadt Wien, 1987.
Wallach, Luitpold. *Liberty and Letters: The Thoughts of Leopold Zunz.* London: East and West Library, 1959.
Wein, Martin Joachim. *History of the Jews in the Bohemian Lands.* Studies in Central European Histories 61. Leiden: Brill, 2016.
Weinberger, Leon J. *Jewish Hymnography: A Literary History.* London: Vallentine Mitchell, 1998.
Weinstein, David. "Nineteenth- and Twentieth-Century Liberalism." In *The Oxford Handbook of the History of Political Philosophy*, edited by George Klosko, 414–35. Oxford: Oxford University Press, 2011.
Weinstein, Roni. *Kabbalah and Jewish Modernity.* Portland, OR: Littman Library of Jewish Civilization, 2015.
Weir, Todd H. "The Specter of 'Godless Jewry': Secularism and the 'Jewish Question' in Late Nineteenth-Century Germany." *Central European History* 46, no. 4 (2014): 815–49.
Weiss, Avi. "Defining 'Open Orthodoxy' within Judaism." *Tablet Magazine,* June 29, 2015.
Weiss, Tzahi. "The Reception of Sefer Yetsira and Jewish Mysticism in the Early Middle Ages." *Jewish Quarterly Review* 103, no. 1 (2013): 26–46.
Weissler, Chava. *Voices of the Matriarchs: Listening to the Prayers of Early Modern Jewish Women.* Boston: Beacon Press, 1998.
Wendehorst, Stephan, ed. *Bausteine einer jüdischen Geschichte der Universität Leipzig.* Leipzig: Leipziger Universitätsverlag, 2006.
Wertheimer, Jack. *The American Synagogue: A Sanctuary Transformed.* New York: Cambridge University Press, 1987.
———. *Jewish Religious Leadership: Image and Reality.* New York: Jewish Theological Seminary, 2004.
———. *A People Divided: Judaism in Contemporary America.* New York: Basic Books, 1993.
Wiedemann, Albert. *Die sächsischen Eisenbahnen in historisch-statistischer Darstellung.* Leipzig: Thomas, 1902.
Wiese, Christian, ed. *Redefining Judaism in an Age of Emancipation: Comparative Perspectives on Samuel Holdheim, 1806–1860.* Studies in European Judaism 13. Leiden: Brill, 2007.
Wilke, Carsten. *"Den Talmud und den Kant": Rabbinerausbildung an der Schwelle zur Moderne.* Hildesheim: Olms, 2003.
———. "Modern Rabbinical Training: Intercultural Invention and Political Reconfiguration," in *Rabbi – Pastor – Priest: Their Roles and Profiles through the Ages,* edited by Walter Homolka and Heinz-Günther Schöttler, 83–110 (Berlin: de Gruyter, 2013).
Wistrich, Robert S. *The Jews of Vienna in the Age of Franz Joseph.* Oxford: Littman Library of Jewish Civilization, 1990.

———. "Socialism and Judeophobia: Antisemitism in Europe before 1914." *Leo Baeck Institute Year Book* 37 (1992): 111–45.

Wolf, Gerson. *Die Juden in der Leopoldstadt ("unterer Werd") im 17. Jahrhundert in Wien*. Vienna: Herzfeld & Bauer, 1864.

Wolf (Wohlwill), Immanuel. "On the Concept of a Science of Judaism (1822)." *Leo Baeck Institute Year Book* 2 (1957): 194–204.

———. "Ueber den Begriff einer Wissenschaft des Judentums." *Zeitschrift für die Wissenschaft des Judentums* 1, no. 1 (1822): 1–24.

Woolf, Jeffrey R. *The Fabric of Religious Life in Medieval Ashkenaz (1000–1300): Creating Sacred Communities*. Études sur le judaïsme médiéval 30. Leiden: Brill, 2015.

Yerushalmi, Yosef Hayim. *Zakhor: Jewish History and Jewish Memory*. Samuel and Althea Stroum Lectures in Jewish Studies. Seattle: University of Washington Press, 1982.

Ziegler, Dieter. *Eisenbahnen und Staat im Zeitalter der Industrialisierung: Die Eisenbahnpolitik der deutschen Staaten im Vergleich*. Stuttgart: Steiner, 1996.

Zimmermann, Moshe. "Zukunftserwartungen der deutsch-jüdischen Gesellschaft im langen 19. Jahrhundert." *Aschkenas: Zeitschrift für Geschichte und Kultur der Juden* 18/19 (2008/2009): 25–39.

Zunz, Leopold. *Die gottesdienstlichen Vorträge der Juden, historische entwickelt*. Berlin: Asher, 1832.

———. *Die synagogale Poesie des Mittelalters*. 2 volumes. Berlin: Springer, 1855–1859.

———. *Zeitschrift für die Wissenschaft des Judentums*. Berlin, 1822/1823.

———. *Zur Geschichte und Literatur*. Berlin: Veit, 1845.

Zweig, Stefan. *Die Welt von Gestern: Erinnerungen eines Europäers*. Stockholm: Bermann-Fischer, 1942.

Index

1848 Revolutions, 23
   generation of, 68, 92

Aaron ben David ha-Kohen, 57 (n. 9)
Abarbanel, Isaac, 68, 86
Abraham of Cologne, 61
Abulafia, Abraham, 61, 63–64, 66, 81, 82
Akiva, 91–93
Alharizi, Judah ben Solomon, 61
Allgemeine Zeitung des Judentums, 71
Amalek, 184–85
Anti-Semitism, 13
Aquinas, Thomas, 61, 80, 81–82
Arabic
   Jellinek's interest in, 55–56, 77
   Kabbalah and, 56, 60–61, 66–67, 72, 74
Arama, Isaac, 68
Auswahl kabbalistischer Mystic, 61, 67

Back, Aron, 22
Back, Sarah, 22
Bähr, Yisachar, 57 (n. 9)
Balerio, Samuel, 57 (n. 9)
Baron, Salo W., 125
Beiträge zur Geschichte der Kabbala, 60, 66, 72, 75
Bendavid, Lazarus, 47
Beer, Bernhard, 67
Berlin, 13, 22, 24
   Haskalah in, 31
   seminary in, 33
Bernhardt, L., 47
Bet ha-Midrasch, 4, 51, 53, 65, 69–70, 77, 80, 84
   messianism in, 83
   preface to third volume of, 95
Botarel, Moshe, 57 (n. 9)
Breslau, seminary in, 33, 51, 154, 155

Broda, Tzvi Hirsch, 22
Buchheim, David, 28, 30
Buber, Solomon, 69
Budapest, 13, 22
   seminary in, 33

Caro, Isaac, 68
Central Europe, importance of, 12–14, 18
Chayat, Judah, 68
Chayim ben Samuel of Tudela, 179
Christiani, Pablo, 81
Commentary on Ecclesiastes and the Song of Songs. See Rashbam.
Conservative movement, 8, 154
Creuzer, Georg Friedrich, 78–79

Davidson, Samuel, 77–78, 83
de León, Moses ben Shem Tov, 61–62, 63, 64, 65
   use of language by, 67
Der jüdische Stamm, 137 (n. 42), 147 (n. 16)
Der Orient, 46
   Jellinek's publications in, 51, 56–57
Dresden
   Jewish life in, 41
   rabbinate in, 99, 127
Drslawitz (Drslavice), 21, 27
Dubnow, Simon, 125

Elisha ben Abuya, 91–92
Enlightenment, 12, 16, 149
   liberalism and, 144, 126
   Talmud and, 163
Emancipation, 12, 26–27, 47, 91, 100, 101, 135, 157, 172
Emden, Jacob, 62
Epistles on Philosophy and Kabbalah, 61
Ewald, Heinrich, 147 (n. 16)

225

Fleischer, Heinrich Leberecht, 50, 55, 56, 73
Franck, Adolphe, history of Kabbalah, 59–60, 62, 64, 67, 72
Frankel, Zecharias, 42
   Bet ha-Midrasch and, 71, 73
   Breslau seminary and, 51, 97
   Dresden rabbi and, 99
   Wissenschaft des Judentums and, 48
Frankfurt
   Haskalah in, 31
   seminary in, 33
Freud, Sigmund, 13
Friedlieb, Joseph Heinrich, 78–79
Fürst, Julius, 46, 47, 50, 56, 57, 62–63, 71

Galen, 61
Gans, Edward, 47
Geiger, Abraham, 17–18, 44–45, 49, 50, 73, 154
Gieseler, Johann Karl Ludwig, 59, 73
Gikatilla (Chiquitilla), Joseph ben Abraham, 81
Goethe, Johann Wolfgang von, 100, 101
Goßlar, Naftalie Hirsch (of Halberstadt), 57 (n. 9)
Gottschedstraße Synagogue (Leipzig), 42, 99
Graetz, Heinrich, 49, 61 (n. 20, n. 21), 62, 85, 95, 127 (n. 4)
Gutzkow, Karl Ferdinand, 90–92

Habsburg monarchy, 13
   political reforms in, 25–26
   response to 1848, 24
Halevi, Yehuda, 176
Hamburg Reform Temple, 5, 41 (n. 18)
Hamai Gaon, 61
Hertz, Joseph, 146 (n. 15), 192
Haskalah. *See* Jewish Enlightenment
Hebrew Language, Jellinek's sermons and, 150–54
Hegel, Georg Wilhelm Friedrich, 92, 100, 101
Herder, Johann Gottfried von, 153
Holdheim, Samuel, 154
Holocaust. *See* Shoah.
Humboldt, Wilhelm von, 44, 147 (n. 16)

Ibn Gabirol, Salomon, 64, 81, 82
Ibn Shu'eib, Joel, 68
Institut zur Förderung der israelitischen Literatur, 71
Isaac of Neustadt, 57 (n. 9)
Isaac the Blind, school of, 61

Jabez, Joseph, 57 (n. 9), 68
Jellinek, Hermann, 22
   execution, 24
   political ideas, 23–24
   relationship with Adolf, 24
   writings of, 23
Jellinek, Isak Löw, 22
Jellinek, Moritz, 22
   in Budapest, 23
Jena, 24, 49
Jesus, 5, 44, 45, 150 (n. 25), 184
Jewish Enlightenment, 12, 30–31
   Spain and, 115
Jewish modernity
   definition of, 8–12, 13, 14
   as discourse, 10
Jewish mysticism
   Hekhalot and *Ma'asei Merkava*, 83–85
   Jellinek and, 4, 52–53
Jewish ritual/practice, 8
   women and, 3, 132–33
Joseph II, Edict of Tolerance, 26
Jost, Isaak Markus, 4 (n. 2), 49 (n. 41), 51 (n. 50), 52 (n. 53), 55, 59 (n. 13), 71, 73, 85, 95
   on Jellinek's scholarship, 66 (n. 36), 72

Kabbalah, Jellinek's studies of, 51–52, 53, 57–60, 64–65, 77, 78–79, 83, 116
King, Jr., Martin Luther, 148
Kirschheim, Raphael, 73
Kalonymus, Kalonymus ben, 179

Landauer, Meyer Heinrich Hirsch, 62–63
   Jellinek's response to, 63–64
Leipzig, 7, 25
   history of, 37–39
   Jewish life in, 39, 41–42
   rabbis of, 42
   University of, 3, 23, 38–39, 50–51, 55

Leipzig-Berlin Synagogue, 99
Leopoldstadt, 107, 109–11
Leopoldstadt Temple (Vienna), 113–14
   dedication of, 117–19
   design of, 116
   preaching in, 138
Liberalism
   citizenship and, 145–46
   definitions of, 143–44
   impact of, 5, 12, 13, 19
   Jellinek's promotion of, 45, 126, 144–46, 155
   political, 8, 25, 26, 100
List, Friedrich, 38
Lonzano, Menahem de. *See Ma'arich.*
Luzzatto, Samuel David
   Bet haMidrasch and, 71, 73, 74–75
   Kabbalah and, 76
Luzzatto, Jacob, 57 (n. 9)

Ma'arich, 61, 67
Mabit (Moses ben Joseph di Trani), 179
Maharsha (Samuel Edels), 179
Mahler, Gustav, 13
Mannheimer, Isak Noa, 104, 105 (n. 5), 120, 121–22, 154 (n. 40)
Maimonides (Moses ben Maimon), 44, 64–65, 74, 176
Mendelssohn, Moses, 12, 48, 149, 161–62, 168, 174 (n. 39)
Midrash, 8
   Jellinek and, 52–53
   Jellinek's sermons and, 148–50
Mishnah, role of the rabbi in, 130–31
Modernism, 9
Monatsschrift für Geschichte und Wissenschaft des Judentums (MGWJ), 48, 67, 71, 72, 77
Moravia, 3, 7, 21–22
   Jewish life in, 25–33
   rabbinate in, 22
Mortara, Marco, *Bet ha-Midrasch* and, 73, 75–76
Moses ben Schem-Tob de Leon und sein Verhältniß zum Sohar, 58, 60–66
Munk, Salomon, 44, 73–74, 86

Nachmanides (Moses ben Nachman), 81

Napoleonic Wars, 2, 27, 35, 135
Neoplatonic philosophy, 80
Neubauer, Adolf, 73
Neuer Israelitischer Tempelverein. *See* Hamburg Reform Temple
New Israelite Temple (Leipzig). *See* Gottschedstraße Synagogue (Leipzig).

Orthodoxy, 8, 12, 18, 120, 156, 181, 185, 194
   Jellinek's relation to, 154–55
   warning to, 185

Passover, sermon about, 100
Philippson, Ludwig, 49, 51 (n. 50), 73, 154
   Bet ha-Midrasch and, 71
Philosophie und Kabbala, 67, 81, 82
Pirkei Avot, 130, 174 (n. 40)
Prague, 3, 7, 22, 23, 24, 33–36
   Jewish community in, 34
   rabbis of, 35
   yeshiva in, 35
Preacher
   Jellinek as, 5, 137–39, 155–57
   Jewish title of, 137–38
Proßnitz, 23, 24, 30–33
   yeshiva in, 26, 31

Rabbenu Tam (Jacob ben Meir), 85
Rabbinate
   role of, 131, 133
   transformation of, 16–19
Rambam. *See* Maimonides.
Ramban. *See* Nachmanides.
Rappaport, Solomon Judah, 35
Rashba (Solomon ben Aderet), 62
Rashbam (Samuel ben Meir), 85–87
Recchi, Emanuel, 57 (n. 9)
Reform movement, 8, 12–13
   Jellinek's relation to, 154–55
   Jellinek's warning to, 185
Reformation, 16
Renan, Ernest, 147 (n. 16)
Rosenfeld, Moses Jehuda, 28, 29
   Jellinek's memories of, 29
Ruth, Book of, 166–67

Sa'adia ben Yosef Gaon, 66–67
Saba, Abraham, 68
Sachs, Michael, 6 (n. 11), 24 (n. 14), 122
Sacks, Jonathan, 192–93
Scholem, Gershom, 4, 61 (n. 21)
Sefer Olam HaKatan, 61
Sefer Yetsirah, 59, 66
Seitenstettengasse Synagogue (Vienna), 104–105, 110
  preaching in, 121, 138
Sermons
  Abraham in Jellinek's, 170–73, 177
  "care of stranger" as theme of, 141, 164–68
  "Christians" as theme of, 168–77
  historical development of, 129–31
  Jellinek's sources for, 139, 142
  midrash and, 148–50
  modern significance of, 134–36
  premodern significance of, 133
  Protestant, 16
  relation to gender roles, 136
  Shabbat HaGadol and, 3, 131
  Shabbat Shuvah and, 3
  "truth, freedom, and justice" as theme of, 142, 161–64, 172–74
  "universalism" as theme of, 141, 142, 147
  weekly, 8, 16
Shadal. *See* Samuel David Luzzatto.
Shoah, 12, 191
Siddur
  changes to, 5
Sofer, Moses, 28, 29, 30
Stadttempel (Vienna). *See* Seitenstettengasse Synagogue (Vienna).
Stamm (tribe), 145
Steinschneider, Moritz, 31 (n. 38), 49, 51 (n. 50), 73, 75 (n. 16), 76, 95, 97
Sulzer, Salomon, 120
Synagogue, 15, 19
  aesthetics of, 114–16
  definitions of, 131–32
  urban reinvention of, 112–13, 116–17

Tischendorf, Constantine von, 76–77, 78, 83

Thomas von Aquino in der jüdischen Literatur, 81
Torah, 8, 21
  Hebrew language and, 153
  Platonism and, 80
  "the stranger" in, 164–65, 167

Ungarisch-Brod, 21, 23, 24, 27–29
  rabbis of, 28–29
Urbanization, 2, 3, 5, 13
  Jewish communal, 8, 15–16, 40–41
  religious freedom because of, 181–82
Uriel Acosta: A Tragedy in Five Acts, 91–93
  Jellinek's discussion of, 93–95

Vienna, 13
  Haskalah in, 31
  Jellinek and, 3
  Jewish community in, 105
Vienna Rite, 121–22
Vital, David ben Solomon, 57 (n. 9)

Wanefried, Moses Katz, 30, 31–32
Weimar, 9, 12, 24
Wissenschaft des Judentums, 8, 12, 42–49, 71
  ideals of, 82, 95–96
  Jellinek's critique of, 95–97
  relation to university, 51
Wolf (Wohlwill), Immanuel, 46, 47
Wolf, Israel, 28

Zakuto, Abraham, 62
Zeitschrift für die religiösen Interessen des Judenthums, 72
Zeitschrift für die Wissenschaft des Judentums, 46, 47
Zohar
  Abulafia as possible author of, 63–64, 82
  Jellinek's studies of, 51, 53, 57, 58–66, 79, 81, 83, 87, 139
Zunz, Leopold, 46, 47, 70, 71, 73, 97
  Die gottesdienstlichen Vorträge der Juden, 70

www.ingramcontent.com/pod-product-compliance
Lightning Source LLC
Chambersburg PA
CBHW021943290426
44108CB00012B/941